THE CENTURY PSYCHOLOGY SERIES
Richard M. Elliott, *Editor*
Kenneth MacCorquodale, *Assistant Editor*

Principles *of* Psychology

Principles *of* Psychology

A SYSTEMATIC TEXT IN THE SCIENCE OF BEHAVIOR

Fred S. Keller

and

William N. Schoenfeld

DEPARTMENT OF PSYCHOLOGY
COLUMBIA UNIVERSITY

New  York

APPLETON-CENTURY-CROFTS, INC.

EDITOR'S INTRODUCTION

Psychologists have been ardent professionals, an eager, easily converted lot. No wonder the cry is often heard among them "There is news in the land of Babel," meaning "Here now is *the* psychology!" So it has come about that there are mechanisms of automatic defense against the asserted exclusiveness and the propaganda of behavior theorists. Chief among them is undoubtedly negative adaptation or, as the authors of this book would have it, with greater illumination, "absence of reinforcement."

I grant the serviceableness of such defenses in preserving common sense and healthy skepticism, yet I am sorry for the psychologist who misses this out-of-the-ordinary textbook. He may be one whose own work lies far afield. But no matter what that work may be, it would enhance his vision and build his morale to know that it has been possible already to demonstrate, operationally and therefore beyond challenge, so much lawfulness of behavior on the single assumption that all the features of learned behavior are but the routes, straight routes and detours, down which an organism has been baited. He might quibble over the excessive use of rats and balk at the extrapolations to higher behavior, but he could not deny massive facts that stick.

I especially congratulate you, the thoughtful student, whose first or early exposure to psychology is through this book. Its use as a text is a guarantee that you have an instructor who knows that the basis of every science lies not in talk and proof by say-so, but in experimental methods. At best you are going to learn psychological science by your own sciencing, in a laboratory. If circumstances deny that privilege, your instructor will still see to it that you get the next best by perfectly feasible demonstrations in the classroom. Finally, if this book arouses in you the tingling enthusiasm that in an earlier form it has plainly evoked in many students, you are on your way to insights of the greatest value. They will be of use to you whether you become a psychologist, teacher, lawyer, sales-man, philosopher, doctor, or just a person who feels the need to see beneath the seeming chanciness of human behavior.

RICHARD M. ELLIOTT

PREFACE

This book is a new kind of introduction to psychology. It is different in that it represents for the first time a point of view that is coming to guide the thinking and research of an active group of psychologists in this country. The members of this group are mainly experimentalists, laboratory workers, who spend much of their time in observing and measuring the behavior of organisms—rats, dogs, guinea-pigs, apes, pigeons, and, of course, human beings. They are unflaggingly on the lookout for fundamental principles of behavior—principles that hold true for the white rat as well as the college student, for the dog in laboratory harness as well as the patient on the psychoanalyst's couch, for the tribal savage as well as the sophisticated product of our own culture. Already they have discovered some of these principles and have brought them together in the beginnings of scientific theory. Other principles are, at present, only suspected, and the search goes on at an ever faster pace. In this book, we try to tell about the ones of which we are certain; we describe some of the research they are based on; and we point out the way in which they may be organized to give a meaningful picture of human conduct. We hope that something of interest and use, perhaps even something of adventure, will be found in our account.

This has not been an easy book to write. Our aim, at the outset, was clear enough: we wanted to construct an elementary text in psychology that would be suitable for our own use and, hopefully, for the use of a rapidly growing number of like-minded teachers. We had felt, for some time, the need for a book that would integrate classical and contemporary thought in a way that would adequately represent the dominant theoretical trend of today. But when, at last, we undertook to write it ourselves, we soon became aware of the difficulties involved. We had no models to work from, no tradition to follow, at the undergraduate level of exposition. With respect to the content as well as the form of our text, we had to rely upon our own judgment, again and again—often with misgivings.

We found, too, that several readers had to be kept before us as we wrote. There was the beginning student, the object of our greatest concern, who might never go beyond an introductory course. There was the advanced undergraduate, even the graduate student, who had not yet been acquainted with our way of thinking. And, finally, there were our colleagues, watching us to see how well we would be able to carry reinforcement theory to the student.

Now, with our book in the hands of the publisher, we are well aware that it reflects our struggle with these problems, rather than their complete solution. No one could think otherwise. We will have to be content, at present, with something less than the loaf we intended to put on your table. On the other hand, we think there is something nutritious in it. How well it has been kneaded, and how well baked, the reader must judge.

All books are indebted to more people, for more things, than the authors can remember. At this juncture, we recall most clearly Richard M. Elliott, whose confidence in our project never faltered and who was most generous with his reinforcements; Thomas W. Reese and Kenneth MacCorquodale who, with gentle painstaking, rooted out errors and added their thoughts to our own at many points; and Murray Sidman and James A. Dinsmoor who, with great kindness, took up the double burden of illustration and indexing. More than by any other man, we have been guided and inspired by the work and thought of Burrhus F. Skinner, who led us into the field of behavior theory, and whose influence has so perfused this field as to be lost to a proper contemporary perspective. We are aware, too, of how much we owe to our own students—those men and women, working alongside us—whose vitality and creativity have been a recurrent source of our own enthusiasm.

F.S.K.
W.N.S.

We are aware, too, of how much we owe to our own
students—those men and women, working alongside us,
whose vitality and creation have been a recurrent source of

Pour atteindre à la verité, il faut une fois dans
sa vie se défaire de toutes les opinions que l'on a
reçues et reconstruire de nouveau, et dès le fonde-
ment, tous les systèmes de ses connaissances.

René Descartes

CONTENTS

1

PSYCHOLOGY AND THE REFLEX

NATURE WITH its myriad phenomena assumes a unified aspect only in the rarest cases; in the majority of instances it exhibits a thoroughly composite character...; it is accordingly one of the duties of science to conceive phenomena as made up of sets of partial phenomena, and at first to study these partial phenomena in their purity.

P. Volkmann, *Erkenntnistheoretische Grundzüge der Naturwissenschaft,* 1896

Preliminary

The purpose of this text is threefold: (1) to acquaint you with a number of well-established psychological principles; (2) to show you how these principles are related, one to the other; and (3) to suggest how you may apply them in the analysis of everyday human activity. In addition, we hope that you will draw from it some notion of where the frontiers of our science lie, of what important problems remain to be solved, and, perhaps, an idea of how you can help in furthering their solution.

With certain matters of theory and practice commonly considered in elementary texts, we shall not be concerned. You will find in this book no chapters on the workings of the human nervous system, the structure and function of our sense organs, or the measurement of intelligence. These are interesting matters for advanced study, but they do not rightly belong within a text devoted to fundamental problems and basic principles of psychology.

For the general reader, there are excellent surveys and samplings of the various fields and problems of psychology, which provide a bird's-eye view of the science. For the advanced student, there are many books that deal exclusively with this or that area of specialized interest. The present text belongs within neither category. It aims simply to furnish the beginning student with a solid foundation and a trustworthy framework for thinking about, or dealing with, human nature as he finds it in his daily life. And, needless to say, it should also prepare him for further, more intensive, study in our field.

As you make your way, step by step, through this book, you will notice certain outstanding characteristics of our approach. These may well be mentioned in advance, as a preparation for things to come. Our approach is biological, experimental, and systematic. *Biological,* in that our basic principles will often be drawn from the study of animal behavior, and will be found to apply at various evolutionary levels; *experimental,* in that these principles will be derived, not from casual observation or untested opinion, but from laboratory studies in which the important factors are isolated and varied in such a manner as to permit scientific lawfulness to be discovered; and *systematic,* in that the interrelation of experimental facts will be one of our major concerns.

The Subject Matter of Psychology

Tentatively we may define psychology as *the science of the behavior of organisms.* Such a simple statement, however, is both incomplete and misleading. Psychologists are not, as a rule, equally interested in the behavior of *all* organisms. Their attention is usually focussed primarily upon the human being and a few of his near-relations in the animal kingdom —for example, the rat, the cat, the dog, the monkey, and the chimpanzee. The *comparative* psychologist makes it his business to examine differences and similarities of behavior throughout the evolutionary scale. We, however, shall have little interest in the activities of animals markedly different from man, or in those infra-human activities which throw no light on *human* conduct.

Moreover, the psychologist studies behavior *in its relation to environment.* Behavior alone would hardly constitute the subject matter of a science. Imagine, for a moment, the sense-lessness of a motion-picture record of an organism's behavior from birth to death, with every indication of the world in which it lived carefully blotted out! Only when we begin to relate behavioral to environmental happenings does the possibility of a scientific psychology make its appearance.

Stimulus and Response

But we must go still further. Behavior and environment are unwieldy terms, too broad in their meaning to be very useful. As soon as we attempt to deal with either, we find ourselves asking *What sort of behavior? What aspect of environment?* This is but another way of saying that, whenever we try to describe either the behavior or the environment of an organism, we are forced to break it down into parts. *Analysis* is essential to description, in our science as well as others.

Through analysis, psychologists have arrived at the concepts of *stimulus* and *response.* A stimulus may be provisionally defined as "a part, or change in a part, of the environment," and a response may be defined as "a part, or change in a part, of behavior." We shall recognize, however, that a *stimulus* cannot be defined independently of a response. An environmental event becomes a stimulus by virtue of the fact that it is followed by a response. Activities of our muscles and glands (the so-called bodily effectors) make up our responses. These terms provide the specificity we desire and make a study of the environment-behavior relation feasible by giving us things to observe and to measure. Stimuli and responses are the basic units of our descriptions and provide the starting point for a science of behavior. We would not go far astray in asserting that modern psychology itself is essentially a stimulus-response psychology.

The Reflex

Physiologists have supplied us with a very useful word with which to designate any specific stimulus-response relationship. The word is *reflex,* and, in the chapters to follow, we shall employ it frequently. For example, we shall speak of the *salivary reflex* when we refer to the fact that food, in the mouth of a hungry man, quickly evokes a flow of saliva. We shall even extend the use of the term to denote responses for which related stimuli are not clearly observable. Thus, we shall give the name *reflex* to the response made by a child in clapping his hands, even when we have no way of knowing exactly what stimuli are responsible for the act. But more of this later.

The Response Mechanism

Between the stimulus and the response there are obviously bodily happenings. It is well recognized today that stimuli affect sense organs (called *receptors*) and that sense organs, when excited, cause nerve impulses to be transmitted over nerve pathways to the brain or spinal cord and thence to the muscles and glands (*effectors*). This sequence of events results in those responses which we, as psychologists, are interested in relating to stimuli. The structures involved—the receptors, the nervous system, and the effectors— make up what is commonly known as the *response mechanism.*

The detailed function of the response mechanism is of principal concern to the *physiologist.* He tells us that the receptors or sense organs are of three main types:

1. *Exteroceptors,* small structures within the eye, the ear, or the skin, which are excited by stimuli external to the organism.

2. *Interoceptors,* tiny organs which lie mainly within the alimentary tract, and which are excited by internal stimuli.

3. *Proprioceptors,* which are located within the muscles,

joints, and tendons, as well as the inner ear, and are excited, that is, stimulated, by movements of the body or its parts.

In line with this distinction, stimuli themselves are often described as exteroceptive, interoceptive, or proprioceptive. This gives us greater specificity than is conveyed merely by the word *environment*.

We are also told that the nervous system has subdivisions. One part of it, the *somatic* nervous system, serves primarily to transmit nerve impulses from the sense organs to those muscles of the body which are employed in walking, talking, writing, and the like—responses which are highly specific and of great importance in making changes in our environment. The other part, the *autonomic* nervous system, is essentially an extension of the somatic nervous system, but serves mainly for the conduction of nerve impulses to the glands and the so-called "smooth" muscles of our bodies —for example, the digestive glands and the muscles of the blood-vessel walls, the stomach, and the iris of the eye. The action of part of this autonomic system is extremely diffuse and is most conspicuously responsible for the widespread internal changes which occur in all of us when under strong emotion.

The Reflex Arc and the Reflex

Anatomists and physiologists have analyzed in detail the structure and function of the response mechanism. Their interest in filling the gap between stimulus and response has led them to the conception of a *reflex arc,* in order to distinguish it from the observed relation of stimulus to response which we have called the *reflex*. The simplest conceivable chain of structures between our two end-terms, stimulus and response, is presumably one that includes (1) a receptor element (cells or cell groups in the sense-organ tissues), (2) a sensory or afferent nerve element (nerve cells or neurons) for conducting impulses to some nerve center in either the brain or the spinal cord, (3) a motor or efferent nerve element for conduction from nerve center to effector, and (4) the effector itself, a muscular or glandular element (muscle or gland cells) that accounts for the final response.

This chain or arc of structural elements—receptor cells, sensory and motor nerve cells, and effector cells—has sometimes been called a reflex, and some theorists have maintained that it is the organic basis of the stimulus-response relation. We need not here examine the evidence for such an argument, which has often been disputed, but it is important that we make a clear distinction between the reflex as a *relation* actually observed and the reflex as a hypothetical *mechanism*. Confusion will be avoided if we use *reflex* in the former case, and *reflex arc* in the latter.

The newcomer to psychology will gain little from further discussion of physiological matters. It is true that psychologists have long been interested in relating behavior to receptor, effector, and nervous-system function; and *physiological psychology* is today a thriving field of study for the advanced student. But as far as general principles of behavior are concerned, this area of investigation has not as yet been very helpful. It is, in fact, the case that our knowledge of the stimulus-response relation has more often preceded than followed our knowledge of its physiological counterpart.

Extension of the Reflex Concept

The reflex, as well as the reflex-arc, concept grew up in physiological science. Muscular movement, originally attributed to supernatural forces and later ascribed to a power residing within the muscles themselves, was gradually recognized as due to the action of successively excited parts of the response mechanism. Also, the importance of an initiating stimulus was demonstrated, and it became clear that many animal reactions were a direct and almost inevitable result of stimulus presentation. Observation of such phenomena as the writhings of a decapitated lizard in response to mildly injurious stimulation of its skin led to the search for stimuli to other reactions of operated animals, and soon disclosed a considerable number of comparable stimulus-response relations. The advocates of scientific determinism were thus encouraged to extend their researches into the realm of normal, intact animals and, eventually, to man himself. It became obvious that, regardless of the physiological activities involved, stimuli and responses were often associated in a definite and openly observable cause-effect sequence. Lists of animal and human reflexes were compiled, and psychologists, as well as physiologists, turned to the task of further exploration and study.

By 1919, it was possible for John B. Watson, an American pioneer in the objective, natural-science approach to psychology, to suggest that the identification, enumeration, and classification of stimulus-response relations was the principal concern of our science. In effect, he proposed a cataloguing of reflexes as basic to the prediction and control of human and infra-human behavior. In the furtherance of such a program, Watson himself made extensive observations on the 'unlearned' reactions of newly-born human infants to various simple forms of stimulation.

Watson's proposal is now deemed impracticable. Even if we assumed that the entire reflex repertory of a given organism might some day be determined (which is very unlikely in view of the effects of training and the extreme difficulty in identifying the stimuli for many common forms of response), we would still be unable to formulate general principles of the sort that we require. We need a dynamic, rather than a static, picture of the behavior of organisms. To describe process, not to inventory elements, is our major concern. A more productive approach has been one that takes for granted the basically reflex character of our behavior, selects a few examples for observation, and examines their dynamic properties in some detail. This is the approach that will be taken in the present text.

Some Reflex Properties

We begin our account with a few facts that are so simple and ubiquitous that they might easily be overlooked. Yet they actually have the status of fundamental principles. They are readily demonstrable in any experimental situation where the intensity of a stimulus can be controlled and the magnitude of a response can be measured, and they may also be crudely observed under the non-quantitative circumstances of everyday life.

Take, as an example, the *scratch reflex* of a *spinal dog* in the laboratory of a physiologist. In such an animal, a severed spinal cord permits movements of the hind legs which are free from any influence stimulating the fore part of the body. When a touch stimulus is applied to the dog's hind ribs, a rhythmic flexion and extension of the right hind leg will take place. This response resembles a normal dog's reaction to the bite of a flea, but since it is uncomplicated by the effect of any stimuli concurrently exciting the dog's eyes or ears, it has a somewhat artificial appearance. Nevertheless, it is easily elicited and very useful in illustrating properties of reflex action in general.

The Threshold or Limen

One of the first facts that may be demonstrated with such a reduced animal is that *a stimulus must be of a certain intensity before it can elicit a response*. The intensity just sufficient to excite is called a *liminal* or *threshold* intensity. Lesser intensities are called below-threshold or sub-liminal since, when applied singly, they never evoke a reaction. Correspondingly, greater intensities are called above-threshold or supra-liminal.

All of the elicited responses of organisms (either operated or intact) show this dependence upon stimulus level, and great effort has been expended throughout the past century in determining the liminal intensities of visual, tactual, auditory, and other stimuli. Indeed, an entire field of research, *psychophysics,* has been oriented about such measurements. Workers in this field have dealt not only with *absolute* thresholds, the kind defined above, but also with *difference* thresholds, in which one studies the organism's capacity to detect differences in the intensity of stimuli that are at the outset well above absolute-threshold value.

We shall come back to thresholds later, in Chapter 5. At present, it is enough to note that many common observations point to their existence. When we raise a watch to our ear to hear the tick, when we find the first star in the evening sky, or when we observe the dimming of theatre lights, we are dealing with the fact of absolute or relative intensity limens. Other instances will quickly occur to anyone who thinks about the matter.

Latency

A short interval of time elapses between the application of a stimulus and the arousal of a response. This interval is called the *latency* or *latent period.* In the scratch reflex of the spinal dog, the interval may range from 140 ms. (milliseconds) to 500 ms. (half a second) , depending upon the intensity of the stimulus employed. In such a reflex, strong stimuli reduce the latent period and weak ones lengthen it. Other reflexes may show a different range of latency values, but for any single reflex of this sort conditions may be so controlled as to produce a fairly constant value. This constancy is important since it gives us a measure of the effect of changing the conditions.

Although this relation is quite dependable in such cases as that of the spinal dog's scratch reflex, there is another type of stimulus-response connection where changes in stimulus intensity are not so clearly reflected in alterations of latency. When the driver of a car responds to a green light by making the movements which set his car in motion, the latency of the response does not appear to be directly related to the intensity of the light. He starts up as quickly for a weak light as for a strong one. The process involved in such a case requires, as we shall see, its own explanatory treatment.

We shall return to the matter of latency in Chapter 5, when we discuss some experimental studies of *reaction time*—a term that may already have suggested itself to you. We shall then see that latency and reaction time are not unrelated, the latter being a variation of the former. For the present, however, the distinction should not be prematurely pressed.

Stimulus Intensity and Response Magnitude

If the scratch reflex of our spinal dog is elicited by a barely supra-liminal stimulus, the latency, as stated above, will be relatively long. This will not be the only effect observed. The flexion of the leg may be limited to a single short excursion or, at most, to two or three. If, now, the stimulus intensity is raised to a higher value, there will ensue an increase in both the amplitude and number of scratching movements. Within limits, *the magnitude of the elicited response is dependent upon, that is, is a function of, the intensity of the stimulus.*

As in the case of latency, however, the response magnitude is not always seen to bear such a neat relation to the stimulus variable. In a snake-infested cave, a faintly heard rattle may evoke as vigorous a reaction as the report of a revolver; in a tropical jungle, the hum of a mosquito may sometimes elicit as strong an emotional response as the roar of a near-by plane. Such observations point to other controlling factors, and the laboratory bears this out. A different, but nonetheless lawful, relation will occupy our attention later.

Reflex Strength

There are properties of reflex action other than those just described, and they too may be observed in the behavior of a spinal animal. We need not, however, consider them in this text, since we are here concerned with bare essentials, and

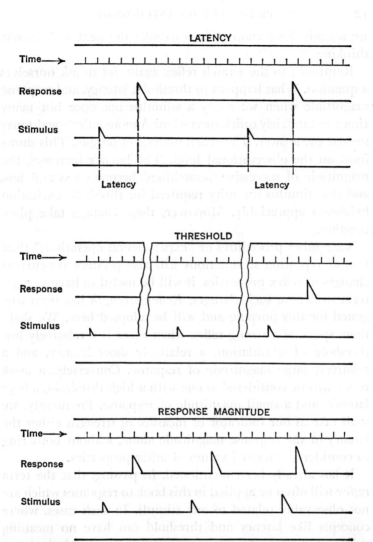

FIG. 1. Schematic tape records of three reflex properties. The height of a spike on the stimulus line indicates stimulus intensity; that on the response line, response magnitude. The distance between the stimulus and response spikes on the constant-speed tape gives the latency. The time line is made by an automatic marker which ticks off any desired unit of time. The broken threshold tape shows that the stimulations were very widely spaced to prevent possible summation of stimulus effects.

we already have enough facts to take the next step in our thinking.

Returning to the scratch reflex again, let us ask ourselves a question. What happens to threshold, latency, and response magnitude when we apply a stimulus not once but many times and in fairly quick succession? A moment's thought may suggest the answer. The reflex undergoes *fatigue*. This shows itself on the observational level. The latency increases, the magnitude of successive 'scratchings' becomes less and less, and the stimulus intensity required for threshold excitation heightens appreciably. Moreover, these changes take place together.

Since other procedures or "experimental operations" than that of repeating stimulations will also produce concurrent changes in reflex properties, it will be useful to have a single term to denote such changes. *Reflex strength* has been suggested for this purpose and will be adopted here. We shall, then, speak of a *strong* reflex when there is a relatively low threshold of stimulation, a relatively short latency, and a relatively large magnitude of response. Conversely, a *weak* reflex will be considered as one with a high threshold, a long latency, and a small magnitude of response. Frequently, we shall take as our indicator or measure of strength either the latency or the response magnitude alone, without bothering to consider the related values of other properties.

It has already been mentioned, in passing, that the term *reflex* will often be applied in this book to responses which are not observably related to any stimuli. In such cases, where concepts like latency and threshold can have no meaning (since they depend upon a stimulus-response relation), we shall nevertheless speak of *reflex strength*. *Frequency of occurrence* will then become a very important measure of strength. Until we come to Chapter 3, however, this matter needs no further discussion.

A Few Remarks

So much by way of preliminaries. This is a short chapter, but you should now be able to say something about (1) the general aim of this text; (2) the subject matter of psychology; (3) the concept of the reflex; (4) the nature of a few basic reflex properties; and (5) the meaning of *reflex strength*. All this is essential to your understanding of what will be treated in the pages to come. Each step in our exposition will depend upon what has gone before. Unless you have understood the earlier facts and principles, you will almost surely have trouble with the later. For this reason it will often be helpful for you to go over again a paragraph, a section, or a chapter previously read, in order to strengthen your foundation for the topic at hand or the topics to come.

It will also be wise, in reading the coming chapters, to divest yourself, as far as possible, from preconceptions concerning psychology. Our everyday language is shot through with purportedly psychological terms and concepts. Most of these are lacking in scientific significance, because they are either poorly defined or unrelated to anything else, and they will find no place in our account. You are asked here, as you would be in physics, chemistry, or biology, to learn a new language. The power of this language can be appreciated only by the one who applies it consistently and rigorously, avoiding the contamination of ill-defined or long-discarded terms.

NOTES

In the back of this book, along with the subject index, is an alphabetical list of some of the more important books and articles to which we have referred in preparing our chapters. We have adopted the practice of mentioning, in the text, authors' names and the dates of their publications (e.g., Hilgard and Marquis, 1940). The complete reference is provided in our list—thus "HILGARD, E. R., and MARQUIS, D. G. (1940). *Conditioning and learning.* New York, Appleton-Century-Crofts, xi, 429 pp." After each reference you will find, in italics, the page numbers on which the contribution is cited in this text.

The introduction to psychology provided by this book is something of a departure from the usual approach, and you may at some time be interested in comparing it with other texts. Three very popular elementary accounts are those by Munn (1946), Ruch (1948), and Woodworth and Marquis (1947). Two other well-known books, by Garrett (1941) and by Crafts, Schneirla, Robinson, and Gilbert (1938), are often used as collateral reading in beginners' courses. Any one of these will give you a good idea of the range of topics to which students are usually exposed in their first course, but in none of them will you find a serious attempt to show how the topics are interrelated or integrated within a unified whole. Only a few authors have made an effort similar to ours (e.g., Muenzinger, 1942).

The systematic position portrayed in the present text is best described as *reinforcement theory,* which is the dominant viewpoint in modern behavior theory. Our own account leans heaviest on the work of B. F. Skinner (*The behavior of organisms,* 1938), but is not uninfluenced by other expositions—as found, for example, in the writings of E. L. Thorndike (1911, 1932) and the recent teachings of C. L. Hull (1943).

The student who does not mind reading something of a more technical stripe than we offer may go to Skinner's book. There, in the first two chapters, he will find further discussion of such topics as the data of psychology, the need for analysis, the concept of the reflex, the structure of psychological theory, and related matters. The viewpoint in Hull's *Principles of behavior* (1943) provides a stimulating contrast.

Our systematic position has not kept us from looking at facts in other theoretical contexts. Good data are good data, regardless of theory, and we have been happy to draw upon the experimental findings of our colleagues whenever it seemed profitable, regardless of the viewpoint that guided their research. Therefore, if you are one who likes to "go to the original," do not be surprised if you occasionally find an article written in terms with which you are unfamiliar. If you can push aside the interpretations and discussions, and attend to the experimental procedures and results, you will see why we thought the article worth consideration. Later on, if your interest in psychology continues, you will be better able to evaluate the explanations and debated points.

2

RESPONDENT CONDITIONING

TAKE A hungry horse; expose the duct of the parotid gland on the side of the jaw; nothing will come out—the gland is at rest. Now, show the horse some hay, or better, make some movement indicating that his meal is coming. Immediately a steady flow of saliva will start ...

Claude Bernard. *La Science Expérimentale,* 1878

Pavlov and the Conditioned Reflex

In the history of science, it often happens that the facts, principles, or methods of one field are put to account in the development of another. This is especially true of a young science. In psychology, the boundaries of which have only recently been established, borrowings from other fields have been numerous. Since 1879, when Wilhelm Wundt set up the first psychological laboratory in Leipzig, Germany, our science has often drawn upon her elder sister, physiology. An example of this was cited in Chapter 1: the concept of the reflex actually emerged as a result of purely physiological interest in the functioning of organisms.

We must now acknowledge another debt, again to physiology, for one of our keystone concepts. This is the principle of the *conditioned* reflex, first clearly stated by the Russian physiologist, Ivan Petrovich Pavlov (1849-1936), as the outcome of investigations begun in Petrograd (now Leningrad) during the closing years of the last century.

In 1904, Pavlov received the Nobel Prize in medicine for his studies of the digestive activity of dogs. During these studies, he noticed something that suggested to him an experimental solution of some of the problems of *brain* function.

15

Drawing about him a number of co-workers, he soon launched a large-scale program of research—a program that took up the remaining years of his life and won him grateful recognition from biological scientists throughout the world. Psychologists, however, have profited more from this research through the light it shed upon *behavior* than through the speculations Pavlov advanced concerning brain function.

Pavlov's basic observations were simple. If food or certain dilute acids are put in the mouth of a hungry dog, a flow of saliva from the appropriate glands will soon begin. This is the *salivary reflex,* long known to exist in various animals, including man. But this is not all. Pavlov noted, like others before him, that the animal would also salivate when food had not yet reached the mouth: food *seen* or food *smelled* would elicit the same response. Also, the dog would salivate merely upon the appearance of the man who usually brought his food.

For Pavlov, these observations raised important experimental questions. How did it happen that the mere sight of the person who fed the dog was enough to evoke a salivary secretion? Surely, this was not an innate or inborn stimulus-response relation, typical of all dogs and as uneducable as the scratch reflex of a spinal animal. On the contrary, it seemed obvious that the effect of such a pre-food stimulus could be understood only in terms of the individual experience of the organism. Somehow, an originally ineffective stimulus for salivary response must have taken on new significance for this animal; it must have come to *signalize* the approach of food. Also, it seemed to *prepare* the animal for the food by starting the digestive process.

This led Pavlov to develop an experimental method for studying the *acquisition* of new stimulus-response connections. In practice, this method requires no small degree of laboratory control and technical skill, but it may be outlined rather simply. First, a normal dog is familiarized with the experimental situation until he shows no disturbance when placed in a harness and left alone in a room especially designed to cut off unwanted outside stimuli. A small opening or fistula is made in the dog's cheek near the duct of one of the salivary glands. When the fistula is healed, a glass funnel is carefully cemented to the outside of the cheek so that it will draw off the saliva whenever the gland is activated. From the funnel, the saliva then flows into a glass container or falls, drop by drop, upon a lightly balanced recording platform. The magnitude of responses to various stimuli can be measured by the total volume or the number of drops secreted in a given unit of time. The experimenter, who sits in an adjoining room, can make his measurements, apply what stimuli he desires (including food), and observe the dog's behavior through a window.

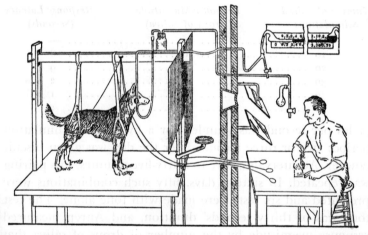

FIG. 2. Representation of a Pavlovian situation for conditioning the salivary response in a dog. (After Dashiell, 1949.)

When everything is ready, the dog is exposed, on successive occasions, to a pair of stimuli. One stimulus, say a small portion of powdered food, initially elicits a flow of saliva each time that it appears and the dog eats. The other, say a tone, has no such effect, but may cause some other behavior, perhaps a twitching of the ears or a turning of the head toward the source of sound. The combination of the two stimuli is presented at irregular intervals over a period of days, always at a time when the dog is hungry. The purpose, of course, is to determine whether one stimulus (the tone) will acquire the power of eliciting the same response as the other (the food). So, after a certain number of pairings, the originally ineffective stimulus (tone) is presented *alone,* to see if it will produce salivation.

Table I gives data from an experiment by Anrep (1920), one of Pavlov's pupils; and it shows what happens when such an experiment is carried out. In this study, a tone of 637.5

Table I

ACQUISITION OF A CONDITIONED SALIVARY REFLEX
(Anrep, 1920)

Number of Paired Stimulations	Response Magnitude (Drops of Saliva)	Response Latency (Seconds)
1	0	—
10	6	18
20	20	9
30	60	2
40	62	1
50	59	2

cycles per second was sounded for a five-second stimulation period; two or three seconds later the dog was given biscuit powder. At intervals of five to thirty-five minutes, this pairing was repeated. In sixteen days, fifty such combinations were presented and six tests were made with tone alone. The test tone was of thirty seconds' duration, and Anrep measured response magnitude by the number of drops of saliva that were secreted in this period. In addition, he recorded the latencies of the response, in seconds.

From this table you can see that the amount of salivation in response to tone-alone increased from a zero value, after a single combination, to sixty drops in the test interval following the thirtieth combination. Along with this increase in response magnitude, there was a decrease in the latency of the response to tone, from eighteen to two seconds. Little change occurred as a result of further pairings of tone with food, showing that the tone-salivation tie-up was well established by the thirtieth combination.

Experiments like this led Pavlov to formulate a new principle:

If any casual stimuli happen, once or a few times, to accompany stimuli which elicit definite inborn reflexes, the former stimuli begin of themselves to produce the effect of these inborn reflexes. . . . We designate the two sorts of reflexes, and the stimuli by which they are elicited, as *unconditioned* (inborn) and *conditioned* (acquired) respectively. (Pavlov, 1923, translated by E. B. Holt in *Animal drive and the learning process,* 1931, p. 24) .

A schematic picture or paradigm of Pavlovian "conditioning" may be helpful at this point.

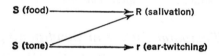

In this paradigm, three reflexes are represented. The food-salivation and the tone-ear-twitching reflexes are "unconditioned"; the tone-salivation reflex is "conditioned." The letters S and R refer, of course, to stimulus and response. The use of r is merely to show that the ear-pricking response to tone is of no great importance in this conditioning process; it may even disappear during the repeated application of the tonal stimulus. The important response, and the one that is measured, is the one belonging to the salivary reflex.

Early in their studies, Pavlov and his students found that this sort of conditioning could occur only when the food-salivation reflex was stronger than the reflex elicited by the "casual" stimulus. For example, an intense electric shock (rather than a tone, a light, or a touch) would not become a conditioned stimulus for salivation because it produced a violent emotional upset in the animal. This led Pavlov to say that a conditioned reflex must always be based upon an unconditioned reflex that was "biologically more important" or "physiologically stronger." The stronger of the two unconditioned reflexes is the one that strengthens or *reinforces* the new stimulus-response relation. The stimulus of the stronger unconditioned reflex is often called the "reinforcing stimulus."

Pavlov's principle has been restated, by Skinner (1938), in a way that highlights the importance of the reinforcing stimulus, and points up the fact that a new reflex is formed by combining elements of the two that were already present in the organism's repertory.

The approximately simultaneous presentation of two stimuli, one of which (the "reinforcing" stimulus) belongs to a reflex existing at the moment at some strength, may produce an increase in the strength of a third reflex composed of the response of the reinforcing reflex and the other stimulus. (Skinner, *The behavior of organisms,* 1938, p. 18.)

Temporal Factors in Conditioning

In the above statement, as in Pavlov's, a close relation of the two stimuli in time is specified. One stimulus is to "accompany" or be "approximately simultaneous with" the other. We are tempted to ask further questions about this relation. Does conditioning proceed more rapidly with simultaneous than with successive stimulus presentations? If successive stimulation is effective, which of the two stimuli should come first for best results? Is conditioning still possible when considerable time elapses between the two?

Answers to these questions have been sought by several investigators and we now know that a strict simultaneity of the two stimuli is unnecessary for the rapid development of a conditioned reflex; and that a close succession of stimuli, one being presented two or three seconds after the other, is probably the most effective arrangement of all. We know, too, that a conditioned reflex is set up only with very great difficulty, if at all, when the conditioned stimulus *follows* the unconditioned, even by a fraction of a second. In terms of our tone-food example, the tone should *precede* the food (as it did in Anrep's experiment) if the conditioning procedure is to take effect.

As to how far in advance of the unconditioned stimulus the other one may come, research does not yet give a final answer. What evidence we have makes it seem likely that a limit would soon be reached. Two types of Pavlovian procedure bear upon this problem. In one, the salivary response is first conditioned to a sound or some other stimulus by the method of "simultaneous" presentation. Then, as the pairing continues, the unconditioned stimulus is not provided until the conditioned stimulus has been steadily present for a given period of time, say three minutes. Eventually, under such circumstances, a "delayed" conditioned reflex may be established: the animal will respond with salivation only after the conditioned stimulus has been present for two minutes or more of the three-minute interval. One is led to say that he can now "tell the time" with considerable accuracy.

The second type of procedure is similar to the first, but with one important difference: the conditioned stimulus is *not maintained continuously* during the interval of delay, but is presented only *at the beginning* of the interval. As in the case of the delayed reflex, however, long-continued pairings of this sort will bring about a temporal discrimination: the dog will not salivate until the time for reinforcement approaches. Pavlov called this a "trace" conditioned reflex, arguing that the immediate cause of salivation was some trace of the conditioned stimulus that had been left in the nervous system of the animal.

Related to these two procedures, because of the time discrimination shown, are the following observations, also made in Pavlov's laboratory. (1) A dog was fed regularly at thirty-minute intervals. When this routine had been well established, food was withheld at the usual feeding time. Salivation was nevertheless noted to occur at approximately the end of the thirty-minute period—the time when the food would ordinarily have been provided. In Pavlov's terms, a "time

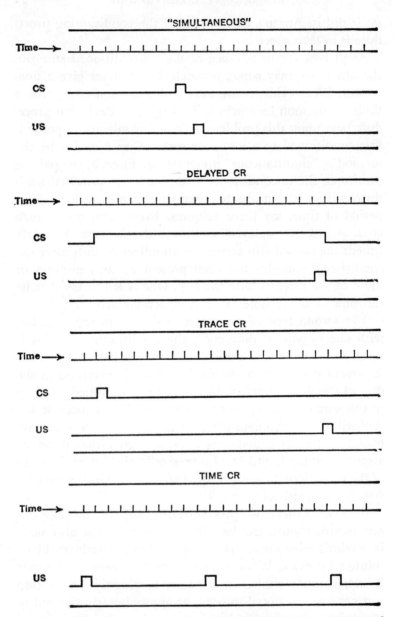

FIG. 3. Time relations in respondent conditioning. CS = conditioned stimulus; US = unconditioned stimulus.

reflex" was formed. (2) In another case, the same thirty-minute interval between feedings was used, but the food was always presented to the accompaniment of a metronome beat. After repeated pairings of metronome and food, salivation was conditioned to the sound, as you would expect, but it was also dependent upon the time-since-feeding. If the metronome was sounded alone early in the period between feedings, no salivation would occur; if it came slightly later, a small magnitude of response might be produced; and, as the end of the period approached, the effect would be correspondingly greater. Finally, with long training, salivation-to-metronome was elicitable only at the very end of the between-feeding interval; the response was conditioned, so to speak, to metronome-plus-thirty-minutes.

These rather astonishing results tell us that the dog can make an extremely delicate time discrimination, but they do not bear upon the question of the maximal possible delay between the conditioned and the unconditioned stimulus. The experiments on the delayed and the trace conditioned reflex are more to the point. The fact that a three-minute lapse between stimuli results in conditioning only after many pairings probably indicates that the limit was almost reached. Certainly, under the usual conditions of Pavlovian experimentation, in which the pairings of stimuli do not come at regular intervals, we would not expect to train a dog to salivate to a tone that preceded food by half a day!

Compound Stimuli

In Pavlovian conditioning, a relation is established between a response and some stimulus that accompanies the reinforcing stimulus. Why, then, you may ask, does the response link itself exclusively to the tone, the light, or the touch provided by the experimenter; are there not other stimuli in the situation which regularly accompany the presentation of food? This is a simple enough question, but the answer is complex, having at least two major aspects. First, these "other" stimuli may be present not only when reinforcement is given, but also under conditions of *non*-reinforcement, in which their eliciting power would be expected to dissipate itself (in accordance with the principle of *extinction*, to be treated in Chapter 4). Secondly, a number of experiments from Pavlov's laboratory have pointed to the fact that when certain *compounds* of stimuli, such as light-plus-sound or sound-plus-touch, are regularly paired with food, it is possible that *only one* member of the compound will become a conditioned stimulus. For example, Palladin conditioned salivation to a combination of touch-plus-temperature. Then he tested separately the elicitive function of the two components. The tactual stimulus was found to elicit as strong a response as the compound, but the thermal stimulus was without the least effect (Pavlov, 1927).

Such findings have opened up a brand-new field of research in conditioning, but one into which we need not enter here. We shall, however, return to the problem in another connection, when we consider the stimulus control of another type of conditioned response (Chapter 8).

The Extension of Pavlovian Research

Pavlov and his collaborators studied many other aspects of salivary conditioning than the ones we have mentioned. Some of this research is of interest only to the specialist in this province, and we may ignore it here. We cannot, however, leave the basic principle without some general remarks about its extension, its significance, and the influence it has had upon psychological thought.

We know today that the principle may be demonstrated in the behavior of many more animals than the dog. Hardly a species has been studied in which conditioning cannot be established. Even one-celled organisms seem to display similar changeability. Special experimental conditions may be needed. Thus rats, guinea pigs, and other small animals require apparatus and techniques that are clearly unsuitable for human beings. But the broad generality of the principle is not to be questioned.

Extension of the procedure has also involved the use of reflexes other than the salivary response to food (or acid) as the "biologically stronger," reinforcing reflex. Since 1916, a number of investigators, mostly American, have shown that the constriction of the pupil of the human eye, which results naturally from stimulation with strong light, can be conditioned to the sound of a bell, or some other stimulus. Others have demonstrated that changes in the electrical resistance of the skin (through sweat secretion), elicited by such stimuli as a mild electric shock or a fairly loud buzzer sound, may readily serve as a basis for new reflexes. Still others have worked with such reinforcing reflexes as blood-vessel constriction in response to stimulation with cold objects, changes in pulse beat resulting from electric shock or skin injuries, and so on.

Many agents have been used as conditioned stimuli, within the sense-fields of sight, sound, touch, taste, and smell—even proprioceptive stimuli, aroused by movements of the legs, hands, or arms, have been employed. In several experiments, responses have been conditioned to *words*, either spoken by the experimenter or *by the subject*. A couple of these experiments may be described briefly because of their intrinsic interest and their relation to the problem of 'controlling' bodily changes.

Hudgins (1933) seems to have been the first to condition a response to self-initiated verbal stimuli. He used, as his basic unconditioned reflex, one with which Cason (1922) had already worked in human experimentation: the constriction of the pupil of the eye in response to bright light. In a rather complicated sequence of stimulus pairings and combinings, he was able to condition this pupillary reflex to (1) the sound of a bell; (2) a vigorous contraction of the hand and fingers; (3) the word *contract*, as spoken by the experimenter; (4) *contract*, when spoken by the subject himself; (5) *contract,* when whispered by the subject; and, finally, (6) the subject's silent, or sub-vocal, *contract.* Which is to say that, through a conditioning procedure, the subject came to control his own pupillary contraction—a feat that is ordinarily thought impossible for human beings.

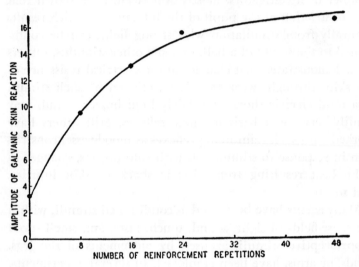

FIG. 4. An acquisition curve showing the magnitude of the conditioned galvanic skin response after varying numbers of reinforcements. The CS was a tone; the US for this respondent was an electric shock to the wrist. (After Hull, 1943, based on data of Hovland, 1937d.)

Menzies (1937) conditioned changes in the skin temperature of human subjects by a very ingenious technique. Unconditioned stimulation was applied by immersing a subject's hand in a beaker of ice-water, and the measured response was the elicited change in temperature of the subject's other hand. (It had been known, since 1858, that a fall in the temperature of one hand is regularly accompanied by a similar change in the temperature of the other.) With this stimulation was paired, in various parts of Menzies' experiment: (*a*) the sound of an electric bell or a buzzer; (*b*) a visual pattern of illuminated crosses; (c) verbal stimuli—the meaningless word *prochaska*, spoken aloud by the experimenter and repeated in a whisper by the subject, or merely whispered by the subject alone; and (d) the proprioceptive stimulation provided by extension of the arm, clenching of a fist, or holding the head in a thrown-back position. Conditioning was effectively established, in from nine to thirty-six pairings, for twelve of the fourteen subjects. (In one of the two 'failures,' conditioning was doubtful; in the other it did not take place, presumably because the unconditioned stimulus itself was not always effective.) It was set up to verbal stimuli as readily when the subject whispered the word to himself as when the whispering was combined with the experimenter's spoken word. Moreover, in three subjects who had been conditioned to respond to the visual pattern, the temperature change could be induced by asking them to "recall" or "think about" the stimulus! In short, Menzies showed convincingly that a conditioned thermal change could be set up easily in his subjects with all of the stimuli that he tried, both exteroceptive and proprioceptive.

Such experiments as these raise some important questions concerning the nature of "voluntary control," but this is not the place for their consideration. At this point, it is probably enough to say that the problem will not be solved on the basis of Pavlovian conditioning alone, since this type of conditioning fails to tell us how the controlling word (*contract* or any other) itself comes to be strengthened.

Physiologists tell us that all the reflexes thus far mentioned are alike in one important respect: they depend upon *autonomic nervous system* function. They involve the action of glands and smooth muscles (e.g., the secretion of sweat and the contraction of blood-vessels). Since the action of such effectors is often associated with states of emotion (in "fear," the saliva dries up, the sweat pours out, the skin cools, the pupils of the eyes dilate, etc.), it will come as no surprise for you to learn, in later chapters, that these states may be conditioned in Pavlovian fashion.

Yet, a few reflexes do not require autonomic function and may apparently be reinforcing. Foot-withdrawal at the onset of electric shock is neither a smooth-muscle nor a glandular response, but it has been used as a basic unconditioned reflex by Russian and American workers in many experiments. Bechterev (1857-1927), one of Pavlov's contemporaries, was the first to work extensively with this response and, in this country, through the studies of Liddell and others, it has become a common form of conditioning procedure.

The experiments of Liddell and his collaborators, using sheep as subjects, are of particular interest in showing the relative complexity of the behavior involved in such "motor" conditioning situations. A common technique in their studies is one in which the sound of a metronome is paired with an electric shock to the animal's left foreleg. At first, only the shock will elicit a flexion of the leg muscles, but, after a few stimulus combinations, the beating of the metronome is in itself sufficient to evoke the response. (Along with this effect there may also be measured a conditioned change in skin resistance and breathing rate.) This is, to all appearances, a simple and straightforward case of Pavlovian conditioning. It may be shown, however, that seemingly minor alterations in the experimental procedure are enough to produce dramatic changes in the subject's behavior. In one experiment, when shock regularly followed a five-second series of metronome beats, an increase in the daily number of stimulus pairings from ten to twenty resulted in an entirely unpredicted change in the sheep's behavior. Formerly a steady and tractable animal, he suddenly began to show distinctly "neurotic" symptoms. He resisted being led into the laboratory; once in the experimental harness, he became quiet, but only for as long as the experimenter remained in the room; when left alone, and before any stimuli had been applied, he began to make foreleg movements as if in expectation of the shock;

the effect of the shock, when actually given, was to quiet the animal for a minute or more but, as the time for the next stimulation approached, the frequency of the leg movements increased. In spite of a reinstatement of the earlier experimental conditions, this deviation from normal behavior became daily more pronounced, and was alleviated only by a long vacation in pasture (Anderson and Liddell, 1935).

Observations of this sort, on other animals and over a period of years, have raised important questions concerning the origin, development, and cure of neurotic behavior—questions already raised by Pavlov in his studies of the discriminative capacities of dogs (see Chapter 5), and questions to which Liddell himself has given much attention (Liddell, 1938). They also suggest the presence, in an apparently "pure" Pavlovian set-up, of factors which have not as yet been fully identified. Certainly the results of such experiments as Liddell's are strikingly at odds with those obtained in the conditioning of salivary and other autonomic functions.

The latter suggestion is supported by several recent demonstrations of *pseudo-conditioning,* in which motor responses not unlike foot-withdrawal have been employed, and in which "conditioning" occurred without any pairing of stimuli. For example, Reinwald (1938) has observed that white rats, after jumping and running in response to a few electric shocks, will react similarly to a tone that was initially without observable effect upon their behavior. Had this effect resulted from a succession of tone-shock combinations, it could easily have been mistaken for true conditioning. Certain strong unconditioned stimuli may, apparently, be so generally disturbing as to render an organism sensitive to influences which, under other circumstances, would not have been felt.

Indirect evidence of the complexity of supposedly simple extensions of Pavlov's technique to responses that involve action of the somatic, rather than autonomic, nervous system will be presented in the following chapter. You will see that it is possible, in some such instances, to point to the operation of another basic principle of conditioning—one that clearly applies to most of our everyday actions and is often found in combination with the one now under discussion. You will also be able to understand why one theorist (Skinner, 1938) has suggested that Pavlovian conditioning is limited exclusively to autonomic responses.

Respondent Behavior

Whatever the strengths or limitations of the Pavlovian principle, one point stands out clearly: this type of conditioning always depends upon the *elicitation* of response. Food elicits salivation; strong light elicits a pupillary constriction; shock elicits foot-withdrawal; and so on. The unconditioned stimulus is observable, and the basic reflex occurs with a regularity and automaticity comparable to the reaction of a spinal dog. Also, as with a spinal reflex, strength may be measured in terms of such properties as latency and response magnitude.

The name *respondent* has been given to stimulus-elicited behavior in order to contrast it with behavior for which no stimuli can be identified. We have adopted this term and will use it in the succeeding pages of this book. By introducing it here, we justify the title of the present chapter and pave the way for later discussion. Since all the reflexes thus far mentioned involve the action of identifiable eliciting stimuli, we may use *respondent* as the equivalent of *Pavlovian* conditioning, and we may speak of *a* respondent when referring to a specific instance of such conditioned or unconditioned behavior.

Higher-Order Conditioning

It was reported from Pavlov's laboratory, early in the twenties of this century, that a conditioned reflex, once set up, might serve as the unconditioned-reflex basis of another; and a distinction was made between *primary* and *secondary*, or *higher-order*, conditioning. Frolov, one of Pavlov's co-workers, conditioned salivation to both the sound of a buzzer and the beat of a metronome. When these two *first-order* conditionings were well established, he used them in building a second-order reflex—salivation in response to a *visual* stimulus, a black square. Great caution had to be exercised in presenting the stimuli: an interval of fifteen seconds had to elapse between the black square and the sound of the 'reinforcing' metronome beat or no conditioning was possible. Also, the secondary reflex never became very strong: the latency was great and the response magnitude was small. But some effect was discernible, in spite of the fact that the black square was never paired directly with the original food stimulus.

In another experiment, Foursikov used the foot-withdrawal response to electric shock as his basic reflex and was able to obtain results that pointed to the possibility of *third-order* conditioning. The withdrawal response was first conditioned to a tactual stimulus, then to the sound of bubbling water, and, finally, to a tone of 760 cycles per second, with each new reflex based exclusively upon the preceding one. This is schematized in the three paradigms shown on this page, where Roman numerals I, II, and III indicate the successively conditioned reflexes. Again, however, the effect required highly controlled experimental conditions, was rather unstable, and grew less as the order went higher. Also, prolonged attempts by Foursikov to set up a *fourth-order* reflex were entirely without success.

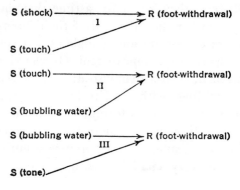

It is possible that the facts do not clearly prove the existence of higher-order conditioning. Conceivably, the findings are due to other factors in the situation than stimulus combination. In Foursikov's study, one might point to the sensitizing effect of electric shock and the similarity of the sound of tone to that of bubbling water for at least some of the effects of the conditioning procedure. Be this as it may, the influence of higher-order conditioning could hardly be expected to play much of a part in the everyday behavior of organisms, where conditions are seldom well controlled.

Pavlov's Place in Psychology

The principle of respondent conditioning, firmly established on an experimental footing, had many repercussions in psychology. It appealed especially to the objectivists in the field as a welcome replacement for the older, subjective "association of ideas"—a legacy from British philosophy. Men like John B. Watson saw in the concept at least a partial explanation of the fact that many stimulus-response relations, not discoverable in infancy, are present in adult life. Ignoring the problem which this raised for anyone who sought to identify, in any adult, *all* the stimuli for his responses, they seized upon the principle to show that everyone's behavior repertory is the final product of countless stimulus substitutions. Overwhelmed by the vision of a natural-science explanation of behavior that had previously been attributed to 'psychic' or 'mental' influence, they forgot for a time that they were at the beginning, rather than the end of their labors.

The apparent demonstration of higher-order conditioning gave added impetus to this movement. Overlooking the difficulties involved in such a demonstration, they accepted the experimental findings with alacrity as evidence of the all-embracing power of Pavlov's formulation. If the mere combination of stimuli, even if remote from the one that was initially reinforcing, sufficed to set up new stimulus-response connections, the very citadel of subjectivity—the "higher mental processes" of imagination and thought—might soon be stormed.

Pavlov himself, although not unaware of the behavioral implications of his work, was more interested in the light he thought it shed upon the functions of the brain. Conditioning, for him, depended upon the rigorous control of experimental variables—time of stimulus presentation, number of reinforcements, strength of the basic reflex, and other factors —all of which were to be studied in detail by laboratory methods. Wherever he looked, he saw *problems,* the analysis of which required research, and more research. On the other hand, his most ardent psychological admirers saw only *solutions,* answers to age-old questions. When these early enthusiasts recognized any scientific problem, it was merely the old one of identifying the stimulus components of every environmental situation and describing the responses associated therewith. And such a problem does not readily give way to experimental attack.

Nowadays we view the matter in a different way. Modern psychologists, although less interested in the physiological implications of their studies in this field, tend to lean in Pavlov's direction. That is, they have wholeheartedly adopted his experimental attitude and in general are wary of extending the principle into territory not already cleared by laboratory research. Gradually, they have taught us to see the limitations as well as the strength of Pavlov's work.

Respondent conditioning is now a well-accepted principle of behavior. Pavlov would deserve a place in the history of psychology, if for no other reason. Fortunately for us, his work did not stop at this point. When we consider, in the chapters to come, such concepts as those of "extinction," "generalization," and "discrimination," we shall again have occasion to pay homage to this Russian genius. He did not give us a complete system of behavior. In fact, we shall see that other, non-Pavlovian, principles have actually become more important in the development of such a system. But he carried us a great step forward in the path we were destined to follow in the scientific study of animal and human conduct. In retrospect, it is interesting to consider that a *physiologist* should have been the man to do so much in promoting our enterprise. We are in no position to weigh his contributions within his chosen field; we can say very little about the degree to which he cleared up the mystery of brain action; but his work will stand for many generations as a landmark in the analysis of behavior.

NOTES

The best single source-book for English-speaking students of respondent conditioning is Pavlov's *Conditioned reflexes: an investigation of the physiological activity of the cerebral cortex,* a translation from the Russian by G. V. Anrep, published in London by the Oxford University Press in 1927. Another book, a collection of Pavlov's Lectures on Conditioned Reflexes, translated by W. H. Gantt, was published in New York by International Publishers in 1928. Besides the lectures themselves, this volume includes a short biography of Pavlov (by Gantt) and a bibliography of nearly two hundred different articles which emanated from Pavlov's laboratory between 1903 and 1926. Before 1927, however, psychologists in this country had a very incomplete picture of Pavlov's work, and his influence was felt only gradually.

It has been pointed out recently, by Hilgard and Marquis (1940), that the work of Vladimir M. Bechterev actually aroused more interest in this country than did that of Pavlov himself. Bechterev, as mentioned in your chapter, dealt with responses like foot-withdrawal to electric shock. Since his publications were often in German, and occasionally in French, they were more accessible to American readers. Having been a student at Leipzig under Wundt, he retained a strong interest in psychology and an acquaintance with its problems; and he used human as well as animal subjects in his experiments. His most important book, *Objective psychology,* was translated into French and German in 1913, and his teachings are now available in English (*General principles of human reflexology,* 1932). Since 1927, however, with the appearance in English of Pavlov's monumental work, Bechterev's influence has gradually disappeared. Modifications of his basic technique are still used in many laboratories in the United States (at Yale, Cornell, Rochester, and Indiana, to mention but a few), but researchers have quite generally adopted the terminology and systematic concepts of Pavlov.

Among the names associated with the early development of interest in Pavlov (and Bechterev) in this country are those of R. M. Yerkes and S. Morgulis (1909), J. B. Watson (1916), K. S. Lashley (1916), W. H. Burnham (1917), F. Mateer (1918), S. Smith and E. R. Guthrie (1921), H. Cason (1922), and F. H. Allport (1924). You will find an excellent review of this development, together with a summary of some important Pavlovian concepts, in the first two chapters of *Conditioning and learning* (Hilgard and Marquis, 1940).

A good review of early studies in stimulus compounding (in Russia and elsewhere) is available in a paper by G. H. S. Razran (1939c). This is one of many reviews by Razran, whose scholarly interests and acquaintance with the Russian language have permitted him to render invaluable service to his American colleagues. Except for the translations of Pavlov's books, our principal contact with Russian research has been made through Razran's efforts.

3

OPERANT CONDITIONING

Suppose, now, that in putting out its head to seize prey scarcely within reach, a creature has repeatedly failed. Suppose that along with the group of motor actions approximately adapted to seize prey at this distance, . . . a slight forward movement of the body [is caused on some occasion]. Success will occur instead of failure. . . . On recurrence of the circumstances, these muscular movements that were followed by success are likely to be repeated: what was at first an accidental combination of motions will now be a combination having considerable probability.

Herbert Spencer, *Principles of Psychology,* 1855

Thorndike and the Law of Effect

In 1898, five years before the term *conditioned reflex* appeared in print, an important psychological monograph was published in the United States. Its title was "Animal Intelligence: An Experimental Study of the Associative Processes in Animals," and it was written as a doctoral dissertation by Edward Lee Thorndike (1874-1949) at Columbia University. This study was important for two main reasons: (1) it introduced an experimental method of investigating the problem-solving behavior of animals; and (2) it attempted to account for such behavior in terms of *associations* (stimulus-response connections) that were strengthened by their results.

In Thorndike's experiments, cats, dogs, and chicks were subjects, but, in the present account, we shall limit ourselves to his studies with cats, which may be taken as typical of his work. With these animals, fifteen different forms of "problem box" were used as apparatus, representing as many different problems for solution. Most of the boxes were crate-like affairs, about twenty inches long, fifteen inches wide, and twelve inches high. At the top of each was a trap-door through which a cat might be dropped into the box, and on one side was a door through which he might escape and get to a small bit of food (meat or fish) on the floor outside. The door was held in a closed position by a bolt or a bar, but could be opened from within when some release-mechanism—a latch, a wire loop, a lever, or some other simple device—was properly manipulated by the cat.

The experimental procedure for any given task was roughly as follows. A hungry cat was dropped into the box and left there until, in the course of his activity, he happened to operate the appropriate release-mechanism—for example, until he pulled a loop or depressed a lever that opened the door. As soon as he left the box and ate the morsel of food that awaited him outside, he was taken up by the experimenter and put back in the box, the door of which had again been locked. After a second escape and feeding, the procedure was repeated; and so on.

For each problem, Thorndike noted the time required by the animal to escape from the box on each successive trial. Figure 5 shows, graphically, the number of seconds needed by one cat on each of twenty-four trials to make a loop-pulling escape response.

This curve, which is fairly representative of results obtained with other cats and other problems, helps us to understand what took place in these studies. First, we see an overall reduction in the time per trial required for the animal to get out of the box. The number of seconds needed for the first escape was 160; for the twenty-fourth, it was only seven. The amount and the rapidity of the drop was greater for some problems and some animals than it was for others; and there was a wide variation in the number of trials required before the escape-time became minimal. Secondly, it appears that, in spite of the general decrease of time as the number of trials increased, there was considerable irregularity. Setbacks in the animal's progress were fairly common. Thus escape from the box on the second trial required but thirty seconds, whereas, on trial three, which followed immediately, ninety seconds were needed. In some of Thorndike's other experiments, these irregularities were even more pronounced and continued for many trials before a consistent, quick solution developed.

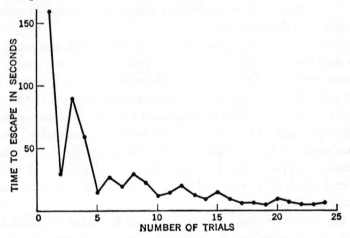

FIG. 5. Time taken to escape by one of Thorndike's cats on successive trials in a problem box. (After Thorndike, 1898.)

While gathering the time records, Thorndike did not fail to observe the behavior of his subjects. He noted, for example, that a cat, when first confronted with his problem, commonly made vigorous attempts to escape confinement. "It tries to squeeze through any opening; it claws and bites at the bars or wire; it thrusts its paws out through any opening and claws at everything it reaches; ... For eight or ten minutes it will claw and bite and squeeze incessantly." (*Psychol. Monogr.*, 1898.)

In the course of such activity, nearly all the cats hit upon the response that opened the door and gave access to food. When returned to the box for the second test, the struggling recommenced, and continued until a second solution was achieved. Gradually (in some cases, rather suddenly), with successive confinements and escapes, the amount of useless activity diminished and the cat's behavior became clearly oriented toward the release-mechanism. Finally, a well-directed and stereotyped mode of response developed: the "problem" was solved.

According to Thorndike, the solution of such a problem by cats and other animals involved the formation of an association between some aspect of the stimulus-situation, such as the wire loop or the wooden lever, with the specific movement that led to door-opening. Further, he argued, the stimulus-response relation that finally appeared was obviously influenced by the outcome of this movement. The pleasure experienced by the animal in getting out of the box and to the food served to stamp in the connection between stimulus and response that led to the pleasure. By the same token, stimulus-response connections that did not lead to a pleasurable after-effect were not strengthened, and tended to drop out.

Here was the first approximation to a basic principle of behavior. Thirteen years later, when Thorndike republished his monograph as part of a book on *Animal intelligence* (1911), the same idea was presented formally as the *Law of Effect:*

Of several responses made to the same situation, those which are accompanied or closely followed by satisfaction to the animal will, other things being equal, be more firmly connected with the situation, so that, when it recurs, they will be more likely to recur; those which are accompanied or closely followed by discomfort to the animal will, other things being equal, have their connections with the situation weakened, so that, when it recurs, they will be less likely to occur. The greater the satisfaction or discomfort, the greater the strengthening or weakening of the bond. (Thorndike, E. L., *Animal intelligence: experimental studies.* New York, Macmillan, 1911, p. 244.)

By this time, Thorndike had joined the staff of Teachers College at Columbia University and had embarked upon a long career of productive research in psychology and education. A man of strong practical interests, powerful motivation, and striking originality, his yearly output of work was enormous in bulk and varied in content. From his early experiments with animals, he was led to problems of human learning, classroom procedures, dictionary construction, intelligence testing, and vocational guidance. Wherever he turned, he never lost sight of his fundamental principle and, from time to time, he brought forth specific evidence of its operation.

The law of effect was not Thorndike's only answer to the way learning takes place in animals and human beings. Early in his thinking (1898), he recognized a *law of exercise* according to which connections are strengthened through mere repetition and weakened through disuse. By 1932, however, he was led by his own research to renounce his former position and to argue against exercise as a factor working independently of effect. Also, in 1913, he proposed a *law of readiness,* but this was little more than a guess, in terms of "conduction units," as to the physiological conditions underlying the operation of his basic principle, and never played a very important rôle in his research. Somewhat more interesting and more empirically grounded were five subsidiary laws which were intended to supplement the primary ones. One of these, that of *associative shifting,* is the Thorndikian counterpart of Pavlov's principle, and another *(response by analogy)* bears some resemblance to the principle of *generalization* with which we shall deal in Chapter 5. In the main, however, he left these subordinate laws in a relatively undeveloped state and we need not give them elaborate treatment here.

The law of effect was, then, Thorndike's major contribution, and the beginner in psychology generally accepts his formulation without question. "Trial and error, with accidental success" seems to describe satisfactorily a great deal of problem-solving behavior as he knows it in his everyday life. He is usually quite ready to believe that many of his own reactions to stimulus situations are firmly implanted because of their effects. In fact, he may tell you that, long before he heard of Thorndike, he had assumed the operation of some such general principle and could have told you about it if you had asked him. How else, he may say, does one find his way about in a strange city, 'learn the ropes' of a new occupation, solve a Chinese puzzle, or master any complicated skill, except through the effect of the success that attends his trial-and-error behavior?

You may, therefore, be surprised to hear that Thorndike's principle was challenged by psychologists in many quarters. How can it be, said one group of critics, that "pleasure" or "satisfaction," which are *mental* states, exercise an influence upon such clearly *physical* phenomena as responses to stimuli? How, said others, can the *results* of an action have any effect upon the action itself when the action is over and done with before the results are apparent—what sort of cause-effect relation is this, in which the effect has to function as the cause? Still others, less concerned with the philosophy or logic of Thorndike's position, argued that his formulation was lacking in generality and not always supported by fact. Observations were brought forward to show (1) that trial-and-error was typical only of a very restricted form of problem solving—one in which "insight" into the situation was prohibited by the very conditions of the experiment; (2) that, even with Thorndike's cats, the solution of a problem was not always "hit-or-miss" and gradually achieved, but was, at least in some cases, practically reached on the very first trial; and (3) that learning is possible without *any* effect—as when rats, given a chance to run a maze prior to the introduction of any food reward, showed by their speed of learning in later, rewarded runs that they had profited from their 'unrewarded' explorations.

In view of later developments, such arguments, and a great deal of the research that they fostered, were somewhat beside the point. They served to obscure, rather than clarify, a fundamental principle; to delay, rather than hasten, an important line of investigation. A full appreciation of Thorndike's contribution did not come until thirty-odd years after his first monograph was published, when the principle was re-affirmed and placed clearly within a larger body of theory.

Skinner and Operant Conditioning

In 1930, there was published, in the Proceedings of the National Academy of Science, a short paper on the eating behavior of white rats. The author was B. F. Skinner, then a graduate student in psychology at Harvard University. Skinner described, in his paper, an experimental method that, in slightly modified form, has become a fixture in modern experimental research. It involved simply (1) a device for giving a small pellet of food to a hungry white rat each time that the animal pushed open the swinging door of a food-bin at one end of his experimental chamber; and (2) a recording mechanism that caused a vertical movement of a pen upon the paper-covered surface of a slowly revolving cylinder (a kymograph drum) whenever the rat opened the door of the bin to obtain the pellet. The vertical pen marks were made at right angles to the drum movement and were cumulative— that is, each upward distance that the pen moved was added, by a ratchet device, to the preceding one. Since a short period of time was required for the eating of each pellet before the next door-opening took place, and since the drum continued to revolve steadily during this period, each mark was displaced slightly to the right of the preceding one. This provided a step-wise record, of the sort shown in Figure 6. The vertical lines (of equal length) indicate successive door-opening responses and the horizontal lines (not necessarily equal in length) indicate the time elapsing between responses. Since the pellets were of a constant size and weight (about $\frac{1}{15}$ of a gram), an *eating rate* is represented.

The step-wise effect is very obvious in Figure 6 because of the size of the time-units and response-units we have selected. If the units had been smaller, the effect would have been less pronounced. Figure 7 is copied from an actual record ob-

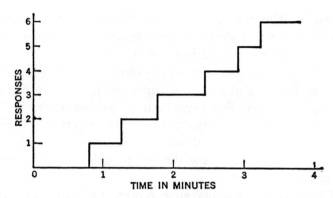

FIG. 6. Illustrating the construction of a cumulative record of bar-pressing responses.

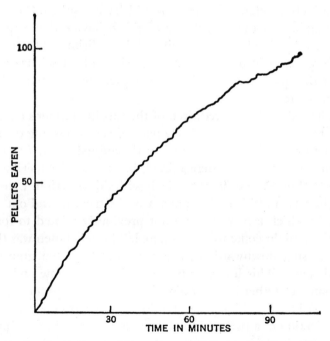

FIG. 7. A cumulative record of a rat's food-getting responses (bar-pressing for pellets) during a daily eating period. (After Skinner, 1938.)

tained in Skinner's experiment. In this case, the steps are so close together that they are imperceptible in our copy and a fairly smooth *curve* of eating results.

Such a curve is characteristically obtained when a rat is fed daily with pellets at a regular time, and is deprived of food during the intervening periods. It shows that, under such a regimen, the animal begins by responding at a relatively high rate and gradually slows down as he nears the point of satiation. The curve is, to use the mathematician's term, *negatively accelerated*.

The curve does not, of course, represent *all* eating behavior in rats. Had the animals been permitted to live in the experimental box and eat whenever their hunger led them to do so, they would probably have eaten at a somewhat slower but very constant rate on each occasion: *straight-line,* rather than negatively accelerated, curves would have resulted. The important fact is the *orderliness* of the behavior that appears under a specified set of experimental conditions. The search for orderly relationships is characteristic of all science and, with the discovery of a single example, one is often led to hunt for more.

The only behavior required of the rats in Skinner's experiment was the simple and fairly natural act of pushing open a door to reach food. How or when the animal *learned* to perform this act was not determined, but a second experiment, reported by Skinner in 1932, dealt with this question. Using a modification of his earlier apparatus, he tried to find out the way in which a new act, one not previously related to food-getting, might come to be so related. The act chosen was that of pressing downward, with a force of about ten grams, a small lever. This lever, or bar, was situated at one end of a response chamber in a sound-resistant and light-proof experimental box (see Figure 8). Its downward movement caused the ejection of a pellet of food, from a magazine in an adjoining chamber, into a small metal cup or tray. With every activation of the food-magazine by the bar depression, a record was made on a kymograph drum outside the experimental box. The record was cumulative, as in the study of eating rate.

The experimental procedure involved (1) a preliminary acclimatization of the hungry animal to the response chamber, with a supply of food in the tray, until he moved and ate freely in the situation; (2) further sessions in which the rat was accustomed to eating pellets, when they were discharged, one at a time, from the food-magazine by the experimenter; and (3) training in the bar-pressing response. Stage 3, the important one in this experiment, was conducted as follows.

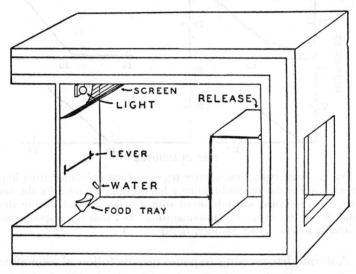

FIG. 8. An early model of Skinner's bar-pressing apparatus. (From Skinner, 1938.)

After twenty-four hours' deprivation of food, the rat was placed in the response compartment of the box. The bar was present, the food-magazine was filled with pellets, and a water supply was obtainable from a small tube near the tray, but the tray itself was empty. When the rat approached the tray, as he had learned to do in stages 1 and 2, and found no food, he soon engaged in exploratory behavior of one sort or another within the chamber. In ten or fifteen minutes, often sooner, this exploration led to a depression of the bar, usually accomplished by one or both of the rat's forepaws as he raised himself to sniff at the wall above the tray or at the slots through which the bar entered the chamber. The bar-depression was accompanied by the click of the food-magazine (to which the rat was accustomed in stage 2) and the ejection of a pellet into the tray. At the same time, the response was recorded on the kymograph drum outside the box.

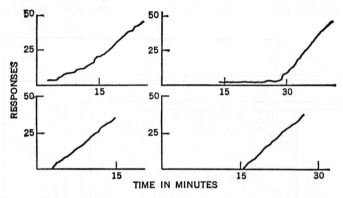

FIG. 9. Some typical cumulative response curves obtained from hungry rats on the day of conditioning a bar-pressing response for the first time. Each response was reinforced with a pellet of food. Notice that conditioning is commonly "instantaneous," and that the response rate is usually steady. (After Skinner, 1938.)

A second bar-pressing response usually followed soon after, in some cases immediately after, the first pellet had been seized and eaten, and the animal quickly developed a maximal rate of pressing and eating. The sample records in Figure 9 illustrate this clearly. The two lower curves in this figure show the immediate development of a maximal response rate; the upper curves show a slight *positive* acceleration at their beginning, with a few responses occurring before a constant eating rate appears.

It is clear from these curves that the rats quickly learned to press the bar when food resulted from the act. Indeed, if we were unaware of the preliminary stages of the experiment—the acclimatizing of the animal to the apparatus and the training to approach the tray when the magazine was operated—we might conclude from some of the records that the rat had already solved the bar-pressing problem when it was first presented. Except in those animals that produced positively accelerated curves, the learning process was practically instantaneous. And in no case was there anything comparable to the gradual and irregular progress that typified the behavior of Thorndike's cats.

Skinner called his study an experiment "On the Rate of Formation of a Conditioned Reflex." It was obvious to him, however, that the rat's behavior could not adequately be described in terms of the conventional Pavlovian paradigm. A number of insurmountable barriers stood directly in the path of such an analysis. A practical exercise will convince you of the difficulties in applying Pavlov's principle to the bar-pressing situation. Construct for yourself the paradigm, after the model in Chapter 2, labeling each S and R appropriately to show how the reflex is established. What are the two reflexes with which you begin? Where is the third reflex, the conditioned one? How does the 'conditioned' stimulus come to act as a substitute for the 'unconditioned' in eliciting the response to the latter? Be sure that you limit yourself to *observable*, rather than purely hypothetical, stimuli and responses.

As an outcome of his own struggle with this problem, Skinner proposed, in 1935, and again in 1937, that we recognize *two* types of conditioning: Type S and Type R. Type S is no more than the classical Pavlovian conditioning, in which reinforcement is always related to the presentation of a *stimulus*—for example, food is given when a tone is sounded. Type R, which is represented in the acquisition of bar-pressing behavior, involves a relation between reinforcement and a specific *response*—thus, food is given when the bar is pressed.

A paradigm suitable for Type R conditioning is shown below, along with the familiar Type S schema. A comparison of the two will help you to understand some of the ways in which the two types differ.

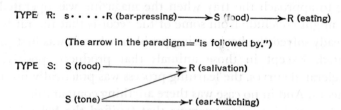

(The arrow in the paradigm = "is followed by.")

Type S conditioning, as we have seen, involves the *elicitation* of a response (salivation) by an identifiable conditioned stimulus (tone) that is under the experimenter's control. In Type R conditioning, the specific stimulus that initially evokes the response (bar-pressing) *cannot* be identified. This is indicated by the small *s* of the Type R paradigm. We need not assume that bar-pressing has no cause or that it can bear no relation to environmental stimuli; we shall see, in Chapter 5, that stimuli may "set the occasion" for this response. But, for all practical purposes, the response just *occurs,* is initially *emitted,* without relation to any specifiable stimulus agency.

Type S conditioning involves *stimulus substitution* and the formation of a *new reflex.* The tone, in our example, comes to act as a substitute for food in eliciting salivation; and tone-salivation is the new reflex. In Type R conditioning, however, there is merely the strengthening of a reflex that already exists in the organism's repertory. Bar-pressing, for instance, occurs with *some* frequency prior to any reinforcement with food. At any rate, no substitution is involved and no new stimulus-response relation is formed.

Type S conditioning *prepares* the organism for reinforcement. The tone comes to elicit salivation in advance of the food, paving the way, as it were, for its digestion. Type R conditioning *procures* or *produces* the reinforcement—bar-pressing provides the rat with a food pellet. The two processes may take place concurrently, although our observation is usually limited to one of them. Pavlov himself noted that Type S conditioning was commonly accompanied by "motor reactions" of head-turning and the like which we would now ascribe to the development of a Type R conditioning. More recently, another investigator (Brogden, 1939b) has shown that when dogs are reinforced with food for making a leg movement (Type R conditioning) in the presence of a tone, there is the simultaneous development of conditioned (Type S) salivation.

With respect to this last distinction, a simple example may not be superfluous. A hungry boy, home from school, is met at the door with the odor of freshly baked cookies. In accordance with his history of Type S conditioning, his 'mouth waters,' preparing him for what may follow. But *nothing* will follow unless he has been conditioned in Type R fashion to make his way to the kitchen and exhibit the verbal or other behavior which, in the past, has been productive of cookies.

The Law of Operant Conditioning

These differences between Type S and Type R conditioning are associated with a broader distinction, mentioned briefly in the preceding chapter, between two fundamental classes of behavior. One of these, which includes all those responses, conditioned or unconditioned, that are *elicited* by known stimuli, we called *respondent*. The other class, comprising all those responses that are *emitted* more or less independently of identifiable stimuli, we may now call *operant*. The spontaneous movements of an infant organism, human or otherwise, are mainly of the latter type; and so are the "voluntary" acts of human beings. In fact, most of our behavior in the routine affairs of everyday life is clearly operant, in that it *operates* or acts upon the environment to produce the satisfaction of our basic needs. Respondent behavior is much less commonly observed and seldom, it ever, operates upon the environment to produce anything.

Operant behavior is conditioned primarily, if not exclusively, in Type R fashion; respondent behavior is usually conditioned in Type S fashion. Hence, when its suits our convenience, we may speak of Type R as operant conditioning, in the same way that we speak of Type S as respondent. Again, just as we refer to any single example of respondent behavior as *a* respondent, we shall refer to each example of operant behavior as *an* operant.

We have seen, in Chapter 2, that the *strength* of a respondent is commonly measured in terms of latency and response magnitude. Neither of these measures is satisfactory in determining the strength of an operant. Latency can have no meaning in the absence of an identifiable stimulus from which to measure the *S-R* interval; and the magnitude of an operant response does not change during conditioning in the orderly manner that typifies the respondent. The amount of saliva secreted by a dog in response to a tone may increase gradually with successive tone-food combinations, but the force of a bar-pressing response may be as great on its first appearance as it is on its fifty-first, and it may fluctuate throughout a long series of emissions.

Our best measure of operant strength is *frequency of occurrence*. An operant is strong when emitted often within a given period of time; it is weak when emitted rarely. We have, in a sense, assumed this already, in the case of bar-pressing: a steady, high rate of responding implied a strong response-tendency, whereas a slow, uneven rate implied a weak one. In the case of a respondent, frequency is a useless measure—in fact, no measure at all—since the response rate is determined solely by the rate at which the eliciting stimulus is presented to the organism.

"If the occurrence of an operant is followed by the presentation of a reinforcing stimulus, the strength is increased." (Skinner, 1938.) We can now begin to grasp the significance of this statement of the principle of Type R conditioning. Bar-pressing is an operant. It occurs with a certain low frequency prior to any experimental procedures that we may apply. Its strength is increased when it is followed by reinforcement. Increased strength means merely that it occurs with higher frequency than it did before.

Table II
COMPARISON BETWEEN TYPE S AND TYPE R CONDITIONING

Type S	Type R
Paradigm: $$S_1 \longrightarrow R_1$$ $$S_2 \cdots\cdots r_2$$	Paradigm: $$s \cdots\cdots R \longrightarrow S \text{ (reinforcement)}$$
Response is elicited.	Response is emitted.
Stimulus substitution.	No substitution of stimuli.
Formation of new reflex.	Strengthening of reflex already in repertory.
"Preparation" by conditioned stimulus for the unconditioned reinforcement that follows. The response does not manipulate the environment.	Response "procures" the reinforcement. The response "operates" on the environment.
Commonly, if not always, is mediated by the autonomic nervous system, involving smooth muscles and glands.	Mediated by somatic nervous system, involving skeletal muscles.
Usually measured in terms of reflex latency or magnitude.	Usually measured in terms of reflex rate; sometimes, latency.

Operant Conditioning and the Law of Effect

When you compare the work of Skinner with that of Thorndike, you may be impressed by the numerous dissimilarities. The two men used different species of animals, different apparatus, and different experimental procedures. Yet, when you consider that both situations required a manipulation of some environmental object; when you note that the presentation of food was in each case contingent upon this manipulation; and when you compare the principle of Type R conditioning with the law of effect, you may notice a striking agreement. Both formulations emphasize the influence of the outcome of a response upon its strength: Thorndike calls it "satisfaction" and Skinner speaks of a "reinforcing stimulus." Skinner's formula seems to be the narrower of the two, since it contains no equivalent of Thorndike's "discomfort," yet Thorndike himself later came to discount the weakening effect of discomfort—a point to which we shall return later.

There is still another similarity. In spite of Thorndike's emphasis upon a connection or bond between situation and response, it is perfectly clear that he does not refer to the Pavlovian type of connection. He would have been the last to suggest that the loop-pulling or other manipulative behavior of his cats was elicited in the same way that food elicits salivation, a shock elicits foot-withdrawal, or a cinder in the eye elicits tears.

This last point requires some elaboration. Throughout much of the present chapter, we have underlined the fact that a large proportion of an organism's behavior is emitted rather than elicited, and is conditioned in Type R rather than Type S fashion. We may have led you to think that responses like loop-pulling and bar-pressing can have no relation whatever to stimuli. If such was your impression, it should be corrected. Operant behavior, however spontaneous in its initial occurrence, very soon becomes associated with stimuli. The cat that has learned to pull the loop, or the rat that has learned to press the bar, reacts to stimuli or stimulus combinations, even if we cannot specify them completely. In the absence of a loop or bar, the animal seldom paws the air. But these stimuli are *not* eliciting: they are not related to their responses in the same way that salivation is related to food or foot-withdrawal is related to electric shock. It is just that the responses are *more likely to occur* in the presence of such objects. To use an expression quoted earlier, these stimuli *set the occasion* for responses. Later on, when we consider this matter in more detail, we shall refer to them as *discriminative* stimuli.

The Runway Technique

In the discovery and demonstration of basic principles, everything depends upon the kind of method that we employ. We seek, first, to find lawful relationships between known variables. This is the aim of all scientific endeavor. But, at the same time, we hope that our findings can be related to each other, within an integrated whole, and that our generalizations will apply to less restricted experimental situations than the one from which they were initially drawn. In these respects the bar-pressing technique has proved especially useful, as you will see again and again in the pages to come. It is, however, by no means the only method to which experimental psychologists have appealed in their attempts to analyze the behavior of organisms.

A relatively simple means of studying operant behavior, and one in which Type R conditioning is readily apparent, is the *runway* method. In this procedure, as recently employed by Graham and Gagné (1940), hungry rats are used as subjects. After several periods of acclimatization to experimental conditions, the animal is placed in a starting-box, the sliding door of which opens to an elevated wooden pathway, three feet long and three-quarters of an inch wide. At the other end of the pathway is a food-box, identical in its dimensions with the starting-box. The rat's task is merely that of running from the starting-box to the food-box when the door of the former is opened by the experimenter. Upon entering the food-box, the door of which is then closed behind him, he is reinforced with a bit of food. When the food is eaten, the boxes are carefully interchanged and, after a pause for equalizing the between-run intervals and baiting the new food-box, the procedure is repeated.

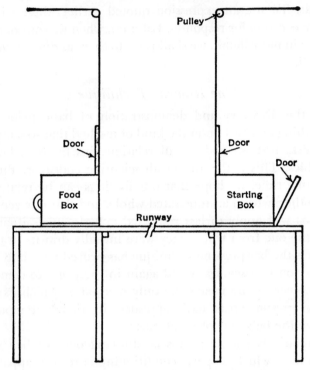

FIG. 10. A version of the Graham-Gagné apparatus. (After Raben, 1949.)

Progress in this task is measured in terms of the time elapsing between the opening of the starting-box door and the rat's
passing of a point four inches along the runway. This time
interval was found by Graham and Gagné to decrease on successive runs. For a group of 21 animals, the average (geometrical mean) value obtained on the first run was 71 seconds.
The second trial required only 17 seconds and, by the fif-
teenth run, the low value of 2.8 seconds was reached. These
data are represented in Figure 11.

It is obvious, in this study, that operant conditioning
occurred, through the reinforcement of the running response
with food. Yet the situation is different in certain important
respects from the one used in bar-pressing studies. For ex-

ample, in the Graham-Gagné method, the experimenter, as well as the subject, determines the frequency of the running response. Only at certain intervals is the response made possible. This is essentially the trial-by-trial procedure employed by Thorndike in his problem-box experiments; and Thorndike, too, used a time-measure of progress. It is interesting to note that, although the curve of Figure 11 is an averaged record of 21 rats, it resembles closely that of Figure 5 (page 38), obtained by Thorndike with a single cat.

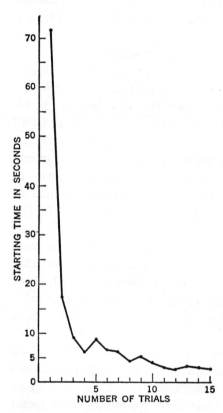

FIG. 11. A plot of average starting times on successive trials by a group of rats on the Graham-Gagné apparatus. (From data provided by Graham and Gagné, 1940.)

Another point of difference between the runway and bar-pressing techniques lies in the fact that the runway requires conditioning of a *series* or chain of responses (see Chapter 7) that take more time and are presumably greater in number than in the case of bar-pressing. Consequently, the reinforcement of the bar-pressing response is more immediate and direct than the reinforcement for leaving the starting-box when the door is opened. It is probably for this reason that the whole runway performance is learned more gradually than is bar-pressing.

The Maze Technique

You have probably recognized that the bar-pressing technique is actually a simplified form of the problem-box method, in which the trial-wise procedure is replaced by the more useful "free operant" arrangement—that is, the animal determines his own response rate. Similarly, the *runway* method may be considered as the final stage of another important line of development in the investigation of operant behavior. In 1901, when Thorndike was busy with his problem-solving studies at Columbia, W. S. Small, at Clark University, was exploring the trial-and-error behavior of rats with a device that was soon to enjoy tremendous vogue among American psychologists. Even today, when the popularity of this device has greatly decreased, the beginning student of psychology generally expects any reference to rats to be followed by talk about *mazes*.

Interest in mazes or labyrinths is understandable. The early Greek equivalent of "labyrinth" was applied to intricate underground passages and networks of chambers, which never fail to stir the imagination. From the great Egyptian labyrinth, described by Herodotus as containing 3,000 chambers, to the decorative garden mazes of eighteenth-century France and England, and the amusement-park mazes of modern times, men have been intrigued by such devices. It is not strange that Small, in his search for a task the mastery of which would be slow and measurable for animals that spend most of their lives in dark and winding passages, should have hit upon this form of apparatus.

The maze that Small built was a crude, wire-mesh affair, with a sawdust-covered floor. In design (see Figure 12), it was modeled after the famous hedge maze on the grounds of Hampton Court Palace in England. Like most mazes used since, it comprised a series of straight-aways, turns, choice-points, and blind alleys, with a reward at the end of the route. Progress can be shown by the reduction of running-time on successive trials, or in the number of blind-alley entrances. Small's own studies were not extensive, but suggested several lines of research. He noted that rats decreased their

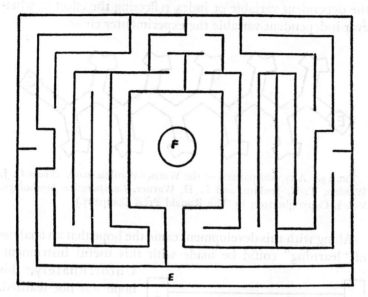

FIG. 12.   Design of the Hampton Court maze used by Small. The animal starts at *E*, and finds food at *F*. (From Small, 1901.)

running-time and errors with continued practice; that they adopted a short-cut provided by the pattern (at the fourth choice point); that lessened hunger brought greater variability of behavior; and that they seemed to depend less upon sight and smell than upon touch or movement (proprioceptive) cues. All these matters were subjected to later study by other investigators, who improved and standardized the training procedure and developed new and more reliable apparatus (see Figure 13) . Maze units were equalized in length and increased in number; one-way doors were introduced to prevent retracing of paths; extra-maze distractions were eliminated; motivation was more rigorously controlled; and so on. Such studies were undertaken to determine the influence upon maze-learning scores of such factors as age, sex, previous maze experience, sense-organ participation, distribution of practice, and brain destruction. Maze performance was, thus, the dependent variable or index reflecting the effect of whatever independent variable the experimenter chose.

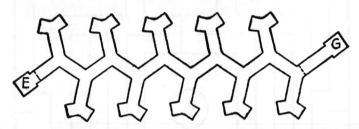

FIG. 13. A typical pattern of the Warner-Warden maze. (From C. J. Warden, T. N. Jenkins, and L. H. Warner, *Comparative psychology,* Vol. I. Copyright 1935 by The Ronald Press Company.)

Along with this development came the hope that an analysis of "learning" could be made with this useful instrument.

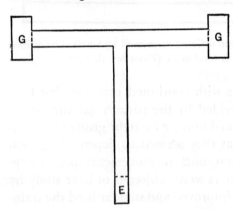

FIG. 14. A T-maze with a single choice point. The animal starts at *E,* and reinforcement is located at one of the endboxes (*G*).

Unfortunately, this hope was not realized. It gradually became clear that maze-learning was an exceedingly complicated affair, and that the maze itself was not the simple device that it had seemed to be. Even when attention was centered upon the behavior of a rat at a single choice point, the problems involved were too great for the kind of description most desired by the scientist.

We shall return to the problem of maze-learning in a later

chapter, after you have become acquainted with the concepts required for its explanation. For the present, we may limit ourselves to the statement that, for a *close* analysis of behavior, the maze is useful only when reduced to its very simplest form—that is, when it becomes no more than a runway or a single T.

Quick Learning

It was noted, earlier in this chapter, that the bar-pressing response of a white rat may be conditioned with a single reinforcement; and two cases of this were pictured in the cumulative response curves of Figure 9. This is not an unusual finding. Suppose you were to use a modification of the Skinner apparatus (see Figure 8) in which the animal's living-cage is transformed into a response chamber by the mere insertion of a bar. Under such circumstances, with hungry animals, and with only the briefest of acclimatizing and pre-training periods, "one-trial learning" is commonly observed. Seldom does conditioning fail to occur within a few minutes after the bar is first presented. The rat, one might say, "gets the point" immediately, often reaching a steady response-rate after the discharge of but one pellet into his tray.

This kind of behavior has sometimes been likened to the sudden, "insightful" achievements of animals higher than the rat in the phylogenetic scale. For example, Wolfgang Köhler (1925) presented chimpanzees with a variety of fruit-getting problems—stacking boxes, using sticks, taking detours, and the like. He noticed, and described vividly, many instances in which the apes, after a preliminary survey of the situation, attained their objectives quickly and conclusively, in almost-human fashion, without any discernible "trial and error." Such results are in sharp contrast with the slow, stepwise progress of rats in mazes and cats in problem-boxes, and Köhler argued that his own animals, by virtue of the experimenter's choice of problem situation, were permitted to show their true intelligence or use of "insight."

Today we can say that the sudden or one-trial mastery of *any* problem is due to one, or both, of two factors: (1) the *similarity* of the problem to one that was solved on an earlier occasion, or (2) the *simplicity* of the problem itself. Köhler's findings are probably attributable, in large part, to the first of these factors. He took samplings of behavior, like those taken in human intelligence tests; and the success of his animals may be ascribed to their past history of conditioning (see our treatment of similarity in Chapter 5). Rapid acquisition of the bar-pressing response, on the other hand, is traceable primarily to the relatively uncomplicated nature of the task. Bar-pressing has considerable unconditioned strength to begin with: it occurs with more than zero frequency prior to any reinforcement that we provide. Moreover, the specific movements involved are very few in number, and this is a good reason for calling a problem "simple." We could easily complicate matters in the bar-pressing situation, say by demanding a greater force of response, or by placing the food tray at some distance from the bar, so that the animal would have to leave the vicinity of the tray to obtain the next reinforcement. By requiring this additional activity, we could undoubtedly lengthen the learning time, *unless* the rat had had experience in getting food under similar circumstances.

In the case of human beings, the solution of problems may be speeded up by a special set of conditions. It is too early for us to consider these conditions here, but we may note that the possession of *language* is often of help in reducing the time required or the number of errors made in the mastery of certain tasks. Thus, the person who 'verbalizes' his choice-responses while finding his way through a complicated maze will make a performance record definitely superior to that of a person who does not employ such aids (Warden, 1924). Apparently, verbal sequences can be memorized by the human learner faster than the purely manual or locomotor pattern. These verbal sequences arise from his movements and then come to direct the chain in a discriminative fashion. In some instances, the rate of improvement is so dramatic as to obscure the fact that essentially the same basic principles are involved in verbal as in non-verbal behavior.

Positive and Negative Reinforcement

Thorndike, in his 1911 statement of the law of effect, spoke of the strengthening effect of "satisfaction" upon the bond between situation and response. Today, avoiding controversy about the nature of "satisfaction," we would say that the food he gave to his cats for opening a problem-box door was *positively* reinforcing. On the observational level, this would mean exactly what Thorndike meant—that the effect of the food was to increase the frequency of the response that produced it. We know, too, that water, for a thirsty animal, would have had a similar effect. Food and water belong to a class of positive reinforcers.

This is not all that Thorndike said. He spoke also of the weakening effect of "discomfort" upon situation-response connections. Certain stimuli (electric shocks, loud sounds, strong lights, etc.) serve to *decrease* the frequency of responses in the wake of which they follow. Nowadays, we call them *negative* reinforcers, but they are not best defined in terms of their weakening function. By 1932, Thorndike himself argued that "rewards" and "punishments" are not opposed to each other in the manner implied by his earlier formulation; and we shall offer evidence, in the next chapter, to show that the weakening effect of negatively reinforcing stimuli is not permanent.

Another, and probably a better, way of handling the matter is to define *positive* reinforcers as those stimuli which strengthen responses when *presented* (e.g., food strengthens bar-pressing or loop-pulling behavior), and *negative* reinforcers as those which strengthen when they are *removed*. Experimentally, a number of responses have been conditioned in animals entirely on the basis of escape from, or reduction of, certain stimulus conditions. Mowrer (1940) showed, for example, that a panel-pushing response could be rapidly set up in white rats when it was reinforced by the removal of electric-shock stimulation; and Keller (1942) obtained similar results when he conditioned bar-pressing in rats by the simple device of turning off a bright light for sixty seconds whenever the response was emitted in its presence. At the everyday level, too, we often see the results of this kind of strengthening. We move out of the heat of the noonday sun; we close the window that shuts out the roar of traffic; we take off the shoes that pinch our feet; and we kindle the fire that will warm our hands. In each case, we perform an act that has previously been strengthened because it produced the cessation of a "noxious" or "annoying" stimulus.

We have, then, two ways of defining negative reinforcers: the first is in terms of the weakening effect they have when presented; the second is in terms of the strengthening effect of their removal. The effect is upon *operant* behavior; an operant is weakened in one case and strengthened in the other. Yet, it should be noted that the *same* operant cannot simultaneously undergo both changes. A strong light, applied briefly whenever a bar-pressing response occurs, will depress the frequency of the pressing (Schoenfeld, 1947); if the same light is continuously applied until a bar-pressing response occurs, and is then immediately extinguished, the response will be strengthened. But the response cannot produce and remove a stimulus at one and the same time.

Operant-Respondent Overlap

Coincidental with their effect upon operant behavior, negatively reinforcing stimuli may exercise another function: they may serve as *eliciting* stimuli for *respondent* behavior. Two cases arise: (1) elicitation may accompany the *weakening* function of a negative reinforcer, as when a strong electric shock inhibits bar-pressing and, at the same time, elicits foot-withdrawal, squealing, blood-pressure changes, and so forth; and (2) it may accompany the *strengthening* function, as when a shock elicits a foot-withdrawal, which is then strengthened operant-wise by the shock-removal. The second case is represented in the accompanying paradigm.

S (shock) ⟶ R (flexion) ⟶ S (shock-removal)

Another combination of elicitation and operant strengthening is seen in an experiment reported by Konorski and Miller (1937). Using an electric shock just intense enough to elicit a leg-raising response in a dog, they gave food to the animal after each elicitation. The scheme, then, would be this:

S (shock) ⟶ R (flexion) ⟶ S (food)

Here the shock elicits flexion and the flexion 'produces' food. We are therefore prepared for the finding that "after a few reinforcements the animal starts to raise its leg independently of electrical shock—as soon as it finds itself in the given experimental situation." (Konorski and Miller, 1937, p. 266) Such cases of overlap may be hard to understand unless you perceive that, with the use of shock, one elicits responses of those very muscles which are used in operant behavior.

A question often occurs in connection with operant-respondent overlap: since a skeletal-muscle or 'motor' respondent, such as foot-withdrawal to shock, may be conditioned in a Type R manner, cannot an autonomic respondent, like salivation or the galvanic skin response, be strengthened by the same procedure? Very little information exists on this point, but the answer is probably No. One may apparently strengthen an operant which will in turn produce the conditioned stimulus for a respondent, as in the Hudgins and Menzies experiments (see pages 25-27), but we do not thereby liberate the respondent from its dependence upon an eliciting stimulus. As for the reverse effect, it is not clear, at this time, that a motor respondent can be conditioned by a Type S procedure. The possibility of sensitization (see page 29) or some kind of operant reinforcement, such as shock-removal, has seldom been eliminated in experiments designed to test this matter.

Related to the latter point are some unpublished observations by Reinwald (1941). A dog was first trained, by a Type R procedure, to lie quietly on his right side, with his left leg suspended by a harness in such a way as to permit its unimpeded movement whenever the patellar tendon of the leg was tapped lightly with a small hammer. Then, in an attempt to condition this patellar reflex or knee jerk, taps to the tendon were combined with visual stimulation—a moderately intense light just in front of the animal's eyes. The procedure thus conforms to the Pavlovian paradigm:

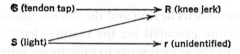

One thousand combinations of the conditioned and unconditioned stimulus were presented to the dog over a period of many weeks, with the following result: *no evidence of Type S conditioning was obtained.* Although the tendon tap regularly elicited the knee jerk, the light never came to exercise the least effect upon the response. Results of this sort should not be hastily generalized, since the patellar-reflex findings may not be typical, but they do suggest a critical scrutiny of the alleged cases of respondent conditioning when somatic or "motor" responses are involved.

The Importance of Operant Conditioning

The principle of operant conditioning may be seen everywhere in the multifarious activities of human beings from birth until death. Alone, or in combination with the Pavlovian principle, it is involved in all the strengthenings of behavior with which we shall be concerned in this book. It is present in our most delicate discriminations and our subtlest skills; in our earliest crude habits and the highest refinements of creative thought. It accounts, in large part, for our abnormal 'fixations' as well as our normal 'adjustments'; for our parades of power and our shows of weakness; for cooperation no less than competition. It may be seen in our friendly relations with, and our withdrawals from, our fellows; in our expressions of bigotry and toleration; in our virtues as well as our vices.

We do not expect you to accept this appraisal without question or reservation at this time. We have scarcely begun our analysis of behavior. Only a few experiments have been cited, most of them drawn from the laboratories of animal research. Other principles and other findings have yet to be considered, and these in turn must be related to the ones already treated. Nevertheless, so basic and so far-reaching is the law of operant conditioning that, even now, you should be able to find, in your own experience, many illustrations of its action. Later on, as we deal with ever more complex problems, you will be more, rather than less, aware of its explanatory power.

NOTES

We have ignored, in our discussion of Thorndike's work, his many studies of connection-formation in human beings, where the mere announcement of *Right* or *Wrong* by the experimenter was used as a reward or punishment for some response, usually verbal, on the part of the subject. This omission will be understood after you have seen, in Chapter 8, how words and other stimuli, not initially reinforcing, may come to exercise such an effect upon operant behavior. Also, in our treatment of the runway and the maze, no mention has been made of the way in which results from these devices have exemplified, even clarified, the operation of other principles than the one to which this chapter is devoted. This, too, will be corrected as we go along.

The way in which we have treated the concept of "insight" deserves a word of qualification. Köhler's fascinating reports of chimpanzee behavior (*The mentality of apes*, 1925) were once widely regarded as convincing demonstrations of the inadequacy of conditioned reflex theories. His *Umweg* or *detour* method of experimentation, in which animals were required to use crude tools (sticks, strings, etc.) or *round-about* approaches to their food-objectives, was hailed by some as the best of all instruments for analyzing 'intelligent' behavior. Today, however, we see that Köhler's method left much to be desired, since it involved no study of the relation between known variables, as presupposed in scientific inquiry. His observations did little more than suggest problems for further research. Conditioning principles may be expected to apply to them as well as to any other instance of everyday problem-solving.

The distinction between operant and respondent conditioning, although anticipated in the writings of many psychologists, was not sharply drawn until 1935, in an important paper by Skinner. Since then, it has been endorsed and discussed by a number of authorities in this area of research (Schlosberg, 1937; Hilgard, 1937; Razran, 1939a; Hilgard and Marquis, 1940; and Mowrer 1947). The terms *classical* and *instrumental,* employed by Hilgard and Marquis, are rather widely used equivalents, respectively, of *Type S* and *Type R* conditioning.

Hilgard and Marquis have described four categories of instrumental (operant) conditioning. (1) *Reward training,* in which responses are strengthened through the presentation of positively reinforcing stimuli; (2) *escape training,* in which they are strengthened through the termination or reduction of "noxious" (i.e., negatively reinforcing) stimuli; (3) *avoidance training,* which is accomplished when "the learned reaction prevents the appearance of a noxious stimulus"; and (4) *secondary reward training,* in which strengthening results from presenting stimuli which have previously accompanied positive reinforcements. You will note that we have already considered the first two of these categories; *avoidance* behavior and *secondary reward training* will be treated in Chapters 8 and 9.

Some psychologists prefer not to use the term *conditioning* in connection with the strengthening of operant responses, bar-pressing or otherwise. They speak of *trial-and-error, law-of-effect,* or, simply, *effect* learning. We need not object to these terms, as long as the reference is clear, but we think it more appropriate to adopt the notion of two types of conditioning: (1) the Pavlovian case, in which a reinforcing stimulus (e.g., food) is provided in connection with the presentation of a *stimulus* (e.g., tone); and (2) the Thorndikian case, in which the reinforcing stimulus is contingent upon a *response.* The important thing, for us, is that there are two reinforcement contingencies—one with an S and one with an R.

In connection with the concept of positive reinforcement, it has been argued (e.g., by Hilgard and Marquis, 1940) that our quoted principle of operant conditioning on page 50 is circular. We use *reinforcing stimulus* to explain the strengthening of an operant; but we *define* a reinforcing stimulus in terms of its strengthening effect. The fact of the matter is that some stimuli strengthen the responses they follow, and others do not. To the former alone do we apply the term *reinforcing.* A less debatable wording of our principle might run as follows: *There are stimuli which have the power to strengthen the operant responses that produce them. This strengthening may be termed 'operant conditioning,' and the stimuli may be referred to a class called 'reinforcing.'* This is the essence of our quoted principle, and the circularity is superficial.

4

EXTINCTION AND RECONDITIONING

Never suffer an exception to occur.... Each lapse is like the letting fall
of a ball of string which one is carefully winding up; a single slip undoes
more than a great many turns will wind again.

> William James, on the making and breaking
> of habits, *Principles of Psychology*, 1890

The Adaptability of Behavior

So long as life endures, a creature's behavior is a clay to be
molded by circumstances, whimsical or planned. Acts added
to it, and other acts which fall out, are the means by which
it is shaped. Like the two hands of an artisan, busily dabbing
and gouging, are the two processes, *reinforcement* and *extinction*.

Reinforcement is the indispensable condition for strengthening reactions. But, as we know, its effect is exercised in the
presence of *all* of the stimuli existent at the time it occurs.
Some of these stimuli (such as the day's temperature, passing
odors, and momentary illumination) may be irrelevant in
that they are not the ones necessarily correlated with reinforcement. They may, on later occasions, be quite different
while the reinforcement continues to be associated with only
one stimulus. If irrelevant stimuli were perpetually to arouse
the response, we would have a picture of sheer biological in-
efficiency: energy spent uselessly, time lost, and impaired
chances for survival. The adaptability of behavior to *critical*
stimuli depends on the possibility of diminishing the response
to non-critical ones. Such a decline in reaction strength fol-

lows the withholding of reinforcement. This is called *extinction,* and is the process we have now to examine.

Respondent Extinction

Just as a Type S reaction is strengthened by the presence of the unconditioned stimulus, so it is weakened by its absence. Suppose we halt the concomitant presentation of conditioned and unconditioned stimuli, but continue to present the conditioned stimulus. When this is done, and we measure the magnitude of the response, we find that on successive tests the response to the conditioned stimulus decreases and eventually reaches zero. This is what Pavlov called *experimental extinction,* and the principle may be stated as follows:

> *If a conditioned reflex of Type S is elicited without the presentation of the reinforcing stimulus, its strength decreases.*

A response, then, is said to be extinguished when, as a consequence of its dissociation from reinforcement, the conditioned stimulus has lost its eliciting power.

The table below shows the phenomenon as reported from Pavlov's laboratory. A dog was conditioned to salivate at the sight of meat-powder, through many trials in which he was shown the powder and then allowed to eat some. Extinction was then carried out, with thirty-second showings of powder which were never followed by eating. In a few trials, the

Table III

EXTINCTION OF A CONDITIONED SALIVARY REFLEX
(Data from Pavlov, 1927)

Successive unreinforced stimulations	Number of cc. of saliva secreted in each thirty-second period
1	1.0
2	.6
3	.3
4	.1
5	.0
6	.0

conditioned stimulus lost its power to elicit salivation. You will note that some extinction occurred with each unreinforced stimulation, and that the drop in response went rapidly at first, and then more slowly. This progression is typical of the various Type S connections which have been set up and broken down in many laboratories since Pavlov's early experiments.

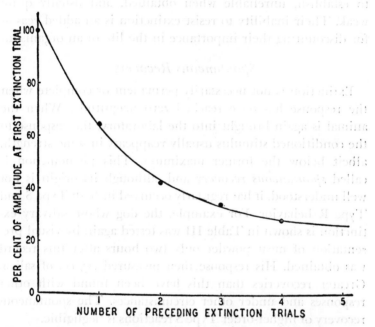

FIG. 15. Average extinction curve of the conditioned galvanic skin response obtained from 20 human subjects. The ordinate is in per cent, so that for no preceding extinction trials (i.e., on the last conditioning trial) the amplitude of the GSR is given the value of 100 per cent. The unconditioned effect of the CS (tone) accounts for the curve's failure to drop to a zero level. (From Hull, 1943, based on data supplied by C. I. Hovland.)

The actual speed of extinction depends on several factors. (1) Fully-conditioned reactions extinguish more slowly than those based on only a few reinforcements, and over-conditioned reactions more slowly than those just brought to full strength. (2) Extinction seems to take fewer trials when un-reinforced elicitations come close together than when distributed over a longer time. (3) Higher-order conditioned respondents are very susceptible to extinction: a few presentations of the stimulus without reinforcement from the preceding conditioned stimulus, and the reaction is at zero. (You will recall that higher-order Type S reflexes are difficult to establish, unreliable when obtained, and usually quite weak. Their inability to resist extinction is an added reason for discounting their importance in the life of an organism.)

Spontaneous Recovery

Extinction is not necessarily permanent or complete when the response has once reached zero magnitude. When the animal is again brought into the laboratory, the response to the conditioned stimulus usually reappears in some strength, albeit below the former maximum. This phenomenon is called *spontaneous recovery* and, although its origin is not well understood, it has regularly occurred in both Type S and Type R behavior. For example, the dog whose salivary extinction is shown in Table III was tested again by visual presentation of meat powder only two hours after this record was obtained. His response then measured .15 cc. of saliva. Greater recoveries than this have been found with other responses and under other circumstances. The spontaneous recovery of higher-order Type S reactions is negligible.

Extinction following spontaneous recovery is faster than original extinction. If there is a second recovery, it is less in magnitude than the first and is extinguished more rapidly. As a rule, only a few extinction sessions are needed to overcome the diminishing recoveries and to reduce the response strength to a stable zero.

Operant Extinction

Conditioned operants are extinguished by severing the relation between the act and the effect. As successive responses fail to produce reinforcement, the recurrence of the response is less and less likely. The principle of Type R extinction may be put as follows:

The strength of a conditioned operant may be diminished by withholding its reinforcement.

As in the case of operant conditioning, the principal measure of operant extinction is the frequency of the response in time. The loss in strength is seen in a fallen rate of emission. This is portrayed clearly in the cumulative response curve of Figure 16. As responses come more and more slowly, the cumulative curve bends over and takes on a characteristic shape.

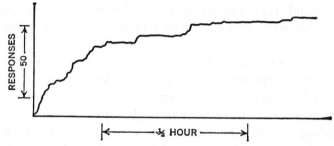

FIG. 16. Typical cumulative response curve for extinction of bar-pressing by a white rat following about 100 reinforcements. (After Skinner, 1938.)

The extinction curve for a response hitherto regularly reinforced (that is, with a reinforcement for *each* emission) is usually, if not always, rather uneven. It begins with a steeper slope (higher response rate) than that during regular reinforcement, partly because responses are no longer separated by eating time, and partly because the animal is apt to attack vigorously the now-unrewarding bar. Thereafter, the curve is marked by wavelike changes in rate which distort it in detail but still permit the drawing of a smooth 'envelope' to describe the over-all trend. These bursts and depressions of response might be called emotional in character, the counterpart of more complicated frustrations and aggressions seen in man. Consider, for example, the frustration-aggression pattern in the behavior of a child who struggles with knotted shoe-laces or an unyielding door, or the effect of an unresponsive listener in coldly dousing our dinner-party stories.

Resistance to Extinction as a Measure of Strength

A strong habit is one that tends to persist after the reinforcement has been discontinued, whereas a weak one succumbs more quickly. Taken by itself, emission rate under regular reinforcement is not a good indicator of operant strength. With bar-pressing for food, for example, rate is greatly affected by such incidental things as the size and hardness of the pellets—which determine chewing time. On the other hand, resistance to extinction serves to disclose quite well what strength an act has acquired during a training period.

But how to measure this resistance? We can use the total number of responses emitted in extinction, or the number required to reach some arbitrary *extinction criterion* such as the first five-minute or ten-minute interval in which no responding occurs. The number of responses in a complete extinction is generally more satisfactory, since any short-time criterion excludes possibly important data contained in the rest of the extinction curve. On the other hand, extinction criteria have the advantage of being time-saving and experimentally convenient, and are therefore frequently employed.

Resistance to extinction after regular reinforcement is governed by a number of factors, among which are the following:

1. *The number of reinforcements applied to the response.* Williams (1938) trained five groups of rats to press a bar for food. The animals in each group were allowed a given number of reinforcements before extinction was begun, the low-number group receiving but five reinforcements, and the high-number group, 90. In Figure 17 is plotted the mean number of unreinforced responses made by each group up to

a criterion of five minutes of no response. Resistance to extinction is seen to increase with number of reinforcements up to a point beyond which additional reinforcements produce very little increment in strength. (In mathematical terms, an *asymptote* of strength is approached.)

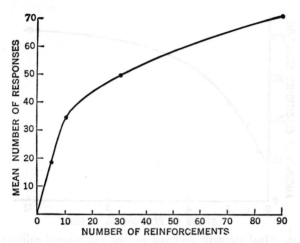

FIG. 17. Curve showing the relation between number of reinforcements and number of extinction responses. The number of responses made is taken as the measure of strength of conditioning. (After Williams, 1938.)

2. *The amount of reinforcement given for each response.* This factor has recently been investigated by Zeaman (1949). Four groups of rats were given one run a day on a Graham-Gagné runway for twenty days, with a different amount of food reinforcement for each group (.2, .4, .8, and 1.6 grams). Zeaman was able to show that the amount of reinforcement received during training was related to the highest speed of starting (see page 54) that each group ultimately attained. The group given a small amount of food did not reach as low a starting-time level as the group given a large amount. These results accord with those from an early study by Grindley (1929) which indicated that chicks will traverse a runway faster for six grains of rice per trial than they will for one

grain. Similarly, Wolfe and Kaplon (1941) found that chicks learned a maze faster when a whole kernel of popcorn was given for each run than they did when only a quarter of a kernel was provided. At the end of the training period in Zeaman's experiment, when the starting-times had decreased

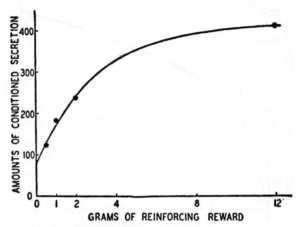

FIG. 18. Final strength achieved by the conditioned salivary reflex in the dog as related to the amount of food reinforcement used in the conditioning. One dog was used with four different CS's, each CS being reinforced by a different amount of food. The training schedule involved presentation of all four stimuli in random order, but each stimulus was always associated with its own amount of food. The curve shows the limit of response strength reached for each stimulus, and indicates that respondent as well as operant conditioning is influenced by the amount of reinforcement employed. (From Hull, 1943; data supplied by W. H. Gantt.)

to a minimal value for each group, the running response was extinguished. Although extinction began with the groups at different levels, and although the number of non-reinforced trials was insufficient for a complete test, Zeaman's analysis suggests that an increase in amount of reinforcement goes with an increased resistance to extinction.

3. *The degree of motivation present during extinction and conditioning.* You will see, in Chapter 9, that resistance to extinction depends upon the motivation (hunger, thirst,

etc.) present at the time. Suppose a group of animals, equally hungry, are conditioned with the same number of reinforcements. If they are then extinguished under different degrees of hunger, the hungrier ones make more responses than do the less hungry (pages 265-266). That is, resistance to extinction is greater when extinction is carried out under high motivation than under low (Perin, 1942). Oddly enough, however, when groups of animals are *conditioned* under different degrees of (hunger) motivation and extinguished under the *same* degree, the extinction responses do not reflect the differences in training conditions. A certain low degree of motivation is required for *any* conditioning, but added increments do not seem to give added strength (Strassburger, 1950).

Table IV

THE EFFECT OF VARYING DRIVE LEVEL AT TIME OF CONDITIONING UPON
THE STRENGTH OF CONDITIONING

(Data from Strassburger, 1950)

Number of Reinforcements	Hours of Deprivation at Conditioning					
	½	1	4	11	23	47
30	—	—	128.3	111.4	128.1	123.5
10	74.4	94.3	68.5	—	99.4	—
1	—	42.4	—	39.0	45.0	51.8

The table summarizes the experimental design and findings. Each entry in the table represents one group of animals conditioned in bar-pressing under the indicated length of food deprivation and with the indicated number of reinforcements; the numerical value of the entry gives the mean number of bar-pressing responses made in the first hour of extinction. Ten to twelve animals were used in each group. Extinction was carried out at the same drive level (23 hours of deprivation) for all groups. None of the values in any row is significantly different from the others in that row by statistical test. Thus, for a given number of reinforcements, the drive level at time of conditioning did not affect the strength of the response (as measured by resistance to extinction). Note, however, that there is a relation shown between the number of reinforcements and resistance to extinction. This latter finding corroborates that in Figure 17, page 73.

When Is a Response Extinguished?

An operant must exist in some strength before it can be conditioned; it must be emitted once in a while at least, in order for us to reinforce it. This unconditioned rate of emission may be called the *operant level* for that response, and it appears as part of the general activity of the organism. It determines the quickness with which a response can be reinforced: if the act comes infrequently, there is a long wait; if the first reinforcement does not take hold, conditioning is inconveniently delayed.

From the fact of operant level, it follows that *an extinguished response will not reach a zero rate*, but will return to one that existed before reinforcement. Thus, the cumulative response curves for bar-pressing extinction in the rat will approach or reach a slope that approximates the one that existed prior to conditioning. For this reason, experiments which aim to compare numbers of responses in extinction after different kinds or amounts of training must take account of the operant level. Unconditioned emission rates must be determined for all animals before the experimental factor is introduced. The groups may be equated for prior level, or a correction may be applied to the final data.

Spontaneous Recovery of a Type R Response

Suppose that, on a given day, after conditioning, a period of extinction has reduced bar-pressing to a low rate. The next day's session, with all conditions the same, will give another, but smaller, extinction curve. This observation has been made in a number of studies. Youtz (1938), for example, extinguished bar-pressing in rats to a criterion of no response in twenty minutes. One day later, in a second extinction session, he obtained as much as 55 per cent of the responses emitted in the first. The amount of recovery diminishes, however, with successive extinctions until none is discernible apart from that which arises from general activity.

Further consideration of this spontaneous recovery suggests that the number of responses 'recovered' does not add up to more than would be expected from an extension of the original extinction curve; in other words, if the extinction curve had been continued without interruption, the number of responses would have been about the same as that obtained from a spaced succession of shorter extinction periods. This may, or may not, be true; there is some evidence to the contrary (Ellson, 1939; Keller, 1940). It does appear, however, that the longer the interval between original extinction and a later one, the greater the accumulation of unexpended re-

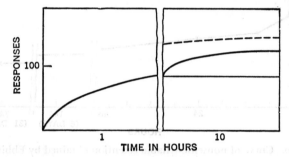

Fig. 19. A schematic curve illustrating how spontaneous recovery after a lapse of 8 hours might approach the extinction curve (dashed line) that would have been expected if extinction had not been interrupted. (After Skinner, 1938.)

sponses, and the greater the apparent recovery. This effect may be quite pronounced, even for intervals measured in minutes, if extinction is interrupted very soon in the first session. At that time, responses are coming out at a good clip and, consequently, many will pile up in a short space of time. An example of this is afforded by Ellson's (1938) study in which extinction was carried out to a five-minute period of no responding. (Such a criterion is reached before the process is very far advanced, and many responses are still to come.) Subsequently, four groups of his animals were given recovery intervals of 5.5, 25, 65, and 185 minutes, after which extinction was resumed to the same five-minute criterion. The average numbers of responses accumulated in the respective groups were 7.6, 14.4, 19.5, and 24.4.

Extinction and Forgetting

The beginner in psychology often takes *extinction* to be synonymous with *forgetting*. A close examination of forgetting shows us, however, that matters are not quite as simple as this. Let us look, briefly, into the history of the problem. Back in 1885, Hermann von Ebbinghaus published a volume

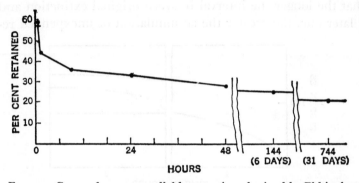

FIG. 20. Curve of nonsense-syllable retention obtained by Ebbinghaus with the "savings method." This method takes the difference between original time taken to learn and relearning time after some period, and computes the "per cent time saved" (here called "per cent retained") by dividing the time difference by original learning time. Each period represents the learning and relearning of a different list of nonsense syllables. Ebbinghaus served as his own subject. The first three points plotted are for intervals of .33, 1.00, and 8.8 hours, respectively. (After Ebbinghaus, 1885.)

entitled *Ueber das Gedächtnis* or, in English, *On Memory*. In this book he proposed methods for the quantitative study of human verbal learning and the retention of learned material, together with a large body of data he had painstakingly amassed in studying his own ability to learn and relearn series of nonsense syllables (*rop, fim, zeb*, etc.). We shall consider, in Chapter 7, the actual process of serial learning, and will have occasion to refer again to Ebbinghaus. In the present connection, we may note that one of the problems to which he addressed himself was that of forgetting. The curve in Figure 20 shows how he found the amount of retention of nonsense syllables to depend upon the amount of time that passes between initial learning of a list and later relearning to a given degree of perfection. It indicates that the major loss in remembering occurs quickly after learning, but some small residue can be expected to survive for a long time.

Despite Ebbinghaus' results and the supporting evidence later provided by other investigators, objections soon arose. We now know that his 'forgetting curve' is not broadly applicable to other than nonsense material. Many observers have pointed to the recall of supposedly dead memories in dreams, hypnosis, and reveries. Psychiatrists have convinced us that, with suitable prompting, persons may recover memories that had at first seemed hopelessly lost. Experimentalists, too, have added evidence which indicates that 'meaningful' material, such as prose and poetry, does not fade with time in the manner suggested by the Ebbinghaus curve.

Scientifically, the meaning of forgetting should probably be restricted to the weakening of response which results exclusively from the lapse of time between conditioning and some later test of strength. Simple conditioned responses, operant or respondent, lend themselves to the study of this phenomenon. After the response is established, any length of time may be allowed to elapse before it is tested again and compared with its former strength. If forgetting takes place during the interval, the loss in strength should be reflected in, say, a decreased resistance to extinction of the response. The upshot of several studies has been that the *mere disuse* of a conditioned response yields very little diminution in strength over periods of months or years. Figure 21 presents averaged extinction curves of bar-pressing in two groups of rats. The upper curve was obtained on the day following the one in which 100 responses had been reinforced; the lower curve was obtained forty-five days after initial conditioning and the same number of reinforcements. Experimental extinction is, apparently, far more effective in weakening a response than is a period of passive disuse. Today, many investigators believe that, given ideal control over a creature's activity during the interval between learning and testing, a conditioned response would show no weakening at all.

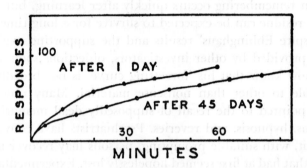

FIG. 21. Average cumulative response curves for bar-pressing extinction in two groups of rats extinguished after different periods of time following original conditioning. Only slight loss of strength results from the mere lapse of time. (From Skinner, 1938.)

The seeming dilemma is not insoluble. The crucial difference between the Ebbinghaus results and the conditioned-reflex results lies in the type of materials employed. Nonsense syllables, in long lists, memorized individually in a fixed serial order, are subject to much mutual confusion and blocking. The intervals between learning and relearning in Ebbinghaus' work were undoubtedly filled with verbal behavior—of which nonsense syllables are special cases. These syllables probably cannot be isolated or protected from blending with other speech, and this would involve, in time, a loss of their identity. This is probably related to the fact that we 'forget' foreign languages and our school-day mathematics, but not how to swim or ride a bicycle.

If we ask now whether there is such a thing as forgetting, the answer is probably No. A simple and distinct act probably does not expire through disuse; an intricate set of reactions may suffer, if not rehearsed, from internal attrition. If, in the interval, other things are learned or practised which conflict with the original responses, 'forgetting' will be the result. The everyday use of the word *forgetting* does not, of course, distinguish between lapse of time and other factors that may account for a loss in retention.

Regression: a By-product of Extinction

Occasionally we see an adult behave, as we put it, "like a child"; or a youngster who, seeing his parents' attention turn to a new infant, may once again wet himself, insist on being hand-fed, and refuse to sleep in a dark room or in his own bed. These and other instances have seemed to psychiatrists to illustrate in common a mechanism which they describe as a *regression* or going-back. They consider regression to be a retreat from one's more recently acquired behavior to that of an earlier period. From the critical writings on this subject, we may extract a central idea: If present behavior is not capable of getting reinforcement, one reverts to older forms of response which were once effective. An individual whose best efforts fail to reach a solution of his difficulties is thrown back upon other resources, and these resources are the ones he once used successfully but outgrew with maturation or social training.

Clinical observations are always complex and it is dangerous to entertain over-simplified explanations of them. Nevertheless, the notion of regression has led to a search for a possible prototype which would give some degree of validity to the idea. Mowrer (1940), in the study cited earlier (page 61), believed he found such a prototype. In his experiment, rats were conditioned to push a panel in order to turn off a shock coming from the cage floor. The first response to the shock, before panel-pushing was learned, was a tiptoe posturing or dance, which reduced the severity of the shock. With further training, this response diminished in favor of the more effective response to the panel. In a later extinction series, when panel-pushing was itself no longer reinforced by shock-removal, the animals went back to the earlier mincing steps which had been their partially satisfying mode of coping with the noxious stimulus. Such findings as these have been reported by Hull (1934) and a number of other investigators (e.g., Masserman, 1946); and we shall have occasion to return to this matter later in connection with the problem of 'chaining' (Chapter 7.).

One-Trial Extinction

Extinction, as we have been describing it, is a pretty slow process, but it may have occurred to you that many of our own responses show a *rapid* decrement when reinforcement ceases—that you, for example, would very soon stop making a response that no longer got results. With the exception of the feeble-minded (Mitrano, 1939) or the very young, no human being is likely to waste many coins on a vending machine that is out of order; and few of us will blindly persist in turning a key that no longer opens a door, or scratching matches that never light.

It is undoubtedly true that extinction of an operant may be very rapid, even complete in a single emission (how many of us put two nickels in a coin box when the first is not returned?), but this statement is deceptive because it ignores the fact that immediate extinction is not a property of original behavior. We *learn* the signs of failure by virtue of long training, and these signs come to govern the number of responses made in extinction. We *discriminate*, that is, between reinforcing and non-reinforcing situations (see Chapter 5).

An analogue of such behavior can be found in lower organisms. At the beginning of an experimental hour, a rat is given a set number of regular reinforcements, say ten or twenty, for bar-pressing and then extinction is carried out for the rest of the hour. The same procedure is followed on the next day, and the next, for as long as we wish. The number of responses made in extinction on successive days decreases markedly, indicating that the very failure to obtain the reinforcement begins to act as a signal to cease responding (Bullock and Fischer, 1950). It is basically this process, which human beings improve upon over the rat by direct verbal instruction, that enables a response to be dropped at once. To speak of it without qualification as one-trial extinction is incorrect. It would be equally erroneous to do so in the case of a conditioned Type S reaction like salivation which, in successive extinctions following reconditioning, may get to a point where a single non-reinforced elicitation is enough to drop the response to zero magnitude (Pavlov, 1927).

Periodic Reconditioning

The interspersal of conditioning and extinction that we have just been discussing leads us into an extremely interesting area. The regular reinforcement of response is not the world's rule; and some important properties of behavior should arise from periods of extinction that are broken into by occasional reinforcements. Laboratory research has, in fact, disclosed that this is the case; and we may now examine some of the results obtained by the systematic repetition of conditioning and extinction.

One such procedure, which has proved to be a valuable research tool, is based upon the use of single reinforcements that are periodically provided throughout the experimental session. The schedule may be of two kinds: in one, the reinforcements are separated by a fixed *time interval;* in the other, they are separated by a fixed *number of unreinforced responses.* Let us take them up in order.

Periodic Reconditioning at Fixed Intervals

To illustrate the first procedure, we take a hungry rat and our representative bar-pressing response, and we choose three minutes as a between-reinforcement interval. The animal's first response to the bar is rewarded with a food-pellet, but none of the responses in the next three minutes is permitted to be effective. The very first response after the interval is

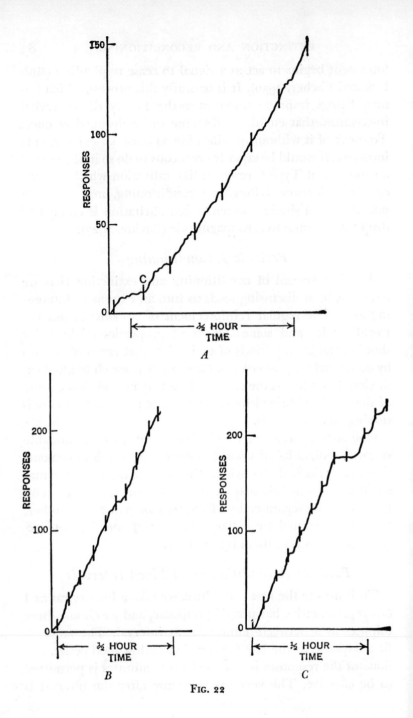

FIG. 22

reinforced, and the responses in the next three minutes again go unreinforced. And so on, for as many cycles of reinforcement and non-reinforcement as we desire. (The interval of extinction responses is not *precisely* 'fixed,' of course, since the rat may not always respond at exactly the time when the food-pellet becomes available, but excessive delay is very rare because of the steady high rate of responding which usually develops.) If we are patient and do not cut the procedure off too soon, we get an interesting set of changes. The cumulative response curve passes through three stages.

1. At first, the intervals of unreinforced responding are likely to contain little curves which bend over, and which are actually small extinction curves. Each reinforcement brings out some responses, but not many, and they dwindle during the interval. Figure 22-A reproduces a record obtained under these conditions. You will observe that the little curves sum up so as to give a positively accelerated trend to the over-all curve.

2. When reconditioning has been continued for a while, the positive acceleration comes to an end, and the rates within the intervals fuse into a steady stream of responding. The temporally spaced reinforcements suffice to maintain a consistent strength of response which accounts for the straight-line appearance of the cumulative record. The beginning of such a rate is seen in the later portion of Figure 22-A, and throughout Figure 22-B.

LEGEND FOR FIG. 22

A. The first stage of P-R (periodic reconditioning) training for a white rat. The vertical strokes in the curve mark the reinforcements. Note the extinction-like shape of the cumulative response curve in the first few periods, and the later suggestion of a steady rate.

B. The practically linear cumulative response record obtained as the second stage in P-R responding. The P-R interval was three minutes, and this portion of the record occurred after about 60 reinforcements.

C. The third stage of P-R responding, showing the presence of a temporal discrimination. This record is from the same rat as in *B*, and was obtained after 17 days of training (one hour, or 20 reinforcements, per day). (After Skinner, 1938.)

3. After many reconditioning sessions, the response curves during the three-minute intervals take on a scalloped appearance opposite to that in stage 1. Right after a reinforcement, the animal delays his response for a time, but, as the seconds slip away, he starts up again, slowly at first, and then faster, until the interval is over and the next reinforcement is received. This shows that a *temporal discrimination* has been formed. The responses just after eating a pellet are weakened because they are never reinforced, whereas later responses are strengthened because the reinforcement is given later. The animal comes to "tell the time" at which responding is more likely to succeed. Since, in this case, reconditioning is *periodic,* some degree of temporal discrimination is unavoidable in the long run. The curve in Figure 22-C, obtained after seventeen one-hour sessions of periodic reconditioning, shows this clearly. You will note the essential similarity of this finding to that described in our treatment of the *trace reflex* in Chapter 2. In the course of trace-reflex formation, salivation to the conditioned stimulus is increasingly delayed until it comes just before the reinforcement.

The close examination of curves, like that you have just made, is an example of honoring small details, an occupation that has paid rich dividends in the history of science. Let us, then, consider another example. (And let us, for convenience, adopt the practice of using "P-R" for "periodic reconditioning.") Figure 23 presents a telescoped P-R curve for the same animal that provided the curves for Figures 22-B and 22-C. It gives us an over-all view of response rate during twenty-four experimental hours. With the details washed out, another trend emerges. (This can best be seen by raising your book in the horizontal plane and sighting along the curve from its near end.) The curve bends over slightly with continued training, as the number of unreinforced responses falls off. This is not unlike the drop in response frequency mentioned earlier in connection with "one-trial" extinction, but it is much less marked. Apparently the temporal discrimination which controls the number of responses is, in this case, slow to form. One might say that it is harder to 'tell when' the next reinforcement is coming than to 'tell that' there will be no more. Even single reinforcements, properly spaced, keep the response strength high for a long time.

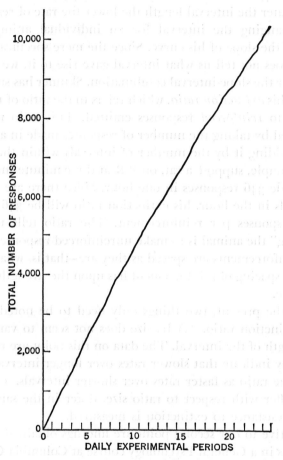

FIG. 23. Cumulative response curve under three-minute P-R over an extended period of time. Note the slow over-all negative acceleration that probably shows the control over responding gradually assumed by the temporal discrimination. Figures 22-B and 22-C are enlarged portions of this curve. (After Skinner, 1938.)

Response Rate and P-R Interval

In the above illustration, a fixed interval of three minutes was used. You may wonder what the effect would be if the length of this interval were changed. The answer to this query has been given tentatively by Skinner (1938). Within limits, the greater the interval length the lower the rate of response; and changing the interval for an individual animal will change the slope of his curve. Since the mere specification of slope does not tell us what interval gave rise to it, we need a term for the slope-interval combination. Skinner has supplied this in his *extinction ratio,* which refers to the ratio of *unreinforced* to *reinforced* responses emitted. This ratio may be obtained by taking the number of responses made in an hour and dividing it by the number of intervals within the hour. For example, suppose a rat, on P-R at three-minute intervals, has made 346 responses in one hour. Since there are twenty intervals in the hour, his extinction ratio will be 346/20, or 17.3 responses per reinforcement. The ratio tells us how "willing" the animal is to make unreinforced responses when the reinforcements are spaced as they are—that is, what effect a given spacing of reinforcement has upon the strength of the response.

For the present, two things only need to be noted about the extinction ratio. (1) Its size does not seem to vary with the length of the interval. The data on this point are meagre, but they indicate that slower rates over longer intervals give the same ratio as faster rates over shorter intervals. (2) Rats that differ with respect to ratio size, differ in the same way when resistance to extinction is measured.

Relative to our second point are findings obtained by 120 students in a General Psychology course at Columbia College in 1946. Each student worked with a single rat and, in one class experiment, a two-minute P-R was employed to determine the extinction ratio for each animal, after which the bar-pressing response was extinguished. The 120 rats were

ranked for size of extinction ratio and for number of responses during one hour of extinction. The coefficient of
correlation between the two ranks was +.72, indicating that
if a rat gives a large number of unreinforced responses during
P-R he will also give a large number in extinction. This had
been predicted by the class, and the results bore out the prediction, but the finding needs to be checked with a more
rigorously controlled experiment.

Extinction After Periodic Reconditioning

One thing is very certain: P-R increases the resistance of a
response to extinction. This finding comes out of experiments
like the following. One group of hungry rats is given twenty
regular reinforcements with food for bar-pressing, and the
response is then extinguished. A second group also receives
twenty reinforcements before extinction, but these reinforcements are spaced out in a three-minute P-R schedule. Suppose
that extinction in both cases is carried out for four hours, one
hour per day on successive days. When all the extinction responses of the two groups are added up, the second group
comes out far ahead in the total number made.

This simple experiment leads to some additional com-
parisons. As we saw earlier, extinction following regular
reinforcement starts with a sharp initial spurt in rate,
exceeding that which prevailed during regular reinforcement.
Afterwards, the extinction curve is marked by wave-like
depressions and accelerations in responding. In contrast, periodic reconditioning gives rise to an extinction curve which
does not noticeably exceed the previous P-R rate. If we compared the two extinctions for only a brief period after reinforcement had ceased, regular reinforcement would appear
to have generated a greater resistance to extinction than P-R.
Such a conclusion, however, would be unjustified, since a con-
tinuation of extinction would reveal that the responding after
P-R goes on unabated for a considerable time, whereas that
after regular reinforcement soon tapers off. Here, as in other

circumstances, it is wise to wait until all the returns are in.

Not only is extinction after P-R more resistant, but the curve is also smoother than that after regular reinforcement.

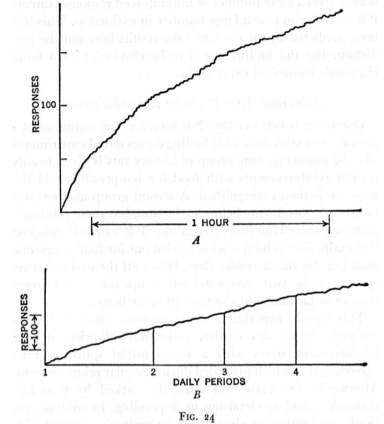

FIG. 24

A. Cumulative response curve of extinction immediately following P-R. Note the smoothness of this curve as compared with extinction after regular reinforcement (Fig. 16).

B. Cumulative response curve of extinction following P-R. Compared with extinction after regular reinforcement, responding goes on unabated for a considerable time. (After Skinner, 1938.)

The vacillations between aggressive attacks on the bar and depressions in responding, which come after regular reinforcement is discontinued, do not occur so markedly after

P-R. The greater smoothness of extinction suggests that P-R increases a creature's "frustration tolerance." Intrinsic to P-R is the recurrence of periods of non-reinforcement during which "frustration" is repeatedly experienced and overcome by continued responding. We might expect the same sort of result in training children. Occasional reinforcement gives stability to behavior, and persistence in the face of failure. Skinner has argued that this stability, as well as the increased resistance to extinction following P-R, is a significant property of our normal behavior, and responsible for "equanimity in a world in which the contingency of reinforcing stimuli is necessarily uncertain." He points out that our behavior "would be clumsy and inefficient if the strength of an operant were to oscillate from one extreme to another with the presence or absence of its reinforcement" (*The behavior of organisms,* 1938, p. 138.)

Fixed-Ratio Periodic Reconditioning

In addition to withholding reinforcement for a fixed interval of time, we can make it wait upon the emission of a certain *number* of unreinforced responses—that is, we can establish a *fixed ratio* of unreinforced to reinforced responses. This procedure brings to mind cases in which a set task must be carried out before we reap a reward. If we use it carefully within the laboratory, it should enable us to make some interesting discoveries about our own behavior.

The experimental scheme is as follows. A rat is first trained under P-R at a fixed interval of, say, five minutes, until his response rate is stabilized. Suppose we find that his extinction ratio is 10:1 (ten unreinforced responses for each reinforced one), and we then decide to change over to fixed-ratio reinforcement, making food contingent upon a given number of responses. Three alternatives are open to us: we can set a fixed ratio (1) less than, (2) equal to, or (3) greater than the extinction ratio.

If a reinforcement is given for *less than* ten responses, it

will come *sooner* than usual within each interval—that is, it
will take him less than five minutes to get his pellet. If it
comes sooner, there will be more frequent reinforcement, and
this will result in an increased rate of response just as it does
with shorter fixed-interval P-R (see page 88). The new rate,
in turn, will bring reinforcement even more quickly, and the
process will repeat itself until a limiting high rate of response
is achieved. The more the fixed ratio falls short of the extinction ratio, the faster the acceleration in rate and the earlier
the final rate-limit will be reached. Figure 25 shows this
schematically for four fixed ratios below our assumed extinction ratio of 10:1.

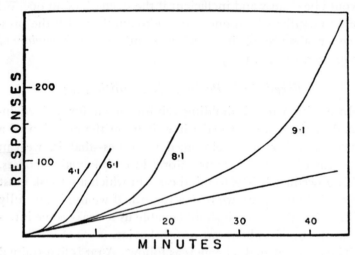

Fig. 25. Hypothetical curves showing acceleration of the response
rate under several fixed ratios smaller than the 10:1 extinction ratio
represented by the straight-line P-R curve. (From Skinner, 1938.)

Consider, now, the hypothetical effect of using a fixed ratio
which is the *same* as the extinction ratio—that is, 10:1. Presumably, the frequency of reinforcement will continue to give
us the same slope of curve as the five-minute P-R with which
we started out, since the fixed ratio calls for the same number
of unreinforced responses as would be emitted, on the aver-

age, in the five-minute interval. This turns out to be the case, at least for a while. After a time, however, there is an acceleration like that which occurs when the fixed ratio is less than the extinction ratio. A rat may maintain his fixed-interval slope for as long as three experimental hours, whereupon he may (sometimes suddenly) assume a new and higher rate of responding. What could have 'informed' him that reinforcement was contingent upon the number of responses rather than the interval, and that he might rather respond rapidly? The answer lies in the fact that the extinction ratio varies from time to time. Ten-to-one was an average ratio; at one time or another it was certain to be more than that—sufficiently so to trip off the circular accelerative process. Such variations are especially common in an animal's natural habitat, and are accentuated by fluctuations in his level of motivation which, in turn, determines the size of the extinction ratio (see Chapter 9).

When the fixed ratio is *greater than* the extinction ratio, we require *more* than ten responses before we reinforce. This means that reinforcements come, on the average, less often than every five minutes. The rate of responding should, therefore, go down. But a lower response rate at fixed ratio decreases the reinforcement frequency still further. We have a circular interaction in which response rate continually decelerates and finally extinguishes. The rapidity of the extinction will depend upon how much the fixed ratio exceeds the extinction ratio. Although reinforcements will be received every now and then, the response rate, cannot be sustained. Even if it were sustained, a high fixed ratio might involve more loss of energy than the single reinforcements could offset, and the animal would waste away because of this unfavorable balance of food intake and energy output.

The running response in an apparatus like that of Graham and Gagné (page 54) also reveals the basic properties of fixed-ratio reinforcement. Since the runway is of fixed length, we can think of it in a rough way as demanding a certain number of steps for traversal. The distance is short, so the fixed ratio of unreinforced steps is comparatively small. The decreased running time on successive trials represents an acceleration in rate of step-responding, that is, the rat emits his running steps with increasing speed up to a limit. Although, unlike bar-pressing, the animal moves into a new stimulus-situation with each running response, the parallel between the two procedures is striking.

The 'Ceiling' of Fixed-Ratio Responding

In the example just considered, where the fixed ratio exceeded the extinction ratio, we said that the response extinguishes. This happens whenever the fixed ratio is *suddenly* set at a value *far above* the extinction ratio and the same effect would be achieved with the runway apparatus if we were suddenly to lengthen it to, say, a thousand feet. But there is another procedure, of a more gradual sort, by which we can establish very high fixed-ratio values. Taking our rat with the assumed extinction ratio of 10:1, let us begin with a fixed-ratio schedule of 8:1. The response rate will accelerate, as described above. Once the rate is up, consider the situation that exists. What is being reinforced? The responding, of course, but also the *high rate itself* is now feeling the effect. Every time a reinforcement comes it impinges upon responses coming out at a certain rate, so that not only the response is kept strong, but the rate, too, is being conditioned. The animal "learns" that bar-pressing is rewarded when it is fast. This is an aspect of Type R conditioning which we now meet for the first time, and it may pay you to stop for a moment to think it through.

With our animal now responding at a high rate, we may raise the fixed ratio to a new level, perhaps of fourteen responses. Bridging the small gap from eight to fourteen is not hard, because the animal is already conditioned to a high response rate, and the exact number of responses is somewhat elastic. He tends to keep up a high pressing speed until the reinforcement is forthcoming. After the new ratio is strongly practised, it is raised once more; after a time, we increase it again. If the increases are not too great at any one step, a ratio can be reached far beyond the starting point. In one experiment (see Figure 26), it was actually possible by a process of gradual approach and thorough training to reach and sustain a ratio of 192 responses per reinforcement, without extinction! (Skinner, 1938.) Figure 26 also reveals in each curve

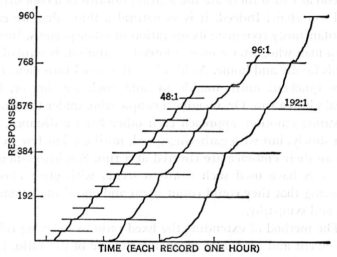

Fig. 26. Reinforcement at several fixed ratios. The cumulative response curves are for one rat that was gradually worked up to the ratio of 192:1. The horizontal lines indicate reinforcements. (After Skinner, 1938.)

the acceleration of response during periods of non-reinforcement. This acceleration resembles that shown in the P-R curve on page 84 and has a similar origin. Actually, a temporal discrimination, although of no "use" to the rat in fixed-ratio P-R, is nevertheless formed, since the experimental arrangement never permits one reinforcement to follow immediately after another. Or, think of it this way: receipt of a pellet is never followed immediately by another reinforcement, so the animal holds off further responding for a while.

But, when responding is resumed, the speed picks up again because reinforcement is less delayed by a quick completion of the fixed ratio than a slow one. In the vernacular, we would say that "the rat becomes more eager for the food pellet as he gets closer to winning it."

This phenomenon is not alien to our everyday experience. Faced with a monotonous, routine job of definite length, like mowing a lawn, we are apt to hasten our work as we approach its end at which there are the waiting rewards of a cool drink and soft chair. Indeed, it is so natural a thing that we can spontaneously recognize its operation in other persons. Imagine a man who, after a long enforced separation, is returning to his family and home. As his objective comes into view, his pace quickens until, unable to hold back any longer, he breaks into a run. Or, imagine a couple who, under the stress of strong emotion, approach each other from a distance, at first slowly, but with gathering speed, until the last few steps before their embrace are covered at a run. Sensitive cinema directors have used such wordless scenes with great effect, knowing that they could count upon audiences' understanding and sympathy.

The method of extending the fixed ratio by delaying reinforcement and gradually advancing the size of the ratio, has been employed with rats in other than bar-pressing situations. A caged rat may be taught to pull a string to which a piece of food, lying outside the cage, is attached (e.g., Tolman, 1937). As sureness and speed develop in the short pulls, the string may be lengthened by slow degrees. Eventually, the string may reach a length well beyond that which the animal could initially have been conditioned to pull, but he hauls away heartily and persistently on each occasion. Or, a rat may be taught to dig sand from a tube through which he has previously run unimpeded to obtain food (Stone, 1937). Once the response is well established, more and more sand may be let into the tube. If the increase is not too precipitous, a truly enormous amount of sand may be removed by the rat between reinforcements. The extension of the fixed ratio by a judicious manipulation of reinforcement bears a resemblance to the type of response training called "differentiation" (see Chapter 6).

Extinction Following Fixed-Ratio Reinforcement

Fixed-ratio reinforcement leads to extinction curves which are different from those following either regular or periodic reinforcement (fixed interval). The curve begins steeply, and maintains a maximal rate until the responses, quite abruptly, come to an end. Figure 27 shows this for one rat that had been working at a high ratio, and for one at a low ratio. The reason for the difference between these and the more usual extinction curves may not at first be obvious. You will remember, however, that fixed-ratio reinforcement strengthens not only the individual response, but also the *rate* of response. When a reinforcement comes, the rate is usually maximal. A high rate of responding is usually followed by a reinforcement and, adopting a term from the following chapter, we can say that the animal "discriminates" his own rate of responding. In his world, the occurrence of fast responding marks the time when reinforcement can be 'expected,' hence it sets the occasion for more responding. When extinction has begun and he reaches the end of his fixed ratio, no pellet is discharged, yet the situation is the normal one for reinforcement. Consequently, he keeps on responding rapidly because, in his history, reinforcement has come on such an occasion. Each new response makes the occasion still more appropriate for further responding, with the result that the responses continue to come out at a sustained maximal rate. This cannot go on indefinitely, because past training has given the response only a limited strength with which to resist extinction. When the break comes, it comes suddenly. A tempting analogy is that which likens the response tendency to a reservoir that is draining off at full flush under high constant pressure right up to the point of total depletion.

In contrast with this process, extinction following fixed-interval P-R or regular reinforcement shows little influence of a special "discriminative value" attached to the rate of response. The effect of reinforcement is primarily to strengthen the individual response, irrespective of rate, while non-reinforcement decreases that strength. In fixed-ratio reinforcement, each non-reinforcement adds to the 'occasion' for more responding and hastens the appearance of the next response. These different consequences of non-reinforcement arise, of course, from the opposed training procedures. Since reinforcement is connected with different features of responding, we can expect different extinction characteristics.

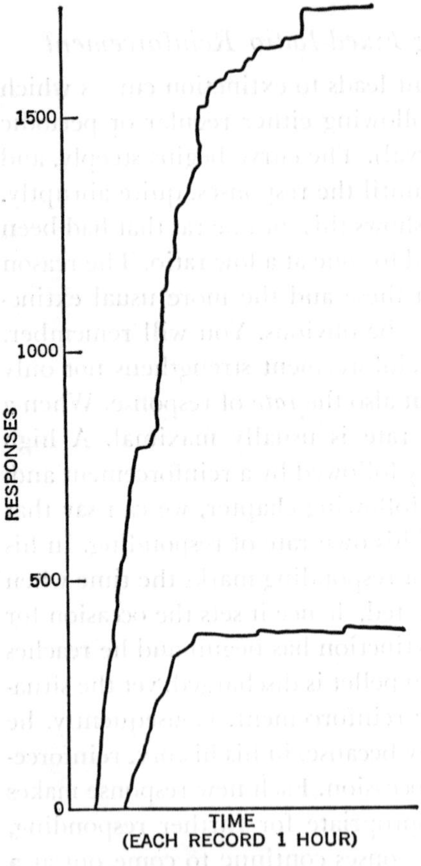

FIG. 27. Cumulative response extinction curves of two rats after fixed-ratio P-R. (After Skinner, 1938.)

The Effect of Aperiodic Reinforcement

Outside of the laboratory, regular reinforcement is by no means the rule, but neither is strictly periodic reinforcement. It is hardly to be expected that a schedule of any fixed interval or any fixed number of responses would be scrupulously honored by an environment so crowded with different events. We may well ask, then, whether the results of *aperiodic* reinforcement are the same as those of *periodic* or *regular* reinforcement.

Following Skinner's (1933) early studies of P-R with rats, a number of other scientists tried out modified forms of intermittent reinforcement with other organisms and other responses. Brogden (1939a), using dogs as subjects, conditioned salivation, or foot-withdrawal from shock, with regular reinforcement. Subsequently, the animals were given training with aperiodic reinforcement. He found that response strength was maintained at a high level even when no more than 40 per cent of the responses were reinforced. Apparently the effect of the aperiodic procedure was strong enough to offset that of the relatively small number of reinforcements provided.

Humphreys' (1939) experiments in this field are of especial interest because he used human subjects. He studied the conditioning of an eye-wink response and, later, the galvanic skin response (change in electrical resistance of the skin). In the first experiment, a light of short duration was followed, after 400 milliseconds, by a puff of air to the eyeball. Conditioning was assumed to be present when the eye-closure, originally elicited by the air-puff, occurred regularly in response to the light and in advance of the puff. One group of subjects was regularly reinforced, the air-puff following each presentation of the light on ninety-six occasions. Another group, given "partial reinforcement," received the air-puff after the light only 50 per cent of the time—that is, on forty-eight of the ninety-six occasions. In spite of this difference in the number of reinforcements, the conditioning was set up as readily in one group as in the other.

In conditioning the galvanic skin response, Humphreys paired a tone with a mild electric shock (the unconditioned stimulus for the change in skin resistance) under two reinforcement schedules. Members of a regular (100 per cent) reinforcement group were given sixteen combinations of tone and shock; and members of an aperiodic (50 per cent) reinforcement group were given only eight combinations, randomly interspersed with eight presentations of tone alone. Test trials, with tone alone, followed each training period. Again, the results showed the two schedules to be about equally effective in maintaining response strength.

Extinction trials were given at the conclusion of each of these experiments and, in both cases, a greater resistance to extinction was shown by the aperiodically reinforced responses. The effect was more striking with the conditioned eye-wink, but was clearly present with the galvanic skin response—a finding confirmed in a later study (Humphreys, 1940). This is probably what you would expect, since aperiodic would seem to resemble periodic more than regular reinforcement, but these experiments do not entirely satisfy our curiosity. One of them dealt exclusively with respondent conditioning, and the other involved operant-respondent overlap. Neither was based upon the emission of straight-forward operant responses such as make up the bulk of our everyday behavior.

When we turn to the relatively unrestricted or 'free' situation provided in the bar-pressing type of experiment, we find only a few published studies to date (Humphreys, 1943; Mowrer and Jones, 1945; Jenkins and Clayton, 1949; Skinner, 1950). The effect of such a reinforcement schedule can be described, however, with some assurance. If bar-pressing is reinforced at intervals of four, three, two, and one minutes, together with some reinforcements that come immediately after a reinforcement (a 'zero interval'), with these intervals appearing in random order, a very steady rate of responding will quickly develop. Even after many days of training, the straight-line character of cumulative-response curves will be maintained, since no time discrimination is present to give the records a scalloped effect like that observed in fixed-interval or fixed-ratio P-R. Also, a great resistance to extinction will be built up by such a procedure—possibly a greater resistance than that which results from P-R at fixed intervals or fixed ratio. The extinction curve itself will show little, if any, initial acceleration, and its course will be marked by only minor fluctuations in rate. Under certain conditions, as when the organism has been accustomed to relatively long intervals of non-reinforcement in his training sessions, the rate during a large part of the extinction curve will be indistinguishable from the rate that preceded extinction.

Casual observation suggests, of course, that the operant behavior of human beings in their daily affairs is greatly affected by aperiodic reinforcement. In very few spheres of human activity is reinforcement either regular or strictly periodic, and, in certain cases, the effect of this aperiodicity is dramatically impressive. The chronic gambler, whose infrequent winnings do not keep him from trying his luck again; the "punch-drunk" pugilist who stumbles into the ring long after his fistic power has waned; even the oft-disappointed farmer who tills his land once more in the hope of a bumper crop—do not these all suggest the strengthening effect of occasional, unpredictably spaced rewards?

With the facts of P-R in hand, you should be able to make some critical deductions about educational procedures which strive to control behavior. You should, for example, see how one would go about teaching a child to be persistent in the face of failure. One would make sure, in training for skill, for confidence at work, or for willingness to persist in social activities, that the child is guaranteed some measure of success and approval—regularly at first, but later only occasionally, so that he will not give up in the face of setbacks. In the case of emotion, where Type S reactions play an important rôle, you should be wary of using fear stimuli, like talk of bogeymen, to make the child obedient. Once conditioned, fears are difficult to extinguish; and great care must be taken thereafter to avoid even accidental reconditioning by stimuli which would have gotten little notice prior to conditioning. Also, if some unwanted behavior in a child is to be extinguished, even one surrender by the parent, in a moment of fatigue or embarrassment, might renew the behavior strength more than it would have if extinction had not been undertaken in the first place. To one who would break a habit, we might paraphrase William James and say: Never suffer reinforcements to occur during the extinction process, else you may inordinately strengthen the very response it was your aim to weaken!

Superstition: An Experimental Example

Superstitions may be considered as beliefs or practices based upon assumed "if ... then" relations which are either false or undemonstrable. *If* a black cat crosses my path, *then* I shall have a bad day; if I take a turn around the table, my luck at cards will change; if there is a solar eclipse, disaster will befall the tribe; rain on this day means rain each day for the next forty; a newborn infant must not be praised aloud, lest spirits overhear and harm him through jealousy. Cause-effect connections, or sequences of events, are thought to operate which have no basis in fact. In groping to understand the troubles and joys of life, men often invent explanatory forces or causes which they hope can then be dealt with by placation or counter-measures. Superstitions are frequently based on anxiety about what a dimly-grasped natural environment holds in store for us, and it is this emotional quality which secures their unreasoning acceptance and unshakable grip. Some superstitions are widely held, a social heritage of beliefs taught us by our elders, but others are private convictions arising, we think, from valid personal experiences.

One class of superstitions is that in which the supposed cause-effect relation involves some act of our own as the agent in producing a given environmental effect. This effect may be the procurement of a positive reinforcer or the averting of a negative. If I wish down a well, my wish will come true; if I carry a rabbit's foot, no harm can befall me; if I pierce the manikin's heart, my enemy will die; if I perform this ritual in the morning, I insure against failure during the day. Such instances spring from the temporal contiguity of a response and a reinforcement in the individual's own history or in his observation of others. As you are well aware, a reinforcement will strengthen any act which precedes it, and this is true even when the contingency is accidental. The correlation may be 'false,' but this will not side-track the conditioning. So far as the organism 'knows,' his reaction was indeed the effecting agent. With strengthening, the response appears more frequently, and the probability of another coincidental reinforcement increases. Thereafter, only occasional contingencies are needed to keep up the 'magical' response at some strength.

This situation has been duplicated experimentally in a simple manner (Skinner, 1948a). The method of establishing a 'ritualistic superstition' is essentially that of periodic reinforcement, except that the reinforcement is not made to depend upon the emission of any arbitrarily selected operant. Into a hungry pigeon's cage a small portion of food is presented at fifteen-second intervals. The presentation is governed automatically by a clock and, once the mechanism has been started, requires no attention from the experimenter, who may even retire from the scene, leaving the animal to its own devices. An hour or so later, if he returns to observe the result, he will find some interesting behavior. The bird may be walking systematically in circles; he may be tossing his head repeatedly, or swinging it from left to right in a pendular motion; he may be making regular brushing movements with his beak in the direction of the floor, or poking it into the upper corners of the cage. He has been caught, as it were, by the accident of reinforcement, supplied by an unwitting environment, at a chance-point in his on-going behavior. He has acquired a 'personal superstition.' The response is conditioned faster with shorter between-reinforcement intervals, when the chance of extinction and the emission of alternative responses is lessened. Once the response is established, however, this interval may be lengthened to, say, one or two minutes without changing the behavior. Moreover, a great resistance to extinction may develop. In one animal, more than 10,000 emissions of the response (a side-to-side hop) occurred before a fifteen-minute period of non-responding appeared.

Punishment and Extinction

Almost any discussion of the control of behavior eventually runs head-on into the question of the part played by "punishment." At various times and in various places, men have based their ideas of formal education, discipline, and social training upon the premise that punishment affects behavior in a manner the opposite to that of reward. In other words, it has been supposed by many to "stamp out" behavior just as reward "stamps it in." On the other hand, throughout the years, isolated observers and thinkers have been skeptical about the long-term effectiveness of this kind of behavioral control. As a rule, these men did not deny that punishment influenced behavior, but they questioned the permanence, as well as the desirability, of such influence.

Sigmund Freud, the psychoanalyst, was one whose clinical experience led him to the latter view. He believed that one's early development is of great importance in shaping his adult personality; and he argued that, during this development and later, many desires and acts (mainly sexual) must be kept from overt expression if one is to become a socially acceptable human being. Overt expression is prevented by punishment or the threat of punishment, but the wishes and tendencies toward the forbidden behavior are not thereby done away with. They remain alive and forceful, although one may be unaware of their existence within him. Freud described this banishment of acts from overt expression as "repression" to the "subconscious."

Thorndike, on the basis of human learning experiments, also came to doubt the efficacy of punishment as a means of permanently weakening behavior. In 1931, he modified his famous 'law of effect' so as to exclude the idea that annoyers were the opposite of satisfiers in their effect upon response, asserting that "Annoyers do not act on learning, in general, by weakening whatever connection they follow." Again, in 1932, he stated that "a satisfying after-effect which belongs to a connection can be relied on to strengthen the connection . . . but there is no evidence that an annoyer takes away strength . . . in any way comparable to the way in which a satisfying after-effect adds strength."

Neither of these men can be said to have solved the problem of punishment to the satisfaction of the laboratory scientist. Thorndike's experiments were concerned almost entirely with the effect of a spoken *right* or *wrong* upon the strength of verbal connections such as those formed when one memorizes a series of word-number associations; and Freud's view was part of an elaborate conceptual system which laid no claim to experimental support—either in its origins or its implications. The net result of their teachings, as you might guess, was not the blind acceptance of doctrine, but a quickening and a broadening of laboratory research; and it is out of such research that the true status of punishment may be expected to emerge.

We can best approach this matter here by referring back to our discussion of positive and negative reinforcement. It was pointed out, in Chapter 3, that certain stimuli, such as loud sounds or electric shocks, belong within a class of *negative reinforcers:* when presented, they weaken operant behavior; when removed, they strengthen it; and they also possess eliciting power. Let us examine, more closely than before, the *weakening* effect of such stimuli.

Negative reinforcement can be made contingent upon a response—that is, the response can *bring it on*. This is an important type of "punishment," as the word is commonly used. The contingency may be provided by nature (a child's finger is always burned when thrust into a flame) or through the behavior of another organism (the hand may be slapped when the finger is placed in the mouth). In either instance, the child is "punished," but psychologists have, naturally, been more interested in the social than the non-social case.

Punishment may be applied to an operant under two general conditions: while the response is (a) undergoing positive reinforcement (regular or otherwise) to see if it will nullify the effect of positive reinforcement; and (b) when it is being extinguished, to see if it will subtract from the strength already possessed by the response. Both cases are interesting, but the latter has more practical and theoretical significance, since it is closely related to the age-old question of the permanency of punishment's effects. We begin, therefore, by asking whether punishment, applied to an operant during extinction, will have a short- or a long-term influence upon the strength of the response.

This problem was first attacked, in an exploratory way, by Skinner (1938), in connection with his studies of operant behavior in the white rat. Two groups of animals were given periodic reconditioning for three days. Extinction was then carried out in two periods, of two hours each. With one group, all responses made in the first ten minutes of the first period were punished; with the other group, extinction took place in the usual way, no responses being punished. The punishment for the first group consisted of a slap administered by the bar itself whenever it was depressed. This slap was given to the animals' forepaws by a sharp return kick of the bar provided when an electric hammer struck against the bar shafts outside the response chamber. Figure 28 shows the average extinction curves for the two groups. The remarkable thing in these curves is that the effect of the slaps in suppressing the response was only temporary; the two groups eventually came out even in the total number of responses emitted during extinction. Apparently punishment did not subtract from the over-all strength of the response, and Skinner concluded that the experiment gave "no evidence whatsoever for a process of negative conditioning directly the opposite of positive conditioning."

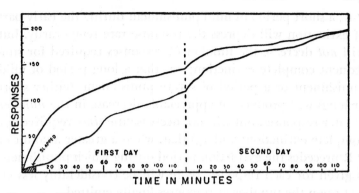

Fig. 28. The effect of punishment on extinction. Experimenter's comment: "The two curves are from groups of four rats each, with the same experimental history. All responses made by one group during the first ten minutes of extinction were slapped. The rate is depressed for some time but eventually complete recovery is made." (From Skinner, 1938.)

That more remained to be learned about the effects of punishment was indicated by a second experiment in which four rats, after P-R training, were given five extinction periods of one hour each. During the first two days and forty minutes of the third, no responses were slapped. For the last twenty minutes of the third day, and the entire hour of the fourth, all responses were slapped. On the fifth day, unpunished extinction was resumed. The average curve for the four animals is given in Figure 29. It is plain that there was no recovery from the punishment during the fifth day. It appears that a prolonged period of slapping had a more lasting effect than the short one employed in the first experiment. We cannot say, however, that the effect was permanent, since no further extinction tests were given.

A recent extended and significant research dealing with the punishment of operant behavior is that of Estes (1944). This investigator, taking off from Skinner's observations, concerned himself primarily with the effect of electric shock upon bar-pressing rate. In a long series of experiments, he showed (1) that, after two or three one-hour sessions of fixed-interval

P-R, a short period of mild punishment during the early part of extinction will depress the response rate temporarily, but will *not* decrease the number of responses required for subsequent complete extinction; (2) that a long period of mild punishment or a period of severe punishment (either short or long) will produce an appreciable decrease in the *number* of later responses, but will not decrease the *time* required for complete extinction; and (3) that, when a greater amount of P-R precedes the extinction period during which punishment is given for each response, there will be considerably less effect upon the number of responses finally emitted.

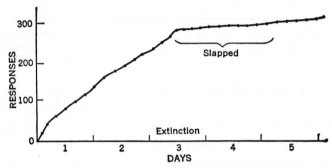

FIG. 29. The effect of extended punishment on the average extinction curve of four rats, the extinction being carried out after P-R at fixed intervals. (After Skinner, 1938.)

These results tell us that the effect of punishing the bar-pressing response is not permanent, at least in terms of the *time* required for extinction when punishment has been stopped; and that, if the response is strongly conditioned in advance, it may not even reduce the *number* to be emitted later. But Estes' next finding is still more dramatic. (4) The effect of electric shock was no greater when bar-pressing brought it on than when it was delivered independently of the response. When shock was given only at times when the animal was not pressing the bar, there was the same immediate depression of rate and the same slow recovery as when the response itself was punished. In a word, the effect was non-specific. To Estes, this suggested that the important relationship was not between the punishment and the response, but between the punishment and the general situation in which it occurred.

According to this analysis, shock is an unconditioned stimulus for a "changed state of the organism," involving emotional respondent changes and accompanied by a decreased frequency of bar-pressing. (See the following scheme.)

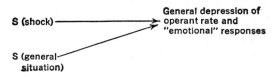

Since the shock is delivered in a "general situation"—the rat's cage environment—this situation becomes, for all practical purposes, a conditioned stimulus for the behavioral changes evoked by the shock itself. Moreover, if this analysis is correct, it would follow that the mere presentation of the 'conditioned situation,' unaccompanied by shock, would lead to extinction of the effect.

In support of this hypothesis, Estes found that when bar-pressing was punished in the usual way during a short period of extinction, and this was followed by a two-hour period in which the rat was left in the response chamber, *with no bar present and no further punishment,* the effect of the shock was almost entirely absent when the bar was re-introduced and extinction was resumed. Leaving the rat in the chamber without the bar led to a nearly complete dissipation of the emotional upset caused by the shock. Except for a small depression at the start, the final extinction curve was in no discernible way different from that provided by animals that had never been shocked.

The just-mentioned small remainder of shock-effect was not ignored by Estes, who explained it in the following way. Punishment had been given to the bar-pressing response; and its effect had presumably been conditioned to *all* aspects of the stimulus situation which were present when the response was made. Extinction of the effect had occurred in the presence of most of these conditioned stimuli, but not all. The bar itself was absent during this extinction, and so was the response of pressing. Hence, the stimuli provided by the bar and the pressing movements themselves had not had a chance to lose their conditioned-stimulus status. Consequently, when the bar was returned to the chamber for the final extinction of the operant, the bar-stimuli and the (proprioceptive) pressing-stimuli were still able to exercise a small but measurable influence upon the response rate.

Estes' "changed state of the organism" was, as he said, "of the sort commonly called 'emotional,'" and we shall have more to say about this effect of punishment later, when we attack the general problem of emotion (Chapter 10). Already, however, we can see some interesting parallels of his rats' behavior, in the field of everyday human conduct. Consider, for example, the not-uncommon experience of bringing down upon ourselves, through something we have said, the strong disapproval of others. (Disapproval itself may be negatively reinforcing—Chapter 8.) The ill-chosen words have been uttered and the damage is done; we are covered with embarrassment and confusion at the outcome. We are 'emotionally upset' and we seek escape from our predicament (as the rat often tries to climb out of his chamber) by one means or another. If our attempts fail, we remain to face the music, but for some time after the *faux pas,* and even when disapproval is no longer in evidence, our behavior may be seriously depressed (just as the rat needs time to recover from his shock). If we do escape from the embarrassing situation, we need only to enter it again in order to re-experience the upset that it caused; indeed, the mere reinstatement of the fateful words, at some other time or in some other circumstances, may rearouse the old emotion in what seems to be full force. Repeated exposure to the situation or utterance of the previously 'punished' words will, in time, cause the disturbance to vanish just as, in the rat's case, repeated returns to the response chamber and further pressings of the bar will lead to an extinction of the effect and a recovery of operant strength.

The major conclusion to be drawn from these studies is, of course, that the effects of punishment are likely to be impermanent. When the emotional disturbance resulting therefrom has disappeared, the punished act may still need a long period of extinction before it is eradicated from the organism's repertory. If this is true, and if it applies to men as well as rats, we cannot but wonder why the use of punishment has been so widespread throughout the ages: why this truth received so little recognition. A moment's thought, however, will suggest two answers. First, if one disregards the restrictive and biologically uneconomical effects of punishment, he may use it in depressing "wrong" behavior and thereby pave the way for the strengthening of "right" behavior. This is a technique still commonly met with in educational practice and often supported by experimental studies in human and animal learning (Bunch, 1928, 1935; Dodson, 1932; Warden, 1927; Gilbert, 1936, 1937; and others). Various researchers have shown that a combination of reward and mild punishment will reduce the time or the errors involved in the solution of problems.

The second reason is not often mentioned: the use of punishment is *positively* reinforcing to the *user*. There is no gainsaying that punishment has its advantages in the control of others. Given the requisite physical strength, or the symbol thereof, we can always force others into a state of submission —at least temporarily. Whatever annoyance they have provided for us is thereby eliminated, and *we* are positively reinforced. On the basis of this fact alone, it is easy to see why we live in a world where punishment or threat of punishment is the rule; where power or the signs of power are considered all-important in achieving social control.

Concluding Remarks

Two new principles, those of operant and respondent *extinction,* have been introduced in the present chapter, and we have shown how they operate in conjunction with operant and respondent *conditioning* to build up reflexes of exceptional strength; extinction, as well as conditioning, is involved in the procedures of periodic and aperiodic reconditioning. We have also presented evidence to show that the weakening effect of negative reinforcement (punishment), when added to that of non-reinforcement, is probably temporary. By now you should begin to appreciate the kind of analysis of behavior that we are attempting. Our aim, throughout this text, is to show how the complex may be explained in terms of the simple. This will be even more apparent as we move along. Not many new principles will be added in later chapters; but these will be required for your understanding of a great many aspects of human nature which, for the average person, are often shrouded in darkness.

NOTES

Related to the effect of different amounts of reinforcement upon *extinction* (page 73) is the effect, reported by Jenkins and Clayton (1949), of different amounts upon the rate of response when aperiodically reinforced. Pigeons, trained to peck at a response key for food, were given either two or five seconds of eating time at irregularly spaced intervals. The mean number of pecking responses in half-hour sessions was found to be 1205 for the two-second amount and 1557 for the five-second amount. Unpublished observations of white rats in the Columbia laboratory indicate that a comparable effect may be obtained under aperiodic reinforcement with one *versus* two pellets of food.

In discussing the relation between response strength and the amount of motivation present during conditioning, we mentioned only Strassburger's (1950) study, which we felt to be the most conclusive treatment of this matter to date. We neglected, perhaps unfairly, to describe (1) the initial attack upon this problem by Finan (1940), who also used the bar-pressing technique; (2) a later study by MacDuff (1946), who used the maze; and (3) a still later study by Reynolds (1949) with the runway method. Finan found that conditioning under twelve hours of food deprivation provided the greatest response strength in his rats, with twenty-four-, forty-eight-, and one-hour deprivations decreasingly effective. MacDuff's order of effectiveness, from most to least, was forty-eight-, twenty-four-, and twelve-hour deprivations. Reynolds, who has certain objections to both the Finan and MacDuff studies, concludes, from his own data and his predecessors', that we cannot yet say whether response strength is, or is not, a function of motivational strength at the time of conditioning.

Characteristics of unconditioned or operant-level bar-pressing (see page 76) by rats when motivated by hunger have been described by Hefferline (1950), and have also been investigated by Schoenfeld, Antonitis, and Bersh (1950b) who obtained measures of such activity under both hunger and thirst.

In the text, we said that forgetting is caused by what *happens* during the passage of time to interfere with, block, or extinguish the material-to-be-recalled. A more detailed statement, and some relevant data, may be found in Guthrie (1935) whose theoretical viewpoint is nevertheless different from the one we have adopted.

In our discussion of aperiodic reconditioning, we cited experiments by Brogden (1939a) and Humphreys (1939) in which avoidance responses were conditioned. Regular reinforcement was, in both cases, presumably compared with aperiodic reinforcement in its effects. This is, as you may have recognized, an over-simplification of what took place. Anticipating our later treatment of avoidance behavior (Chapter 9), we may say that neither the shock nor the puff of air constituted the reinforcement in these experiments. Rather, the leg-flexion and the eye-wink were strengthened by the *removal* of stimuli which had been regularly or irregularly associated with the shock or the air-puff. The periodicity or aperiodicity involved in such studies is of a different sort from that which is involved when bar-pressing is reinforced with food.

Many investigations, not mentioned in this chapter, have been carried out for the purpose of determining whether punishment is an aid or a hindrance in the mastery of complex learning problems. Electric shock has been the favorite punishing agent, and, for obvious reasons, animals have been the principal subjects. Mazes and discrimination boxes (see page 137, Chapter 5) have been the most popular forms of apparatus; and the shock has commonly been applied in connection with an animal's choice-point behavior—for example, a rat may be punished before, after, or at the moment of making a right or a wrong turn in a visual-discrimination test (Muenzinger, *et al.*, 1934, 1935, 1936, 1938). With respect to the solution of such problems, it now appears that there is no single answer to the question of how punishment affects learning. This will be quite understandable when you see that learning, in these situations, involves much more than mere conditioning, either operant or respondent. In addition, and still more important, is the fact that such a stimulus as electric shock may have any one of several functions. It may depress the response that *it* follows, or its removal may strengthen—as you already know. But it may also be informative, acting as a discriminative stimulus for a specific response (see Chapter 5). Under certain conditions, it may even be *positively* reinforcing when applied (Chapter 8). Any or all of these functions may be exercised in the maze or the discrimination box, depending upon the degree of shock employed and the kind of time relationship with stimuli and responses that may be provided. This has been made especially clear in the studies conducted by Muenzinger and his co-workers.

The strongest opposition to the use of punishment in education comes from Thorndike's many studies of human learning. Thorndike argued that the effect of *Wrong* or other mild 'annoyers' is often to strengthen, rather than weaken, the responses they follow. Admitting that intense punishment might sometimes have a suppressive effect upon behavior, he pointed out that it was always a dangerous weapon, being most effective with sensitive persons, who need it least. At best, Thorndike argued, punishment is successfully applied only when it leads one "to shift to the right behavior and enjoy it, or to have such expectations from the wrong behavior that he is more comfortable to avoid it than to enter upon it." (The full import of the last part of this quotation will be clearer when you have read the discussion of *avoidance* behavior in Chapter 9 of this text.)

5

GENERALIZATION AND DISCRIMINATION

INSTANCES of this kind are so plentiful everywhere, that if I add one more, it is only for the pleasant oddness of it. It is of a young gentleman, who, having learnt to dance, and that to great perfection, there happened to stand an old trunk in the room where he learnt. The idea of this remarkable piece of household stuff had so mixed itself with the turns and steps of all his dances, that though in that chamber he could dance excellently well, yet it was only whilst the trunk was there; nor could he perform well in any other place, unless that or some such other trunk had its due position in the room.

John Locke, *An Essay Concerning Human Understanding*, 1690

Stimulus Generalization

This chapter begins with a single fact or characteristic of behavior: When an organism is conditioned to respond to one stimulus, it will respond in the same way to certain others. We call this *generalization* and, as we proceed, we shall find that it helps us to explain a great deal of behavior that seems, at first glance, to be very complicated.

The existence of stimulus generalization was discovered early in the history of psychology. Before 1910, Pavlov and his co-workers had observed it and reported upon it in these words: "If a tone of 1000 d.v. is established as a conditioned stimulus, many other tones spontaneously acquire similar properties. . . . The same is observed with stimulation of other receptor organs. This spontaneous development . . . we have termed . . . generalization of stimuli . . .". The fact is now so well established in both respondent and operant behavior that we may state it as a principle

An increase or decrease in the strength of one reflex,
through reinforcement or extinction, is accompanied
by a similar but smaller increase or decrease in the
strength of other reflexes that have stimulus properties
in common with the first.

A little thought will convince you that this principle is of importance to any organism in its daily life. Our environment is in perpetual flux, and it is very unlikely that any stimulus ever recurs in identical form. The visual stimuli supplied by a running rabbit to a pursuing fox, or by the face of a friend as you see it from moment to moment, are subject to countless variations in pattern, movement, brightness, and so forth, yet the fox continues its chase, and you do not feel yourself confronted by a procession of strangers. In the ever changing environment, the generalization of stimuli gives stability and consistency to our behavior.

Stimulus Discrimination

On the other hand, the behavior of organisms would be equally ineffective and unadaptive if it could never get over the barrier of generalization. An organism must be able to respond differently to different objects in its environment; and common observation tells us that it does. The fox pursues the rabbit, but not the hound; and we distinguish one friend's face from another's. Behavior can show a specificity with respect to stimuli, and when this specificity is developed in the face of generalization, we speak of *stimulus discrimination*.

An organism manifests a discrimination when it comes to respond to one, but not to the other, of two previously generalizing stimuli. To be called discriminative, the response to the first must be maintained while the response to the second is weakened. In the laboratory and in everyday life, the development of this difference depends upon the reinforcement, or lack of reinforcement, that attends responses. The basic principle may, then, be stated as follows:

*A reflex strengthened through generalization may be sep-
arately extinguished, so that an organism responds to
one stimulus and fails to respond, or responds less
strongly, to another.*

In contrast with generalization, the process of discrimination
gives our behavior its specificity, variety, and flexibility.

Forming a Respondent Discrimination

"Generalization" and "discrimination" are a natural pair,
like the opposite poles of a magnet. Pavlov's (1927) way of
showing how discriminations are formed is embodied in the
"method of contrasts," which combines the procedures of reinforcement and extinction. A hungry dog is first conditioned
to salivate to a 1000-cycle tone (or some other) by the usual
Type S technique. Such a conditioning, as we already know,
will be generalized—the dog will salivate, to a lesser degree,
when other tones are presented. One stimulus, say the 1000-
cycle tone, is then chosen as 'positive' (to be followed by
reinforcement) and another, say the 900-cycle tone, as 'negative' (never to be followed by reinforcement). The two
stimuli are then presented, in haphazard order, on many occasions. The outcome is a difference in the strength of the
two reflexes—in other words, a discrimination is formed.

An indispensable part of this procedure of selective reinforcement or "contrasts" lies in the random alternation of
the stimuli to be discriminated. Too many successive presentations of either tone alone will not overcome generalization.
Frequent interchange of 'positive' and 'negative' stimuli is
essential if a discriminative response is to be established.

The formation of a discrimination is, then, a double process. Through generalization, each direct reinforcement of
stimulus A adds to the eliciting power of stimulus B; each
extinction of stimulus B subtracts a little from the power of
A. Further reinforcements give more power to A than B; and
further extinctions take more from B than A. As the stimuli

draw apart in their power, a discrimination is in the making. The gradual accumulation of differences in the strength of the two reflexes is the heart of the process.

Generalization and Discrimination in Operant Conditioning: The "Discriminative Stimulus"

We now return to our representative operant, bar-pressing. You saw, in Chapter 3, that this response was emitted, not forced; and that its strength could be increased through reinforcement. You saw, too, in the case of the runway operant, that a connection developed between the running behavior and the opening of the starting-box door. This door-opening stimulation was called "discriminative," rather than "eliciting," and we are now in a position to make this distinction clearer.

Suppose, in the bar-pressing situation, that we take two stimuli, a bright light and a dim light, and arrange an experiment in which they are turned on alternately within the rat's response compartment. The rat has been conditioned previously to press the bar for food. He is hungry again and, when placed in the box, begins to respond immediately. This time, however, the conditions are different. Although he is free to respond at any time, we reinforce the response *only when the bright light is on.*

In such a case, neither stimulus *elicits* bar-pressing. The bright light merely sets the occasion on which reinforcement will follow *if* the response is made; the dim light, on the other hand, provides the cue for *not* responding and sets the occasion for non-reinforcement. Each is a *discriminative stimulus.* Adopting conventional notation, we may refer to the bright light, in the presence of which reinforcement occurs, as S^D (ess-dee) and the dim light, in the presence of which there is no reinforcement, as S^Δ (ess-delta).

Let us continue the procedure. Periodically, the bright light (S^D) comes on and stays on until the animal presses the bar. At the response, food is delivered and the light goes off.

For five minutes, the light is dim (S$^\Delta$) and no response during that time is reinforced. Then, S^D appears again, the next response is reinforced, and the cycle is repeated—for as many times as we desire.

As in the case of respondents, generalization occurs. A reinforcement in the presence of S^D increases its effectiveness as a cue, but it also increases, to a lesser degree, the effectiveness of S$^\Delta$; an unreinforced response to S$^\Delta$ decreases its effectiveness and weakens slightly that of S^D. Continued alternation of S^D and S$^\Delta$ causes them to draw apart in their evocative power.

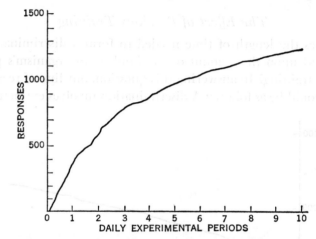

FIG. 30. The formation of a light-dark discrimination by one animal following two sessions of P-R at fixed intervals. (After Skinner, 1938.)

Here, again, *extinction* is the hallmark of discrimination—responding to S$^\Delta$ extinguishes while responding to S^D is maintained. A cumulative response curve should therefore reveal, by its shape, the formation of the discrimination. That is, it should resemble a curve of extinction. It is because extinction, as opposed to conditioning, is the important process in discrimination, that our experiment provided such relatively long periods of S$^\Delta$.

Figure 30 presents such a curve, made by a single rat, during a ten-day period of experimentation in which light was the S^D and darkness was the S^Δ. The discrimination, which appears as a relatively slow change in response rate under S^Δ, followed two days of periodic reconditioning (in the dark) at five-minute intervals. One hour of training was given per day, and approximately six hours were required for the amount of responding in successive five-minute periods to reach a minimal value. Responding under S^Δ never disappears entirely, and the S^D responses are of course included in the cumulation; hence, the curve never reaches an operant level comparable to that of a simple extinction curve.

The Effect of Previous Training

Does the length of time needed to form a discrimination depend upon the amount or the kind of an organism's previous training? In answering this question, our line of reasoning would be as follows: A discrimination involves extinction;

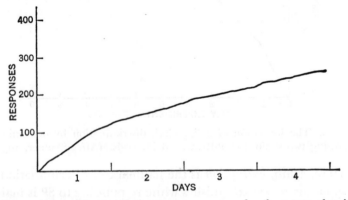

FIG. 31. Average cumulative response curve for four rats showing the formation of a light-dark discrimination following 50 regular reinforcements and one period of extinction. (After Skinner, 1938.)

resistance to extinction varies with the kind and amount of training, hence the time required for a discrimination to develop will depend upon previous training. In Figure 31, we have an average discrimination curve for four rats. Before the discrimination began, these animals had received fifty regular reinforcements, followed by a period of extinction. The strength of the response was therefore much less than in the case of the rat (see Figure 30) that had previously received two days of periodic reinforcement when the discrimination training was introduced. Figure 31 shows that the discriminative process for this group was practically complete by the end of the second day.

An interesting result, not so easily predicted, arises when we attempt to teach a discrimination without *any* previous training in bar-pressing. Here, on the first occasion when the bar is accessible, the S^D is present. The first response is reinforced, the S^D is replaced by S^Δ for a five-minute interval, and the cycle is then repeated. A sample curve for a single animal is given in Figure 32. It shows that the generalization to S^Δ

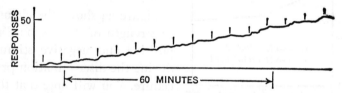

FIG. 32. The formation of a discrimination without previous conditioning. The vertical strokes over the cumulative response curve indicate reinforcements in the presence of the S^D. (After Skinner, 1938.)

is almost *nil*, so that there is nothing to extinguish. We conclude that, under suitable conditions, a discrimination may be formed immediately. The basic requirements are that neither reflex is strengthened in advance of the training procedure, and that the first reinforcements occur in the presence of S^D.

A Human Discrimination Analyzed

When human rather than animal subjects are taught to make discriminations, it is not always easy to identify the changes that occur, but an experiment by Hilgard, Campbell, and Sears (1938) offers convincing evidence that the same fundamental processes are involved in each case. A visual stimulus (a light in the left one of two small windows) was presented on sixty occasions to fourteen subjects, each presentation being followed by a puff of air to the eyeball (the eliciting stimulus for the eye-wink reflex). After this training, when the subjects were responding to the light in advance of the air-puff about 75 per cent of the time, another stimulus (a light in the right-hand window) was introduced and randomly alternated with the first during sixty trials of discrimination training. The left-hand light was positive (always followed by the air-puff) and the right-hand light was negative (never followed by the air-puff).

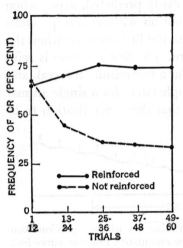

FIG. 33. Progress in forming a discrimination by human subjects. The conditioned response employed was the eye-wink; the stimuli to be discriminated were visual. (After Hilgard, Campbell, and Sears, 1938.)

Figure 33 shows the change in strength of the response to positive and negative stimuli during the discrimination procedure. You will note that the responses to S^D and S^Δ draw apart gradually in their frequency, and that the major change is one of extinction—a weakening under S^Δ. Except for a slight drop in the S^D curve at the very beginning of the discrimination trials (possibly due to a generalization from the extinction of response to S^Δ), the eye-wink occurs with the same frequency as at the end of the conditioning trials.

Abolishing a Discrimination

If we wish to abolish a discrimination, we must restore responding to S^Δ. Two procedures are available. (1) We may keep S^Δ present continuously and reinforce every response, thus reconditioning the extinguished response. (2) We may return to periodic reconditioning at the same interval employed in discrimination training but without the use of S^D. This kind of abolishment gets the response back to its original P-R rate.

Extinguishing a Discriminative Operant

Abolition of a discrimination is different from extinguishing the discriminative response. When we abolish, S^D and S^Δ are equalized through reinforcement of both (responses under S^Δ are reconditioned); when we extinguish, the equalization of S^D and S^Δ is accomplished by the weakening of the response to S^D. To illustrate the latter, suppose that we have a well-formed discrimination, in which S^D regularly evokes the response and S^Δ seldom does. The response to S^D is, then, our discriminative response. It may be extinguished, like any other, by withholding all reinforcement in the presence of S^D. But what kind of an extinction curve would you look for? You might expect, at first thought, a great resistance of the response to extinction, since S^D responding has been reinforced, say, at five-minute intervals, and this is like the procedure of periodic reconditioning. On second thought, you will see that the response has *always* been reinforced under S^D—the only non-reinforcement was under S^Δ. The curve of extinction to S^D should therefore resemble that of extinction after regular reinforcement—which it does.

The Meaning of "Similarity"

British philosophers of the seventeenth and eighteenth centuries made much of two "laws" through which "ideas" were associated: *contiguity* and *similarity*. The influence of these philosophers is still apparent in our everyday speech, as when we say that one idea calls up another because of their likeness or because they were once associated in time or place, but a modern objective psychology does not find the concept of the "association of ideas" very useful. We do find, however, that a contiguity of *stimuli,* or of *stimulus and response,* is essential to Type S conditioning or operant discrimination. Can we give an objective meaning to "similarity" as well?

If you will pause to consider the matter, you will see that "similarity" and generalization are the same thing. In everyday affairs, we talk as if stimuli could be similar in themselves, but actually their similarity depends upon our own behavior; they are similar when, and only when, we make the same sort of *response* to them. Similarity does not reside in stimuli alone, any more than in "ideas."

Stimuli, it is true, may have common physical properties and, in a physical sense, are therefore "similar." But when people say that things are similar they mean that they tend to *react* to them in the same way. They are really reporting this tendency with the words *They are similar.* This is quite different from the physical similarity which is often, though not necessarily, present when the responses are similar.

Related to this point is an experiment by Plotkin (1943) on the learning of International Morse Code by college students. Before their instruction began, these students were presented with pairs of code signals and asked to rate them on the degree of their "similarity." Later, during the actual code training, he found that the confusions of signals with each other (generalizations) were directly related to their previously estimated "similarity." For example, the signals for the letters C ($-.-.$) and Y ($-.--$), which were commonly generalized during training, had already been judged to be very much "alike"; whereas, the signals for A ($.-$) and O ($---$), which had been rated as dissimilar, were never confused with each other. The identity of "similarity" and generalization was quite clearly indicated, and gives weight to Hull's (1943) statement that "the common-sense notion of similarity and difference is based upon the presence or absence of . . . generalization."

When two or more stimuli are found to generalize, so that a response conditioned to one is made to the others of the group, we may of course try to identify the property that they have in common. It is sometimes difficult, or even impossible, to do this. Stimuli are known to acquire their functional equivalence from several sources. We may, for example, generalize two visual stimuli on the basis of wave-length, energy, size, shape, or location. Also, if they are composite stimuli, they may generalize through the identity of their parts. Apparently, too, they may generalize on the basis of the emotional or other responses that they arouse within us (as in the case of "mediated" generalization, to be mentioned later). These and other factors play a part, singly or in combination, in determining the degree to which stimuli are equivalent in evoking response. You may well imagine that the problem of identifying them in any given case is one that challenges the best efforts of specialists in the field of discrimination.

The concept of generalization has been extended to more complex problems of human behavior. Psychiatrists and clinical psychologists often encounter striking instances of respondent generalization, in which emotional upsets originally connected with a single event in a patient's history come to be evoked by stimuli commonly met in the daily routine of living. In one case, a phobia that prevented a woman from looking into the eyes of anyone, whether friend or stranger, was traced to a single experience. Some years before, when surreptitiously opening the drawer of a chest in the home of a blind aunt, she was confronted with a pair of staring glass eyes. The panic induced later by the sight of any eyeball stemmed from this "trivial" but "similar" incident.

Up to this point we have emphasized the *strengthening* action of generalization. But the opposite effect may also occur. Experiments show that reflexes, strengthened through generalization, may be weakened when the originally conditioned reflex is extinguished. Also, if a number of different stimuli, say a tone, a touch, and a sound, are attached to the same response through conditioning, the extinction of any one of them will decrease the strength of the rest.

Into the details of such experiments we need not go, but it may be mentioned that psychiatrists, again, have apparently utilized this principle. A number of their curative techniques, as when they probe repeatedly with verbal stimuli into the lives of their patients, clearly provide for the extinction of emotional respondents. Through generalization, the emotional responses to these upsetting stimuli when encountered outside of the clinic are also extinguished to some degree in spite of obvious differences in the stimulus situation.

Generalization Gradients

Generalizing stimuli may be classed in terms of the sense-organs involved—visual stimuli, for example, involve the function of receptors in the eye. Within each of these 'sense departments,' stimuli may form series, like the series of pitches, colors, loudnesses, brightnesses, warmths, and distances apart on the skin surface. Now, if we inquire how, after any one member of a series has been made a conditioned stimulus, the effects of generalization spread out over the rest, we discover an interesting fact: there is a *gradation* of effect, depending upon the physical proximity of the stimuli to the one conditioned.

Pavlov (1927) noted this early in his studies of generalization: "If a tone of 1000 d.v. is established as a conditioned stimulus, many other tones spontaneously acquire similar properties, *such properties diminishing proportionally to the intervals of these tones from the one of 1000 d.v.*" (The italicizing is our own.) This gradation effect has led to the term *generalization gradient*.

In addition to a gradient for *strengthening*, Pavlov also reported one for extinction, obtained from the following experiment. Along the hind leg of a dog, five spots were selected, the first at the paw and the others spaced three, nine, fifteen, and twenty-two centimeters from the first. By direct reinforcement, the four spots were equalized in their effectiveness as conditioned stimuli for salivation, while the paw spot was extinguished. When this state was reached, the paw spot was given three more unreinforced stimulations, and the other four spots were separately tested. The generalized extinction was greatest for the three-centimeter spot and decreased progressively to the twenty-two-centimeter spot.

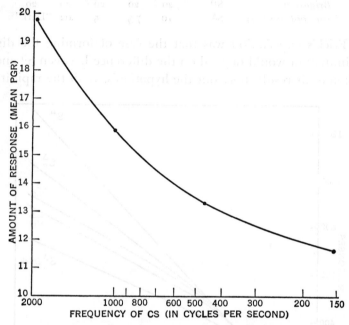

FIG. 34. Average generalization gradient for tonal pitch obtained from 10 human subjects. The conditioned response was the galvanic skin response, labeled PGR (psychogalvanic reflex) on the ordinate; the US was electric shock. The response was first conditioned to a tone of 1967 c.p.s., and generalization was tested to tones of 1000, 468, and 153 c.p.s. The abscissa is logarithmic in scale to keep the figure down in size. (Data from Hovland, 1937a.)

Both conditioning and extinction generalization gradients have been found for human respondents by American investigators (Bass and Hull, 1934; Hovland, 1937a). Moreover, gradients for discriminative stimuli have been demonstrated in studies of operant behavior. Frick (1948) put five groups of rats on a discriminative training schedule in which S^D and S^Δ

were alternately present for two and a half minutes each. S^D and S^Δ were lights of different brightness, and each group of animals was trained with a different pair, as shown below:

		I	II	III	IV	V
		GROUPS				
Brightness	S^D	20	20	20	20	20
(in foot-candles)	S^Δ	10	7.5	5	.02	"Dark"

Frick's expectation was that the ease of forming the discrimination would depend on the difference between S^D and S^Δ; and his results bore out the hypothesis. Both the rapidity

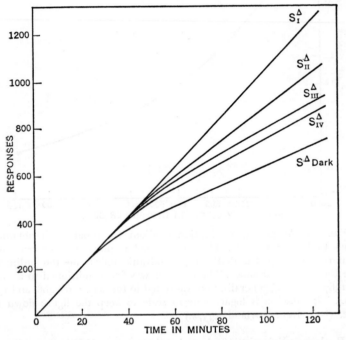

FIG. 35. Average cumulative curves for S^Δ responding by the several groups in Frick's experiment. The curve for S^Δ_I is linear and does not differ from the P-R rate before discrimination training began (i.e., the difference between S^D and S^Δ_I was not discriminable). The separation of the curves is an indication of the varying degrees of generalization. The curves are composites of a number of experimental periods. (After Frick, 1948.)

with which responding to S^Δ extinguished and the completeness of the extinction were increased as the difference between S^D and S^Δ grew larger. Similar results have been secured by Raben (1949), who used the Graham-Gagné runway and a technique developed by Verplanck (1942).

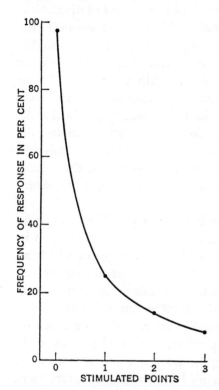

FIG. 36. Average generalization gradient of tactual stimuli varying in distance from a conditioned spot on the skin of human subjects. (After Gibson, 1939.)

Evidence for generalization gradients with human subjects and discriminative stimuli was collected, in 1939, by Gibson. In one experiment, the S^D was a vibratory stimulus, applied to the subject's back. After a verbal response (a spoken nonsense syllable, *dut*) had been connected with an S^D at one spot on the skin, the vibration was presented at spots four, eight, and twelve inches distant in a straight line down the subject's back. Each subject was instructed to respond with the syllable *only when* the stimulus was felt at the initial position. Generalization was measured in terms of the percentage of *dut* responses to the stimulus at each of the other positions. The average percentage values obtained for the four points were, respectively, ninety-eight (at the 'conditioned' spot), twenty-five, fourteen, and nine, indicating a steep but continuous gradient (Fig. 36).

The Study of Discriminative Capacity

A proper understanding of discrimination must develop along two lines: first, an analysis of the *process* of discrimination and the factors influencing this process; secondly, the investigation of the discriminative *capacities* of organisms. We have already considered the former, and we now focus our attention briefly upon the latter. Again we shall deal with matters of general validity, not attempting to make an inventory of all the sensory capacities throughout the animal scale, or to catalogue the changes in capacity accompanying the individual development of an organism. Our emphasis will be upon the behavioral aspects of the problem, the experimental methods used, and a few of the more significant concepts.

1. *Capacity and the threshold.* It is possible to alter an organism's environment in a way that has no effect upon its behavior. It is easy to pick a physical change to which an organism cannot be brought to respond at all, or we can choose two stimuli which it will not discriminate no matter how long we continue selective reinforcement. Thus, neither a human being nor a dog would ever respond to a touch on the skin as faint as a dust particle, nor could they ever discriminate a tone of 1000 cycles from one of 1000.01 cycles. The problem of capacity arises from these elementary facts.

The measurement of sensory capacity reduces to two determinations, both of which were mentioned in Chapter 1:

a. The *smallest* value of a stimulus to which a response can be made. Such would be the softest sound, the faintest light, the lowest pitch, the lightest touch. In discriminative terms, it would be the least stimulus which can be discriminated from *none at all*, so that a response cannot be conditioned to a lesser value. As noted in Chapter 1, these least values have been called "absolute thresholds" or "absolute limens."

b. The least *difference* between two stimuli, each above

the absolute threshold, that can be discriminated. Two stimuli may be so close together that, behaviorally, they are identical; the difference between them must reach or exceed a certain value before a response to one but not the other may be established. An extension of the metaphor of "threshold" led naturally to the designation "difference threshold" or "difference limen." Both types of threshold are stated in terms of some physical measure of the stimulus, whether energy, frequency, pressure, temperature, or some other. Stimulus values may be thought of as "supra-liminal," just "liminal," or "subliminal" for both types of threshold. Nevertheless, it should be kept in mind that the meaning of threshold lies in an organism's *behavior*. We define in physical terms those stimuli which are or are not adequate for discriminative responding. The behavioral data are always prior and necessary to the concept of capacity; and stimuli which are not discriminated even after arduous training are *held* to be below capacity level. We speak *as if* stimuli can or cannot be discriminated because of the limitations of capacity, but we *intend* that capacity be defined by the behavioral evidence of stimulus discriminability.

2. *The 'psychophysical' methods.* Historically, the study of human sensory capacities was the first to get under way in psychology with an adequate set of methods. By 1860, Gustav Fechner, an outstanding German scientist of his day, had formulated several experimental procedures which are still the backbone of human sensory research. Designed to test the limits of discriminative capacity, these methods aim to determine both absolute and difference thresholds. Fechner himself thought of them as a means of determining the relation between "mental sensations" and the "physical world" (hence "psychophysics"), but we see them today, not as a solution to a philosophical problem, but as important contributions to the measurement of sensory capacities.

The psychophysical methods differ in their complexity, their usefulness under given circumstances, and in the type of threshold they measure. Because Fechner realized that a subject's sensitivity varies from moment to moment, the methods each provide for measurements to be repeated as often as desired in order to secure reliable average estimates of threshold. They are alike, too, in presenting to a subject either single or paired stimuli. The subject is asked to report whether he can perceive the stimulus at all, or whether he can tell that two stimuli are different. Repeated stimulus presentations and statistical treatment of responses finally yield an estimate of his threshold and the consistency of his responses, both of which are measures of his accuracy or capacity.

The psychophysical methods are unquestionably endorsed by common sense. They are characteristically human in their reliance upon verbal behavior. They do not ask how such behavior is acquired and how words come to be discriminative responses. Nothing seems more reasonable on the surface than to ask a person whether he can or cannot perceive a stimulus or a stimulus difference. In this case, however, as in many others of unanalyzed human intercourse, common sense does not reveal the actual complexity of the experiment or the tacit assumptions upon which we proceed. The very feasibility of the methods, in which 'instructions' to the subject are indispensable, depends upon a long history of verbal behavior in both experimenter and subject which circumvents the need for training a new discriminative response such as would be necessary with lower organisms. The former "asks" the latter to "observe," "perceive," "pay attention," "judge," "coöperate," and so on; and the subject's only reinforcement is "social approval." Truly, there is material for analysis here. Yet, despite their naiveté, the psychophysical methods give a very fine measure of human sense acuity. The reliance upon verbal behavior is amply justified by the lawfulness and dependability of the results.

With human or animal subjects, and with respondent or operant methods, threshold determinations are subject to the influence of many important variables. These experimental situations include far more than the stimuli to be discriminated or the receptor organ being tested. Variables within the organism and in the experimental situation may count heavily in determining results. Hence, it is always premature to conclude that the absolute or difference threshold obtained is a final and immutable value. A failure to discriminate with one method does not mean that the organism would fail with a different method. Human subjects, for example, may improve their thresholds when given information on their performance during the experiment. Only recently, too, the use of a conditioned respondent has revealed for the first time the existence of color vision in the rabbit, when other methods had failed (Brown, 1936). Such instances will undoubtedly occur in the future.

3. *Some examples of human acuity.* Studies of human receptor sensitivity have turned up some dramatic facts. Our senses are really much more acute than we commonly imagine. Indeed, they frequently prove to be more responsive to small environmental energies and changes than most of the modern physical instruments which we regard with awe. Under good experimental conditions, a person with normal eyes can tell two colors apart when they differ by as little as two or three millimicrons in wave-length (a millimicron is a millionth of a millimeter); the brightest light which permits ordinary good vision may be 2.00×10^8 times as bright as the absolute threshold value; and a wire $3/32$ of an inch thick can be seen at a distance of half a mile.

Hearing is initiated by the impact of sound waves against the ear-drum. It has been computed that the faintest sound we can hear arises from impacts which do not greatly exceed in force the casual collisions of air molecules against the drum. With a little more sensitivity, we could actually "hear" the molecular movement of the air. As for pitch, some subjects can, with 100 per cent certainty, discriminate two tones which, at the 200-cycle level, are separated by only one-eighth to one-half of a cycle.

The sense of smell is also extremely acute, despite popular misconceptions. One sniff suffices to tell the presence of a substance like mercaptan when the amount of material involved is much less than can be picked up with a spectroscope. For odorous gases injected into the nasal passages, a rise in pressure of a few millimeters of mercury is enough to make some subjects unfailingly distinguish the smell where before they were completely insensitive.

In some of our sensing, we are excelled by lower animals, like the dog; in others, we stack up quite well against our biological contemporaries. This is true, however, only for acuities measured under rigid experimental controls. In everyday life, our senses function under crude conditions and we do not usually have occasion to fall back upon their extreme capacities. For these reasons, we do not learn our full potentialities until the laboratory tells us its story.

4. *Other methods.* Since the capacities of infra-human organisms cannot be gauged by way of verbal responses, we resort to the basic procedure of forming a discrimination. For example, using a respondent like the salivary reflex, we begin with two visual stimuli and the method of contrasts. The "positive" stimulus is a luminous circle, the "negative" an ellipse. The ellipse has a minor axis equal to the circle's diameter, but the major axis is twice that length. The discrimination between the two stimuli is easily formed. Then, by small steps, we bring the ellipse nearer and nearer to the shape of the circle, reinforcing regularly the response to the latter and never reinforcing the response to the former. At some point in the progression, the major-minor axis ratio of the ellipse will be such that the animal no longer responds to it any differently than to the circle—that is, we come to his *difference threshold.* Pavlov (1927) found this ratio to be about 9:8. By a similar procedure of selective reinforcement, we may determine the *absolute threshold* (e.g., for a sound) by seeing how small a stimulus magnitude can be made into a conditioned stimulus.

The basic experiment for *operant* discrimination may also be used in determining thresholds. The difference limen is obtained by bringing S^D and S^Δ to the point where, with a slightly smaller difference between them, the cumulative response curve shows exactly the same properties as the ordinary P-R curve. That is, extinction to S^Δ does not occur and the reinforcement of only S^D responses sets up a periodic cycle. The absolute threshold is determined when we find the least value of S^D which, when paired with an S^Δ of zero mag-

FIG. 37. One of Elder's subjects, earphone adjusted over left ear, in position for tests. The experimenter, who is behind the screen, raises the inclined sliding door at the ape's right, exposing the telegraph key. When the key is correctly pressed by the subject, his reward is delivered automatically through the chute at the left. (After Elder, 1934.)

nitude, still permits a discrimination—or, to turn it around, the greatest value of S^D which, with S^Δ equal to zero, gives only a P-R curve. (This method, as well as the preceding one for respondents, tells us how the difficulty of *forming* a discrimination changes as the stimuli approach liminal values.)

Variations of the operant procedure have been used in studying the discriminative capacities of organisms higher in the scale than the rat. Elder (1934), for example, determined the absolute threshold for tonal intensity in several chimpanzees by having them press a telegraph key whenever the "positive" stimulus sounded in their ear-phones. A "ready signal" (the opening of a door which gave access to the key) preceded exposures to S^D and S^Δ (silence). The S^D was presented until a response occurred, after which the door to the reaction key was closed and the ape was given a bit of fruit; S^Δ was presented for short periods only—eight seconds of silence following the signal, or until the subject responded "falsely"— after which the door to the key was closed again. An equal number of S^D and S^Δ presentations were provided, in random order, and threshold determinations were based on the percentage of correct responses at different intensity levels. The threshold values for seven tones, ranging in frequency between 128 and 8192 cycles per second, showed that, on the whole, the apes were equal in their sensitivity to human beings of a comparable age group.

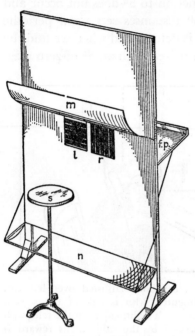

FIG. 38. The Lashley jumping apparatus. *s*—animal's stand; *n*—net; *f.p.*—food platform. (Reprinted from Crafts, Schneirla, Robinson, and Gilbert, *Recent experiments in psychology*, as redrawn from Lashley, 1930. Copyright, 1938. Courtesy of McGraw-Hill Book Company.)

A more complicated form of operant technique comes under the heading of "choice-reaction." There are several variations of this technique, but none is intended to give, nor does it give, a picture of the discriminative *process*. The stimuli to be distinguished are simultaneously presented, and one observes merely the all-or-none event on each trial in which the response is made either to S^D or S^A. A growing preponderance of responses to S^D as against S^A indicates an emerging discrimination. The technique is adequate to show whether a discrimination is possible, hence to supply a measure of threshold.

Two rather widely employed examples of the choice-reaction method are the "jumping apparatus" (Lashley, 1930)

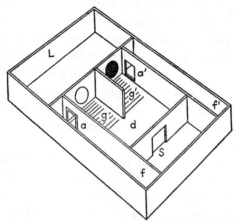

Fig. 39. An apparatus for teaching a visual discrimination. The animal starts at S; d is the choice point; g and g′ are electric grids; a and a′ are doors to the food alleys f and f′; L is the light box; the stimuli to be discriminated are the differently illuminated round windows. (Reprinted from Crafts, Schneirla, Robinson, and Gilbert, *Recent experiments in psychology,* as redrawn from Lashley, 1929. Copyright, 1938. Courtesy of McGraw-Hill Book Company.)

and the "T-box" (Yerkes and Watson, 1911). In the first, a hungry rat is taught to jump from a ledge through either of two identical loose curtains, behind which it lands on a platform and is reinforced with food. After conditioning, the curtains are changed so that they bear different stimuli, such as a circle *versus* a square. A jump to the arbitrarily 'correct' stimulus carries him through the curtain to food; an 'incorrect' jump dashes him against a door which is closed behind the curtain and drops him into a net. The stimuli may be equated in all respects (brightness, color, etc.) save the one to be discriminated (shape), and are frequently interchanged in position to avoid the strengthening of response to irrelevant cues or the growth of a 'position habit.' The method could, of course, be used without employing negative reinforcement for the 'wrong' response but simply omitting positive reinforcement.

The T-box is essentially a bifurcating alley in which the animal starts at the foot of the shaft, moves down, and turns right or left into one of two end-boxes, one being correct in that it contains food, and the other incorrect in that it leads to no reinforcement or to negative reinforcement like electric shock. The correct turn is signalled to the animal by the S^D in use, and, again, care is taken to avoid mere position habits. As in the case of the jumping technique, some criterion of successive correct choices is taken as the measure of discrimination.

Both the T-box and the jumping technique may be employed in studying the effect of various factors (brain operations, drug injections, motivation, past history, etc.) upon discriminative capacity, but the T-box has had the greater usefulness. It permits the testing of more sense functions and a wider variety of animals. In addition, it may be noted that the T-box is essentially a one-choice maze (a simple T-maze) and is suitable for at least the exploratory investigation of still other influences upon operant behavior.

Discrimination and "Experimental Neurosis"

Much attention has been paid in recent years to aberrations of behavior which appear when animals are forced to their discriminative limits. Pavlov (1927) observed, in the ellipse experiment mentioned above, that when his dog reached the 9:8 ratio of axes, an attempt to push this discrimination completely disrupted the dog's behavior. He became violent, bit the apparatus, whined, and barked; in the investigator's opinion, he presented "all the symptoms of acute neurosis." One of Pavlov's students obtained a similar effect in a pitch-threshold experiment, a visiting psychiatrist agreeing that the animal was "neurotic." These induced disorganizations are now called "experimental neurosis," and have since been established in rats, cats, sheep, pigs, and even human beings. They point to a closer integration of psychopathology with the theories and laws of general behavior.

Experimental neurosis may be obtained in both respondent and operant discriminative conditioning. In the latter, the disruption of behavior is accentuated if, in addition to going unreinforced, the responses to S^Δ are punished. Forcing a response in the jumping apparatus by goading the animal with a blast of air or pushing him off the ledge, may have this result. When negative is combined with positive reinforcement in this fashion, the amount of "conflict" increases as the threshold is neared or the difficulty is increased. There is no choice but to respond, and a "wrong" response is costly in terms of punishment.

The symptoms of experimental neurosis include refusal to work, excitement, cowering, disturbances of breathing and heartbeat, irregularities of activity and rest cycles, rigidity, trembling, convulsions, and spasmodic muscular twitchings ('tics'). Oftimes, the animal will seem normal when outside the experimental situation, but the abnormalities erupt as soon as it is put back. In some instances, the disorganization is carried over into the animal's routine environment (Liddell, 1938), and may slowly disappear with prolonged vacation, only to emerge with full force when the experiment is resumed. Once set up, the neurosis may not only affect the discrimination of threshold stimuli, but an even cruder discrimination (e.g., an ellipse ratio of 2:1) may be disturbed.

Human beings cannot, for obvious social reasons, be subjected to extreme experimental neurosis. In Pavlov's laboratory, however, small degrees of upset were produced in a child of six by requiring a discriminative motor response to metronome beats. Rates of 144 and 92 beats per minute were easily discriminated, but after narrowing down the difference to 144 and 120 per minute, the child became surly, disobedient, and uncoöperative. Other children, organically impaired by encephalitis or cretinism, were also brought to the point of mild behavioral disruption by being required to make overly fine discriminations. Such manifestations are not unlike those sometimes observed when human adults are repeatedly compelled to attempt delicate discriminations in psychophysical experiments or in certain occupational training. Students of radio code, for example, have been known to show deviations from normal behavior which, in extreme cases, warranted a psychiatric classification of "code neurosis."

It is still too early to judge the implications of this line of research for the whole range of human maladjustments. To many psychologists, it seems a good beginning. The precipitating causes of human abnormality often appear similar in principle to the experimental observations. The work is being actively pressed in many laboratories, by psychiatrists as well as psychologists. Phobias, compulsions, anxieties, and other long-recognized disorders are fast becoming the concern of the experimentalist as well as the therapist and the clinical investigator. We may look forward with some optimism to a day of mutual aid and understanding between workers in these two historically unrelated fields.

Discriminative Reaction Time

In our study of discrimination, we are interested in how a response depends upon stimulus conditions. When we come to analyze this dependency, several measures of response are possible. For example, there is *response frequency*, in the now familiar bar-pressing situation, when animals are involved. In psychophysical experiments, we use the frequency-of-detection of stimuli or stimulus differences. *Latency* of response affords another measure—one which has historically been called *reaction time*.

How fast can a person react to a discriminative stimulus?

This question is ordinarily answered in the laboratory by the following procedure. We instruct a subject to respond as quickly as he can; we give him a 'ready signal' so that he can get 'set'; and we deliver the stimulus. We may use a light, a sound, a touch, or any other stimulus we wish; and the subject's response may be pressing a telegraph key, calling out a word, or any other operant that we can conveniently record. The time between the stimulus and the response is his "reaction time."

The study of reaction time was not launched by psychologists. During the nineteenth century, before the advent of modern registering devices, astronomers were vitally concerned with this matter. In attempting to note the exact moment at which a star passed the meridian, they had to observe its movement and respond immediately when it crossed a hairline in the objective of a telescope. Over the space of many years, they struggled with the problem of cutting down discrepancies in the observations of different persons; and they bequeathed to us the expression, "personal equation," for individual differences in reaction time among various observers. Also, H. L. F von Helmholtz, a brilliant investigator in physics, physiology, and other fields, attempted, in 1850, to determine the speed of nerve-impulse conduction in human beings, with a reaction-time method modeled after one he had employed on a nerve-muscle preparation excised from a frog's leg. A subject's skin was stimulated at points differently distant from the brain, and to each stimulus he was instructed to respond as quickly as he could. By dividing the difference in estimated length of nerve for two skin spots by the difference in the two reaction times, Helmholtz arrived at an approximate speed of conduction. His final figure of about sixty meters per second was surprisingly close to currently accepted speeds (about sixty-eight meters per second), although his data were so variable that he would not trust them.

It was not until 1868, however, that Donders, another physiologist, pointed out that several *types* of reaction time might be investigated. He saw that increasingly complex stimulus and response alternatives should have their effect upon reaction time, and he set down what he thought were the three typical experiments.

1. *The A-reaction.* The subject makes only one specified response, say pressing a key, and a single stimulus is used each time. This is the so-called *simple reaction time.* It has been used as an index of the effect of drugs and fatigue; in comparing response speeds with stimuli belonging to the different senses; in determining the importance of stimulus intensity; and under other experimental conditions.

2. *The B-reaction. Two* stimuli are employed, each with its own appropriate response. For example, a subject may be asked to respond with his right hand when shown the color green, and with his left when shown red. On successive trials, the stimuli are interchanged at random. The subject, on each occasion, discriminates which is being presented, reacting with the appropriate hand. This is sometimes called the "disjunctive" reaction time, because of its either-or character—that is, the subject responds in one way or the other.

3. *The C-reaction.* This is another disjunctive reaction time, sometimes known as the "discrimination" reaction time. Two stimuli are used, and the subject must discriminate by responding to one, but *not* to the other. This is essentially the discriminative situation that we described earlier in connection with bar-pressing and Elder's (1934) study of auditory acuity in the chimpanzee.

If you think this over, you will probably conclude that the order of increasing complexity in Donders' types is not A-B-C, but A-C-B. The C-reaction adds a discriminative factor to the A-reaction; and the B-reaction adds a response factor to the C-reaction. The average reaction-time values for the three cases come out as you might expect: A is fastest, C is intermediate, and B is slowest.

Other investigators went further. It seemed reasonable that two things should hold. In modern terminology, we would say that (1) reaction time might be used as a measure of degree of stimulus generalization; and (2) reaction time should increase with the number of different responses brought into play. The correctness of both assumptions has been well established. In one series of studies, Henmon (1906) studied the B-reaction, using pairs of colors, tones, and lines. Members of the pairs were different in varying degree. One pair of lines, for example, might be nearly the same in length, whereas another might be quite different. The subject was instructed to respond to a specified color or line of the pair with the right hand if the stimulus was on the right, and with the left hand if the stimulus was on the left. With the tones, a right-hand reaction was called for if the second of the two tones was higher in pitch, and a left-hand reaction if lower. The kind of results obtained are typified by those shown below.

Stimuli to Be Discriminated	Average Reaction Time (milliseconds)
Tones differing by 16 cycles	290
" " " 12 "	299
" " " 8 "	311
" " " 4 "	334

The importance of increasing the number of responses (better, stimulus-response units) has been demonstrated in several ways. One experimenter (Merkel, 1885) used a separate stimulus and reaction key for each finger. The stimuli were five Arabic and five Roman numerals, visually presented, and each was associated with the reaction of a specific finger. In the simplest situation, only one stimulus and only one finger movement was employed; in the most complex situation any of the ten stimuli might appear and the appropriate reaction had to be made. The average reaction times in the ten different cases were as follows:

Stimulus-Response Units		Average Reaction Time (milliseconds)
1	(simple reaction)	187
2		316
3		364
4		434
5	(disjunctive	487
6	reactions)	532
7		570
8		603
9		619
10		622

Merkel's experiment, and possibly Henmon's, have a bearing upon another problem, that of *response* generalization ("induction"), to be discussed in the following chapter. The evidence is clear, however, that discriminative difficulty, arising from stimulus generalization, is reflected in reaction time. The greater the generalization, the slower the reaction time.

Reaction Time and Operant Latency

Every reaction time is an operant latency. More specifically, it is the *minimal latency* of an operant response to a discriminative stimulus. As in the case of threshold determinations, the measurement of minimal *human* latencies is enormously facilitated by previous conditioning to verbal discriminative stimuli. The subject is instructed, he understands, and he coöperates by doing his best. He has long been reinforced for rapid response when such requests or their equivalents form a part of the discriminative-stimulus compound. It is even possible that, finding himself in a laboratory, face to face with an experimenter, and so on, he may not even require "instructions" to respond with all speed. He "sets himself," we say, for the task; he "assumes" that it is the quick response that is wanted.

The animal usually behaves otherwise. Reduced latencies are ordinarily obtained only after considerable training. But the basic procedure is the same. The reinforcement of a response is made contingent upon the occurrence of that response within a given time after S^D is presented. We start with the animal's normal range of latencies and get him to speed up by withholding reinforcement for the slowest responses. By gradually eliminating the longer latencies through extinction, while continuing to reinforce the shorter ones, we ultimately reach a latency that is minimal—beyond which selective reinforcement is no longer effective. We have then determined his reaction time for this S^D. The process may have required several hours, distributed over several days, whereas a human reaction time could have been determined in a single experimental session, but the outcome is the same; in each case we have achieved a minimal latency through selective reinforcement.

Latency and the Discriminative Process

The normal operant latency of response to an S^D in the bar-pressing situation may fluctuate considerably from one stimulus presentation to another, depending at least in part upon the animal's location and ongoing activity at the time of stimulus onset. One might, however, expect that, in *forming* a discrimination, there would be a change in latency of response to S^D and S^Δ, the former decreasing, the latter increasing, as training progresses. If this were so, we would have another way of analyzing the process besides that provided by the cumulative response curve.

Unfortunately, the findings on this score have not been very helpful. While a change in latencies does occur in the bar-pressing experiment, it is quite small, it comes in very early, and it stops long before the discrimination is firmly established. In other studies, where a running operant is used, the situation is apparently different. In teaching a discrimination with the runway apparatus, the end-box contains a reinforcement only if an S^D (e.g., light over the runway) is present, and S^Δ (no light) runs are not reinforced. On successive S^D trials, the animal starts out more and more quickly after the release door is opened; whereas interspersed S^Δ trials give progressively slower starting times, increased vacillation, and more instances in which the animal does not leave the starting box at all. The technique is a trial-by-trial affair, like that of the T-box and the jumping apparatus, with no free operant to be observed in process of change; but, if we treat starting times as operant latencies, we do observe a trend of times which is somehow related to the formation of the discrimination. The problem of bringing a latency measure into closer harmony with a rate measure is yet to be settled.

Workaday Reaction Times

In everyday behavior, most of our responses are not emitted under such favorable conditions as those of the laboratory; and the demand for high-speed reactions is made only occasionally, as in athletics, military combat, and the control of such machines as the airplane and the automobile. For several reasons, the values reached in human reaction-time experiments are seldom approximated, even in these pursuits. Warning signals are often lacking; one may not know from what direction the stimulus is coming; one is usually engaged in doing something else when the response is suddenly demanded; the response may involve the action of large, rather than small, muscle groups; the stimulus may be very weak, or so strong as to cause "freezing"; and so on. Thus, a group of football players in uniform may average as much as 400 milliseconds in getting off a scrimmage line at an auditory signal (Miles, 1931); and the reaction time of automobile drivers may rise to several seconds when an impending accident requires a shift of the foot from gas pedal to brake.

Individual differences in reaction time have long been recognized, and attempts have often been made to use these differences as a basis for selecting men to be trained in special skills. If one could predict the success of radio operators or fighter-plane pilots from their performance on a short speed-of-response test, then one would pick only the fastest men for schooling and thereby save the effort and expense of training those men who would ultimately "wash out" or become combat casualties. When used for such purposes, however, reaction-time tests have proved of indifferent value, probably because other factors (discriminative capacity, motivation, adequate training procedures, etc.) are also important for success in these occupations.

Multiple Discriminations

Although an analysis of discrimination necessarily begins with simple cases, our behavior is usually guided by stimulus combinations that are quite complex. Many S^D's may sometimes operate in *succession* and we may be unable to respond to all of them properly. At other times, they may operate *simultaneously* and our response is to the compound rather than any single element. Again, a response may be made to one or a group of S^D's which are constantly changing. In any or all of these cases, the basic processes of discrimination remain as we have outlined them, but their working out often presents difficult problems.

1. *Successive discrete S^D's.* We can illustrate the first type of discriminative complexity by what is encountered when one tries learning to receive International Morse Code. As everyone knows, this code consists of short and long sounds ("dots" and "dashes") which are combined in various ways to form distinctive patterns. A beginner needs to learn thirty-six of these patterns or signals—twenty-six for the alphabet, plus ten for the numbers 0-9. His job is to become able to discriminate each well enough so that he can write down, or "copy," the appropriate letters or numbers as the signals are sounded one at a time and in random order. At first, many of the signals sound alike, and the student puts down the wrong character. These are obviously cases of generalization. A table of errors made for a class of beginners in code will show that these generalizations fall within certain categories

depending upon the dot-dash composition of the signals (Spragg, 1943; Keller and Schoenfeld, 1944). The problem for the learner is very largely a discriminative one, since his responses—the writing or printing of letters and numbers—are usually well established ("differentiated") long before he hears code.

An example of the sort of generalization that occurs in code mastery has already been given earlier in this chapter when we considered the concept of "similarity." In Table V below are given several other instances of the kind of confusion that makes trouble for beginners. These are typical, but not the only ones that occur. Most of the signals actually generalize with *several* others. Thus, the signal for P may generalize not only with the one for J, but also with the ones for F, L, C, (—.—.), Q, X, and perhaps a half dozen more in the early stages of training. Moreover, this generalization is reduced by training less readily for some signals than for others. Long after W, P, and F are discriminated, 5 and 6 may give trouble by generalizing with H and B respectively, 4 (...–) will continue to generalize with V (...–), and so on.

Table V

GENERALIZATIONS COMMONLY MADE BY BEGINNERS IN LEARNING TO RECEIVE INTERNATIONAL MORSE CODE

Signal		is generalized with	Signal	
.——	(W)		.—.	(R)
.——.	(P)		.————	(J)
..—.	(F)		.—..	(L)
..———	(2)		...——	(3)
.....	(5)		....	(H)
——.—	(Q)		——..	(Z)
—..—	(X)		—...	(B)
—....	(6)		—...	(B)

As with all discriminations, the speed of learning code can be increased by making reinforcement as immediate as possible for the correct discriminative response. (For more on delayed reinforcement, see pp. 208-209). This fact is utilized in the "code-voice" method of teaching now employed by the U.S. Army Signal Corps (TM 11-459). After each signal is sounded, there is a pause of two or three seconds during which the student writes down, if he can, the character that was represented. Then the character is identified vocally by the instructor and the next signal is presented. Eventually,

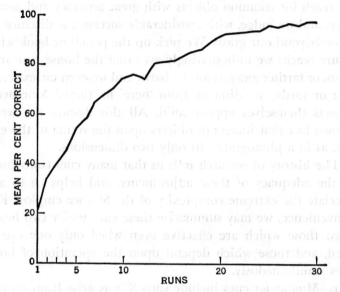

FIG. 40. Progress curve for a group of beginning students learning to receive International Morse Code by the "code-voice" method. The data plotted are the average per cent correct responses on successive training "runs" of 100 randomized signals each. Prior to the first run, the 36 signals were identified once, and this is one reason the curve does not start at zero per cent correct. (After Keller, Christo, and Schoenfeld, 1946.)

under this form of tuition, the student accurately anticipates each announcement, and the use of the reinforcing "voice" may be discontinued. Figure 40 shows the sort of progress that may be expected of college students when given one hour daily of this kind of training.

2. *Compound S^D's.* This category of multiple discriminations includes some cases which seem so natural to us that

we do not often think to inquire about them, and other cases which are the basis of some amusing and unusual effects. Let us consider, as our first example, that of *depth perception*. We accept unquestioningly the fact that we can see objects in depth or, better, that we react appropriately to the third-dimensional aspect of objects. Under ordinary circumstances, we reach for common objects with great accuracy and assurance, and we judge, with considerable success, the distance of those beyond our grasp. We pick up the pencil or book with a sure reach; we unhesitatingly aver that the house is nearer to us, or farther away, than the barn; and we even estimate, in feet or yards, the distance from 'here' to 'there.' Moreover, objects themselves appear solid. All this despite the well-known fact that images of objects upon the retina of the eye are, as in a photograph, in only two dimensions.

The history of research tells us that many cues contribute to the adequacy of these adjustments, and helps us to appreciate the extreme complexity of the S^D's we employ. For convenience, we may summarize these cues under two headings: those which are effective even when only one eye is used, and those which depend upon the operation of both eyes simultaneously.

1. *Monocular* cues include such S^D's as arise from (*a*) the *interposition* of objects (the nearer object hides, in part, the object that is farther away); (*b*) *size* and *perspective* (the far-away object is smaller than the one near-by, and the continuous change in object size with distance is perspective); and (*c*) the *distribution of light and shadow* (concavity and convexity, which are third-dimensional characteristics of objects, commonly depend upon this cue). These and one or two others have long been recognized by painters who sought to represent depth upon canvas.

2. An important *binocular* cue is that provided by the fact that our two eyes, being apart, cannot be stimulated in exactly the same way by a single solid object. The depth provided by this disparity may be demonstrated dramatically

with a stereoscope. This device, a fixture in the old-fashioned parlor, permits two slightly different bi-dimensional views to stimulate the two eyes separately, with a resultant tri-dimensional effect that may be very striking. 'Stereoscopic vision' provides us with one of our most subtle cues.

Not all of these cues (and we have omitted several others) need to operate at one time to guide our adaptive reactions, although many of them are commonly available. Numerous experiments have shown that one or two may function, often very effectively, in the absence of the rest. The loss of an eye, which automatically eliminates all binocular cues, does not thereby render the loser helpless; it merely makes him more dependent upon the cues that remain.

Some of the depth S^D's are apparently learned in the early movements and experiences of the child. As he reaches and crawls, for example, he soon learns the importance of inter-position, perspective, and the movement cues provided by the muscles of the eyes. Some are so obscure that, even with coaching, they are not easily appreciated. Yet the effectiveness of our movements in space is clearly dependent upon them, and these movements are continually being reinforced by their outcome. After awhile, we think nothing of reaching for objects and finding that our hand has gone just the right distance and in just the right direction to make the contact; or we throw a ball with considerable accuracy without once stopping to attend to the discriminative basis of the act.

Another instance of the operation of compound S^D's is seen in the fact that a given object, under changing stimulus conditions, seems to retain its proper character. A man standing on the sidewalk across the street seems as tall as a man should be, although his image on the retina of your eye is much smaller than it would be if he were standing close by. This phenomenon is referred to as "size constancy"; but other object properties than size lead you to behave in a 'constant' way. In a similar fashion, you can judge with great accuracy the *shape* of an object despite the changing stimulation it supplies as it moves about in your environment. You have no difficulty in seeing a dish as round, although its projection on your retina is usually elliptical. The *brightness* of objects provides still another example. Your handkerchief looks white whether you see it in the sunlight, in the classroom, or in a dim corridor. The important point about all forms of constancy is simply that, in responding to the physical properties of objects, your responses are the product of the discriminative stimuli arising not only from that object but also from as much of the environment as is available. If you were asked to judge the size of a line of light in a completely dark room, you would find the task difficult—you would ask to know, or you would try to guess, its distance from you before you ventured an estimate. Under strict experimental control, the dish *can* be made to look like an ellipse, by cutting off all cues of its tilt with respect to other environmental objects and with respect to your own person. And brightness constancy can be destroyed by a similar reduction in the number of cues (such as prevailing illumination of the environment) upon which you ordinarily depend, so that the handkerchief will look black under special conditions.

"Redintegration" is another case in point. It is easy to show that when S^D compounds are the basis of a response it is possible to obtain that response to a *portion* of the compound. The recognition of a work of pictorial art may be based on only one detail, or the identification of a symphony may be made with only a few notes carrying a simple melodic line. Redintegration is a case of generalization through partial identity. It is not, as was once thought, a separate principle of discrimination, but is to be thought of in terms of generalization and elements of compounded S^D's.

3. *Changing S^D's.* Our third category of discriminative complexity is that in which S^D's are in a continuous state of change, and a few examples will suffice to show its prevalence. To a tennis player, a bounding ball gives an infinite and continuous series of stimuli, but his response to them must

be sure and quick. To the sportsman who brings down a duck or shatters a clay pigeon, or the skilled machinist who follows the movement of the cutting tool on his lathe, the problem of discrimination is again one of change. For a fighter pilot or gunner, the same is true. A device called a pursuit-meter has been employed in selection tests for gunners and pilots. This apparatus tests the accuracy with which a candidate can follow a moving target through an erratic course. In general, men who do not perform well with such an apparatus are likely to fail in flight or gunnery school, hence may be eliminated in advance in order to save expense and disappointment.

"Higher Units" in Perception

In the laboratory, we seek to isolate the S^D's which enter into complex discriminations like the above, although we know that in ordinary experience they are not so isolated. But we would also like to know how they become integrated. In learning Morse code, for example, the student progresses to a point where he is no longer responding to discrete signals, but is hearing a number of them together. An indication of this is the fact that, with plain-language transmissions, he can "copy behind" with considerable ease, the extent of his lag being an indication of how much he can grasp at one time—that is, how big his *unit* is. A burst of signals sounds to him like a *word* and he does not pause to break it up into separate letters. In early studies of code learning (Bryan and Harter, 1899), it was observed that before a student could pass beyond a certain word-per-minute proficiency he might spend a good deal of time during which he made no apparent progress. If he persisted, he could resume his advance, this time going on to a new level of mastery in which he could handle groups of signals or short words. Periods of no progress were called "plateaus" and it was at first thought that these were necessary stages in which the learner consolidated smaller units or elements into higher units. Today we believe that such intervals of no progress can be largely avoided by carefully and systematically combining signals and giving him practice on higher units, rather than allowing the student to form them himself on the basis of accidental combination and by dint of mere perseverance. Higher perceptual units in vision can also be studied in connection with the so-called *span of apprehension.* Flash for one-tenth of a second a number of letters on a screen before a student who has been instructed to call them back. If he is tried on one, two, three, or more, we can quickly determine the largest number that he will apprehend without error, and how his accuracy diminishes when we exceed this number. Suppose we find that a given subject can unfailingly report correctly as many as six letters. If we change over and flash short words on the screen, we find that he can report about as many words as he did letters. If these words were three-letter words, then he is reporting eighteen letters whereas he could report only six before. Obviously, in the case of the words, the letters are no longer functioning as separate elements, but this time the words are elements. We have here another instance of the combination, through training, of simple S^D's into compounds or higher units.

Concept Formation

What is a "concept"? This is another term which has come into psychology from popular speech, carrying with it many different connotations. We shall have to be careful in using it, remembering that it is only a name for a kind of behavior. Strictly speaking, one does not *have* a concept, just as one does not *have* extinction—rather, one demonstrates conceptual behavior, by acting in a certain way. Our analysis should really start with a different question: What type of behavior is it that we call "conceptual"? And the answer is that when a group of objects get the same response, when they form a class the members of which are reacted to similarly, we speak of a concept. A child's concept of "horse" may be such that his first sight of a cow, a mule, or a camel may all result in his saying "Giddap" or "Whoa," or simply "Horsie." A group of events may also be responded to in the same way and thus form a concept, such as "war." Classes of objects or events, differently responded to, develop different concepts. "But," you may say, "this is only generalization and discrimination all over again"—and so it is. Generalization *within* classes and discrimination *between* classes—this is the essence of concepts.

1. *The growth of concepts.* It is important that we maintain an objective attitude toward concepts, that we see them in terms of behavior. A good way to do this is to note how some concepts develop in human children. At birth, the world of the child may be, as William James said, no more than a "booming, buzzing confusion," but very soon he responds in different ways to different parts of his environment. For example, at the age of about three months, he seems to show the rudiments of a 'social smile'—that is, he smiles at other human beings. We like to think, at this stage, that he 'knows us,' and parents fondly believe that they alone can evoke the expression. A test will quickly show, however, that the child is responding to the *moving* or *noise-making* aspects of parental behavior; moving animals and rattling toys will also set off the reaction. We may, if we wish, think of this as a primitive conceptual distinction between moving and non-moving objects. Later on, the child may reserve his smile for members of the family, even crying at the approach of strangers, but many months of learning must precede the advance of his discrimination to this stage.

An interesting set of studies by Piaget (1929) traced the changes in the child's concept of living *versus* non-living objects. This was done by asking children of various ages what they thought was alive and why, whether objects feel hurt when kicked or become sad when locked in a closet, and so forth. It turned out, as you would expect, that the criteria used for defining living and non-living objects change with age and the accumulation of experience. At one time all moving objects are called alive. Later on, a distinction is made between things that move when pushed and things that move 'by themselves' (brooks, clouds, trees in the wind). Only gradually, and never completely, do they approach in their conceptual behavior the 'realism' so highly prized by modern man. Since our own movements of locomotion, respiration, speech, and the like are perhaps the first, and certainly the most important, to occasion the response "living," it is not strange that we find the brook 'running,' the wind 'sighing,' the trees 'whispering,' and the table 'groaning' under its load of viands. 'Animism,' which is opposed to 'realism' and which is said to involve the ascription of the properties of animate things to those that are inanimate, is readily seen to be another case of generalization. Rigorous discriminative training is required before a concept of living objects can be formed which excludes this primitive extension.

Through education, formal and informal, our concepts are altered and enlarged. Where once we thought that trout, eels, sharks, and whales were all "fish," we learn in school that these organisms fall into different categories, and our concept of "fish" is radically changed. Similarly, our concept of airplane once included heavier-than-air craft with propellers, wings, engines, fuselage, and tail. Today we are modifying this category to include pilotless planes that are jet-propelled and without the conventional engine. Apparently the presence of wings is the indispensable part of our concept of airplane, since wingless ships, like rockets, do not evoke the name. In these cases, and in others, the difficulty of classifying often becomes acute. For example, we know what "fighting" is, but we may be unable to say whether puppies, engaged in rough-and-tumble, are "fighting" or "playing."

2. *Experiments on concept formation.* In the laboratory, studies of concept formation fall roughly within two major classifications. As an example of the first, we have an experiment by Hull (1920) in which subjects were taught to re-

spond with nonsense words (*li, ta, yer,* etc.) to different Chinese characters. Six lists, of twelve characters each, were memorized successively by each subject. The seventy-two characters were different in total composition, but each of the twelve characters of the first list had a component (a 'radical') which was present in one of the characters of each later list, and the same response word was required whenever this radical appeared. Thus, the word *li* was applied to six different characters (one in each list), all of which possessed the same radical. The point of the experiment was to see whether the learning of successive lists would be facilitated as the subject was given more and more experience with the basic radicals. The results showed that the process of mastery was indeed speeded up as each new list was learned. The subjects came to 'form concepts' in the sense that they generalized on the basis of the key radicals in the different characters. Moreover, some subjects who were able with very few errors to respond to the characters of the sixth list were unable, when asked, to identify the radicals to which they were correctly responding. Evidently, this kind of conceptual behavior may be established without a subject's being able to state in words just what he is doing. This is most informative when we consider that in common speech we normally tend to identify the 'possession' of a concept with one's ability to verbalize it, even if only approximately.

In the second major type of experiment on concept formation, a subject may be shown a number of objects and *instructed* to find the common characteristic which establishes a category. Thus, Smoke (1932) studied the formation of ten concepts each of which concerned a certain type of geometrical design having a nonsense name. A "pog," for example, always contained a circle within a rectangle, although a series of "pogs" might differ in the size or some other aspect of the circle or rectangle. The subject examined one "pog" after another when they were presented and advised the experimenter when he was ready to define the class. He was then asked to state what a "pog" was, to draw two examples, and to select from a list of sixteen test figures those which fulfilled the "pog" requirements. Although the ease of the generalizations depended upon the kind of geometrical design employed, the subjects were usually able to single out those containing the same basic components. Moreover, in agreement with Hull's findings, they were sometimes unable to *define* a class satisfactorily when they had already 'passed' the other tests.

3. *Non-verbalized concepts.* In view of the fact that a subject may behave conceptually without being able to tell us the basis of his discrimination or generalization, it is natural to ask whether concepts are peculiarly human. From observation and theoretical analysis, we are led tentatively to conclude that lower animals exhibit fundamentally the same behavior. Consider a hunting dog, being trained to pursue rabbits. Early in his training he may fail to discriminate adequately and find himself embarrassed in an encounter with a polecat or a hedgehog. When we say, later, that he is properly trained, we mean, among other things, that his concept of rabbit will exclude these other creatures. In the laboratory, we may train animals, as well as young children, in concept formation, when there is no possibility of verbal definition. A child, for example, may be taught to reach toward a triangular figure for a piece of candy, while reaching to a circle goes unrewarded. Later, if we substitute different shapes of triangles and different sizes of circles, his response remains correct. Animals may also be taught to generalize on the basis of triangularity (Fields, 1932) . We approached this matter before, in our treatment of "similarity" and stimulus equivalence, and now we can see that equivalent stimuli is what we mean when we speak of a concept.

The "transposition" experiment provides us with another instance of this sort (Spence, 1936; Jackson, 1939). A child or an animal is trained to approach the brighter of two discs. After thorough conditioning, the brighter disc is removed and in its place another, dimmer, one is added so that the same ratio of brightness exists between them as previously did between the earlier pair. The organism will respond to the disc which is now the brighter one, although it was formerly the dimmer. This experiment has been spoken of as an example of the concept "brighter than," but the essential fact is not altered. We are here dealing with the generalization of stimulus patterns.

It is curious to note the resistance that may be shown to the notion that the term *concept* need not be limited to matters capable of being verbalized or found only in the behavior of human adults. We seem to have here a problem in our own behavior. *We* have formed a concept of conceptual behavior which is based upon such factors as the age of the subject, his ability to verbalize, and the fact that he is human. It is true that our verbal behavior as adults becomes very complex and that, in philosophy, for example, we may wrestle with the identifying characteristics of such verbal concepts as justice, virtue, and wisdom. In such highly sophisticated discourses, we have an example of the attempt to reach agreement as to the criteria of the just, the virtuous, and the wise —to enumerate the essential S^D's for evoking these words. Disagreements arise through differences in individual discriminative histories. The problem is not unlike that faced by writers on semantics; if we wish to know whether two persons 'have in mind' the same thing when they use the same word, the answer will lie in the overlap of discriminative stimuli which evoke the word from each. The fact that two persons using the same word may agree on some of its meanings and disagree on others should not be surprising—they have, after all, not had identical training, and the conditions which evoke the word in one may disagree in part with those which evoke it in the other.

We have been dealing with concept formation as a resultant of stimulus generalization and discrimination. This is all right but, especially in the case of adult human beings,

it is not the whole story. An important sector of adult behavior is verbal in nature, and the analysis of this behavior
must precede a fuller understanding of conceptual activity.
In the concluding chapter of this book, a brief sketch will be
offered of a promising theory of verbal behavior that is in
accord with the general principles you have learned. After
you have read that sketch, you might profitably turn back to
review what is said here.

4. *Concepts and mediated generalization.* Generalizations
are said to be mediated when they are based upon a stimulus
equivalence which results from training (Cofer and Foley,
1942). Some concept formation is an example of such equivalence. The words *vase* and *urn* have few stimulus properties
in common. If we were to condition a respondent or an
operant in a young child to the sound of one of these words,
there would be very little generalization to the sound of the
other. An adult, however, who has learned that these words
are almost synonymous and may be used interchangeably, is
likely to show considerable generalization. Following the
lead of Razran (1939b), who first explored this area, Riess
(1940) conditioned the galvanic skin reflex initially to one
stimulus word and then tested for generalization to two other
words, one of which was a synonym and one of which was a
homonym of the first. For the stimulus words themselves (*style,
freeze, surf,* and *urn*), there was an average gain of 346 per
cent in magnitude of skin response through conditioning.
The synonyms (*fashion, chill, wave,* and *vase*) gained 141 per
cent through generalization; and the homonyms (*stile, frieze,
serf,* and *earn*) gained 94.5 per cent. Whereas the generalization to the homonym illustrates simply stimulus generalization, that to the synonym illustrates mediated generalization
based upon the previous training which produced the 'meaning' equivalence of these two words. (We shall have more to
say about 'meaning' in Chapter 7.) Riess (1946) was also able
to show that, for children below twelve years of age, there
was more homonym than synonym generalization—a finding

that accords well with the generally accepted belief that the meaning value of words increases with age.

Table VI
MEDIATED GENERALIZATION IN THE CONDITIONING OF THE GALVANIC SKIN RESPONSE TO VERBAL STIMULI IN SUBJECTS OF VARYING AGE
(Data from Riess, 1946)

	Mean Age			
	7 yrs. 9 mos.	10 yrs. 8 mos.	14 yrs. 0 mos.	18 yrs. 6 mos.
Number of Children	21	22	25	24
Word	222	227	243	281
Homonym	159	65	60	52
Antonym	139	97	77	103
Synonym	129	60	110	149

In the experiment, the GSR (measured in microamperes) was first conditioned to a word; after which generalization was tested to a homonym, an antonym, and a synonym of that word. Exposure of the stimulus words was visual, and of three-second duration. The table is to be read as follows: The 21 children aged seven years and nine months (average) showed an increase in GSR to the word after conditioning of 222 per cent of their pre-conditioning GSR to that word; the degree of generalization between the word and its homonym is shown by a GSR to the homonym of 159 per cent of the homonym's pre-conditioning GSR value; between the word and its antonym, 139 per cent; between the word and its synonym, 129 per cent. At this age, stimulus (auditory) similarity between the word and homonym outweighs the 'meaning' similarity: but, by the age of 14, the order of generalization is reversed, with mediated generalization through 'meaning' being the largest.

Generalization and Discrimination in Education

The process of education is greatly concerned with generalization and discrimination. It is possible that, at the beginning of life, all stimuli may generalize to produce mass and profuse responses in the infant. As he matures and learns to discriminate objects in his environment, those generalizations which persevere during his pre-school years will probably be adequate for most of his gross adjustments, but they must be broken down later in the interests of his educational progress. The new generalizations and discriminations will in turn undergo change as his schooling continues. From his science teachers, for example, he will learn that falling stones and falling paper obey the same law, that fish breathe in a way very similar to ours, that an alley cat and a lion have much in common. In fact, from one point of view, the whole business of science will be seen as the arrangement of nature's facts into new categories, with a stress upon the important but not obvious similarities and a disregard for the obvious but unimportant dissimilarities. Even changes in the fundamental theories of science are of this nature. The history of great discoveries is one of the reorganization of facts into new classifications on the basis of related properties. Planetary movements are tied into one general law with the motion of falling bodies. Electric currents are tied to the behavior of ions in chemical solutions. Nerve impulses are shown to be electrical phenomena. The behavior of *all* organisms follows the same basic laws. On simple and complex levels of animal and human behavior, the operation of generalization and discrimination are among the most important phenomena with which we deal. The Army dog that growls at men in strange uniform but greets its own soldiers; the child who learns to tell "Daddy" from "Mommy" (and may then call all men "Daddy"); the student who learns that bats and whales are both mammals, not bird and fish; and a psychologist who cites three apparently different instances of behavior as examples of the same basic laws—all of these are doing very much the same thing.

NOTES

A very readable source on respondent generalization and discrimination may be found in Pavlov's (1927) own book, especially in Chapters VII and VIII. The statement of the principles as we have given them (for both operants and respondents) have been drawn, however, from Skinner (1938).
If you are interested in the technical details of the psychophysical

methods, Woodworth (1938) offers a thorough account. A comparison of human sensory capacities with those of animals at various phylogenetic levels has traditionally been dealt with by the comparative psychologist. For numerous illustrations in this area, you may consult Warden, Jenkins, and Warner (1935-1940).

The early history of the "personal equation" and the study of reaction times has some entertaining features, well brought out by Boring (1929) and Woodworth (1938).

Among the first to recognize the importance of a systematic attack upon the problem of "mediated generalization" were Cofer and Foley, in 1942 and later. The problem has not yet been investigated, however, to the degree that its importance would seem to justify.

6

RESPONSE VARIABILITY AND DIFFERENTIATION

After E. R. Guthrie and G. P. Horton, *Cats in a Puzzle Box,* 1946

Introduction

In this chapter, we shall deal exclusively with operant behavior. We shall concentrate upon the behavior itself, rather than the stimuli that set the occasion for its emission. Indeed, we shall deal with changes in behavior that take place *irrespective* of the S^D situation. Our major concern will be with three related matters. First, we shall consider the fact, perhaps obvious, that operant responses may differ on successive emissions, even when positive reinforcement is regularly applied. Secondly, we shall try to relate this variability to the influence of *negative* reinforcement that results directly from the emission of the operants themselves—an influence that may accompany the positive reinforcement. Finally, it will be shown that different strengths may be given to different variations of a response by applying positive reinforcement in a selective manner. In treating these matters, our task will not be simple, because the data are incomplete and still a source of conflicting opinion; but the problems are important and cannot be by-passed, even in a text for beginners.

Variability versus Stereotypy

Suppose that, in the situation where a white rat obtains food by pressing a bar, the first response to be reinforced is that of bar-biting, rather than a leaning, pressing, or climbing response. We would expect, would we not, that this response would be strengthened: that it would be more likely to appear at a later time—that it would gain a definite advantage over other possible modes of bar depression? We would expect, too, if it did recur and was again reinforced, that its probability of further recurrence would increase even more. Eventually, we would look for a considerable automatization or stereotyping of the rat's bar-pressing behavior. We would expect a single, fairly restricted mode of response to develop.

Although the degree of automatization actually achieved in this situation is not as great as the above paragraph suggests, observation indicates that, within limits, something of the sort actually does take place regularly in the case of the rat, and there are supporting data from experimental studies of other organisms. Guthrie and Horton (1946) observed and photographed approximately 800 solutions of an escape-to-food problem by 52 cats, obtaining camera records of all the "escape postures" used by thirteen of their subjects. Solving the problem required that the cat's responses bring about a slight inclination of an upright pole within an otherwise unfurnished response-chamber. A small deviation of the pole from the vertical position was enough to open a door in the glass front of the chamber, whereupon the animal was free to obtain a bit of salmon from the top of a table a few inches away from a point of exit. Contact of any sort with the release device occurred "inadvertently" on the animal's first trial, after a period of sniffing, clawing, or pawing at the glass door, and after various turns about the chamber. This was apparently a rough equivalent of the behavior described by Thorndike many years earlier—note the quotation on page 38. The final, and effective response of the series took many accidental forms. One cat brushed the pole with his flank; one stepped on the base of the pole with his hind foot; another backed into the pole; and so on. After escape and feeding, the animal was again permitted to enter the response-chamber from a starting-box. On this occasion, and on later ones, the cat's

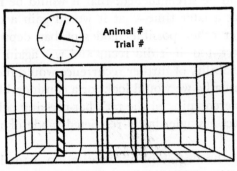

Animal #
Trial #

FIG. 41. The apparatus used by Guthrie and Horton in their photographic study of response variability in cats. The front wall of the "puzzle box" was made of glass to allow the taking of pictures. The striped pole, when pushed in any direction, would operate the door-opening mechanism and allow the animal to emerge from the box to reach a food reinforcement lying outside. The clock gave the time taken to get out after the animal was put in. (After Guthrie and Horton, 1946.)

behavior often seemed to be a *"detailed repetition"* of that observed on the first trial. In not a few cases, one sample of release behavior of a given animal was indistinguishable from another in practically every aspect. Some variation in response was noted: minor differences in escape postures were fairly common and, in some cases, markedly different modes of escape were used by the same animal on successive trials. Guthrie and Horton were, however, most impressed by the stereotypy of the behavior, rather than the variations in it. (The variations were accredited by them to the influence of slight changes in the stimulus situation occasioned by different approaches to the pole, accidental distractions, and other "interfering" factors.)

Somewhat different from the Guthrie-Horton study was an earlier one by Muenzinger (1928), who taught thirteen guinea pigs to press a bar in a three-chamber problem box. Each animal entered the response-chamber from a starting-box and was given access to a food-chamber whenever he opened the door to it by pressing a lever. As soon as the food was eaten, the animal returned or was forced back to the starting-box where he remained until the experimenter was ready for the next trial. As a rule, fifteen trials were given to each of the pigs daily and a total of either 600 or 1000 solutions of the problem was accumulated. These solutions were not photographed, but Muenzinger was able to distinguish nine different "patterns" of successful response (three right-paw and three left-paw patterns, a two-paw pattern, a head-movement and a biting or gnawing response). He found that only one animal, a pig that never made the biting response, failed to display all nine patterns at one time or another during the experiment; and he noted that the animals changed from one pattern to another as frequently at the end of their training as they did in the earlier trials. Some degree of stereotypy did appear; there was a decrease in the average *number* of different patterns displayed from the beginning to the end of the experiment, and most of the responses at the end fell within one or two of the nine categories. But Muenzinger emphasized the "plasticity" rather than the "mechanization" of the behavior. Even when the *same* pattern occurred on many successive occasions, he tells us that it was seldom duplicated exactly from trial to trial, and might be suddenly supplanted by an entirely different pattern. Only three of the thirteen animals showed a preference for a single response pattern from start to finish.

Close examination of these studies suggests that the observed behavior of Muenzinger's guinea pigs closely paralleled that of the Guthrie-Horton cats. The principal difference involved seems to be one of descriptive emphasis. In one case, the stereotypy or mechanization of response is stressed; in the other, the variation and plasticity. Muenzinger, in addition, seems to have been more alert to the *changes* in variability that occurred as a result of prolonged training. Both experiments, however, raised questions of real importance to our understanding of behavior. Some of these questions will be considered here; others are still to be investigated.

Response Induction

We have seen, under the heading of generalization in the preceding chapter, that the reinforcement of a response in the presence of one stimulus will strengthen it in the presence of other stimuli when these have properties in common with the first. There is, apparently, something like this on the side of response. The strengthening of one response may bring about a strengthening of certain others, where there is no change in the external stimulus situation. Thus, the reinforcement of one act of bar-pressing will affect, to a lesser degree, the strength of other acts which differ from the reinforced one in several identifiable aspects.

One way in which a response may differ from another is in *topography,* by which we mean, in this context, the *form* or *kind* of a response. The movement of one leg, for example, is topographically different from the movement of another, or from the movement of an arm or a finger. Also, responses, even when topographically similar, may differ in their *force* or their *duration,* properties which may be subjected to quantitative measurement. Thus, the bar-pressing response, even when quite stereotyped, will vary appreciably in its intensity or force, as well as in the amount of time that the bar is held down on each successive response. The question we now ask is this: will the strengthening of a response having a certain topography, force, or duration lead to or 'induce' a strengthening of responses which differ from it in one or more of these properties?

Let us begin with topography. Kellogg (1939) conditioned the flexion of a dog's right hind leg to the sound of a buzzer. The response was originally elicited by shock and its strength was maintained through shock avoidance. Along with the establishment of this foot-withdrawal, Kellogg noted that occasional movements of the other legs appeared. The number of such flexions was greatest for the left hind leg, next greatest for the right front leg, and smallest for the left front leg. That is, a sort of 'topographical gradient' was observed. Hilgard and Marquis (1940) have treated this as an example of *response generalization* and have supplied other observations of a similar sort. For ease of reference, we shall speak of such phenomena as cases of *response induction* or, simply, *induction*.

An interesting maze-learning experiment, suggesting response induction, was carried out by MacFarlane (1930). After training one group of rats to *swim* through a maze, he inserted a floor beneath the surface of the water at a depth sufficiently shallow to force them to *run* the maze. For another group, the procedure was reversed. When the rats of each group were tested after the shift, no appreciable increase in errors resulted. Transfer was apparently complete, in spite of the fact that the responses utilized by the animals were observably different under the conditions of swimming and running.

Other cases suggesting topographical induction appear in various experiments commonly treated under the heading of *transfer of training*. Starch (1910) discovered that human subjects who were given practice in tracing the outline of a star-shaped figure, when the figure was seen only in a mirror and a partial reversal of one's customary movements was therefore required, showed a gradual improvement in performance which was not limited to the hand used during practice. In right-handed subjects, the left hand profited considerably even when it had been given no training at all in the tracing task. Other investigators have confirmed these results and added information on the problem. Thus, Bray (1928), employing a technique in which subjects struck at a mirrored target, showed that the transfer effect was not merely bilateral (from the practiced to the unpracticed hand), but also extended to the homolateral foot (i.e., right hand to right foot). Such results remind us of Kellogg's findings with dogs, but they are probably not to be interpreted as simple

FIG. 42. A mirror-drawing apparatus. The subject's hand is hidden from his direct view, but he can see it and the pattern to be traced in the mirror. The reflection, of course, reverses the actual movements to be made in tracing. (Courtesy of C. H. Stoelting Co.)

cases of induction. Bray was able to demonstrate that other factors, such as a "transfer of methods," were involved. Human beings tend to verbalize what they are doing, and any induction that exists between hand and foot in this kind of experiment may be *mediated* or secondary, rather than *direct* or primary.

When we come to consider quantitative induction, the case becomes somewhat clearer. Take the property of response intensity or force. It has been demonstrated that a rat, even after long practice in bar-pressing, will continue to show vari-

ations in the amount of pressure exerted on successive occasions. In an experiment by Skinner (1938), rats were first
conditioned in the usual manner and regularly reinforced
during several training sessions, after which the response was
extinguished. By connecting the bar with a pendulum and
suitable recording apparatus, it was possible to obtain cumulative curves of response intensities during both the reinforcement and non-reinforcement sessions. The slopes of
these curves provided an indication of the average force of
response as well as the degree to which the rats deviated from
this average under the two experimental conditions. It
turned out that, under regular reinforcement, the average
force amounted to 35-40 grams, although many of the responses were weaker or stronger than this. (A ten-gram force
was required to depress the bar, so practically all pressings
were strong enough to be reinforced.) Under extinction,
there was at first a tendency for the animals to respond with
more than the average force during conditioning, but this
was followed by a marked decrease as the process neared completion.

Data on the distribution of forces in such a situation have
been collected by Hays and Woodbury (reported by Hull,
1943) in the Yale laboratory. They reinforced bar-pressing
with food whenever the response intensity amounted to 21
grams or more, until 100 reinforcements had been given. The
frequency with which different intensities appeared, in the
case of one of their rats, is shown in the second column of
Table VII. The third column of this table shows the values
obtained with the same animal when a minimal force of 38
grams was needed.

It is obvious from these data that complete stereotypy in
the force or intensity of the bar-pressing response is not
achieved under these conditions. The reinforcement of a
response having a certain intensity apparently suffices to
strengthen topographically similar responses having widely
different intensities.

Table VII

THE DISTRIBUTION OF RESPONSE INTENSITIES IN THE HAYS-WOODBURY
EXPERIMENT, UNDER TWO CONDITIONS OF REINFORCEMENT
(Data from Hull, 1943, p. 305)

Response Intensity	Intensity Required for Reinforcement	
	21 Grams	38 Grams
13–16 Grams	3 *	0
17–20 "	4 *	1 *
21–24 "	13 †	2 *
25–28 "	20	2 *
29–32 "	37	4 *
33–36 "	16	8 *
37–40 "	12	9 ‡
41–44 "	6	39
45–48 "	0	35
49–52 "	0	11
53–56 "	0	5
57– "	0	3

* No responses reinforced. † Nine responses reinforced.
‡ Seven responses reinforced.

This amount of variation should not be surprising. It is
obvious in most of our own actions and has often been measured. Table VIII gives sample results from an experiment of
Thorndike's (1931) in which subjects, with eyes closed, were
asked to "draw a four-inch line with one quick movement."
During successive sittings, a total of 3,000 lines was drawn by
each subject, under the same experimental conditions and
without knowledge of results, the only reinforcement being
the approval of the experimenter for doing the work. On the
first day, in which 192 responses were made, the range of line
lengths for one subject was 4.1 to 5.7 inches; on the twelfth
day (175 responses), the range was 4.5 to 6.2 inches. The distribution of lengths on both these days is shown in the table.
Aside from a slight shift upward in the average length of
line drawn, which is no more than a daily variation, the two

distributions are essentially the same. If this response underwent any decrease of inductive effect, it must have done so before these periods of prolonged practice were instituted. While the spread of responses in session twelve appears less than that in session one, this does not indicate a day-to-day reduction with practice, since the intervening days show considerable fluctuation.

Table VIII

THE DISTRIBUTION OF LINE LENGTHS DRAWN BY A SUBJECT DURING TWO PRACTICE SESSIONS IN ONE OF THORNDIKE'S EXPERIMENTS.
(Data from Thorndike, 1931, pp. 8-9)

Length of Line (inches)	Experimental Session	
	I	XII
4.10-4.19	2	0
4.20-4.29	1	0
4.30-4.39	4	0
4.40-4.49	3	0
4.50-4.59	11	3
4.60-4.69	11	0
4.70-4.79	21	6
4.80-4.89	26	6
4.90-4.99	30	13
5.00-5.09	20	25
5.10-5.19	22	27
5.20-5.29	16	24
5.30-5.39	12	30
5.40-5.49	7	17
5.50-5.59	3	12
5.60-5.69	2	7
5.70-5.79	1	3
5.80-5.89	0	0
5.90-5.99	0	1
6.00-6.09	0	0
6.10-6.19	0	0
6.20-6.29	0	1

The Why of Variability

One fact emerges plainly from the discussion in the two preceding sections. Under all conditions of reinforcement or non-reinforcement thus far described, some degree of response variability survives—complete stereotypy is never achieved. This appears in the Guthrie-Horton study no less than in the studies of Muenzinger. It is present, too, in all the cases of induction that we have cited. But we are still without an explanation of this variability. Even assuming that the strengthening of one response will strengthen other, slightly different ones, how does it happen that a specific response with one specific set of properties does not, by virtue of more frequent reinforcement, come to be the *only* response emitted in a given experimental situation?

The answer to this question demands that we postpone for a while the consideration of the second major topic of this chapter, and turn our attention to a factor that we have hitherto encountered only in its grosser aspects. Our side trip will not, however, be wasted, because we shall discover some matters of considerable interest and significance.

Variability and Negative Reinforcement

Let us go back for a moment to the Guthrie-Horton experiment. Suppose that, in this study, one of their cats first operated the release-mechanism by falling backward upon the pole while trying to climb the near-by wall. The falling response would presumably be strengthened through its positive reinforcement, but the fall might also provide stimulation of a *negatively* reinforcing sort. The consequences of the fall would thus exercise a depressive effect upon the immediately preceding response, just as a mild electric shock might do. In line with this way of thinking, when the cat re-entered the situation on the next trial, he would not be as likely to reinstate the successful behavior as he would if some other action had brought about his escape from the box and getting of food. Some alternative mode of response, whether previously rewarded or not, would be expected, and another solution might soon be forthcoming.

Or, suppose that the cat's first positive reinforcement came from standing on his hind legs and stretching his body to reach the top of the pole. These straining movements would also provide a negatively reinforcing state of affairs, albeit of a mild degree. With repeated trials, we would look for a more or less gradual reduction in the amount of energy expended in his response to the pole. In everyday language, we would say that the cat should learn to take the easiest, rather than the most awkward or tiresome way of reaching his objective. (It might be, too, that the awkward response would be a somewhat slower one and be at the additional disadvantage of having its reinforcement delayed.)

There is not much evidence in the Guthrie-Horton account, or in Muenzinger's report of the behavior of his guinea pigs, to suggest the operation of this factor in these experimental situations, but Thorndike has given us some dramatic instances. He taught both dogs and cats to lick or scratch themselves in order to escape from the problem box, and found that these operants decreased in magnitude under regular reinforcement until they were mere vestiges of the original. Thus, licking might be reduced to a mere jerk of the head downward. Similarly, Lorge (1936) trained rats to make either a face-washing, standing-up, 'begging,' or scratching movement, reinforcement being escape from a problem box to food. He noted a "short-circuiting" of these responses with successive trials. "The responses became more perfunctory and stereotyped. The 'face-wash' changed from a vigorous wash to a rapid movement of both forelegs to the face; the 'scratch' changed to a rapid flexion of the hind-leg to the flank, only remotely reminiscent of the first response to irritation." When individual rats were trained in all three responses of face-washing, standing-up, and 'begging,' they tended gradually to eliminate the first two responses entirely, securing reinforcement by making a "perfunctory" beg. Related observations were made when other rats were conditioned to touch any one of four differentially accessible projections in their problem box with either forepaw. The animals ended by responding most frequently to the projection that required the least movement and was closest to the door through which reinforcement could be reached. The last-mentioned experiment is remindful of an earlier one by Gengerelli (1933), who trained ring-tail monkeys to depress two (or four) levers in sequence for escape-to-food. He observed that his subjects passed through successive stages of (1) "over-exertion," in which they often climbed up on the levers; (2) two-handed clasping and tugging at the levers; (3) a one-handed grasp-slap combination of movement; (4) a mere downward slap; (5) an ineffectual 'pass' at the lever; and (6) even cases in which the animals "would rush up to the lever, then precipitately turn to run to the next one," without any lever contact.

Still another example, at the human level, comes from an experiment in which Thorndike (1931) required students, during a fourteen-day period, to make 3,360 word completions of a long list of such word-beginnings as *ab, af, bo,* and the like. In some cases, the same beginning was repeated as many as twenty-eight times in the course of the experiment, and it was possible to note any change in the nature of the completion that occurred. Thorndike discovered a strong tendency for the subjects to reduce the length of the complete words as the amount of repetition of the word-beginning increased. Thus, one student, upon the first eight presentations of *el,* responded with *elephant* five times, *elevate* twice, and *elf* once; upon the last eight presentations, he responded with *elf* exclusively. Presumably, the effect of very mild negative reinforcements, in conjunction with the positive reinforcement supplied by any adequate and rapid completion of the task, was sufficient to offset the influence of positive reinforcement for the first-made "long" solutions. This appears to be related to the fact that the most frequently occurring words in the English language tend to be shorter than those appearing less often. It is also reflected in the various truncations and substitutions observed when initially long words come into common use within one or another "verbal community." We speak of our *car*, our *auto*, or our *bus* instead of our *automobile*; we look after a *strep* throat; we send a *wire* or use the *phone*; and we present an S^D rather than a *discriminative stimulus*. In addition, it may account for some of the slurring tendencies often observed in colloquial speech, as when *errors* become *airs*, *flowers* become *flars*, and *borrow* becomes *bar*.

Negative Reinforcement and the "Law of Least Effort"

Another line of evidence for the depressive effect of response-produced negative reinforcement comes from studies of *alternation* behavior in animals, especially the rat. Psychologists have for years been interested in the fact that rats, when given a choice of two equally long routes to food, as in a single-unit T-maze, tend to avoid repetition of the last-made response. Thus, a run to the left or to the right is commonly followed on the next trial by a run in the opposite direction. Some researchers (e.g., Hunter, 1928) have even spoken of an 'innate' or 'natural' tendency of the animals to behave in this manner. Solomon (1948) has recently reviewed the observations in this area and, revising an earlier formulation by Hull (1943), has proposed an explanation that jibes well with the analysis that we have presented in the preceding section. In a choice situation, with conditioned responses of presumably equal strength, the emission of one response provides for its own temporary depression and thus paves the way for the emission of an alternative. Solomon (1946) found that greater "effort requirement in T-maze running is accompanied by a greater frequency of alternation behavior."

One would not expect such a minute amount of response-produced negative reinforcement to be long-lasting in its depressive effect; and the shortness of effect is confirmed in an experiment by Heathers (1940). This investigator found that the amount of alternation in a single-unit T-maze decreased as the time between successive runs in the maze increased.

Various researchers and theorists have treated observations of the sort described here as illustrations of a law of "least action," "minimal effort," or "less work." Such a formulation is non-analytical and should properly be considered as a corollary of something more basic (Hull, 1943); but we are all familiar with the kind of behavior to which it refers. Although these are the more obvious instances, something of the same sort probably accompanies every response, because every response requires effort.

Under certain circumstances, of course, a response will be maintained in considerable strength even when it seems to be inefficient and awkward. This situation occurs when reinforcement has regularly been denied to any easier variations of the response or, as we shall see presently, when motivation is higher. Gilhousen (1931) showed that rats, after having been trained to jump from one small platform to another of a straight-away series leading to food, persisted in their jumping response much longer than was necessary after an unobstructed pathway was set up alongside of their platform route. "Doing it the hard way" is apparently as characteristic of rats as of human beings, and has the same explanation: the hard way has too often been the *only reinforced way available.* Unless negative reinforcement is extreme and is clearly contingent upon a specific mode of response, all of us waste our energies needlessly. Industrial psychologists and 'efficiency experts' are well aware of this, and much of their research is directed toward identifying less effortful ways of reacting which, in the course of daily occupational routine, would never be appreciated or adopted by the individual workers under observation. How many of us would discover, by ourselves, that one brand of typewriter may involve only three-fourths as much work in its operation as another? And how many "hunt-and-peck" typists would be ready to change their style, in spite of the fact that they may know of a better method? The degree of negative reinforcement that accumulates as a result of our hunt-and-peck procedure is not great enough to act as a specific depressant of the responses that brought it about. We may, by ourselves, make notable progress: we reduce somewhat the amount of unnecessary bodily movements; we no longer punch the keys with a force that makes our fingers sore; we may even become two-finger touch-typists, thus eliminating certain movements of the head and eyes. But seldom, if ever, do we attain the efficiency of a well-trained performer who has had the advantage of an experienced teacher. Like Gilhousen's rats, we persist in our energy-wasting ways, and our resistance to change is the stronger because the better way requires, at the outset, an extinction of old, and often very strong, responses as well as a conditioning of new ones. Add to this the fact that reinforcement for the new way is probably not as great, at the beginning, as that provided by the old. It is no wonder that we cling to our own "jumping" responses.

Resistance to the adoption of improved working methods, so often encountered by the applied psychologist, is, one must admit, not always due to the fact that less satisfactory methods have been more often reinforced or that new ones must be conditioned. Sometimes the organism has no choice in the matter. The standard keyboard of a typewriter is undoubtedly inefficient in terms of energy expenditure, yet it is unlikely to be replaced by one that would provide a more equable distribution of effort for the fingers of each hand— for commercial reasons that have nothing to do with the unwillingness of a typist to give up the old and take on the new ways of behaving.

Motivation and Variability

The exclusive reinforcement of a single response variant apparently reduces the probability that other variants will occur, but there is still another factor that deserves attention. Under strong motivation, an increased stereotyping of response may also be observed. In an experiment conducted by Elliott (1934), rats were permitted to reach food at the end of any one of five short alleys that diverged from a common starting-point. The alleys were of equal length and, when hunger motivation was weak, the rats showed no marked preference for one alley over another. However, when hunger was increased, each animal tended to take one pathway to the exclusion of the rest. Moreover, this decrease in variability was irreversible: a return to conditions of weak motivation did not reduce the amount of fixation upon the alley chosen when the motivation was strong.

Quantitative data are lacking for the effect of motivation upon the range of bar-pressing movements, but frequent observations suggest that a narrowing-down effect occurs. For example, when the response removes a noxious stimulus such as a strong light, a well-conditioned rat may be seen to maintain a single, crouching posture close beside the bar during most of the experimental session, even during the faint light of the reinforcement periods, and with all his bar-pressing movements greatly restricted in their variety. Occasionally, he may depart from this routine, possibly because of the negative reinforcement produced by prolonged muscular tension, but his behavior is, in general, strikingly machine-like in quality, and it seems to retain this character for some time after the motivating stimulus has been greatly reduced in its intensity.

Everywhere about us we see human actions that appear to be at least roughly analogous to such laboratory phenomena as these. Heightened motivation seems to be one source of the routinizing and stereotyping that marks our daily habits; and we adhere to such patterns of conduct when the pressure no longer exists. Yet, there is probably no single example that we could give which would not also suggest the operation of more than one factor; and it would certainly be foolish at this time to ascribe to motivation alone all of the tenacity and case-hardening of human behavior that we may observe. What is needed now, more than anything else, is an expansion of research in this very important sphere.

Extinction, Reconditioning, and Variability

A recent study by Antonitis (1950) sheds some light upon the way in which variability is altered during the regular reinforcement, extinction, and reconditioning of operant behavior. Rats were permitted to run from a release box across an open area to a horizontal slot (50 cm. long) in the wall, twelve inches from, and facing, the release-box door. Insertion of the rat's nose into the slot at any point interrupted a

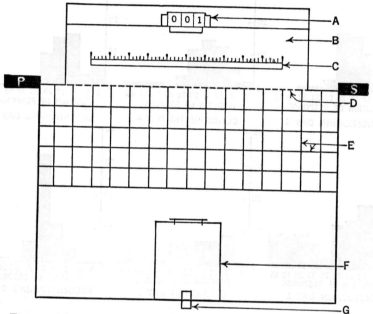

FIG. 43. Plan of Antonitis's apparatus for studying response variability in the white rat. Photographs of each nose-insertion response to the slot allowed the investigator to take two measures of the response: the locus of the response along the slot, and the angle of approach to the slot. Both measures yielded information about the degree of response variability (or its converse, stereotypy); and both measures, as it turned out, told the same story. The labeled parts of the apparatus are as follows: A—electric counter; B—mirror tilted at a 45° angle to the base of the experimental cage; C—reflected image of the 50-cm. response slot; D—clear plastic rear wall containing response slot; E—white lines painted on black floor of cage; F—starting-feeding compartment; G—food tray; S—spotlight; P—photoelectric cell. (After Antonitis, 1950.)

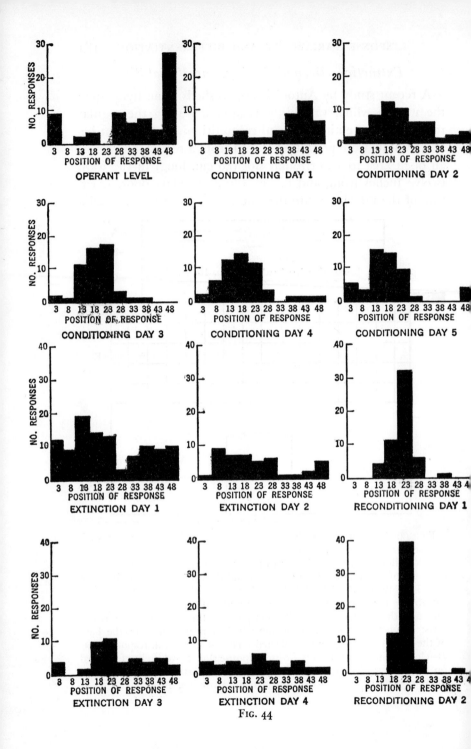

FIG. 44

beam to a photo-electric cell, causing the animal to be photographed in position, whereupon his return to the release box was reinforced with a pellet of food. Experimentation was begun after one operant-level session in which beam-breaking responses were recorded but not reinforced. Five daily conditioning sessions, in which a total of 225 reinforcements was given, were followed by two one-hour extinction sessions, one session of reconditioning (50 reinforcements), two more sessions of extinction, and a final day of reconditioning. Figure 44 shows the way in which the distribution of slot-response positions varied for one animal under these different procedures. During the first five days of conditioning, there was a decrease in the variability of response positions; in the next two days, during extinction, the variability increased; and this was followed by a marked decrease on the first day of reconditioning. This decrease after extinction was characteristic of all the rats and amounted to a greater degree of stereotypy than had been achieved during the five days of conditioning. It remained at approximately the same level in the final reconditioning session, after the third and fourth hours of extinction. A control group of animals, not subjected to the extinction periods but treated like the experimental animals in every other respect, showed no comparable in-

LEGEND FOR FIG. 44

Daily frequencies of response positions along the 50-cm. slot for one of the experimental rats in Antonitis's study. The experimental sequence may be followed by taking the graphs from left to right along each row, starting with the top row. Notice: (a) the wide variability of the operant level responses; (b) the trend toward lessened variability during the five original conditioning days, when each nose-insertion response was reinforced by a food pellet provided in the tray of the starting-feeding compartment; (c) the reappearance of greater variability during extinction days 1 and 2 (as well as the smaller number of responses on extinction day 2 as against extinction day 1); (d) the heightened stereotypy on reconditioning day 1; (e) the return of wide variability on extinction days 3 and 4; and (f) the extreme stereotypy on reconditioning day 2. (After Antonitis, 1950.)

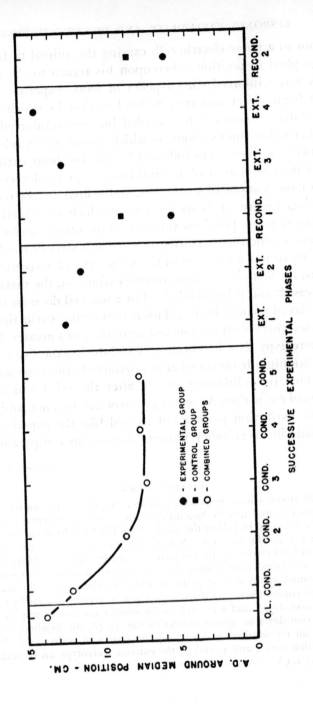

FIG. 45. The course of response position variability throughout Antonitis's experiment. The statistical measure of variability plotted is the average deviation of the individual animals' positions around the group median. The O.L. (operant level) and original conditioning (5 days) data points are based on the combined group of 12 animals, since all received the same training in these stages of the experiment. Variability diminishes (stereotypy increases) as conditioning progresses, with the group approaching a final asymptote. Thereafter, the group was divided into an experimental and control group of six animals each. On extinction days 1 and 2, only the experimental group was extinguished, while the control group remained in its living cages. As seen, extinction raised the variability of the experimental group. On reconditioning day 1, the experimental group's variability falls significantly below what it was both on extinction days 1 and 2, and on original conditioning day 5; while the variability of the control group, which "sat out" the two extinction days, is not significantly different from that of original conditioning day 5. Just about the same effects were obtained on the second two-day extinction session (extinction 3 and 4), which the control group again "sat out," and the second one-day reconditioning session (reconditioning 2). (From Antonitis, 1950.)

crease of stereotypy beyond the first five periods of conditioning.

The Differentiation of Response

Despite the degree of stereotypy that may be achieved through the influences just discussed, a complete mechanization of response is probably never reached. To the person who sets a high premium upon efficiency and precision of movement, this failure may represent a fundamental weakness of our biological function. From another, and wiser viewpoint, it is a boon, since *it permits the development of adaptive behavior that otherwise might never have been included in an organism's repertory.*

The procedure by which we produce *novel* responses in an animal or a human being is simple to describe, although not at all easy to execute. In essence, it amounts to this: we select one (or more) of the "natural" variations of a well-conditioned response and give it *exclusive* reinforcement; the remaining variations are subjected to *extinction.* If we pick out, in advance, a variation that has been of fairly frequent occurrence, and if we apply this selective reinforcement rigorously, we can soon produce an increase in the frequency of the response that possesses the property or properties (for example, the force) that we have chosen. At the same time, we decrease the frequency of those responses that do not meet our specifications.

Skinner (1938) has called this shift in frequency through selective reinforcement the *differentiation of response,* to distinguish it from the discrimination of stimuli, to which it is analogous; and he conducted several experiments on the differentiation of both force and duration of bar-pressing. It will be profitable to consider some of this work briefly, to see how the principle operates. In doing so, we shall limit ourselves to his observations on changes in *force* of response. We take, as our point of departure, the experiment mentioned earlier in this chapter under the heading of induction.

When the normal force of the bar-pressing response, and the range of forces, had been determined by Skinner for a given animal, selective reinforcement was supplied to *above-average* forces that had occurred only occasionally before. The result was an almost immediate shift of response intensities to a higher level. The successful force, which had previously occurred about once in every ten pressings, now appeared as often as once in two pressings. In addition, the entire range of force values was shifted upward appreciably. Something like this may be seen in the Hays-Woodbury figures of Table VII (page 172). The second column of this table, as mentioned above, shows the distribution of forces when there was a 21-gram minimum requirement to obtain reinforcement; the third column tells us what happened in the same animal when a new and greater force (38 gms.) was demanded.

The shift in distribution of forces that takes place under such experimental conditions shows us the way in which we can set up a response that has a force *not previously observed* in the animal's bar-pressing. If, now, we selectively reinforce some of the more intense responses within the new range, we may shift the distribution again; and we may continue in this fashion until our animal is exercising his greatest possible force upon the bar. Skinner was able, through this procedure, to reach a force-level of one hundred grams, nearly one-half of the animal's bodily weight. This could only be achieved, of course, when the force required at a new level had been of sufficiently frequent occurrence at the level preceding; and even then the new level was reached very gradually by the animal. The entire procedure bears a marked resemblance to that described in Chapter 4 for the establishment of high response rates under periodic reinforcement at a *fixed ratio*. Indeed, we would have been justified in treating fixed-ratio P-R in the present context as a *rate differentiation*.

Since force differentiation, in our example, had to be established in the face of the negatively reinforcing effect of the extreme effort involved, setbacks in progress were quite common. This was especially the case at the beginning of a day's experimental session, when considerable 'warming up' was required before the rat reached a level where practically all of his responses produced food. As with the licking response of Thorndike's cat, the animal tended to revert to an easier way of behaving—from which he had to be 'lifted' on each successive day of work.

The warming-up effect observed in differentiated bar-pressing has its parallel in various human activities. Coaches of athletics have long recognized the value of a limbering-up process in such sports as baseball, track, and crew-racing, and this apparently holds for any performance that requires above-normal exertion. Even such small-muscle activities as tapping with the fingers (Wells, 1908) or repeating the alphabet backward (Robinson and Heron, 1924) show similar changes during practice sessions in which a high rate of responding is required.

A study of force-differentiation in a situation comparable to the one used with rats has been made by Murphy (1943) with human subjects. This investigator employed a modification of the well-known "pin-ball" machine in which a small plunger was pulled back against a spring and released to send a twenty-gram marble up a slight incline into a hole. The hole, as well as the course taken by the marble, was hidden from the subject's view, but a flash of light at the front of the machine indicated the correctness of the response. This light-flash was under the control of the experimenter, who could make it contingent upon any degree of plunger-pull or who could eliminate it entirely if he wished. The distance of each plunger movement was recorded vertically and cumulatively on the paper-covered surface of a kymograph drum that jumped ahead horizontally about one-eighteenth of an inch with every completed response. *Rate* of responding was recorded on a separate drum in a manner similar to that used with rats.

Murphy explored (1) the 'normal force' and 'normal rate' of plunger-pulling when all responses were followed by a light-flash; (2) the effect of periodic reinforcement upon response rate and upon the subject's resistance to "shifting" from one required response-magnitude to another; and (3) the difficulty of setting up differentiations when different "margins of error" were permitted. His results were in general agreement with those obtained from rats in the bar-pressing studies, but were different in certain details. For example, the distribution of forces when all responses produced flashes of light bears little resemblance to that obtained by Hays and Woodbury (see Table VII). This is presumably due to the fact, recognized by Murphy, that there were certain differences in the procedure employed in the two studies. In terms of the organism's capacity, the range of response forces was less in this than in the experiment using rats, the practice periods were probably not of comparable duration, the form of reinforcement was different, and so on.

Murphy's study did not involve the reinforcement of all responses above a certain force-level, but specified an upper, as well as a lower, limit of magnitudes. This requirement brings his procedure somewhat closer to the everyday type of human differentiation where the range of response properties must not exceed a fairly narrow band of tolerance if our adjustment is to be effective. The results indicate that (1) as the experimenter restricts the tolerated range the number of incorrect responses required before a correct one is made grows larger; (2) there is an apparent improvement in the ability of subjects to shift back and forth from one response range to another as the number of such shifts increased; and (3) any form of periodic reinforcement is more effective than regular reinforcement in building up a resistance to shifting from one force-level to another. Such findings are clearly consistent with those obtained from studies with rats, and point to the fruitfulness of extending this area of research.

The differentiation of force is, of course, but one form of

change that may result from the selective reinforcement of response. Topographical differentiation is just as common and is considerably more dramatic, since it may lead to actions that are more clearly 'new.' Although few experimental studies have been aimed specifically at this problem, it is obviously present, along with stimulus discrimination, in many forms of training, and it is readily demonstrable at a non-quantitative level. A rat, for example, may be led, by gradual stages, to walk on his hind legs, jump through a loop, carry a marble in his mouth, or perform some other action that would never have occurred in a given experimental setting without the application of a differentiative procedure. The technique is always the same: some one variant of an already conditioned response is selectively reinforced until it becomes more frequent than the others; when this is achieved, a variant of the new response is treated in the same way. Through a series of *successive approximations* to the desired reaction, the behavior is altered until it comes to bear little or no resemblance to the first-conditioned form.

When we think of differentiation, we perhaps think first of animal stunts or athletic skills, but this is much too narrow an application. Teachers of speech or of foreign languages, experts in time-and-motion study, instructors in the various arts and crafts—all these, and many others, are regularly engaged in the formation of differentiated responses. Indeed, there is hardly a human pursuit which, in one aspect or another, does not illustrate the process in some degree.

The accuracy or precision of a differentiated operant is ordinarily, perhaps always, a function of the discriminative capacity of the person who supplies the reinforcement. The teacher of whatever art or skill must be one who can distinguish minute changes in the behavior of his pupil. He must be able to single out that variation of response which is in the direction of the improvement he desires, and he must do this rapidly if he is to make his reinforcement optimally effective. Regardless of his own differentiative ability, he must be able to detect those shades and nuances, those slight deviations and minor refinements in the actions of others which must be strengthened or extinguished when they appear.

Resumé

A word of recapitulation at this point may not be out of order. We have seen, in the present chapter, that organisms characteristically show response variability even in the absence of detectable environmental change. A degree of stereotypy will result from regular reinforcement, but this stereotypy is never complete. We have also seen that the reinforcement of one specific response probably strengthens others (response induction). It has been suggested that the source of variability lies in the fact that even positively reinforced responses are subject to momentary depressions in strength through the negatively reinforcing consequences of their emission—however faint and fleeting these consequences may be. Such depressions pave the way for the emission of alternative responses, some of which may also obtain positive reinforcement and may be even less freighted with negative, so that they take priority in terms of later occurrence. This happens unless there are strong counter-influences—that is, unless the first response has been the only reinforced one or, perhaps, has been established under stronger motivation. This explanation of variability may be related to "alternation" studies and to commonly cited examples of "least effort," but what we need most is further research in this field. With respect to *differentiation*, there is less room for uncertainty than in the discussion of variability. Given a degree of variability, however accounted for, we have no trouble in modifying behavior independently of changes in exteroceptive stimulation. A marked novelty of response may even be achieved simply by reinforcing successive approximations to a desired mode of reaction and withholding reinforcement for responses that do not change in this direction. In this effect we have the basis for developing various skills.

Differentiation and Discrimination

We began our discussion of operant behavior, in Chapter 3, without consideration of the stimuli to which such behavior might be related. Later, in Chapter 5, we showed that operants may come to be emitted in the presence of some stimuli and not in the presence of others. In this chapter, we have argued that responses are never completely stereotyped, and that they may be changed in their character independently of any change in stimulus conditions. Our examples of response differentiation were chosen with an eye to pointing up this independence. Yet it must have occurred to you that many, if not all, differentiated operants are also *discriminative* operants. Very early in an organism's behavioral development a specific mode of response becomes related to a more or less identifiable form of stimulation. Obviously, a rat is unlikely to engage in bar-pressing movements in the absence of a bar that can be seen or touched, just as a human subject in a reaction-time experiment is unlikely to make a key-tapping movement when no reaction-key is present. In many cases, of course, the relation of response to stimulus may not be so apparent, as when a rat is reinforced for standing on his hind legs or a student has been reinforced for raising his hand in class, but even in such instances a correlation may often be discovered; a rat does not emit his standing response when he is no longer in the experimental situation, and a student does not ordinarily raise his hand in the absence of his instructor.

A simple example of the tie-up between discrimination and differentiation is the behavior of an animal in a T-box (page 137). In the presence of one S^D, he turns to the right; in the presence of another, he turns to the left. Similarly, in a reaction-time study, a person may respond with one hand to a green light and with the other to a red one. At a slightly more complex level, we have the subject's behavior in a situation where the specific stimuli and responses are greater in number, as in Merkel's experiment (page 143) which employed as many as ten alternatives. This situation, in turn, resembles the one in which students master International Morse Code, where no fewer than thirty-six basic stimulus patterns are each connected with a differentiated response pattern. When one learns to *receive* code, his problem is mainly *discriminative,* since the written or spoken responses have already been well differentiated; in *sending* code, however, the problem is one of differentiation, since the discriminative work was done when the student learned to read his ABC's.

The early development of a child's vocabulary provides many excellent illustrations of the combined processes of discrimination and differentiation. The vocalization of the child contains, at the beginning, a small assortment of basic sound elements (phonemes). With the maturation of the vocal mechanism, the number of these elements increases and, as they group themselves into patterns by virtue of the principle of "chaining" (see Chapter 7), they are also subjected to differentiation through the selective reinforcement supplied by parents and others. At the same time, the emission of many of these patterns comes to be connected with relatively specific stimulus situations. *Mama* comes to be emitted mainly in the presence of the mother; *dada* may be adopted by the father as *his* name, and so on. At first, the reinforcement for this naming behavior is given lavishly, no great discriminative acuity or differentiative precision being required of the child. Later, as the educational process gets under way, reinforcement is more sparingly doled out, being given only when highly specific responses are emitted in equally specific stimulus situations. In fact, one might say that the educational process itself is largely a matter of establishing connections between well-discriminated stimuli and well-differentiated responses.

In the differentiation of verbal responses, a frequently utilized training procedure is that in which reinforcement is made contingent upon the resemblance of a response to an S^D that is itself the verbal response of another person. We see this whenever a child utters a word in imitation of one emitted by a parent or teacher. The importance of this S^D can hardly be appreciated by one who has never observed the difficulty with which totally *deaf* children learn to speak

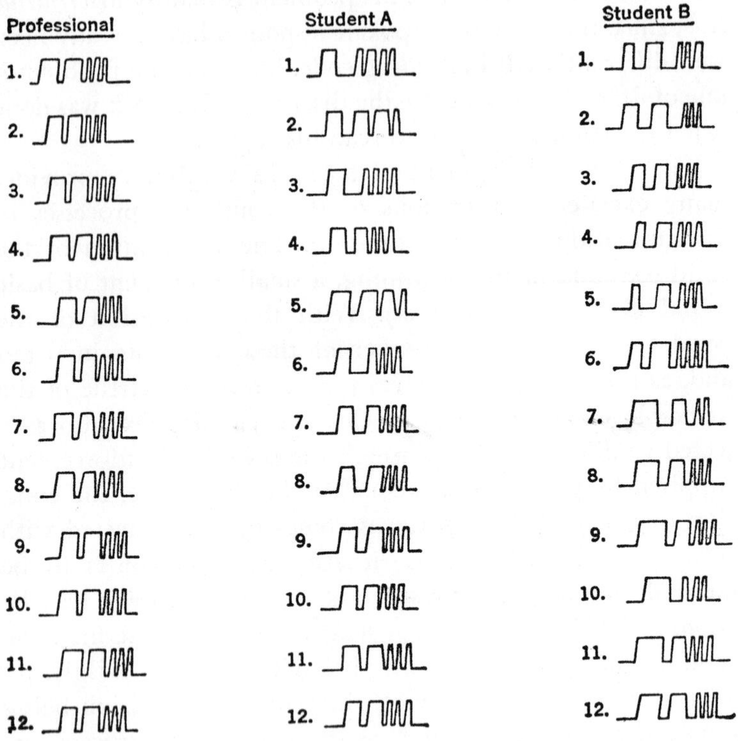

Fig. 46. Actual records of the formation of a differentiated response chain by two students learning to send a Morse Code signal. On each trial the student tried to imitate with his own telegraph key the signal as sounded for him by a professional. The figure shows only the first 12 attempts by these students, who were without any prior experience in receiving or sending the code, but who rapidly achieved an acceptable signal. (Courtesy of M. P. Wilson.)

intelligibly. The very nature of their defect prevents such children from matching their own vocal productions with heard models. A substitute, for the deaf, is provided by vibratory or movement cues given to the child when his hand is pressed to the jaw region of a speaking person. This stimulation may be matched to some extent by the vibrations aroused in the child's own speech apparatus during vocalization; but the match is far from perfect and other cues may also be employed—for example, a visual matching of lip-movements through the child's use of a mirror. Even then, however, the reinforcement provided by the teacher's approval of the approximated sound-pattern remains, for these unfortunates the basic factor in the educative process.

Training in speech differentiation has a close parallel in the procedure through which radio operators learn to transmit code signals. Here, too, a well-accepted teaching device is that in which the student attempts to reproduce a model signal transmitted by the instructor. In the absence of this auditory S^D, progress is seriously retarded, and even a highly trained operator may find his task upsetting when no tone-patterns or associated clickings result from his movements. Although experimental evidence is lacking, there is every reason to believe that, under such circumstances, the intelligibility of his transmission suffers appreciably. As compared with speech differentiation, of course, this skill requires very little precision of movement, but the fundamental process appears to be the same. If adequate responses are to be established or maintained in the absence of heard models, the presentation or withdrawal of reinforcement becomes all-important.

NOTES

Muenzinger's observations of variability in the lever-pressing response of guinea pigs were confirmed in a later study by Muenzinger, Koerner, and Irey (1929). Using a lever the cross-bar of which was removed to eliminate two-paw responses, they noted the persistence of variability in a single mode of response during 600 solutions of the problem. Three pigs were given "guided" training, with only right-paw responses reinforced, and three were given "unguided" training, *any* effective response being reinforced. As you might expect, other than right-paw movements decreased during guided training, but the amount and change of right-paw patterns was about the same for the two groups. One important

difference appeared: there was, in the guided group, a greater development of "accessory" movements—useless responses that accompanied or
preceded the effective ones. Thus, a head movement might accompany
lever pressing with the paw, or a series of light taps might precede a
strong downward push. This unnecessary behavior is attributed to the
greater precision of response required from the guided group, and is
likened to the grimaces and tongue-twistings of a child when learning
to write. Similar observations have, indeed, been reported of human
behavior in learning situations where the tasks were of considerable
difficulty, and it has been noted that the amount of such accessory responding decreases as the task nears completion (Stroud, 1931; Ghiselli,
1936).

Entertaining items, suggestive of response induction, often turn up
in unexpected places. There is, for example, the tale of the British
surgeon who trained his right-handed pupils to perform operations
with the left hand, and who is reported to have said: "Train the left
and the right will look after itself." And there is also the report that an
increase in the muscular development of one arm, as a result of special
exercise, will lead to an increased development of the other. Before
interpreting this to mean a double return for work done, we should
remember that, according to the induction principle, the exercise itself
was not restricted to one arm alone!

Hull's (1943) conception of the way in which a response may produce
its own momentary depression in strength is attributed by him to two
of his former pupils, Mowrer and Miller. Mowrer's version of the idea
is found in a collaborative study with Jones (1943); Miller's is presented
in a book, *Social learning and imitation* (1941), of which Dollard was
co-author. The Miller-Dollard book is a good companion-piece to the
present text, being one of the early approaches to the viewpoint here
outlined. The Mowrer-Jones study dealt with resistance to extinction
as a function of the force required of rats in depressing a bar. Their
findings point to an inverse relation between the variables—the greater
the force the fewer the responses during extinction. Solomon's (1948)
review of the entire problem contains much more material than we
have cited. For example, he connects the principle with studies of work
and fatigue, extinction and spontaneous recovery, discrimination (by
rats) of pathway distances and inclinations, psychophysical judgments,
and the tendency of human beings to avoid the repetition of identical
guesses.

Researchers and theorists whose names have often been connected
with the 'law of least effort' are Wheeler (1929), Gengerelli (1930),
Tsai (1932), Lorge (1936), Waters (1937), Crutchfield (1939), and Zipf
(1948). Hull's interesting treatment of the concept is to be found in
his *Principles of behavior* (1943). Some telling criticisms of 'least effort'
as a basic law may also be found in Guthrie's *Psychology of learning*,
1935.

7

CHAINING

IN LEARNING [the Lord's Prayer] we repeat it; that is we pronounce the words in successive order, from the beginning to the end. The order of the sensations is successive. When we proceed to repeat the passage, the ideas of the words also arise in succession, the preceding always suggesting the succeeding, and no other. *Our* suggests *Father, Father* suggests *which, which* suggests *art;* and so on, to the end. How remarkably this is the case, any one may convince himself by trying to repeat backwards, even a passage with which he is as familiar as the Lord's Prayer.

James Mill, *Analysis of the Phenomena of
the Human Mind,* 1829

The Principle of Chaining

The quotation above, from a famous British thinker, gives us a ready-made introduction to the central theme of this chapter. When stripped of its subjectivity, it constitutes a clear recognition of the fact that responses commonly occur in series rather than as isolated behavioral units. Stated in terms with which you are more familiar, it amounts to this: *one response commonly produces the stimulus for another.*

All along in the preceding pages of this book, we have treated the single response or the single stimulus-response relation as the principal topic with which psychology is concerned. Except for a brief consideration of *compound stimuli* in Chapter 5, we have been careful to postpone the discussion of more complicated matters until the simple ones had been made as clear as we could make them. This has been a necessary approach and the one employed in all scientific exposition, but it may have occurred to you that our treatment was incomplete—that we failed to recognize the fact that one stimulus-response relation is seldom isolated completely from those which precede or follow it. Such a criticism is justified although, in carrying out our scheme of presentation, it would have been premature to discuss the matter before we reached this chapter.

If you were to describe in detail the behavior of a well-conditioned white rat when placed in the bar-pressing apparatus for a period of regular reinforcement, you might come out with something like this:

He ran immediately to the front of the box where he came to a stop in a position facing the bar; then he raised himself on his hind legs and put his forepaws on the bar; with paws in place, he gave a quick downward thrust which depressed the bar sufficiently to activate the food-magazine and discharge a pellet of food into the tray below; then he lowered himself to the tray and seized the pellet with his teeth and paws, after which he settled back on his haunches and began eating the pellet.

In this fairly accurate description, there are at least six distinct reflexes upon which good observers might be expected to agree. Without going into an unwieldy degree of specification, we may list them as follows:

Reflex	Stimulus	Response
5	Bar-location	Approach
4	Visual bar	Rising
3	Tactual bar	Pressing
2	Apparatus noise	Lowering
1	Visual pellet	Seizing
0	Pellet-in-mouth	Chewing

The discriminative stimuli for these responses are not as easily identified as the responses themselves. This is especially the case for the end reflexes in the series (*bar-location* and *pellet-in-mouth* are rather ill-defined stimuli), but it holds also for reflex 1 (the pellet might be touched or smelled rather than seen) and, to a lesser degree, for all the rest. It must be remembered that we are dealing with a series of operants the stimulus control of which is never as strictly or clearly defined as when we deal with respondents. Control may, of course, be established—we have shown this in Chapter 5—and we are safely conservative in assuming the operation of S^D's in the present situation, but a highly specific designation of stimuli can hardly be made in the absence of suitable tests.

The responses of our list are not exactly equal in status. The approach response of reflex 5 will not often occur as a member of the series under conditions of regular reinforcement. After his first bar-pressing response, the rat is in position for the next response and will usually remain so during most of an experimental session. When the food has been swallowed, he will usually raise himself to the bar immediately and press again. We might even expect that the ingestion of food itself would come to serve as an S^D for the reinstatement of the rising response. The other responses of the series are, of necessity, always present and may easily be observed—with a single exception: the chewing response may occasionally be absent (as when the rat loses his pellet) or difficult to detect (as when soft food is used and eating sounds cannot be heard).

In addition to these six reflexes, we could have suggested more. Reflexes of ingestion are known to follow the chewing response; and "approach" is made up of several reflexes rather than one. If we attempted to specify them all, it would be a difficult technical task and no purpose would be served here. In fact, for our present purposes, it will be simpler and equally legitimate to move in the opposite direction and to consider the following list as representative.

Reflex	Stimulus	Response
4	Visual bar	Rising
3	Tactual bar	Pressing
2	Apparatus noise	Lowering
1	Visual pellet	Seizing

This reduction leaves us with a clearly observable and regularly recurring sequence or chain of responses, with stimuli that are effective under ordinary experimental conditions. Yet we know that a visual bar is not a necessity, since a darkened box does not eliminate bar-pressing; similarly, a visual pellet is not essential to eating behavior, because a blind rat would also eat. We know, too, that, in addition to noise made by the apparatus, such as the click of the food-magazine, a discriminative cue may be provided by the sound of the pellet as it drops into the food-tray; and we know that all of these auditory stimuli may be eliminated or reduced in intensity without disrupting the behavior sequence appreciably. Compound S^D's are present at every stage of response; and these S^D's may be exteroceptive, originating outside of the organism, or proprioceptive, arising directly from the muscular movements themselves, that is, inside the organism. The important fact is that each response is undoubtedly dependent upon *some* form of discriminative stimulation.

The paradigm shown below may help you to clarify the operation of our reduced chain. This paradigm may be read as follows:

$$S^{D_4} \longrightarrow R_4 \rightarrow S^{D_3} \longrightarrow R_3 \rightarrow S^{D_2} \longrightarrow R_2 \rightarrow S^{D_1} \longrightarrow R_1$$

S^{D_4} (the visual bar) leads to R_4 (the rising response). This is followed by S^{D_3} (the touch of the bar on the paws), which leads to R_3 (pressing). The pressing is followed by S^{D_2} (apparatus noise), which leads to R_2 (the lowering response); and this response is followed by S^{D_1} (sight of the pellet), which leads to the seizing response, R_1, which initiates eating.

Chains and New Units

Here, then, we have a chain of reflexes in which each response produces the stimulus for the next. A striking aspect of such a chain is the over-all smoothness of transition from one link to another. Indeed, a well-conditioned rat gives the appearance of making, not four responses, but one. There are no pauses, no hitches, no jerks in the sequence. One response seems to flow easily and rapidly into the next. It is not hard to understand why an observer of the animal should speak of a single *act* of bar-pressing in a *field* of stimulation. It is easy to overlook the genesis of the behavior from a series of discrete units linked into a continuous and efficient performance.

The multi-membered nature of the act can be demonstrated, however, even after strong conditioning. Suppose, after considerable training, we permit an animal to press the bar and produce the apparatus noise, but we withhold the food. This is the usual extinction procedure, and you know what kind of extinction curve to expect. In terms of our chaining paradigm, we have broken the sequence at a point between R_2 and S^{D1}. The first three reflexes occur with decreasing frequency until a very low level of strength is reached. But what happens to the fourth reflex, the pellet-seizing? Has it been extinguished too? You can guess the answer: it has not. The rat will still seize any pellet that is placed before him. And this suggests that at least the final link in our chain is functionally separable from anything that preceded it.

But what about the behavior that *preceded* the pellet-seizing; may it not be a natural totality rather than a chain? Again we can put the matter to test. Suppose we begin extinction by permitting the bar-pressing response (R_3) to occur, but not permitting either the apparatus noise or the food to follow. Now, in terms of our paradigm, we have broken the chain at a point between R_3 and S^{D2}, one link in advance of the former break. Suppose, further, that we carry out this extinction until very few pressing responses are being emitted by our rat. When this stage is reached, let us reintroduce the apparatus noise but continue to withhold food reinforcement. Now, when the animal raises himself to the bar and depresses it, he is stimulated by the noise which was formerly a part of the S^D compound that led him to drop down to the tray. What will be the effect of this stimulation upon his subsequent behavior? The question has been answered—experimentally. Following the reintroduction of the apparatus noise, the almost-extinguished bar-pressing will immediately recover strength. That is to say, the bar-pressing is reconditioned for a time and then yields a new extinction curve. This is shown in Figure 47, where the arrow indicates the point at which the apparatus noise was reinstated.

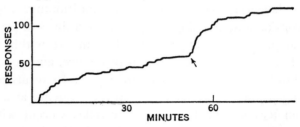

FIG. 47. The separate extinction of chained reflexes. Extinction of bar-pressing was begun in the absence of the S^D (click) for tray-approach. At the arrow, each bar-press was again permitted to produce the click, with a resultant spurt in responding. (After Skinner, 1938.)

Two significant facts emerge from this result. *First*, the mere production of the previously absent S^D strengthens the responses that came before it in the bar-pressing sequence. Why it has this effect is a question to which the following chapter addresses itself, so it need not be answered here, but there is no denying that it does act in such a way. The apparatus noise, under these experimental conditions, clearly serves to reinforce the behavior that, earlier, had been practically extinguished; and it does so in spite of the fact that it is not, during extinction, followed by food reinforcement. *Secondly*, the near-extinction of the first two members of the chain apparently did not affect the third. This answers our question about the totality of the behavior that preceded the pellet-seizing reflex. Whatever the oneness that this behavior exhibited, its chained origin is inescapable. The behavior is made up of elements that are by no means arbitrary and undemonstrable. We can single out these elements if we try.

It would, of course, be wrong to say that a closely-bound chain of responses does not come to function as a unit. When we break a chain at some point, all of the responses emitted up to that point decline in strength together in an orderly fashion. It is this very orderliness that justifies our speaking of *a* response when the entire chain is emitted—although perhaps it would be less confusing if we spoke of the chain as an *act* composed of several responses. Moreover, when viewed by an observer, the elementary components of the act ripple off in rapid succession and with considerable stereotypy on almost every occasion of their emission.

Ordinarily, in such a chain as that involved in bar-pressing, we record the occurrence of only one movement—the actual depression of the bar—but there is no reason why we could not measure the frequency of others. We might, for example, record the approaches to the food-tray which follow the pressings, or the risings to the bar before the pressings. By such means we could study in more detail the building-up and breaking-down of the bar-pressing chain. Further investigation will undoubtedly employ such procedures; indeed, a number of exploratory attempts have already been made (e.g., Arnold, 1947).

An interesting variation in the technique of chaining is shown in an experiment by Gellermann (1931). This investigator found that monkeys, after many practice trials, could solve a *double-alternation* problem in which they had to lift the lids of two adjacent boxes, one at the left (L) and one at the right (R), in a sequence LLRRLLRR, for a food reward that appeared after each response of the series. When this chain was formed, the monkeys displayed an ability to extend the alternation of paired responses well beyond the point at which the series was ordinarily terminated. In a similar experiment, Schlosberg and Katz (1943) demonstrated that white rats can learn to alternate between two upward and two downward pushes of a bar when food is given at the end of a four-membered series. These rats, like the monkeys in Gellermann's experiment, were able to make many successive double alternations.

Relevant observations, although not described in detail, have apparently been made by the psychiatrist, Masserman (1946). He taught cats to obtain food by pressing a pedal three times in succession before running to a food-box. When these "threes" were well established, the procedure was changed to permit a *single* pressing to secure reinforcement. Later, when this new manner of responding had replaced the first-conditioned threes, it was subjected to extinction. As the "singles" fell off in frequency, the cats regressed (see page 81) to the threes. Such observations are interesting and provocative, and they should be checked with follow-up studies.

In the field of verbal behavior, it would seem that nothing is more obvious than the unitary character of chains. Nearly every word on this page is an apparent example of a unit which was originally no more than a vocalized series of unrelated and disjointed elements. What is the spoken word *example* itself but a temporal pattern of sounds that were at first distinct and isolated but are now so well chained as to be practically irreducible except under the special conditions of training in analysis? And this is not all; larger groupings than individual words may act in unitary fashion. *For example, inasmuch as, in fact, and so forth*—all possess this character. Still larger groupings may betray the same cohesion, although to a lesser degree. Complete the following: *bread and* _____; *salt and* _____; *time and* _____; *hue and* _____. Or these: *as quick as a* _____; *as sly as a* _____; *as strong as an* _____; *as wise as an* _____; *as quiet as a* _____. For most of us, the missing link in these oft-recurring chains is quickly added, although the completion will not be the same for every person. A moment's thought will suggest other, and perhaps better, examples.

The problem of the functional unit of behavior, whether verbal or non-verbal, is one that has not yet received the experimental attention it deserves. It would appear that there are many chains of behavior the units of which are themselves chains of still more basic units that have been welded together by the influence of reinforcing agents. Table IX gives data from a study by McCarthy (1930) on the relation between the age of pre-school children and the average number of words used in fifty sentences emitted in a simple observational situation. The figures in this table, which show a regular increase in sentence length with increased age, are typical of results obtained by other investigators for these age-levels. In addition, Davis (1937) has shown that the length of spoken sentences continues to increase with age until, at nine and a half years, the average sentence contains about seven words. When *written* compositions are measured (Heider and Heider, 1940), there is evidence for an increase from about ten words per sentence at the eight-year-old level to about fourteen words at the fourteen-year-old level. All this, of course, is exactly what we would expect if new units of verbal behavior were developed on the basis of the chaining of smaller units. In fact, it is possible that the number of *functional* units employed at different ages does not change very much. A word, at an early age, may be a single unit, whereas at a later age, it may be merely a *part* of a single unit.

Table IX

THE AVERAGE LENGTH OF SENTENCES IN SPOKEN
LANGUAGE AS A FUNCTION OF AGE.

(From McCarthy, 1930)

Age in Years:	1.5	2	2.5	3	3.5	4	4.5
Number of Words:	1.2	1.8	3.1	3.4	4.3	4.4	4.6

Homogeneous and Heterogeneous Chains

Some writers have distinguished between two kinds of chaining (e.g., Arnold, 1947). In one, a given stimulus is followed by a specific response which produces another stimulus which is, in turn, followed by another response, and so on. This type, in which the successive links are different, is called *heterogeneous* chaining. The bar-pressing chain is of such a sort, and so is the chain involved in saying "All men are created equal." On the other hand, we can imagine a chain composed of stimuli and responses which are practically identical in each successive link. This has been called *homogeneous* chaining. The triple pedal-pressing of Masserman's cats approximates such a situation, as does the "rah-rah-rah" of a college cheer.

Cases of pure homogeneity in chaining are rare; strictly speaking, they probably do not exist. Even the "rahs" of a cheer may be discriminably different to the listener in some aspect, say their force; and the successive responses in triple pedal-pressing may differ slightly in one or more of their properties. Moreover, in many instances, the homogeneous links are clearly bounded by heterogeneous ones in the complete chain. Thus, prior to the first of three pedal-pressings is an approach response, and after the third there is an advance to the food-tray. At the verbal level, the rarity of homogeneous links is reflected by the scarcity or complete absence of words in any language where the same syllable is repeated more than twice in succession. In Chinese, which is a monosyllabic language, repetition of the same word three times is so infrequent as to be noteworthy. An exception, *kan kan kan* (Mandarin for *look and see*) is uttered in *almost* a monotone. The Shanghai form, *ku ku ku,* exhibits a greater variation in both stress and pitch.

Related to the above is the difficulty encountered when we attempt to teach rats or other animals to solve the double-alternation problem mentioned in the preceding section. Some experiments make use of the *temporal maze* (see Figure 48). In this maze, the subject may be required to make a left-left-right-right sequence of turns when confronted with the same choice point on four successive occasions during his running. Mastery of the problem may be impossible for some animals because of the similarity of the repeated elements (the S^D's as well as the responses) in the chain. The situation resembles that in which a verbal chain is composed of formally similar responses each of which produces the S^D for the next. "Tongue-twisters" are constructed on this basis. *Pluto, the tutored poodle, practised triple pedal-pressing.* The difficulty of emitting such a verbal sequence rapidly may partially explain the infrequency of polysyllabic English words in which the same syllable precedes two different syllables. Witness the trouble we have with such a common word as *statistics*. We can sympathize with the child who struggled to say to his father: *You put your toothbrush in my cup and you put my toothbrush in your cup!*

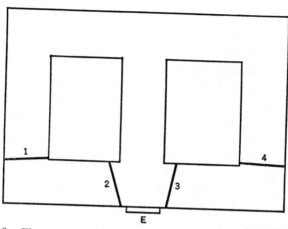

FIG. 48. Floor plan of a temporal maze. *E* is the point of entrance from which the animal moves down the central pathway to the choice point, where he may turn right or left. The hinged doors (1, 2, 3, 4) are manipulated by the experimenter, who prescribes the path by which the animal can return to *E*. Reinforcement, such as food, may be provided at *E* after each run, or only after a series of runs, such as left-left-right-right. (After Hunter, 1928.)

It has been suggested by Skinner (1938) and Mowrer and Jones (1945) that the procedure of *periodic reinforcement* is conducive to the formation of new units, as when a number of bar-pressings are followed by a pellet of food. Mowrer and Jones carried out an experiment in which resistance to extinction of this response was related to schedule of reinforcement. Five groups of rats were used. One group was regularly reinforced during training; one group was aperiodically reinforced; and three groups were reinforced at fixed ratios of 1:1, 2:1, and 3:1 respectively. Their findings led them to conclude that new "patterns" or units of response could be set up; and that the number of *functional* responses during extinction was nearly the same for the different groups of animals, in spite of an increased number of *pressings* as the ratios became larger. How far we can go with this type of reasoning is questionable. It seems unlikely that the rat would be able to make more than two or three bar-pressing responses into a single unit through chaining, but further experimentation ought soon to give us an answer. Close observation should readily disclose whether two or more pressings come to act like one, either during fixed-ratio training or during a subsequent extinction period.

The degree of similarity among the successive links of a chain would seem to set a limit to the size of a unit that can be developed. The number of different responses available to an organism is by no means infinite. Sooner or later, as attempts are made to add links to a chain, generalization and induction will take their toll. More and more discrimination and differentiation will be required, until a saturation point is reached and new links are added only at the expense of the old.

Chaining and Delayed Reinforcement

Facts sometimes lose their simplicity when analyzed but, at the same time, get to be more understandable. We now deal with such a case. At several points in this text, it has been stated, or implied, that an operant is conditioned more rapidly when reinforcement follows *immediately* upon emission of the response. This is supported by a number of investigations and is a truism for animal trainers and educators in various fields. The fact that conditioning is slower as the reinforcement is more delayed has led some theorists, like Hull (1943) to speak of a 'reinforcement gradient' and to specify the limits of delay beyond which reinforcement is no longer effective in strengthening a response.

Delay of reinforcement can now be seen to involve the formation of reflex chains. When we say that a bar-pressing response, for example, has been reinforced after a five-, ten-, or fifteen-second delay, what we really mean is that we have *immediately* reinforced some other response which occurred five, ten, or fifteen seconds *after* the bar pressing. During the time of 'delay,' the animal does not stop behaving; he merely does something else—over which we may have little control. We set up a *chain* of reflexes, of which bar-pressing is an early link. The bar-pressing link cannot be strengthened until we have strengthened the later ones, and this takes time. Even in what we treat as a case of immediately reinforced bar-pressing, there is at least one later link in the chain—the response to the food-tray, which follows the actual pressing and is conditioned first. The immediate reinforcement for the pressing is of a 'secondary' sort (to be described in the next chapter), but it is nonetheless immediate (Spence, 1947; Grice, 1948).

The presence of the last (and first-reinforced) link in such a chain is sometimes unsuspected and may go unobserved. For example, when one conditions a white rat to turn off a light, in the manner described on page 62, the situation is presumably one of 'immediate' reinforcement: the light goes off within a fraction of a second after the bar-pressing response is made. It may be shown, however, that the *reinforcing* effect of light-removal comes later, when the animal is doing something else—holding down the bar, turning away from it, rising above it, and so on. Probably because of the visual lag involved, the effect of light-removal is not felt at the instant of bar-depression. We do not reinforce *first* the response that we are measuring; rather, we make way for a 'superstitious' response to develop, and we are compelled to establish a longer chain than we intended.

A comparable situation exists in certain sports and games, where the first-conditioned response actually follows the effective one. In bowling and in billiards, the last link in the chain is the one often referred to as "body English"—the posture or the movements which are the true accompaniments of a suc-

cessful throw of the ball or shot with the cue. Similar em-
bellishments may be observed in the behavior of amateur
baseball pitchers, basketball players, and golfers.

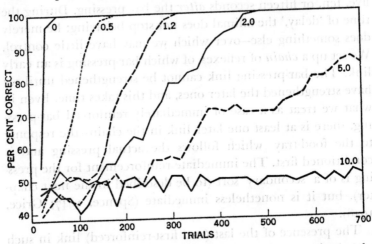

Fig. 49. The effect of delaying the primary reinforcement upon the
rate of mastering a discrimination. Six groups of hungry animals were
trained to make a white-black discrimination in a discrimination box
where the "correct" choice (response to S^D) led to food. The response
to S^D, however, was reinforced after different time intervals, the delays
varying from 0 to 10 seconds. The curves show, for successive blocks of
20 trials, the per cent of correct choices made by the animals in each
group. Note that the longer the delay the slower the learning; until,
with a 10-second delay, the animals do not get past a chance (50 per
cent) performance. This experiment was carried out under conditions
especially designed to eliminate any 'secondary reinforcement' intervening between the choice-point response and the ultimate primary
reinforcement. This elimination reduced the size of the maximum delay
previously thought possible, and was the effect predicted by the experimenter who believed that long delays involved the formation of a
response chain composed of secondarily reinforced units. (After Grice,
1948.)

Exteroceptive and Proprioceptive S^D's in Chaining

The preceding sections may have suggested to you another
distinction that is sometimes made between reflex chains. In
most cases, the obvious discriminative stimuli for the succes-

sive responses of a chain are in the external environment—they belong within the *exteroceptive* class. One response puts the organism in a position such that a new outside stimulus is presented. That is, one response *produces* the external stimulus for the next, as in the behavior of bar-pressing and maze-running. Yet you may have surmised that chains are sometimes composed of responses the principal stimuli for which seem to be *other* responses. This seems to be especially true of verbal behavior. When we repeat a well-worn phrase, it often seems that one word leads to another *directly,* rather than by way of the exteroceptive S^D's (sounds) produced by our speech. We emit the accustomed sequence in a more or less automatic fashion, and we would be hard put to show that each component word depended upon some outside stimulus which the preceding word had produced. We are more likely to say that one response led to another without any reference to changes in the external environment.

We have assumed all along that responses are responses-to-stimuli. Now, when we talk about a response that *leads* to another, we imply that a response can be a *stimulus* for another. But how can we speak of a response as a stimulus without dealing in the worst sort of confusion? Fortunately, there is a well-accepted answer to this question. Early in the nineteenth century it was discovered that we possess a *muscle sense*—that there are actual receptor organs within our muscles, tendons, and joints which are excited by the movements of these effectors. This came to be known later as the *kinesthetic* (movement-perceiving) sense and to it was ascribed our subjective awareness of the position or changes in position of the movable parts of our bodies. As a more objective psychology developed, the term *proprioceptors* was adopted as a name for these sense-organs and *proprioceptive* was applied to the stimuli that excited them (see pages 4-5).

Evidence for the importance of this type of movement-produced stimuli accumulated throughout the years. Today we have every reason to believe that responses may produce directly the discriminative stimuli for further responses, even in the absence of exteroceptive changes. Thus, we are willing to ascribe to the influence of proprioceptive S^D's the fact that eye-movements may provide cues for our judgments that objects are at different distances; that arm, wrist, and hand movements give the cue for judging one lifted weight to be heavier than another; that widespread muscular tensions may set off the responses that help us to maintain posture and right us when we are off balance; and so on. It is difficult to isolate and observe the action of such stimuli, because of the locus of the receptors involved and because they commonly accompany the stimulation of other sense organs, but we can feel relatively safe in asserting that whenever one response leads to another, and no exteroceptive cue can be discovered, a proprioceptive cue can be inferred.

Probably the best examples of chaining in which proprioceptive stimuli may predominate are to be found in the sphere of verbal behavior. Verbal chains, once established, may occur in the absence of exteroceptive stimuli. *Spoken* words, of course, produce sounds which become exteroceptive cues for the speaker himself and thus play an important part in the formation of chains; but when these chains are once set up they may be emitted sub-vocally or sub-audibly, in which case the principal S^D's are proprioceptive. When we silently rehearse a speech or utter a prayer, each response seems to depend upon the preceding one for its emission, which is another way of saying that each response is to the proprioceptive stimulus aroused by the preceding response.

Covert Response

To most persons there is nothing objectionable in the view that overt or observable behavior may be caused by factors that are hidden from the observation of others. They will tell you without hesitation that many of their actions are internally instigated. They will often report a train of "associated ideas" which led to the performance of some overt action.

But they will not as readily identify these "ideas" with muscular responses to proprioceptive stimuli. Common sense tells them that there are ideas *and* actions, either of which may lead to the other; common sense does *not* tell them that associations of ideas are equivalent to chains of reflexes which differ from observable ones only in the magnitude of the responses involved.

Yet, throughout the ages, the notion has often been advanced that thought and action are not always distinct—that some thinking, at least, was no more than *inner speech*. Plato, among the ancients, held such an opinion, and so did others who came later. In the nineteenth century, Alexander Bain, one of the founders of modern psychology, treated thinking as "restrained speaking or acting." Later still, John Watson described thinking exclusively in terms of covert response, either sub-vocal talking or "sub-gestural" gesturing. He argued that children, at first, think out loud and come to speak silently only through parental admonition; that adults who are withdrawn from social contacts tend to think, as well as read, aloud; and that deaf-mutes think and dream with their fingers. He suggested that sensitive measuring instruments would ultimately disclose tiny muscular movements in every instance where thinking occurred.

Support for such beliefs has come, in recent years, from several experimental studies in which minute electrical effects or "action currents" of muscular contractions have been magnified and recorded. Jacobson (1932) gave human subjects extensive training in relaxation (to reduce the general level of electrical discharges from the muscle groups to be tested) and then, with electrodes placed in the region of certain muscles, asked each subject, while in the relaxed state, to engage in imaginal and thinking activities. In one experiment, when the electrodes were fastened near the flexor muscles of the right arm, the subject was told to imagine raising a cigaret to the mouth. When such imagining was carried out, there was a corresponding electrical effect—an effect that was *not* registered in the right-arm electrodes when a movement of the *left* arm was imagined. Similarly, and more strikingly, action currents were recorded from eye-moving muscles when the subject was asked to visualize such an object as the Statue of Liberty or the Eiffel Tower. Finally, with electrodes attached to tongue- and lip-moving muscles, currents appeared when the subjects engaged in mental multiplication or when they recalled, in thought, the words of a song or the meaning of such a term as *incongruous* or *eternity*. These and related observations led Jacobson to conclude that covert muscular response was an essential condition of thought and imagination.

The experiments of Max (1935, 1937) give dramatic support to Jacobson's conclusion. Max used as his principal subjects nineteen deaf-mutes who were adept in sign-language. By attaching electrodes to both forearms of a subject simultaneously, he was able to get action-current records of finger and hand movements under conditions in which no overt response could be detected. Records were taken while the subject was in the waking state preparatory to sleep, and while he was actually asleep. With respect to the sleep records, Max discovered that when strong action-currents appeared and his subjects were awakened immediately thereafter, they almost invariably reported having been aroused from a dream—which they often described in great detail. When, however, they were awakened in the *absence* of these strong discharges, they almost never reported that they had been dreaming. (Contrary to the popular belief that fairly lengthy dreams may take place in only a few seconds of time, Max found that "dream reactions" in his experiment usually involved two and one half minutes or more of responding.) When mild tactual stimuli were applied to the subjects during sleep, covert muscular responses followed in about 65 per cent of the cases. In some instances, these stimuli were sufficient to initiate "dream reactions." Moreover, when deaf subjects, in the waking state, were given various "abstract

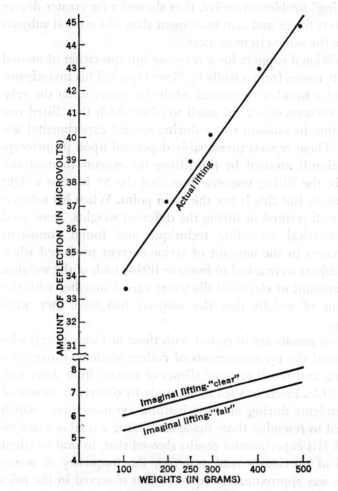

FIG. 50. Action currents from arm muscles during real and imaginal weight lifting. The upper curve is for the amount of electrical discharge when the weights indicated on the abscissa were actually lifted. The two lower curves are for imaginal lifting of these weights, one for times when "clear" images were reported, and one for "fair." (After Shaw, 1940.)

thinking" problems to solve, they showed a far greater degree of covert finger and arm movement than did normal subjects under the same circumstances.

Additional support for a response interpretation of mental activity comes from a study by Shaw (1940). This investigator trained a number of normal adults to report upon the relative heaviness of several small weights which they lifted one at a time in random order during several experimental sessions. These reports presumably depended upon proprioceptive stimuli aroused by the lifting movements themselves— that is, the lifting response provided the S^D for the weight judgment. But this is not the main point. When his subjects were well trained in lifting the different weights, Shaw used the electrical recording technique and found consistent differences in the amount of action-current produced when the subjects were asked to *imagine* lifting each of the weights. The amount of electrical discharge varied together with the amount of weight that the subjects imagined they were lifting.

These results are in accord with those of Ewert (1933) who measured the eye-movements of college students during the reading and *recall* (oral or *silent*) of stanzas from *John Gilpin's Ride*. Ewert was led to his study by observing, in one of his students during an examination, eye-movements which seemed to resemble those made in reading a textbook assignment! His experimental results showed that, in oral or silent recall of previously read material, the frequency of movements was approximately equal to that observed in the original reading. While this study was not concerned with truly covert responses, since the eye-movements (ordinarily unnoticed) could be subjected to direct observation, it does point to the importance of response in what is commonly thought of as an 'imaginal' sort of activity.

Covert Response in Code Learning

We have, then, considerable evidence pointing to the existence, in human beings, of stimulus-response relationships which are ordinarily hidden from objective observation. In view of this evidence, we do not hesitate to affirm the existence of *chains* of reflexes in which at least some of the elements are covert. Even if we refused to trust introspective reports of such chains, we would probably feel justified in assuming their reality.

The assumption of covert chaining serves to clarify and bring within the same conceptual framework a number of apparently unrelated observations. Let us consider, in the present section, the process of learning to receive Morse Code. If, under the code-voice method of training described in Chapter 5 (page 147), one observes carefully the behavior of a beginning code-student, two things soon become obvious. (1) The time required for responding to a signal by printing a character (letter or digit) is gradually reduced as practice continues. Early in training, the student makes use of all the time available between the presentation of the signal and the announcement, by the instructor, of its name. Later on, the appropriate response comes more and more quickly, well in advance of the identification. The latency of the response becomes shorter and shorter. (2) Along with the decrease in latency goes another change. A student may at first exhibit a marked degree of apparently superfluous activity during the latent period. After the signal sounds, and before he prints his character, various interesting reactions may occur. He may tap with his pencil or his foot, make nodding movements with his head, whistle softly to himself, or murmur some equivalent of the signal, such as "di-dah" or "di-di-dit." Only *after* such activity does he make the printing-response. Gradually, however, there is an abbreviation of this activity, until overt intervening responses may no longer be observed. Yet, even at this point, the student may report that he thinks about the signal before he makes his final reaction to it. Thus, he may echo it, visualize it, or respond in some other covert fashion. Ultimately, this covert activity also disappears, and he may report that he prints or "copies" his characters automatically, without any thought of what he is doing.

A tentative analysis of such changes would run as follows. In the first stage of code-receiving, the signal occasions various responses, sometimes overt, which serve in turn as stimuli for the copying response that ends the sequence. Later, these intervening responses become covert, although still present as members of the chain. Finally, they are eliminated entirely, and the observed decrease in latency is thereby made possible. The latency decrease may probably be explained in terms of two principal factors: the failure of long-latency responses to receive reinforcement, and the accumulation of negatively reinforcing effects produced by the continued repetition of (unnecessary) intervening activity.

Covert Response and Reaction Time

In our treatment of reaction times in Chapter 5, we have noted the classic distinction, by Donders, of the A-, B-, and C-reactions. We might also have considered another type, called by Wundt the D-reaction, which was said to be distinguished by the fact that it involved a *recognition* or *identification* of the stimulus prior to the overt response. What was essentially this D-reaction came later to be called the *sensorial* reaction and was contrasted with the *muscular* reaction (the successor of Donder's A-reaction). In the sensorial reaction procedure, a stimulus, say a sound, is presented and the subject responds only after it has been *apprehended;* whereas, a muscular reaction requires the subject to *pay attention* to the response only. The sensorial reaction time was found by Lange (1888) to be about one hundred milliseconds longer than the muscular reaction time.

If you have followed our discussion and are ready to consider the *recognition, identification,* or *apprehension* of a stimulus as basically the same sort of phenomenon as *thinking about* a stimulus before responding to it overtly, you can see why we deferred the treatment of the D-reaction until this time. The reason for the lengthened latency of the sensorial reaction becomes the same as that which holds back the progress of the beginner in copying Morse Code. An intervening covert response—an extra link in the chain—is involved in both cases.

An additional factor adds weight to this analysis. In the history of reaction-time study, the distinction between sensorial and muscular reaction time proved very difficult to maintain under experimental conditions. When subjects were repeatedly asked to make the sensorial reaction, their times tended to approach closely the values obtained for the muscular reaction. Practice seemed to decrease the difference between the two. Just as the code student comes to respond automatically to the presented signal with a minimal latency, so does the laboratory subject find it all too easy to eliminate the *cognitive* activity which characterizes the sensorial reaction. Our explanation of the two changes would be much the same. It is *unrewarding work* to maintain the covert member or members of the chain.

The Context Theory of Meaning

Our mention, in the preceding section, of such matters as *cognition* and *apprehension,* leads quite naturally into the discussion of another problem, that of *meaning.* Common sense tells us that objects, ideas, and actions ordinarily mean something; and the psychologist is not infrequently asked to give his explanation, to say *why.*

One answer to this question is that offered by Titchener (1915), in the early years of the present century, and it may be of more than passing interest to consider his formulation and the bearing of our own position upon it. Titchener was an introspectionist in psychology, who believed that a man's conscious processes were basically analyzable into elements, such as *sensations* and *images;* that these elements were usually compounded within *perceptions* and *ideas;* and that an obvious characteristic of the latter was the *meaning* they possessed. (It was, of course, assumed that sensations, images, perceptions, and ideas were subject to the introspector's personal observation.)

"Meaning," says Titchener, ". . . is always context, one mental process is the meaning of another mental process if it is that other's context." Context itself is nothing more than "the fringe of related processes that gathers about the central group (or "core") of sensations or images." In perception and in idea there is *core plus context,* and the latter "carries" the meaning of the former.

Titchener offers a number of illustrations to show the wisdom of this core-context distinction. Context may, in some cases, be stripped from the core—as when we repeat aloud some word until the context disappears and the word becomes meaningless; context may be added to core—as when we learn the meaning of some strange design or foreign word; context and core may be disjoined in time—as when we know what we want to say but need time to find expressive words, or when the point of a joke is delayed in appearance; the same core may have several contexts—as implied in our worry about the true meaning of a chance remark . . .; and so on. (Keller, 1937)

Titchener had still more to say about the matter. Meaning, as he saw it, is originally derived from an organism's movement: context is initially kinesthetic or muscular sensation, such as that aroused by our bodily orientation toward a stimulus. Later, the context may be visual, auditory, and so forth. Ultimately, however, the meaning becomes almost entirely verbal—when the context is added by something we say (to ourselves) about a stimulus. Or it may even reduce to a "brain habit," without any conscious context; we respond automatically and appropriately, but without any fringe of conscious process which supplements the core.

However strange this theory may sound to you at first, a little thought will make it less so. What Titchener calls *context* is no more than a chain of covert responses which intervenes between the initial, observable stimulus and the final, overt reaction. Recall, for a moment, our code-learning example. A code signal has hardly any meaning for the student at the start; it evokes no more than a kind of "what is it?" response. Later, its meaning grows as the intervening responses (the "di-dahs," the visualizing, etc.) come in. Finally, as these responses drop out, the 'meaning' of the code decreases. Clearly, intervening covert response is the counterpart of Titchener's "conscious context."

You can go on with the translation, point by point—it is not difficult if you have understood the main theme. The translation will not provide you with a complete theory of meaning but it is encouraging to find that an objective science of behavior is able so easily to make use of the findings of pre-behavioral introspective psychology.

The Association Experiment

Related to the principle of chaining, as well as to the reaction-time study, is the well-known *association experiment* —a technique which has been used extensively in psychological laboratories and clinics since 1879, when Sir Francis Galton introduced the basic procedure. Galton presented himself visually with 75 stimulus *words*, one at a time, from a previously prepared list, and measured with a chronograph the time elapsing between his first view of each word and the arousal of the first two ideas which were suggested by it. After each stimulus-response sequence of this sort, he undertook to examine the *nature* of the ideas (whether they were visualizations, verbalizations, or some other acts) and their *origin* in his own life history (whether from boyhood and youth, from subsequent manhood, or from more recent experiences). By repeating his list four times, at one-month intervals, he was led to the following conclusions among others: (1) 45 per cent of his responses were purely verbal, 32.5 per cent were in "sense imagery" (e.g., visualizations), and 22.5 per cent were "histrionic" (postural); (2) the most frequently recurring ideas in the four tests dated from his boyhood; (3) the average time estimated for the recall of a single idea was

1.3 seconds; and (4) some of the ideas recalled were unfit for publication, since they laid bare his "mental anatomy"!

In the modern form of the association experiment, words are still employed as stimuli, but they are always presented by another person, and the time measured is usually that which elapses between the stimulus word and the subject's overt response with the "first word that comes to mind." As a rule, the stimuli are drawn from standard lists and presented to individual members of various groups of subjects previously selected on the basis of their age, sex, occupation, educational level, and so forth. In some cases, the experimenter's principal interest lies in the *nature* of the response words emitted; in other cases, the *reaction times* also receive attention.

One of the better-known studies emphasizing the kind, rather than the speed, of response is that made by Kent and Rosanoff (1910), in which one hundred familiar nouns and adjectives were presented vocally to 1,000 subjects, mostly adults, who were selected, more or less at random, from the general population. When all the response words were tabulated for these subjects, a frequency table was constructed to show, for each stimulus word, the number of subjects who responded in identical fashion. Thus, *light* was given in response to *dark* by 427 of the 1,000 subjects, *night* was given by 221, *black* by 76, and so on. As this example indicates, considerable agreement in responding was shown. The individual stimulus words, however, varied greatly in the number of different responses they occasioned. *Anger*, at one extreme, led to 276 kinds of verbal response, whereas *needle* at the opposite extreme, led to only 72. *Anger*, we might say, has many more meanings than *needle*. Moreover, individual subjects differed markedly in the frequency with which they tended to make unique responses. Some tended to "follow the crowd" while others leaned in the direction of the bizarre and eccentric, indicating very different histories of reinforcement.

Many studies of associative reactions have been made with

the Kent-Rosanoff and other word lists, using a great variety of subjects, a number of different experimental situations, and several systems of classifying the responses. These studies cannot be reviewed here, but a few of the findings may be mentioned as worthy of interest. For example, children, in contrast with adults, respond with (1) more completions of, or enlargements upon the stimulus words (*dark—night, red —wagon, soft—pillow*); (2) more defining responses, often involving several words (*table—made of wood*); (3) fewer opposites (*dark—light, soft—hard*); and (4) more sentence responses (*soft—snow is soft*). Very young children may often show a tendency, not entirely absent in adults, to repeat the stimulus word (*lamp—lamp*).

A thoroughgoing analysis of the association experiment is yet to be made. The basic principle involved is quite clear, however, and has often been recognized, openly or by implication. It may be stated simply. *In the history of an organism, one verbal response, through chaining, becomes the S^D for another.* The stimulus word is part of a chain which has the response word as another member. A single stimulus word may, however, belong within more than one chain, and the likelihood of a given response to such a word will then depend upon a number of factors, operating individually or together. These include: (1) the amount of reinforcement which a specific chain has been accorded; (2) the amount of collateral strengthening due to the presence of certain S^D's in the experimental situation; (3) the presence of strong motives or emotions; (4) the recency with which the response has been reinforced; and (5) the amount of energy expenditure involved.

An example may illustrate the possible operation of these factors. The stimulus word is *dark*. (1) Adults have long used this word in juxtaposition with *light;* children have more frequently followed it with *night;* photographers have often combined it with *room;* and so on. Different responses have different reinforcement histories. (2) Any one of the above responses may be given additional strength by some aspect of the immediate stimulus situation. *Light* may be helped by some conspicuous lighting effect in the experimental chamber; *night* may be partially initiated by the gathering darkness observed outside the laboratory window; and *room* may be aided by the dimness of the chamber (*This room is dark*) or even by some confining aspect of the situation (*Not much room here*). (3) For a hungry subject, growing eager for his meal, *dark* may occasion *meat;* and for a subject in whom dark has become a conditioned stimulus for a violent fear reaction, all responses may momentarily be inhibited. (4) For a subject who came to the experimental session directly from a political discussion or talk of a coming election, *dark* may well evoke *horse*. (5) Finally, of several possibilities, some responses may be less effortful than others. Consider the following hypothetical responses to *dark*:

(1) *the forest primeval*   (2) *complexion*   (3) *light*   (4) *bark*

Classically these responses might be said to fall within a scale of 'meaningfulness-superficiality,' with the most meaningful at the top of the list and the most superficial at the bottom. If 'superficial' is taken as the equivalent of 'economical' (as it sometimes is), and if we see the reactions as running from least to most energy-conserving, they also fit well into an effortful-effortless scale. It is then quite understandable that increased superficiality of response has been claimed by researchers to accompany states of fatigue and repetition of stimulus lists.

Our list of determining factors may not be exhaustive, but it should suggest to you that the emission of a verbal response, like any other, may depend upon a variety of circumstances. More often than not our responses depend upon the joint operation of several factors, rather than the isolated action of one. Clever experimental design and close weighing of probabilities may be required to illuminate the influence of a single variable upon the behavior of an organism with such a complicated past as that of the average adult human being.

When we turn to the matter of *reaction times* in the association experiment, we are immediately confronted with a large body of factual information most of which adds little to the present discussion. Perhaps the two outstanding facts, noted by many investigators, are (1) that the reaction-time values in this type of experiment are usually much greater than in the case of word-reactions to *non-word* stimuli; and (2) that *other-word* reactions are considerably slower than *same-word* (repeating) reactions. Such findings are in accord with the fact that covert response words are commonly reported to intervene between the verbal stimulus and the (overt) verbal response. Moreover, since any stimulus word may have been linked with *several* words in previously established chains, we would expect occasional *interference* of responses—an expectation which is often supported by subjects who claim that response words "get in each other's way." There is also the fact that some stimuli, by virtue of earlier, respondent conditioning, may serve to depress for a short period all operant behavior, including the verbal; and this would obviously lengthen the reaction times of some subjects to some of the words of a stimulus list.

'Complexes' and 'Guilt'

It is partially due to the last-mentioned fact that the association experiment has been used as a *complex-indicator* and as a *guilt-detector*. Carl Jung (1919), the famous Swiss psychotherapist, was the first to see that 'complexes' of repressed behavior might be brought into the open by probing with stimulus-words; and he made an exhaustive analysis of the associative reactions which pointed to the existence of these complexes. His work amounted to a recognition of the fact that certain, ordinarily neutral, words might have become emotionally 'charged' for a patient by virtue of their connection with some earlier experience, generally involving negative reinforcement, and that the responses normally found linked with such words were thereby less likely to occur. When presented with the stimulus words of a 'free-association' test, the patient might respond to some of them (1) with very unusual, far-fetched, or highly personal words; (2) by repeating the stimulus word before making an other-word response; (3) by 'misunderstanding' the stimulus word; (4) by giving exceptionally long reaction times or no word-response at all; and (5) by obvious signs of emotional upset, such as blushing, stammering, whispering the response word, and so on. Jung found that testing and re-testing with carefully chosen stimulus words often aided him greatly in getting at the roots of his patients' troubles, thus paving the road to therapy; and his lead has been followed by many clinicians since.

The clinical use of the association experiment is like its use as a 'guilt-detector,' but with a difference. "The detective knows the crime, but not the culprit; the psychotherapist knows the culprit but not the crime." (Woodworth, 1938). We may add that the 'crime' in question is likely to be crime by courtesy only, since it is more often an affair of the classroom than of the courts. In the simplest demonstration of guilt detection, two students may be drawn from a class and given secret instructions as to their conduct during, say, a ten-minute period outside the room. One student (the 'culprit') is sent into a course of action which is likely to produce embarrassment. For example, he may be asked to enter a professor's office, during his absence, and engage in some trivial activity such as arranging papers on a desk. In the course of this activity a 'mishap' of some sort is arranged to occur and the 'unsympathetic' professor unexpectedly returns. The other student is subjected to no such experience, but, at the end of the ten-minute period, both men are brought back to the classroom and given the free-association test individually. The class is acquainted with the nature of the 'crime,' but does not know the culprit; and the latter has been instructed to hide his guilt if possible. The same set of ordinarily neutral stimulus words is presented to each student, but several of these words have been chosen because of their possible significance to the 'criminal' through his recent experience. Response words are recorded and reaction times are taken with a stop-watch. In this 'experiment' the class, as a rule, has no great difficulty in detecting the culprit, either by his unusual responses to such common words as *ink, desk, office, Professor,* and the like, or by unusually long reaction times. Unfortunately, the validity of this type of detection is not great enough to justify its exclusive use in the detection of real criminals. When carefully administered and accompanied by other data (e.g., changes in blood pressure or the galvanic skin response) it has sometimes been successful in evoking confessions, but it has serious limitations, since it is not sure-fire and may even point the finger of guilt at persons who know about the crime but did not commit it.

Mazes and Nonsense Syllables

A discussion of chaining leads us naturally into two other well-known spheres of psychological research. One of these has been chiefly concerned with the ability of animals (white rats in particular) to run *mazes;* the other has dealt with the rote memorizing of verbal materials (for example, *nonsense syllables*) by human beings. Both have often been cited as cases of "serial learning," which gives you a clue as to the reason for their inclusion in the present chapter.

Hundreds of maze-learning experiments have been carried out since the turn of the century, when the technique was first introduced, with results that often impress observers as small, considering the amount of labor expended. What was considered, at the outset, to be a very simple form of learning, and the possible prototype of habit-formation in human beings, is in reality very complex. Moreover, we now see the problem merely as one calling for the application of explanatory principles.

We are now able (as we were not in Chapter 3) to enumerate some of the more important factors involved in the mastery of any maze habit. We can say, with assurance, that the solution involves the establishment of a *chain* of reflexes, initiated when an animal is placed in the maze and terminated when he arrives at his reward. From our analysis of bar-pressing behavior we can assert that successive *discrim-*

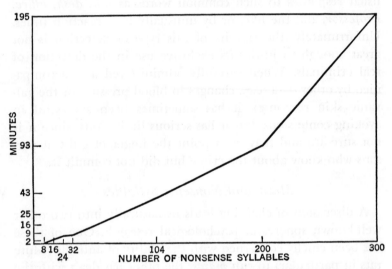

FIG. 51. Curve relating the length of nonsense-syllable lists to the time taken to memorize the lists. The subject was given one trial per day until a given list was mastered. The values on the abscissa and ordinate are the actual lengths-of-list and corresponding memorizing-times. Note the positive acceleration of the curve arising from the ever increasing generalization as the lists (chains) grow longer. (After Lyon, 1917.)

inations and *differentiations* are involved at successive points in the maze pathway; and we can see, as basic to these, the principles of operant *conditioning* and *extinction*. Also, and of extreme importance, we can assume the operation of *secondary reinforcement,* a factor with which we shall deal in the coming chapter.

With respect to rote-learning studies, the situation is much the same. Since 1885, when Ebbinghaus reported his famous experiments, thousands of students have memorized thousands of lists of words or nonsense syllables under various conditions and to various degrees of mastery. Rate of learning, as measured by number of list repetitions or time required to reach a given standard of performance, has been related to length of list, meaningfulness of list material, spacing of practice periods, and many other variables. Similarly, the *retention* of such memorized lists has been studied as a function of time-since-mastery (and the nature of the activity that filled this time), rate of initial learning, amount of over-practice, and so on.

The problem of rote memorization is similar to that of maze learning. It has practical significance because it is like some of the tasks that face us in everyday affairs. Like maze learning, it presents complex matters for analysis (Hull, et al., 1940) and involves the operation of more fundamental mechanisms, but we are not yet at a stage of development where we can do more than suggest the manner of their interaction. The over-all picture is one of verbal chaining, in which the emission of each response comes to depend upon the S^D function of the response, or responses, preceding it in the series.

NOTES

Some exploratory observations by Charles Ferster, in the Columbia laboratory, bear upon the problem of 'homogeneous' chaining and the formation of new response units. Ferster was able to train several rats, with some success, to make paired responses for food reinforcement. He observed, among other things, that, when pairing was well established, the two members of the pair were seldom if ever of the same form. The first response might be with one forepaw and the second with the other; the first might be a fairly protracted push of the bar and the second might be a sharp slap; and so on. Heterogeneity of the two links, rather than homogeneity, was the rule. This gives support to our statements in this chapter concerning the improbability of purely homogeneous chaining.

More than thirty years ago, Swindle (1917, 1919) published several reports on the behavior of animals (e.g., the pecking behavior of cockatoos) in the Berlin zoo. Such responses, in spite of a high degree of stereotypy, showed some variation in force, even when emitted at a very constant rate. Swindle also pointed out that what we call a *reaction time* is dependent upon the number of responses that intervene between the stimulus and the response that we have selected for observation. We are reminded not only of the *associative reaction,* but also of such 'latencies' as are measured in the run-way and the bar-pressing experiments.

An excellent account of the *association experiment* is given by Woodworth in his *Experimental psychology* (1938). You should now be able to appreciate some of the factors involved in this kind of experimentation and find, in Woodworth's examples, plenty of food for thought and some suggestions for future research.

The "dream reactions" reported by Max (page 214) to result from mild stimulation of his sleeping subjects, makes more credible many non-experimental reports of induced dreaming. Thus, it has been said that exposure of a sleeper's feet to cold may evoke dreams of, say, Arctic exploration; that the repeated tipping of a sleeper's bed may lead to dreams of ocean voyages; that the entanglement of legs or arms in bed-clothes arouses dreams of frustrated action; and so on.

Early investigations (e.g., Thorsen, 1925) of the relation between covert response and 'inner speech' or 'thinking' apparently suffered from inadequate experimental technique. Modern methods of recording the electrical changes that arise from covert muscular movement (as in the Jacobson and Max studies) open up a large field of research. Studies by Davis (1948) and others suggest that a frontal attack is possible upon such 'intervening' responses as those involved in associative reactions, meaning, and the like.

One of the first and most elaborate treatments of covert response and its psychological significance is that of Kantor (1924) who found in such response the basis of many allegedly 'mental' activities—perceiving, imagining, thinking, feeling, remembering, and so forth. Kantor's account, although not obviously guided by experimental findings, has many points of contact with the one of this chapter. The advanced student will not let the difficulty of this book deter him from making the effort required to appreciate its contents.

8

SECONDARY REINFORCEMENT

THE CAWING of a rook . . . in itself, is certainly not agreeable. This sound, in the case of those who have lived in the country in early life, and enjoyed its scenes and its adventures, is well known to become a particularly agreeable one.... The explanation is that this particular sound, having been heard again and again among surroundings . . . which have a marked accompaniment of pleasure . . . produces a faint re-excitation of the many currents of enjoyment which accompanied these.

James Sully, *The Human Mind*, 1892

A Pause for Review

The last chapter's discussion of response chaining has no doubt sharpened in your mind a question that was forming earlier. In a chain, each response produces the stimulus for the next response, but why should each producing response be made—what keeps the chain together? The roots of this question go back to our first descriptions of operant reactions, where for the sake of simplicity the question was laid aside so that our analysis of behavior could get under way. We have now come to the point where the problem must be aired and dealt with. In so doing, we encounter a new principle which fills a key place in the jig-saw problem of behavior that we have been carefully assembling in the preceding pages. This principle, if we may name it shortly before explaining it, is that of *secondary reinforcement*. With its aid, we can make new and material progress in rounding out our picture of that extraordinary object of study, the behaving organism.

Perhaps the best way to come at the principle of secondary reinforcement is by a review of the ways in which a stimulus

231

can affect behavior. If we look back over what has been said so far, we can summarize the functions of stimuli quite briefly. Stimuli may be (1) *eliciting,* as in respondent reactions; (2) *discriminative,* in that they "set the occasion" for the emission of an operant response; (3) *reinforcing,* as when a new Type S reflex is brought into being by the unconditioned stimulus, or an emitted operant is strengthened by the presentation of a food pellet. Reinforcing stimuli in Type S reactions are correlated with others which then become capable of eliciting the response. In Type R, the correlation is with a response, the contingency between response and reinforcing stimulus serving to increase the emission frequency of that response. We have not spoken as yet of two other functions of stimuli, the *drive-arousing* and *emotionalizing* functions, but these will be considered in the next two chapters. To the three we have enumerated, however, we wish to add as a fourth that of secondary reinforcement, at times called conditioned reinforcement.

A New Function of the Stimulus

We are led to the realization of a new kind of stimulus control over behavior, by inquiring what the effect upon a non-reinforcing stimulus may be when it accompanies a reinforcing one. When, after many such associations, we apply the erstwhile non-reinforcing stimulus to the organism, we look to see whether its action has undergone a change. The appropriate experiment can be easily arranged. But before any laboratory trial is made at all, a reconsideration of already well-known experiments and observations leads us to the hunch that *a stimulus which is not originally a reinforcing one (or which is not, as we often say, a "primary reinforcement") can become reinforcing through repeated association with one that is.* That is, reinforcing power may be acquired by a stimulus through being present when an original reinforcement is given.

Working from this same hunch, scientists have now established its truth. In the discussion of the principle that follows, we shall report some of the evidence they marshalled for it; we shall consider some of its recent experimental extensions; and we shall indicate, at the same time, its multifold implications for human and animal behavior.

Secondary Reinforcement of Type S Reactions

You may recall that in Chapter 2 we mentioned reports, from Pavlov's laboratory, of higher-order conditioning. In those experiments, conditioned stimuli were used as reinforcements for others in the absence of the original unconditioned stimulus. For example, a buzzer conditioned to elicit salivation was then paired with a visual stimulus like a black square, and presumably sufficed to establish the square as a conditioned eliciting stimulus of the *second order* although the latter was never once reinforced by pairing with the food. The crucial point about these experiments was that a stimulus seemed able to acquire reinforcing power through conditioning, and thereafter to act independently to condition another reflex. Despite the admitted weakness and instability of this higher-order conditioning, the phenomenon aroused much discussion among psychologists. Behavior theorists appealed to the principle in explaining those complex acts of everyday life which are neither initiated nor sustained by unconditioned stimuli like food, water, and sex. Little more was done experimentally with Type S conditioned reinforcement after Pavlov, but it is well that the principle was not lost sight of, because a parallel for it was found in operant behavior—one that assumed even greater importance.

Secondary Reinforcement of Type R Reactions

A stimulus is said to be reinforcing if it possesses the capacity to increase or maintain reflex strength above operant level. In operant conditioning, it must be able to raise the strength of the response producing it, or be able to sustain the strength to some degree in the face of extinction. (In respondent conditioning, it must increase the eliciting strength of a stimulus paired with it.) Here, then, is the criterion to be met by a *secondary* reinforcer: *it must, through conditioning, have acquired the power to condition.* Moreover, we may recognize at once that, as with any conditioned stimulus, a secondary reinforcer used repeatedly without further association with primary reinforcement will extinguish, that is, lose its power to reinforce.

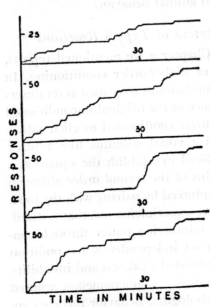

FIG. 52. Conditioning of the bar-pressing response by rats with secondary reinforcement alone. Prior to this, the sound of the food magazine was associated with the delivery of pellets, no bar being present. When the bar was introduced and each press produced the magazine sound, the cumulative response curves shown above were obtained from four animals. (From Skinner, 1938.)

We may summon a few introductory examples to demonstrate the operation of secondary reinforcement. Remembering that the signs of an effective operant reinforcer are an increase in emission rate, or the retardation of extinction, the following experiments illustrate both of them. Thus, Grindley (1929) found that chicks increased their speed of traversing a runway during the first trials of an experiment in which the only reinforcement was the sight of rice grains from which they were blocked off by a sheet of glass. These chicks were accustomed to rice as food, and in the experiment the visual stimulus alone acted as a secondary reinforcement for strengthening the running response. Williams (1929) found that rats, daily trained in using the white compartment of a discrimination box as a route to food, were able to master a fourteen-unit T-maze with no other terminal reinforcement than the white compartment itself. A similar result has more recently been reported by Saltzman (1949); and other investigators have shown that animals will learn mazes or other responses if the reinforcement provided is simply a return to their living-cage homes. Bruce (1932) showed that the extinction of a simple maze performance was slower when food was present though inaccessible (behind wire mesh) at the end of the run than when no food at all was present. Bugelski (1938) got slower extinction of bar-pressing in rats when each response produced an auditory click which had regularly accompanied food-reinforced bar-pressing during conditioning, than when the extinction responses produced neither click nor food.

Still other examples of secondary reinforcement come to light if we suddenly bring to bear upon an extinguishing response a stimulus which had previously been correlated with reinforcement. Thus, if bar-pressing is being extinguished in a rat, and when the response rate has fallen quite low we reconnect the empty magazine so that a response now produces the accustomed clicks (but still no food), the extinction curve shows a burst of responses. This effect was mentioned in the discussion of chaining in the last chapter (page 202), and it is a neat case of secondary reinforcement. Notterman (1950), using rats as subjects in a runway experiment, during the training correlated a light with food as the terminal reinforcement for runs. Later, during extinction of the running response, he re-introduced the light at the end of runs, and found that it acted as a secondary reinforcer since the running speed quickened significantly and durably. Notterman ran control animals to prove that it was not just any stimulus change at the end of a run which could be expected to produce this effect, but that the stimulus used as a secondary reinforcer needed to have a history of association with primary reinforcement.

S^D and S^r

The reader who has trained himself by this time to raise his own questions about details of behavior, will not have failed to ask what we mean by "a stimulus *correlated with* reinforcement" in describing an S^r. (We shall from now on use S^r to denote a secondary or conditioned reinforcement; the symbol S^D, for a discriminative stimulus, is already familiar.) What kind of a "correlation" must it be: what temporal relation to the reinforcement, and what sort of association with it? That mere contiguity with reinforcement is not sufficient to make an S^r out of a neutral stimulus is shown by an experiment of Schoenfeld, Antonitis, and Bersh (1950a). These men trained animals to come to the cage's food tray at the sound of a pellet falling into the tray. After an animal had seized his pellet, and while he was eating it (which took about ten seconds on the average), a light was turned on for one second. One hundred such light-pellet associations were given each animal, and then the possible S^r value of the light was tested by seeing whether bar-pressing could be conditioned by giving only the light as reinforcement. The net result of these associations was zero, and since this type of correlation did not work, it became clear that one had to discover just what kinds of association *could* give rise to a secondary reinforcer. Though not so plentiful as we would wish, all the evidence we have so far points in the same direction. *In order to act as an S^r for any response, a stimulus must have status as an S^D for some response.*

The foregoing sentence, standing alone, is not easy to grasp right off, and three points of explanation probably ought to be made.

1. From the viewpoint of procedure, the training conditions for obtaining an S^r are the same as those for obtaining an S^D. We must first make an S^D of the stimulus we wish to use later as an S^r.

2. The response for which the stimulus is specifically used

as S^D is not the only one for which it can be used as an S^r. For example, in a chain of heterogeneous reflexes, a response which produces the S^D for the next response is thereby strengthened, that is, the S^D for the next response in the chain acts as an S^r on the response producing it even though that response is different from the next. It is worth recalling here that in Skinner's original conditioning experiments the same feature appeared. His rats were first trained to come to a tray for a pellet at the sound (S^D) of the discharging magazine. After being well accustomed to this reaction, the bar was introduced, and pressing was conditioned by the magazine sound which the rat himself produced by his pressing. In these instances, we see the stimulus acting as a reinforcing and a discriminative one at the same time. We shall shortly return to this matter in discussing how chains are cemented together and the "generality of S^r."

3. The equality and interchangeability of the S^D and S^r values of a stimulus are suggested by an experiment of Dinsmoor (1950). This worker gave several groups of rats the same amount of light-dark discrimination training, using the bar-pressing response and food reinforcement. A series of extinction sessions followed in which the S^D established during training was used discriminatively (i.e., preceded the response, and "set the occasion" for it) with one group of subjects, and reinforcingly (i.e., was produced by the bar-pressing responses) with another group. No difference in extinction responding occurred between these two groups. Moreover, in continued extinction sessions, the procedures were interchanged, so that for one group the stimulus hitherto used discriminatively was now used reinforcingly, and vice versa for the other group. This interchange of stimulus functions did not produce any differences in the performances of the groups. Apparently, establishing a stimulus as an S^D establishes it equally as an S^r, and extinguishing its power to function in one way also subtracts, in like degree, from its power to function the other way. This conclusion, tentatively drawn

by the investigator, leads us to wonder how far the exact equality between the S^D and S^r functions of a stimulus may extend. Dinsmoor's study points up the question and provides a basis for further work.

Not only are the S^D and S^r values of a stimulus closely interrelated, but the same stimulus can, as in chaining, exercise both functions at the same time. What, then, is the reason for continuing the distinction between S^D and S^r as "two functions"? The reason lies, of course, *in the way the experimenter is using the stimulus,* that is, whether he wishes it, in relation to some selected response, to act discriminatively or reinforcingly. Once a stimulus has been given a measure of control over behavior through correlation with reinforcement, that control may be used in either S^D or S^r fashion.

That the distinction between stimulus functions on the basis of use is important to retain, can be gathered from the following example of how the two uses may lead to different results. Suppose we have established a stimulus as an S^D for approaching and nosing the food tray in the cage. Afterwards, desiring to test its controlling power, we introduce the bar into the cage for the first time in the animal's experience. If we decide to test the stimulus as S^r, we present it after each pressing and observe that the response rate goes up, subsequently giving an extinction curve (since primary reinforcement is not used to bolster the S^r's power). But, if we decide to use the stimulus as an S^D for bar-pressing, and somehow manage to have it come on before operant-level pressings, we find no increase in rate of pressing, but rather an increase in the rate of the response which the stimulus followed. In short, where we deal with a new response having no previous history of reinforcement, the S^r function can have a specific effect upon the response, whereas the S^D function cannot. This difference in the outcome of the two uses shows that we are still justified in separately discussing the two stimulus functions. After conditioning, a stimulus may perhaps never be divested of its dual endowment, but it is necessary in analysis to isolate the way it is acting in a given situation—just as a material body may possess both mass and extent at the same time, but we do not hesitate to separate the two aspects for study and use.

More about Chaining

We are now in a position to say a bit more about the topic of the preceding chapter. A chain of reflexes is built up by having each response produce the S^D for the next response; it is *held together* by the fact that each S^D acts as an S^r for the response producing it. To indicate the double action of each stimulus, we can give it a double superscript, as $S^{r.D}$, placing the r before the D because its reference is to the prior response, while the D has reference to the following response. The general notation for a segment of a chain would then be like this:

$$\cdots \rightarrow S^{r.D} \rule{1em}{0.4pt} R \rightarrow S^{r.D} \rule{1em}{0.4pt} R \rightarrow \cdots$$

If we number the terms in the formula to correspond to the sequence in which they are built into the chain, we get:

$$(s)\ S^{D_n} \rule{1em}{0.4pt} R_n \rightarrow S^{r_n.D_{n-1}} \rule{1em}{0.4pt} R_{n-1} \rightarrow \cdots S^{r_2.D_1} \rule{1em}{0.4pt} R_1 \rightarrow S^{r_1.D_0} \rule{1em}{0.4pt} R_0 \rightarrow S^{r_0}$$

in which S^{r_0}, R_0, and S^{D_0} are, respectively, the final reinforcement, final response, and final discriminative stimulus in the chain; in which S^{r_1} is the first secondary reinforcement to be "hooked in"; and in which (s) is the operant-level source of the remotest antecedent response in the chain, R_n, to the remotest discriminative stimulus S^{D_n}.

The preceding chapter also emphasized that the $S^{r.D}$ terms in a chain may be either exteroceptive or proprioceptive stimuli. Psychologists have for a long time been interested in the smooth flow and continuity of reflex chains, and have been especially impressed by chains based on proprioceptive cues which are hidden from the experimenter's view. In describing how chains are maintained and carried through, many writers have used such a term as *set*. Organisms were thought of as becoming "set for" a task by way of a "preparatory set," and as being guided or directed in executing a task by a "continuing set." The term itself was never well defined but the observations upon which it was based are to be analyzed from the standpoint of chaining. The initiation of chains by discriminative stimuli, and the sustaining of a sequence by response-produced reinforcing stimuli, are at bottom the real meaning to be attached to "sets," both preparatory and continuing.

In reflecting on the ways in which response chains may be disturbed, we note that there are two. One is that of cutting or breaking the chain at some point by withholding the next $S^{r.D}$—in short, by extinction of all segments up to that point. A second is that of a response producing the "wrong" S^D, that is, not the one necessary for going on with the rest of the chain. This is an occasion for "confusion" or "interruption of the set," so that the completion of the chain is diverted or slowed down, or is temporarily halted while the organism "readjusts," "takes stock of the situation," or "finds another way" to resume the interrupted activity. A hound intently following his quarry through the brush will take some time to regain his composure and return to the trail if he unexpectedly pokes his nose toward a porcupine or a snake. A man's sleepy-eyed morning routine of washing is quickly alerted when, after drowsily squeezing a tube, he tastes shaving cream on his toothbrush; and parents are familiar with the outrage of the child who detects a mistake in an oft-repeated song—as when the weary parent errs: "Simple Simon met a pie-man going home to bed. ..." In these, as in many other cases of interrupted chains, the behavior does not stop completely, but is apt to take, at least for a while, another direction.

The Generality of S^r

In our treatment of secondary reinforcement so far, we have made use of a fact which may now be given the explicit emphasis it deserves. It is this fact that makes the principle of secondary reinforcement so significant for complex activities like the social behavior of human beings. Here it is: once established, a secondary reinforcement can strengthen other responses than that used during its original establishment, *and can do so under other motives than that prevailing during the original training*. This means that an S^r is not limited in its range of applicability, and that it provides us with a "purely general" reinforcement for use under any conditions we desire. We have already seen that a new response can be conditioned by an S^r, and we are now adding the important observation that this may be done even if the motive is shifted (e.g., Estes, 1949a, 1949b). On the animal level, for example, we can correlate a stimulus with water-reinforcement of bar-pressing by thirsty and not-hungry rats, and then use the stimulus as an S^r to condition chain-pulling when the animals are hungry but not thirsty. On the human level, the words "Well done!", or the approval of other people, or money, may act as secondary reinforcers for a variety of behaviors under any prevailing motive.

The fact of S^r independence should not make us forget, however, that (a) an S^r extinguishes or loses its power with repeated application if separated from primary reinforcement and (b) as with any reinforcement, some drive must be present for the S^r to be effective. We need not always pause to identify either the primary reinforcements that continue to support the power of S^r's, or the prevailing drive under which the S^r is acting. Always, however, there is implied the assumption that both are present. In a broad way, you may think of the supporting primary reinforcements as being such things as our daily food and drink, or relief of pain or anxiety; and the operative drives as occasional hunger and thirst, sex drive, and aversive tensions or fears. In a hypothetical environment shorn of primary reinforcements, or in which organisms are devoid of motives, S^r's would either extinguish completely or never act.

Students sometimes offer examples of a social stimulus apparently separated from its primary reinforcement which nevertheless indefinitely retains its control over behavior. Mother is no longer, seemingly, related to food, comfort, and so on, yet she remains a strong controlling stimulus. But we may note that if mother is no longer present, she cannot extinguish as an S^r; if she is present, she often remains associated with primary reinforcement (like "Thanksgiving dinner with the folks"), or she generalizes with other persons who are so associated. Seeming "exceptions" are dangerous when they condense a whole human life in one sentence, not offering sufficient data for diagnosis or discussion. We ought to prefer to remain on firmer ground, using verified principles with proper safeguards against over-extrapolation. The principle of secondary reinforcement, and the fact of its independence, will enable us to take further steps in analyzing complex behavior, and we shall find ourselves employing it in the remaining pages of this book.

One final word on generality. Since the S^r function of a stimulus is closely related to its S^D function, we might hypothesize that the latter should show, to some degree at least, the same generality as the former. That is to say, we might ask whether an S^D once established for a given response under a given drive, is capable of acting as an S^D for other responses under other drives. Again the answer seems to be *Yes,* but subject to the qualification that the response to which the S^D is transferred must already have been conditioned. Thus, Walker (1942) took an S^D previously associated with a running response and presented it during the extinction of bar-pressing. The stimulus had never been related to bar-pressing, but bar-pressing had been conditioned beforehand with the same reinforcement (food) as had the running. The result was an increased rate of pressing during the application of the S^D. Apparently, an S^D which denotes an "occasion" for reinforcement of one response can also be an "occasion" for a second response which has been similarly reinforced but never before connected with that S^D. Data corroborating this finding have been reported by Estes (1943, 1948). Not so definitely answered is the experimental question whether an S^D may be transferred to another response being made under another drive. The proviso would once more hold that the response involved under the new drive must possess some conditioned strength, whether that strength was acquired under the new drive or the one prevailing when the S^D was established. Clearly, the generality of S^D combined with that of S^r adds up to the possibility of greatly extended behavior variety and control.

Some Parameters of S^r

What variables determine the strength of a secondary reinforcement? Of the many we can guess at, experimental information is thus far available on only a few. This area of research is growing, however, and we are sure to increase our knowledge of it greatly in the near future.

1. The strength of a secondary reinforcer may be expected to depend, for one thing, on the *number of times it was correlated with a primary reinforcement*. Bersh (1950) has found this to be so experimentally. Using groups of rats, he paired a light with the dropping of a pellet into the food tray, varying the number of these pairings from 0 to 120 with different groups of subjects. When he later tested the light as an S^r for reconditioning the response of bar-pressing, which had been previously conditioned and extinguished, he found that its strength was greater when its number of correlations with reinforcement had been greater, and that the strength approached an asymptote beyond which an increased number of associations with reinforcement did not carry it.

2. Bersh (1950) has also shown that the *temporal relation* between the S^r and the primary reinforcement with which it is paired during training is important in determining the reinforcing value acquired by the S^r. In one experiment, a light was arranged to begin 0, $\frac{1}{2}$, 1, 2, 4, and 10 seconds before the dropping of a pellet into the tray of the rat's living

cage. When the S^r was later used to condition bar-pressing, the graph of the amount of conditioning obtained rose to a maximum for the S^r which had had an interval of about one second between its onset and primary reinforcement during training. One second is the optimal interval, and intervals

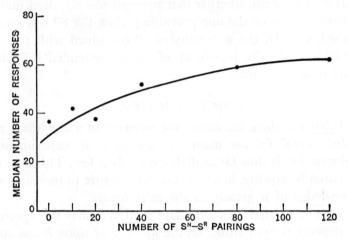

FIG. 53. The effectiveness of a secondary reinforcer as a function of the number of times it was paired with a primary reinforcer. S^N is the neutral stimulus being conditioned as a secondary reinforcer; S^R is the primary reinforcer with which it is paired. (After Bersh, 1950.)

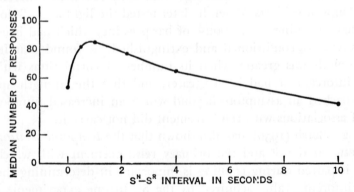

FIG. 54. The effect of the time interval separating S^N and S^R (defined as in Fig. 53) upon the power acquired by S^N to act as a secondary reinforcer. (After Bersh, 1950.)

either longer or shorter are not so effective in establishing a stimulus as an S^r. Another experiment along these lines has been reported by Jenkins (1950).

3. Pursuing the idea that an S^r is established through training as an S^D, Notterman (1950) did an experiment in which the *discrimination training given a stimulus was varied*. He used groups of rats as subjects, a runway as apparatus, and a light as the S^D correlated with food reinforcement while absence-of-light was S^Δ on non-reinforced runs. Each group of rats received the same number of S^D trials (fifty in all over a six-day period), but for each group the number of interspersed S^Δ trials varied. One group got no S^Δ trials at all; another, 10 S^Δ trials; another, 25; another, 50; another, 100. After training was over, each group was extin-

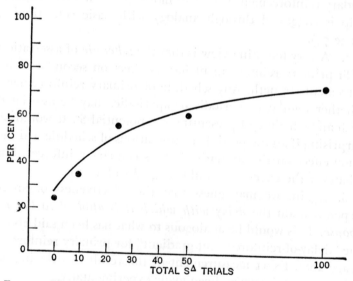

FIG. 55. The effect of increasing discrimination training upon the S^r power of an S^D in Notterman's experiment. The ordinate refers to the amount of decrease in running time when the previous S^D was introduced as the S^r after 94 unreinforced runs under S^Δ. The decrease for each group is expressed as a per cent of that group's running time just prior to the introduction of the S^r. (After Notterman, 1950.)

guished on the runway for 94 trials, each trial being given in the absence of light (S^Δ) and without reinforcement. The light was then introduced as S^r from the 95th trial on to the 105th which was the last, and the amount of facilitation of running produced by the light was compared for the several groups. There was a systematic increase in reinforcing power of the S^r which paralleled the increasing number of S^Δ trials it had been given during its discriminative training.

4. We may guess, in the absence to date of experimental information, that the *amount* of primary reinforcement associated with a secondary reinforcer may also be of significance in determining its strength. Other things equal, if the primary reinforcement is small, then the accompanying stimulus may become only mildly reinforcing; if it is large, the secondary reinforcement may gain more strength. This relationship is suggested through analogy with basic conditioning (page 74).

5. A very tempting view is that the *schedule* of association with primary reinforcement has its effect on secondary-reinforcement strength. Any schedule of primary reinforcement, whether regular or periodic or aperiodic, may be associated with any schedule of presenting the potential S^r. It would be surprising if all the possible combinations of schedule had the same effect on the strength of the secondary reinforcer, but whatever the effect we should be glad to know it.

6. Again, we may guess that the effectiveness of an S^r depends upon the *delay with which it is applied to the response*. This would be analogous to what has been said about the "delay-of-reinforcement gradient" for primary reinforcers (page 208). Exact measurement of the result of delaying an S^r has not yet, however, been made experimentally.

7. There is also to be considered the *nature of the organism* as a determinant of the length and complexity of chains in which secondary reinforcement figures. The organism dealt with in an experiment is one of the conditions of that experiment. He will determine what stimuli may be used at

all for him by reason of his sensory capacities. He will require this or that number of reinforcements to develop a reaction strength which another species might achieve with half that number. His potentiality for acquiring a long chain of reflexes may be quite limited in comparison with an organism far above him in the evolutionary scale. The resistance to extinction of a secondary reinforcement—its longevity—may be enormously different from one level of organism to another: it may endure for life in a man, but expire after several responses in a chicken.

"Token Rewards" and "Sub-Goals"

In analyzing response chains, we noted, among other things, that each S^D in the chain acts as an S^r for the preceding response. We spoke of one response as producing the stimulus in the presence of which the next response is called for. Now suppose that we alter the situation and try to get a chain in which *the next-called-for response is to manipulate or do something with the S^D produced by the preceding response.* What success would we have, and what could we learn from such an experiment?

The experiment, we find, has been done successfully several times, and with a variety of animals ranging from the rat to the chimpanzee. By way of illustration, however, we shall limit ourselves here to studies of ape behavior, since these have been clear, dramatic, and highly suggestive of human conduct. Wolfe (1936) trained chimpanzees to insert small discs (poker chips and brass slugs) into the slot of a vending machine which automatically rewarded each response by delivering a grape. Subsequently, the animals quickly learned to move the lever of a "work apparatus" which provided discs that could be exchanged for grapes in the vending machine. In a number of variations of the experiment, they demonstrated their ability (1) to discriminate food tokens (white discs) from non-food tokens (brass discs); (2) to select blue tokens in preference to white tokens, and white in preference to brass, when the blue procured two grapes, the white procured one, and the brass none at all; and (3) to select tokens in accordance with their prevailing needs—for example, black (food-getting) tokens were chosen when the animals were hungry, and yellow (water-getting) tokens were chosen when they were thirsty. Even when the disc-for-grape exchange was delayed, the subjects stayed at work obtaining discs for a considerable time and saved them until they could be used. Discs that could be 'traded in' immediately had somewhat greater incentive value than those which could not be exchanged until some time later; but the animals would readily lay in a supply of twenty or thirty discs for future use. Cowles (1937) confirmed many of Wolfe's observations and added new data. Most strikingly, he showed that apes were able to form a number of discriminations, some of them quite complicated, solely on the basis of token reward. Thus, they were able to master color, pattern and size discriminations in a standard discriminative situation, after which they carried their tokens to another room and exchanged them for raisins.

There is no reason why you should not have been able to predict in advance the outcome of these studies, since you are already equipped with ample background. The first stage of Wolfe's experiment involved a straightforward operant, disc insertion into a machine for food-reinforcement, that is analogous to the rat's bar-pressing. (This applies also to a host of studies in which a tool or a "manipulandum" is used to obtain food—for example, string-pulling, use of rakes, box-stacking, and so on.) In the preferential selection of blue (two-grape) tokens, the reflex S^D (blue disc)——R has the advantage of a greater amount of reinforcement than the S^D (white disc)——R reflex, just as if there were two bars in a cage, with a rat learning to press one predominantly because it gave more or larger pellets than the other. Related to this choice is also the action of the negatively reinforcing character of the "hard way" (page 177), with the blue disc again benefiting because it gives more-return-for-less-work. In the same situation, the brass disc response is extinguished as the usual result of non-reinforcement, although occasional selection of these discs would be expected (and was observed) on the basis of stimulus generalization. In both Wolfe's and Cowles' studies, the discs were employed in the chain as secondary reinforcements for conditioning other responses. The fact that, after procurement, the next response was a manipulation of the $S^{r.D}$ (the disc) is, on second thought, actually no different from the S^D (visual pellet)——R (seizing) in the chain that follows bar-pressing. The "hoarding" of discs is itself learned through the ultimate, though delayed, reinforcement provided when the discs can once again be exchanged for food. And so on. There is apparently no aspect of this research which taxes unduly the principles with which we are familiar.

Experiments of this sort have also been called "sub-goal" studies. Both "sub-goal" and "token-reward" are ways of denoting the action of secondary reinforcements, and we should not permit ourselves to be disturbed by synonyms. "Token-rewards" were so called merely to distinguish them from "primary" reinforcement. The chimpanzee experiments arouse our interest because they come so close to our own social and economic behavior. In human society, money and other secondary reinforcements such as "prestige" and "community approval" assume, through training, the status of generalized rewards that have potency for practically everything we do. Chimpanzees, like men, will apparently do many things for money.

Secondary Negative Reinforcement

While we have spoken thus far of conditioned reinforcers which act positively, we must not overlook the possibility of conditioning a stimulus as a secondary *negative* reinforcement. In the experimental study of anxiety (see Chapter 9), an S^D is arranged to precede by a fixed time the onset of an inescapable noxious (negatively reinforcing) stimulus like an electric shock. The result, briefly stated, is that bar-pressing in the interval-before-shock is depressed or halted until the shock is past. We ask whether the S^D in this situation becomes also a secondary negative S^r, and we can confirm the fact that it does by showing that an animal can be reinforced by its *removal*.

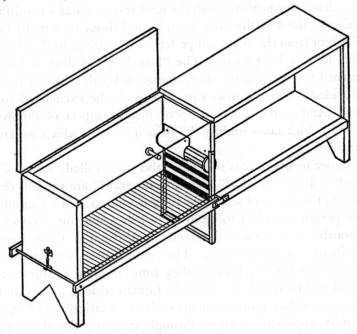

FIG. 56. An apparatus for studying escape from a secondary negative reinforcer. The left compartment is painted white, and contains a floor grid for delivering electric shocks. The right compartment is painted black. The animal can escape from the left to the right by operating a door-opening mechanism in the wall between. (From Miller, 1948.)

Evidence for such an effect has been obtained by several investigators. Hefferline (1950) presented a series of faint clicking sounds regularly in advance of a strong light from which rats could escape by bar-pressing. Whenever an animal responded during the S^D period, the clicking was stopped and, subsequently, no light was presented. After long-con-

tinued combination of clicking-followed-by-light, it became
clear that the bar-pressing response could be kept going for
a time solely because it cut out the clicks. This is related to
an earlier study by Mowrer and Lamoreaux (1942) in which
a buzzer was sounded for six seconds prior to an electric shock
which could be eliminated when the subjects (rats) ran from
one half of an experimental chamber to the other. If the rat
made the running response during the six-second period, the

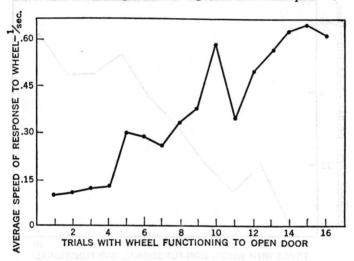

FIG. 57. After considerable shocking in the left (white) compartment of the box in Figure 56, page 250 without any opportunity to escape,
the wheel was made functional, and the animals were permitted to escape
to the right (black) compartment by rotating the wheel to open the
door. The curve shows the average latency changes of the wheel-turning
response on the first 16 trials. (After Miller, 1948.)

sound was discontinued and the shock was not given; if he
did not respond during this period, the buzzer was continued,
with the shock added, until the escape response occurred.
Ten days of buzzer-shock combination, with ten combinations per day, were sufficient to establish the negatively reinforcing effect of the buzzer—that is, to strengthen the running
response through the termination of the sound. In a later
experiment, Mowrer and Lamoreaux (1946) demonstrated

the same effect by conditioning a buzzer-terminating response (jumping into the air) that was distinct from the running response that ended the shock. Still more recently, Miller (1948) showed that both a wheel-rotating and a bar-pressing response could be strengthened when the only reinforcement was escape from a white box (termination of a negative S^r) in which they had formerly been shocked.

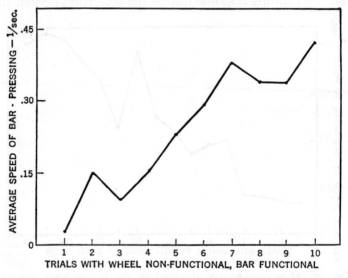

Fig. 58. After the wheel turning response (see Figure 57, page 251) was learned, the wheel was made non-functional and the new response of bar-pressing to open the door was substituted. The white compartment still retained its negative character, since the animal stopped rotating the wheel and acquired the bar-pressing response as shown in this curve. (After Miller, 1948.)

In this connection, we may cite two observations made by Wolfe in the course of his token-reward studies. One of his apes, accustomed to the use of light-blue tokens to obtain 'activity privileges' (return to living-quarters or play with the experimenter), twice employed the discs in what was apparently an attempt to *escape* from the test situation: once when a white rat was introduced into the experimental room, and once when a photographer appeared on the scene to take pictures of the animal's behavior!

One of the commonest appearances of secondary negative reinforcement is in the reflex chains associated with the moving-about of an organism in its environment. Locomotor responses which bring an animal (or human being) into the presence of S^D's which have been correlated with painful or noxious stimuli (primary negative reinforcements) are depressed or weakened, so that he seems to avoid those situations, staying in 'safe' areas. Moreover, an experiment by Bugelski and Miller (1938) showed that rats, placed in a run-

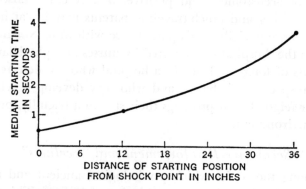

Fig. 59. The tendency to move away from a place where negative reinforcement was applied. The strength of the tendency is measured in terms of the time taken by the animal to get started when placed at three different distances from the point at which he had been shocked. The experimenters refer to this as a "spatial gradient." (After Bugelski and Miller, 1938.)

way at different distances from the point at which they had received electric shocks, ran away with a speed that was proportional to the nearness of the punishment area—the farther from the negative S^r the slower they ran.

We can observe this phenomenon in many other forms of behavior. It is seen especially in the mastery of those skills where a slip means disaster. A choking mouthful of water keeps the beginning swimmer's head up and mouth closed for a long time afterward; and the 'no-hands' cyclist quickly seizes the handle bars when a loss of equilibrium is threatened. 'Safe' places are those in which positive, or at least no negative, secondary reinforcements are found; and they are 'preferred' (the organism spends most of his time in them) to areas in which the S^D's have become negative reinforcers through association with noxious stimuli. 'Home' is such a place to many persons; whereas strange places may be crowded with unknown and untrustworthy S^D's, foretelling unpredictable, even fearsome, events. What we call 'homesickness' may be in good part the absence from one's environment of accustomed, and positive, S^r's. A child raised by much-visiting and much-traveling parents may be 'at home' anywhere, especially if his parents are with him. Not unlike this, is the 'hospitalitis' reported by nurses and physicians in patients of long residence in a hospital who are dejected by the prospect of discharge, and who may develop a relapse, real or feigned, that prolongs their stay in a friendly, protective environment.

Secondary Reinforcement and "Feelings"

Among the topics which psychologists, ancient and modern, have traditionally discussed is that of *feelings*. This topic can take one into many blind alleys, especially if one were to follow the everyday uses of the word. In conversation, the word has no rigorous meaning. We use it in such statements as *I feel reluctant, My feeling is that one should compromise, That feels cold, I feel sad, I feel that I must,* and *Goya's etchings have such feeling!* There are thousands of phrases in which we employ either the verb or the noun, and thoughtful students have long ago agreed that these usages cannot possibly delineate a *single* problem or field of investigation.

Progress in finding a psychological meaning for the term began in the last century and has continued into the present. In one famous attempt to delimit the field, Wilhelm Wundt (1896) proposed a 'tri-dimensional' theory. All true feelings were to be described in terms of three coördinates: degree of subjective pleasantness-unpleasantness; tension-relaxation; and excitement-calm. Thus, any feeling could be adequately described by reference to its place along each of these continua. One feeling might be pleasant, relaxing, and calming; another might be unpleasant, tensing, and exciting; and others would portray still different combinations. This view carried enough prestige to initiate many experimental attempts to find behavioral counterparts (changes in blood-pressure, pulse-rate, respiration, and so on) of each of the alleged dimensions. A great deal of conflicting data resulted, and the whole enterprise is now generally conceded to have been relatively unproductive. Titchener (1908) offered a pared-down introspective account of feelings which eliminated two of Wundt's dimensions, retaining only pleasantness-unpleasantness, but the search for bodily correlates of this dimension was still dogged by failure. Beebe-Center (1932), a present-day authority in this field, finds that no single relation between pleasantness-unpleasantness and either respondent or operant behavior has been accepted without question. The best that he can tell us is that all theories of the relation between feeling and 'locomotor' (his equivalent of *operant*) response "depend on the correlation of pleasantness with seeking, approach, acquisition; and the correlation of unpleasantness with avoidance, withdrawal, rejection."

The bearing of reinforcement upon such verbalizings as "pleasant," "unpleasant," and their synonyms has not been fully explored, but is likely to prove the most profitable approach of all to this problem. Reinforcements appropriate to our "drives" (Chapter 9) commonly evoke "pleasant" or its equivalent—as food when one is hungry; while non-reinforcement, negative reinforcement, and the removal of reinforcement apparently occasion "unpleasant." Even more to the point is the action of secondary reinforcers. Many foods are nourishing but not equally "pleasing" (Mother's cooking is the best!). It would seem that the discriminative stimuli which foretell positive reinforcement raise within us "pleasant and joyful anticipation"; those foretelling negative reinforcement cause "unpleasant and fearful anticipation" or "anxiety." But still we are faced with the task of isolating the S^D's that lead us to emit such words. Theorists have long argued that "feelings" are related, not to objects or other external S^D's, but to the effect they have upon *us* ("If a child is pleased by a new red toy, then both *red* and *pleasantness* are features of his experience, but it is the toy that is red and the child who is pleased"—Beebe-Center). It may be that whenever we say an object is pleasant or unpleasant our statements are based upon intervening responses (of approach, withdrawal, or some other sort) which follow directly upon exteroceptive stimulation and themselves determine the overt spoken outcome. In such a case, "feelings" and "meanings" would have much in common, and the problem of reported "feelings" would be similar to the problem of reported "emotions" (see Chapter 10). This parallel is supported by the fact that reaction times of the verbal responses or judgments 'pleasant' and 'unpleasant' are generally slower than ordinary reaction times—a finding that would be expected on the basis of the intervening response that serves as the S^D for the judgment.

The suggestion is strong that positive secondary reinforcement figures in the explanation of 'joys'—like the joy of revisiting 'the scenes of our childhood.' Apparently the source lies in the reinforcements connected with familiar places, people, things, and actions. The loss or absence of old secondary reinforcers, on the other hand, seems often to be at the heart of our 'sorrows.' Homesickness; dejection at the death of a friend; regret at the passing of old landmarks; yearning for 'the snows of yester-year'—do not these suggest the loss of $S^{r.D}$'s? Indeed, the tie-up of secondary reinforcement and "feeling" seems to pervade our whole lives as social organisms. The process of socialization has to do with acquiring those modes and standards of behavior which are typical of the society in which the individual grows. Because all of our reinforcements occur in a given social environment, and because society often makes reinforcement contingent upon our doing and saying 'the proper things,' we may come to like and prefer as 'naturally pleasing' our own particular way of life, and this or that style of music or art. Even our group prejudices, our small talk, our ambitions, our religion, our special forms of virtue (and vice), appear to have their roots in this basic principle of human behavior. The very language we speak is an edifice reared upon secondary reinforcement. In a foreign land, we thrill to the sound of our native tongue; at home we enjoy the writer or speaker in whose verbal skill dwell many of our strongest secondary reinforcements. We find that poet satisfying who artfully sets up in us the verbal chains that *he* is using, so that his next word, and his next, come almost as the completions of what *we* were about to say! In the verbal interplay between writer and reader, between speaker and listener, it is the writer's or speaker's art to start up in us those 'thoughts' which *agree* with his, bringing us together in the same responses, making us say the same things, or supply the same rhyme. Such an outcome is truly 'pleasant,' even overpowering, because the poet and we have been speaking in the same way together, exchanging our 'desires' and 'passions' and our tears in perfect harmony—a relationship as near to the purely social as we can conceive, and as matchless an example of secondary reinforcement as man can create or find.

Secondary Reinforcement in Social Behavior

As implied above, a stimulus controlling behavior as an S^D, S^r, or $S^{r.D}$ need not stem from the inanimate environment alone. Other organisms (or, the stimuli emanating from them) can act in these ways, too, and therein lies a fact of utmost significance to human as well as other biological life. Social behavior may be described as *behavior for which the reinforcing or discriminative stimuli are, or have been, mediated by the behavior of another organism.* By "mediated" we mean "arising from, or in connection with," and there is no intention of straining the word's connotation. We would neither (1) include as social the delivery of a pellet by the experimenter to a bar-pressing rat—it may be a social situation for the experimenter, but it is not for the rat; nor (2) exclude as non-social the behavior of the marooned sailor who speaks to himself or makes clothes out of skins, since both activities have been socially acquired.

From birth on, social stimuli play a large part in the life of human beings. Many scientists, indeed, have thought that society itself has its origins in the protracted and utter dependence of the human infant. However that may be, parents, and especially the mother, are among the first secondary reinforcers of a social sort to enter the infant's ken. Their discriminative and reinforcing potency are quickly established by their continual association with food, warmth, relief from pain, and the like. If, however, the child is reared by a nurse, then she becomes the ever-present secondary reinforcement, and it is commonly seen that attachment to the nurse replaces that to the mother. Psychiatrists have pointed out that, in adolescence and before, the first sexually interesting objects may be the parents, brothers, or sisters. Within the relatively restricted social environment of the child, the few organisms who serve as the accompanying stimuli when reinforcement is given or withheld can acquire an overspreading and life-long grip on his behavior. With increasing age, the child's widening excursions beyond the home provide an increasing range of secondary reinforcers to control his reactions. School, friends, clubs, and related activities of all sorts—these push upon him the stimuli which are the ever-present signals and accompaniments of ultimate reinforcement, the S^D's and the S^r's which are the warp and woof of his life in society.

Although the theme of *anxiety* will be developed later (see Chapter 9), we should recognize in passing that social stimuli can also act as secondary *negative* reinforcers. As we shall see, the behavior which occurs in the interval between an S^D and a negative reinforcement is characterized by a depression of operant activity and the onset of respondent changes. The laboratory study of anxiety (induced experimentally by using the S^D-negative reinforcement sequence) has numerous implications for everyday affairs. A child raised in a rigid and over-disciplined home, will suffer many punishments through the prescriptions and prohibitions imposed upon him. The adolescent, having to cope with his newly acquired social status, encounters many pitfalls and rebuffs before he learns acceptable modes of behavior. In these and similar instances, *persons* are the appliers of punishment or emotion-arousing stimuli, and, by this association, themselves become secondary negative reinforcements. Through stimulus generalization, other persons may be included within this category. The result may be a depression of activity in their presence, avoidance of people, seclusiveness; in short, there may develop anti-social and maladjusted behavior so alarming to the clinical psychologist or mental hygienist. Where external positive reinforcements of the secondary sort are radically reduced, and where negative reinforcements crowd too strongly upon a man, the final outcome may be complete 'withdrawal from the world'—as seen in the psychosis of schizophrenia. Even in the normal development of children it has long been remarked that age is accompanied by an increase in the sheer number of things feared. The six-month-old infant has few fears; the six-year-old has many. This is the upshot of increasing experience with negative reinforcement in an ever enlarging world, with the consequent multiplication of S^D's for fear. Lower animals may learn most of their fears at the hands of their natural environment; man gets most of his at the heedless or unmerciful hands of his fellow creatures.

Taking Stock and Looking Ahead

Far back in this book we said that human behavior is the final object of interest to most psychologists, as it is to the layman. In reaching our goal, the principle of secondary reinforcement will be of great analytical assistance. When added to the other functions of stimuli, it gives us a powerful and indispensable tool for the solution of many vexing and absorbing problems of human action. It will not escape the thoughtful student that the following points go far toward explaining the elaborate and ramified behavior of organisms high in the evolutionary scale, and of old organisms as against young. Given an undeveloped creature to whom few primary reinforcements may be relevant, the following facts allow us to augment our control over his maturing operant repertory in ever increasing fashion.

1. A stimulus that occasions or accompanies a reinforcement acquires thereby reinforcing value of its own, and may be called a conditioned, secondary, or derived reinforcement. A secondary reinforcement may be extinguished when repeatedly applied to a response for which there is no ultimate primary reinforcement.

2. A secondary reinforcement is positive when the reinforcement with which it is correlated is positive, and negative when the latter is negative.

3. Once established, a secondary reinforcement is independent and non-specific; it will not only strengthen the same response which produced the original reinforcement, but it will also condition a new and unrelated response. Moreover, it will do so even in the presence of a different basic motive.

4. Through generalization, many stimuli besides the one correlated with reinforcement acquire reinforcing value—positive or negative. This point was not stressed in the present chapter but it should require no elaboration here.

Finally, it should be remembered that, in everyday life,

stimuli are not single, that responses are not all alike, and that learning is not all done under the same drive. *Many stimuli* are present when a response is conditioned, all becoming discriminative and secondarily reinforcing; *many responses* are capable of obtaining the same reinforcement; and *more than one drive* (hunger, thirst, etc.) may be satisfied at various times by the same responses and in the presence of the same stimuli. Truly, the study of behavior is a lofty challenge to scientific imagination and method!

NOTES

There is no book on secondary reinforcement to which we can send you for additional information. Hull, however, in his *Principles of behavior* (1943), has devoted a chapter to this important principle. (Almost any text in social or abnormal psychology will, of course, provide you with numerous examples of its operation.) You ought now, however, to be able to follow with little trouble the growing experimental literature in this area. Access to these reports may be gained by way of the *Psychological Abstracts,* a journal that contains short summaries of all articles and books assumed to have any interest whatever for psychologists.

In terms of the relation of behavior to the environment of an organism, the present chapter takes us almost as far as we can go. No more than two functions of stimuli remain to be considered, and nothing new will be said about the basic processes of conditioning, extinction, and the like. In fact, if you have followed our discussion up to this point with moderate success, you possess most of the available tools for behavioral analysis. From now on, we shall be interested in the kind of environmental control that induces changes in the *state* of an organism—as when we deprive an animal of food or water. In our talk of motivation and emotion in the next two chapters, you will see that we do little more than shift the focus of our attention—say, from reinforcement to some previously unmentioned conditions under which stimuli become reinforcing. In Chapter 11, we shall try to point out the direction one might profitably take in carrying the principles into the realm of human interaction.

9

MOTIVATION

It is by the pleasure of exertion, and the pain of inexertion, that we are roused from that indolence, into which . . . we otherwise might sink: as we are roused, in like manner, by the pleasure of food, and the pain of hunger, we take the aliment that is necessary for our individual sustenance; and though the mere aliment is, indeed, more important for life, it is not more important for happiness than the pleasure of activity which calls and forces us from slothful repose.

> Thomas Brown, *Lectures on the Philosophy of the Human Mind*, 1822

A New Line of Inquiry

We have been occupied in exploring the principle of reinforcement and the manner in which the environment controls organisms by way of stimuli. From this single starting point, we have been able to take large strides in understanding why men and lower animals behave as they do. Yet students of psychology, in past times and present, have felt or known that a description of behavior would be incomplete without taking into account another kind of controlling factor which today we call *motivation.*

Common experience reveals the existence of this factor so vividly that men everywhere have evolved a vocabulary and set of ideas for explaining and speaking of it. Growing up in a social community as we do, we are taught the prevailing words and concepts. These seem consequently, to be right, natural, and but common sense. Unhappily, there are few areas in psychology where popular notions contain a more alluring blend of correct and incorrect observations, of valid and biased thinking, of wise and foolish conclusions. Our first task, if we are to make progress in this new line of inquiry, is to begin aright.

Ordinarily, our questions about motives occur in connection with complex types of human interaction. We feel that unless we know the underlying motives we shall not be able to deal effectively with ourselves and others in the many important affairs of everyday life. *Why does each person seek popularity? Why do men marry as they do, and whom they do? Why do men fight and take pleasure in killing?* Our analysis cannot *start* with such samples of behavior, but rather with fundamentals and experimentally verifiable data. The initial aim is to get a proper foundation for further building, not a blueprint for a superstructure which may require endless revision, or may be totally useless, as the basic facts come to be known. Only in this way can we make the scientific progress we want and need.

The Need for the Concept of Motivation

Oddly enough, it is the very first step toward comprehending motives (*drives* is a synonym) which often proves the hardest for the beginning student to take. What is demanded is that he lay aside long-favored personal opinions, and examine *de novo* the reasons for believing that a science of behavior cannot get along *without* motivation! Only if there were observations of behavior not encompassed by the principles set forth in the earlier chapters, would we be required to formulate new concepts to deal with the data. The present chapter is, in fact, devoted to just such observations. Let us take the 'hunger drive' as an example.

Neither rats nor men eat continuously, but at fairly definite intervals and in fairly definite amounts. This fact is banal enough to most persons, who would probably say that an organism eats when 'hungry' and stops when 'full.' But it may do us good to question the obvious, wherein at times have lain concealed some astonishing natural phenomena. So, with a suspicion that this is a phase of behavior worth inspecting, we take to the laboratory; and soon our critical sense is prodded by further discoveries. We find that a bar-trained rat, left in his box or working-cage to obtain all of his meals by pressing, will eat in a fairly regular cycle and only so much at any one time. In a twenty-four-hour period, he may eat on ten or twelve occasions only, each time at a slow but constant rate. When given but *one* meal a day, always at the same hour, a curve like that in Figure 7 (page 43) will be produced. When placed in the box, right after a meal, he will not eat at all. Moreover, an animal cannot be conditioned to salivate (Type S) or press a bar for food (Type R) unless hungry.

These facts may leave you unmoved. Did we not assume all along that hunger or some other drive is required in experiments dealing with stimulus-controlled behavior? Yes, we did; but now we realize that we have on our hands a phenomenon that deserves special consideration. For, trimmed down, our observations are that (1) depriving an animal of food is a way of increasing the strength of a conditioned reflex like bar-pressing; that concurrently, (2) many other reflexes rise in strength, such as reaching, seizing, and chewing; that (3) with sufficient intake of food (*satiation*), these reflexes drop in strength to zero; and that (4) food-deprivation is itself a prerequisite for using food as reinforcement—that a reinforcer is such by virtue of some operation that makes it act so.

It is in this way that the need for the concept of motivation as a new variable in behavior arises. It is because responses can be controlled in other ways than by reinforcement, that a new descriptive term is called for and a new behavioral concept emerges. What shall we say about occurrences like feeding and fasting which affect reflex strength? How many types of such occurrences are there? How can we exercise control over them and, through them, over the organism? How many degrees of each can be set up? How can they be measured? What new experiments do they suggest, and what new knowledge will they generate? How are they related to conditioning, extinction, discrimination, and the like? These questions and many similar ones soon lose their 'obvious' character.

The Nature of Drives

To the question *What is drive?*, we must now answer that drive is the *name* for a fact—the fact that certain operations can be performed on an organism (for example, depriving it of food) that have an effect upon behavior which is different from that of other operations. Drive is not a *thing*, but simply a word we use to show our recognition that behavioral functions which may depend on reinforcement are also modifiable by another influence, one exerted by occurrences which do not involve reinforcement.

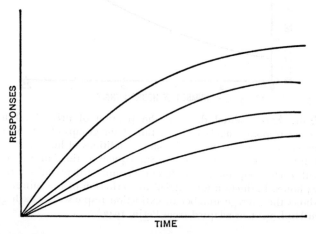

Fig. 60. Illustrating how varying drive levels during extinction act as a parameter of the extinction curve. The higher the drive, the greater the number of responses made and the more rapidly they are emitted.

The observation that 'neither rats nor men eat continuously' requires an analysis that, after all, is rather distant from everyday levels of conversation. Words like *motive* and *drive*, drawn from the common vocabulary, do not explicitly denote the relation with which we are now concerned. Perhaps the idea will become more acceptable as we examine it from different angles and express it in different ways, with a few experimental examples.

1. *Drive in extinction.* It has been quite well established (e.g., Perin, 1942) that the process of extinction is influenced by the drive factor. The experimental design, urged by the initial observation that a bar-trained rat will not press when satiated, is simply this: Expose groups of animals to equal

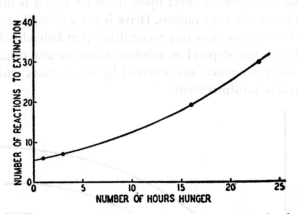

FIG. 61. Experimental data on the relation of drive level to the number of responses made in extinction. Four groups of rats were conditioned to bar-pressing under the same conditions of hunger and given equal numbers of reinforcements. Subsequent extinction was carried out with each group under a different amount of deprivation: 1, 3, 16, and 23 hours. Extinction was carried to a criterion of five minutes. The plot shows the average number of extinction responses for each group. (From Hull, 1943, as adapted from Perin, 1942.)

amounts of training under equal deprivation, and then extinguish the response under different lengths-of-deprivation to see whether the number of pressings they make co-varies with deprivation time at extinction. A fair number of experiments have been made on this question, with good agreement that deprivation time does act as an important variable. The idealized finding is shown in Figure 60 indicating that, in addition to the height of the cumulative response curve reached, the early rate of emission is also affected. Such experiments give substance to the concept of motivation as a determinant of behavior supplementing reinforcement. Technically, we may say that drive, here specified in terms of deprivation time, is a "parameter" of extinction.

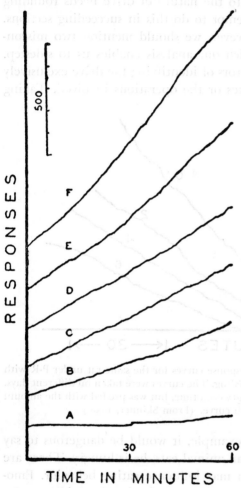

2. *Drive in periodic reconditioning.* Our second example of how the motivation concept derives from the effect of an operation like food-deprivation, is taken from periodic reconditioning. An animal placed on a schedule of P-R at a fixed interval of, say, three minutes, will give cumulative response curves of varying slopes. That is, the rate of responding, within wide limits, increases with increased deprivation (see Figure 62). Similar results are obtained if, instead of varying deprivation time, we deprive all

FIG. 62. Cumulative response curves for one rat under P-R on six successive days in which no food was given beyond the pellet reinforcements during the sessions. The increasing drive is reflected in the rising slopes of the curves. (From Skinner, 1938.)

animals at the same time but provide them with different
amounts of food just before using them in a P-R session (see
Figure 63).

This introduction to the nature of drive needs rounding
out, and we shall attempt to do this in succeeding sections.
Before going on, however, we should mention two misconceptions of drive which our analysis enables us to sidestep.
These are the twin errors of identifying the drive exclusively
with either the reflexes or the operations involved. Taking

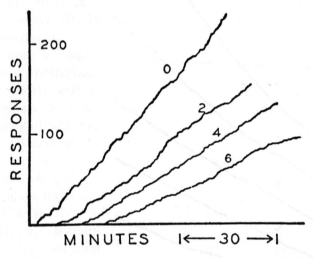

Fig. 63. Cumulative response curves for the same rat under P-R with
varying amounts of pre-feeding. The curves were taken on different days.
The rat was 24-hours hungry each time, but was pre-fed with the amount
in grams indicated on each curve. (From Skinner, 1938.)

hunger again as our example, it would be dangerous to say
that, merely because an animal eats, he is hungry. There are
many variables which may influence eating behavior. Emotional excitement can make an animal stop eating, or the
introduction of another animal into the situation may cause
him to resume eating after he has stopped; and human beings
may eat for social reasons or starve for political ones. Mere
eating at any given time is an inadequate criterion of hunger

unless we know what preceded the eating. On the other hand, identifying a drive with its establishing operation, such as deprivation, is also wrong. There are many deprivations which are of no consequence in determining behavior (for example, depriving a rat of organ music)—which do not establish a drive. The truth of the matter is that when we notice changes in reflex strength we look for corresponding operations, the two things *together* leading us to infer the drive. It is because everyday observation gives us prior knowledge that food deprivation has an effect on response that we accept it alone as 'hunger'. We would gain little from argument as to whether a starving mystic, in the throes of his elation, is 'hungry' or not! And phrases like 'a twenty-four-hour hungry rat' or 'a drive level of sixteen hours,' commonly used as a concession to convenience, should always be understood to mean 'twenty-four or sixteen hours of *deprivation*.'

Drive as an "Internal State"

It would be cumbersome in talking and thinking about drive to have always to do so in long and meticulous statements about its nature as 'a change in reflex strength attributable to some operation performed either experimentally or naturally . . .' and so on. The word *drive* is a shorthand device, a convenience of expression, for both the concept of motivation and the facts subsumed thereunder. We do no harm in using it as long as we know that it is an ultimately dispensable word, and that we can return to our analysis of it when necessary. It is like the word *force* in physics where, in the end, it must be refined and analyzed, but where it is a handy word in many connections. The danger associated with the psychologist's drive and the physicist's force is that of letting oneself be misled into the false issues that are raised by vague everyday references.

Similar considerations apply to the designation of drive as an 'inferred internal state.' This phrase simply recognizes that the effects of an operation like food deprivation are ramified throughout both the physiology and behavior of the organism. Physiologically, there are numberless reverberations and correlates of the operation. These, in a scientific division of labor, are within the province of the physiologist, the chemist, the biophysicist. The concept of drive, however, is a behavioral one; and the physiological effects are not the drive. Behaviorally, a drive is marked by *concurrent changes in the strength of many reflexes*. A food-deprived animal not only presses a bar more frequently and eats more vigorously, but many other reflexes change at the same time (e.g., climbing, sniffing, and running about) if the bar is not present, giving us the impression of increased general activity and restlessness. This makes it appear that the operation has changed the creature in some over-all way, and makes the notion of a 'state of the organism' more palatable.

Very few persons would question that the state is 'inferrable' from the observations, or that it must be 'internal' in nature; and they would probably approve a formula such as this:

Observable *1st Term or Event*	*Construct or* *Intervening Term*	*Observable* *2nd Term or Event*
OPERATION (e.g., food deprivation)	'STATE' (e.g., of hunger)	REFLEX CHANGES (e.g., strengthening of bar-pressing, weakening of grooming behavior, etc.)

Yet, despite the validity of the observations, the phrase 'inferred internal state' adds nothing to our knowledge of drive, because it denotes nothing beyond that which is contained within the observations themselves. It is, once again, a convenience of expression, and we might dispense with the term altogether if it were not for the effort involved in straining for technical purity.

We have given much space to the clarification of the nature of drives, and the difficulties which come from popular usages. If our points are kept in mind, it will be unnecessary for us to forego the advantages of ease and succinctness which inhere in our ready-made and ingrained vocabulary. Instead of devising new symbols, we can adopt familiar speech if at the same time we remember that we have an agreed-upon analysis to fall back on whenever it is needed to reason out new motivational problems or re-examine old ones. We shall, then, henceforth use expressions like 'establishing a drive,' 'reducing a drive,' and others, because they are neat, but in every instance our abbreviated phrase can be translated into the more correct and expanded form that our discussion has supplied.

Discovering Drives

One of the commonest questions asked of students of motivation is *How many drives are there?* To this there is no answer but a tentative one. The number of drives which exist for any species of organism is not determined by any man's say-so, and no list can be given except in so far as the drives are known today. One who wishes to draw up a list must be prepared to defend it by citing his evidence for each one that he includes, since a drive is not a matter of opinion but of proof. He must be able to demonstrate that, as a consequence of some operation, reinforcement and conditioning are made possible; that the operation leads to changes in strength of a previously conditioned reflex and, concurrently, of others; and so on. And, later, if new evidence is forthcoming to show that a drive has been unwittingly omitted, he must be ready to accept it and add it to his list.

The fact that evidence must be found for a drive means, of course, that drives are *discovered*. There is no way of telling in advance how many will be finally found, and all attempts at enumeration are provisional. The situation is not unlike that surrounding the discovery of chemical elements before Mendeleev's periodic table, or since modern atomic research showed how to create new substances. At neither time could the number of obtainable elements be predicted with certainty. The explorer into drives faces two problems. On the one hand, he may set out to discover drive factors in behavior which were not hitherto suspected. An example is that of the so-called "sub-hungers" which are established, not by gross food deprivation, but by particular deficiencies in diet, such as lack of calcium. Sub-hungers act on reflex strength to direct an animal's choice of foods (his selective eating) from among many that are simultaneously proffered. These sub-types of hunger were unearthed in recent years after chemistry and dietetics gave inspiration to the idea and made possible the appropriate depriving operations. On the other hand, the explorer may guess that a drive influence is at work but may not have the establishing operation at his command. The operations for hunger and thirst have been known to all men throughout the ages, but this is not true of such a well-recognized drive as sex. Although, in the females of many species, this drive has long been known to undergo cyclic changes as a function of time, it has only recently been possible to exercise regulation through glandular extracts, surgical incursion into sex tissues, and so on. The discovery, classification, measurement, and study of any drive are inextricably related to the identification of (and, hopefully, mastery over) its establishing operations.

In addition to their incompleteness, lists of drives would be different for different types of living organisms. An operation which strongly affects the behavior of one species may have little or no import for another. Broadly viewed, the amount of similarity in motivation from one species to another depends upon their evolutionary closeness, but this does not alter the need for separate listings and proofs. Fortunately, we are not here concerned with cataloguing, but with an introduction to the nature of drives, to some important ones that human beings share with other organisms, and to the problems of experimental investigation. It is to these ends that our later discussion of a few representative drives is mainly directed.

The Measurement of Drives

If you have followed the preceding points, you should have no difficulty with the next. The matter of measuring drives (or drive level, or drive strength) is always approached incorrectly by one who thinks of a motive as a substantive thing rather than a set of relations between an establishing operation and behavioral changes. You can readily see that what we measure is behavior; that, in practice, any method purporting to measure drive is one that measures reflex strength as it changes with different degrees of a selected operation. The establishing operation is our independent variable, the behavior our dependent variable; the former is specifiable as to kind and degree, the latter is measured for extent of change. The concomitant variation of the two gives rise to, and defines, the concept and the problem of motivation.

It follows, therefore, that there are as many ways of getting at any drive as there are behavioral effects that can be measured. There is no single consequence of an operation like, say, food deprivation, that must be depended on; any concomitant change in response may be taken. In studying or discovering drives, it is important to find an appropriate response that undergoes clear enough, and large enough, changes to yield significant co-variation with the operation. A poor choice can make it seem that the operation has had no effect on behavior (is not really drive-establishing), but trial with another reflex may give immediate success.

It would be superfluous, even if it were possible, to catalog all the reflexes that have been measured in studies of motivation. The particular one selected by an investigator is only incidental to his purpose of learning something about drive. Fortunately, the number of reflex *properties* and characteristics that can be measured is not so great as to make burdensome our task of selection. Here we find, as you would expect, such familiar aspects of responding as rate, latency, force, and the like, all of which are old friends in the analysis of behavior and require no further treatment here. In our later discussion of several representative drives, we shall see with greater clarity and in more detail how these measures are employed.

Two Classes of Drives

As we have pointed out before, many historical observations of human and animal behavior have contained elements of great accuracy and faithfulness to nature. The age-old division of motives into *appetites* and *aversions* is based upon such observations, and remains useful to modern scientists.

The twofold classification of drives arises from certain natural differences. (1) The actual operations which establish drives may be those of *deprivation* (for example, of food or water) or *stimulation* (as by electric shock or painfully strong lights or noises). (2) The types of reinforcement which are effective after, or appropriate to, these two operations also differ. (3) Appetites can be reduced or satiated, whereas aver- sions cannot. Thus, given sufficient food, hunger is erased; but an animal that is aversive to electric shock or strong light cannot be satiated with no-shock or darkness. (4) Most dep- rivations must extend over some length of time before their drive effects become evident. The build-up may require hours, days, or weeks (think of thirst, sex, and the sub- hungers). By contrast, aversive stimuli act, for all practical purposes, immediately. No sooner are they applied than they result in widespread reflex changes and set up the conditions for the strengthening of responses that remove them.

With respect to aversions, it is likely that *any* stimulus, sufficiently intense, may be drive-inducing. The intensity of stimuli forms a physical continuum going from zero to ex- treme magnitudes. At low but supra-liminal values they may serve an elicitative or discriminative function while remain- ing motivationally neutral, in that the animal will neither 'work for them' nor 'seek to get rid of them.' At moderate to high values, they may take on an aversive quality, and re-

sponses may be strengthened by their removal. Extreme
intensities of stimuli may, through their 'emotional' effect,
be no longer suitable for discriminative or aversive purposes.
(For further discussion, see Chapter 10.) At any rate, an
attempt to list the known drives should probably, therefore,
include under aversions a reference to all the stimuli to
which an organism is responsive, with the understanding
that this holds for a given, but as yet indeterminate, range of
intensity values.

Table X

RELATION OF DRIVE-OPERATIONS TO REINFORCEMENT AND SUBSEQUENT
BEHAVIOR

Operation or Natural event } →Drive	Contingency (What the response accomplishes)	Effect of contingency on response strength
Deprivation→Appetite	a. obtaining the subtance (e.g. food): "positive reinforcement."	a. Raises strength.
	b. not obtaining the substance (e.g. food): "withholding positive reinforcement."	b. Lowers strength (or fails to condition), plus possible emotional effects.
Stimulation→Aversion	a. removing stimulus (e.g. shock): "positive reinforcement."	a. Raises strength.
	b. Not removing stimulus: "withholding positive reinforcement."	b. Lowers strength (or fails to condition), plus depressed or emotional behavior.

Some Misconceptions about Drive

The modern conception of motives has taken firm shape only in the last few decades. Before that, motivation was discussed from many standpoints, and, since the available facts were few, it is not surprising that many different conclusions were drawn. Our heritage from those years, as is so frequently the case in the history of science, is a mixture of valuable observations and now-discarded theories. We willingly accept the former, but hasten to correct the latter when they creep into modern thinking. For this reason we must pause here to indicate some outmoded notions of drive which seem especially productive of confusion in a present-day context.

1. *A drive is not a stimulus.* Historically, a stimulus was treated as a goad (*stimulus* is the Latin word for goad) and was often confused with motivation (*motive* means "movement-initiating"). These are, of course, only manners of speaking and are of little factual or theoretical value. A drive has neither the status, nor the functions, nor the place in a reflex, that a stimulus has. It is not a part, or a change in a part, of the environment; it is not, in itself, either eliciting, reinforcing, or discriminative; and it is not correlated with a single response (as is the stimulus) to give us our behavioral *unit,* the reflex. True, the distinction between state and stimulus is hard to maintain when we consider the aversions, which are *stimulus-produced* states, but we must not confuse the effect of the stimulus with the stimulus itself. We would say that the aversive stimulus sets up a drive, one effect of which is to change the momentary strength of a group of reflexes and another to make reinforcement possible. But to say that a stimulus excites one or more stimulus-response relations directly is to deal in absurdity, leading us to such a paradigm as this: $S\text{------}(S\text{------}R)$.

Another difficulty in keeping drives and stimuli distinct lies in the fact that there are internal stimuli which *accompany* drives and may serve as S^D's for a response. Thus, an operation like food-deprivation which establishes the hunger drive also gives rise to internal stimuli which may, in turn, occasion a response of one sort or another—perhaps the verbalization *I'm hungry*. There is no cause to equate two things merely because they co-exist, when actually they have different properties and play different rôles in the control of behavior. A drive is not identifiable with the stimuli it may itself evoke.

2. *A drive is not a response.* Although a motive involves behavioral changes, it is not in itself a response. An organism does not 'respond' (except in a figurative way) to an aversive stimulus or an appetitive deprivation by developing a drive state. Drive is established by these operations, but is not a response to them in any proper sense of the word. To put it in another way, a motive is neither a smooth-muscle or glandular respondent nor a skeletal-muscle operant.

3. *A drive is not a physiological concept.* Everyone acknowledges that behavior is the behavior of an organism, and is consequently accompanied by physiological, chemical, mechanical, electrical, atomic, and other processes in that organism. One must also acknowledge that drive-establishing operations have similar broad consequences. But these facts do not compromise the status of drive as a behavioral concept. The concept arises from behavioral data, and it is in a science of behavior that it is required. The physiologist has no need for drive in his account of, say, blood changes during hunger. He correlates these changes with food-deprivation, just as we do reflex changes; and his correlations are physiological principles, while ours are behavioral ones. The laws of behavior are not the laws of physiology, neurology, chemistry, or physics. Yet, one disadvantage of treating drive, even fictitiously, as a 'state,' is the tendency it fosters in the beginning student to think of it as something physiological which intervenes between the establishing operation and the reflex changes. This habit of thought is readily acquired by one who believes that behavior 'cannot really be understood' without reference to 'underlying bodily processes.' In the end, however, the

'understanding' of behavior depends upon finding lawfulness *in* behavior and, once found, it should not be ignored or renounced in favor of lawfulness in physiology or any other subject matter.

4. *A drive is not pleasure-directed.* Motives involve neither the purposive nor the pleasure principle commonly discussed by the philosopher. When one says that an organism 'wants to obtain pleasure' or 'works to get the satisfying reward,' he uses a manner of speech which dimly expresses the action of reinforcement in strengthening a response. We have noted (page 255) that *pleasant* is a human verbal response that may be attached to certain S^D's and is related to the appropriateness of a reinforcer to the prevailing drive. Hedonic philosophies do not stick close to the facts of behavior in ascribing an objective existence to pleasure, and stressing the procurement of pleasure *per se* as a motive or the purpose of all motives. We do not deprive an organism of pleasure, but of food; we do not reduce hunger with pleasure, but with food, and the purpose of the organism is irrelevant to either deprivation or satiation.

SOME REPRESENTATIVE DRIVES: ACTIVITY DRIVE

Every response, whether operant or respondent, is an activity and, in this sense, every psychological experiment deals with activity. But the terms *activity drive* and *general activity* have a different and definite meaning as they are applied to the motivational and behavioral characteristics of an organism. Activity drive is classed among the appetites, and is the source of action when other reasons for behaving are ruled out or controlled. In nature, periods of activity are preceded by periods of inactivity during which the need increases, just as hunger drive appears in an alternation of eating and not-eating. The fundamental operation, then, is deprivation, and activity drive can be controlled in the laboratory by experimentally varying the deprivation time (i.e., by imposing variable periods of inactivity).

The drive is manifested in general activity, by which is meant the total over-all movement, or getting-around, of the animal. As we shall see, it is not necessary in measuring general activity to dissect it into its component specific responses like running, climbing, scratching, and so on. It may be recorded as though it were a single thing, although actually it is the gross sum of all the reflexes which have been increased in emission rate because of the drive operation. It is possible, however, and desirable in many connections, to use one component of activity as a measure of the whole, because the rise in strength of the component is a reflection of the general increase. General activity is influenced by other motives than activity drive (all drives produce concurrent changes in the strength of many reflexes), and it may then serve as an indicator of the presence of these others. It is only when these others are not present that one speaks of a genuine activity drive.

An Illustrative Series of Experiments

In 1922, Richter introduced a new method for recording the general activity of the rat. This made use of a triangular cage mounted on rubber tambours which were connected by air tubes to a kymograph recorder. As the animal moved about the cage, the shifting weight on the tambours affected the air pressure in the system, producing greater or less agitation of the kymograph pen depending upon the amount of movement, thus giving a measure of total activity.

In one experiment, with other drives and external stimuli controlled, evidence for the activity drive was sought, and found, in continuous twenty-four-hour records of the activity occurring "spontaneously" with the mere passage of time. Active periods were seen to appear (ten to fifteen times per day) with good regularity of spacing and duration. This depended somewhat upon the age of the animal, both young and old animals being less active than those in their prime.

Although there were individual differences among animals at every age, each one revealed typical bursts of activity. The demonstration of pure activity drive has been paralleled with other organisms than the rat, and the drive has turned out to be a factor that has to be reckoned with in a great variety of psychological experiments.

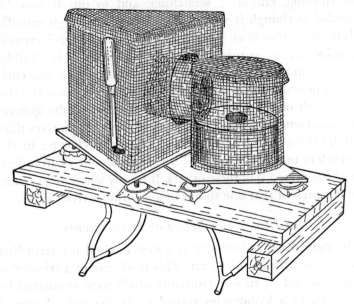

FIG. 64. Richter's tambour-mounted activity apparatus.
(After Richter, 1922.)

With the same apparatus, Richter went on to study the relation of various drive-establishing operations to general activity. He found that his method, although lumping together all changes in reflex strength into the single measure of activity, was sensitive enough to show up the effects of the different operations. Thus, in an experiment with hunger, a group of rats was put on a twenty-four-hour eating rhythm. Each animal was allowed to eat to satiation from an unlimited supply once a day at the same hour, fresh water being always present. Half of the group was then deprived of both food and water, while the other half was deprived of food alone, and the deprivations were continued without break until all the animals were dead. Each rat lived in his own tambour-mounted cage for the duration of the experiment, and continuous twenty-four-hour activity records were taken. The results showed several things. In the first stage of the experiment, the twenty-four-hour rhythmic hunger sent activity above the usual level for satiated animals. Moreover, the temporal pattern of the activity over the day took on a characteristic form, there being a rise about twelve hours after a meal and another as the next mealtime approached. When the continuous deprivation was started, the rats without food and water showed regular *decreases* in activity until the fifth day when all activity ceased (shortly before death), whereas those with food-deprivation only *increased* their activity for the first few days and then dropped off to zero (eighth day). The addition of thirst to hunger, then, gave a different result from a mere increase in the effect of hunger alone.

Richter also tested the effect of temperature on activity. Three temperature levels were used: 10-15°, 23°, and 29-30° Centigrade. The rats were on a twenty-four-hour eating rhythm, with all other conditions controlled. He found less activity at either extreme than at 23° Centigrade. Experiments by other men, and with other organisms, support the general finding that a temperature drive, certainly among warm-blooded animals, is as valid a drive as any. Mass migrations, and the perennial flight of city dwellers to the seaside during a heat wave, bear witness to the power of a few millimeters of mercury in a thermometer column.

In still another experiment, Richter studied the 'nocturnality' of rats, that is, the effect of illumination on activity. The animals spent alternate twelve-hour periods in the light and in the dark, these periods being controlled by the experimenter without reference to the natural day-night cycle. Before recording was started, they were put on a twenty-four-hour eating rhythm. To insure no contamination of the records by activity related to feeding time, half the rats were fed just before the twelve-hour light period and half before the dark. Activity was found to be higher in the dark than in the light, with the difference increasing for older animals. This result has been confirmed by other investigators (Hunt and Schlosberg, 1939) and is related to the depressive effect of light upon bar-pressing (Skinner, 1938), as well as the study of the light-aversion drive to which we shall return presently.

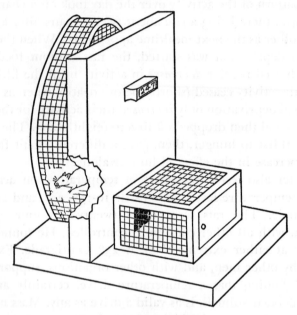

FIG. 65. An activity wheel.

In addition to the tambour-mounted cage, Richter employed a laboratory device which had been in use for some time before his work, the *activity wheel*. This apparatus is an enclosed wheel, suspended by its axle so that it rotates easily, the arrangement being that of a circular tread-mill. From a living cage set by its side, the rat can enter the wheel whenever the door is opened, and run as much and as fast as he wishes, with the wheel turning faster as he runs faster. Each rotation is automatically tallied on a counter, and readings can be taken for any period without disturbing the animal. The wheel does not provide an index of general activity in the same way as the tambour-mounted cage, since only straight-away running is counted and neither lateral movements within the wheel nor partial revolutions are recorded. Nevertheless, data obtained with this device are highly correlated with those from recorders like Richter's, and can therefore be taken as an equivalent measure. Using the wheel, Richter and other workers have confirmed and supplemented the earlier findings on pure activity drive and the effects upon activity of hunger, age, and other factors. Of especial interest is the finding that activity varies as a function of deprivation. If a rat is confined to a small cage and denied access to the wheel except for a short daily period, he will do more running in the time allowed than he would do otherwise; the drive apparently works like any other appetite in this respect.

Other Illustrations of Activity Drive

There are many indications of activity drive in non-experimental situations which point to its reality. Caged animals in zoos have periods of activity which visitors try to catch. Lions and tigers pace, elephants sway and 'dance,' seals swim and dive, monkeys climb and chase—although other drives may be taken care of and the activity may seem 'unnecessary.' City dogs, ordinarily in leash, jump and run and roll on the ground when freed in a park or meadow, not unlike children let loose from school or spending the first hours of a country vacation. Some observers have even reported that human infants, overly restricted in movement, 'work off' their activity in rhythmic swayings, rockings, and jouncings within their play-pens or cribs. Such instances seem reasonably clear in terms of activity drive and activity deprivation.

Activity and the Operant Level

It was noted earlier (page 76) that the operant level of any representative reflex is related to two things: the general activity of the organism, and the ease of conditioning that response. The introduction of a drive like hunger is relevant to both of these. Not only does it put into our hands the power of reinforcement, hence of conditioning, but it also expedites the conditioning by raising the general activity. This rise will, if we have properly chosen our reflex, carry along with it the operant level, so that the response becomes more available for reinforcement and our chances of reinforcing and conditioning it quickly are enhanced.

Other factors, of course, may enter in setting the operant level. There are species differences (think of the relative activity of a turtle and a mouse); there are age differences within any one species; and you can probably think of half a dozen additional determiners. Species differences are especially important when it comes to the form of the response to be conditioned. Pigeons can be taught to peck at targets, rats to press bars, monkeys to turn keys or lift latches, and so forth. The response, naturally, must be within the organism's capacity. Usually we select one that is easy, or natural, for the species in question. If one decides to use a response which, though *possible* for the organism but having an almost-zero operant level, conditioning will be slow and may even require a gradual differentiation.

HUNGER DRIVE

The beginning of scientific research on hunger is of interest, among other reasons, because it shows how, in the gradual refinement of a concept, different paths may be taken by different people; how, by experiment and hypothesis, exploration and reasoning, proof and counter-proof, there is finally left a residue of agreed-upon facts and conclusions which are incorporated within the body of scientific theory. In using hunger as our model in the preceding pages, we have already said a good deal about this drive. We may, however, tell a bit of the early history of hunger research as a setting for some further facts.

Richter's work on activity and hunger drive, together with information already at hand, contained within it the essence of a proper formulation of hunger and, indeed, of all drives. He had performed a deprivation; he had observed concurrent changes in the strength of many reflexes ('heightened activity'); and he had two techniques for measuring these changes (the tambour-mounted cage and the running wheel). Moreover, his techniques were able to measure the *degree* of the drive, that is, they showed the co-variation of amount of response change with amount of deprivation. With this ground-work laid, the concept of drive was ready to be developed. At this point, however, he and other workers were diverted by a strong contemporary interest in the physiological correlates of hunger, and the appropriate behavioral concept of motives was side-tracked for several years. The physiological studies were centered upon events in the stomach resulting from food deprivation, and it was to these that attempts were made to relate the activity changes in hunger.

Hunger and the Stomach

In 1912, a decade or more before Richter began his work, W. B. Cannon, in collaboration with A. L. Washburn, published a paper entitled *An Explanation of Hunger*. Tracing back some sixty-six years the idea that "hunger is the result of (stomach) contractions," they felt that they were able to offer direct proof of the correctness of this view. Their data were obtained by means of a simple apparatus consisting of a small rubber balloon which was swallowed by the subject (Washburn, principally) after his stomach was emptied of food. To this balloon was attached a thin rubber tube that led up the oesophagus and out the subject's mouth. The balloon was then inflated until it assumed the contours of the stomach. With the tube connected to a water manometer, any pressure upon the balloon could be observed and recorded by a floating marker on the water. After some practice, the subjects were able to retain the balloon and tube without nausea, and experimentation was begun.

The findings may be briefly summarized. A few hours after eating, when the stomach is empty, powerful stomach contractions begin. These contractions are of about thirty seconds' duration, and they occur at thirty- to ninety-second intervals. They may go on, in this rhythmical fashion, for thirty minutes or more, to be followed by quiescent periods of thirty to ninety minutes. When the subject, unaware of the record his stomach was writing, obeyed the experimenter's instructions and signalled (by depressing a telegraph key) whenever he 'felt hunger pangs,' his signals were found to come when "contractions were invariably being registered" and near the time when their force was maximal.

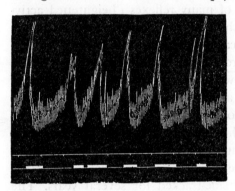

FIG. 66. Portion of a record of human stomach contractions during hunger. The white signals on the bottom line are the subject's reports of "felt" hunger. The reports coincide with peak contractions. The second line is a time line, marked off in minutes. (From Cannon, 1929.)

From their data, Cannon and Washburn came to the conclusion that hunger, which they described as "a dull ache or gnawing sensation referred to the lower mid-chest region and epigastrium," was due to the stimulation provided by the strong contractions of the empty stomach. So great was the impression made by their research, that this stimulus theory of hunger prevailed for many years. We know, today, that there is more to hunger than stomach contractions. It has been shown, for example, that food-getting activity continues with undiminished vigor when the stomachs of rats have been surgically isolated to the degree that stomach contractions could not possibly serve as stimuli for any responses (Bash, 1939); that animals will eat prior to the appearance of the contractions and long after these contractions have disappeared; and that changes in response rate as a function of deprivation are inconsistent with any known properties of stimuli, in the stomach or elsewhere. Yet the stimulus theory of hunger persisted, and so strong was its influence that theorists were led to postulate a stimulus nature for all other drives, even those which, like sex and the sub-hungers, should have encouraged a reconsideration of the evidence and led to a truer conception.

Before Richter's time, there were two major obstacles in the way of a correct interpretation of drive. One was the Pavlovian notion of stimuli as eliciting agents. In looking for the cause of behavioral changes associated with drive, the only known possibility was the elicitative action of stimuli. The recognition of operant behavior still lay ahead. The second obstacle was that the subject, as in the Cannon-Washburn study, could report the 'experience' of hunger pangs. They, and later workers, took the verbal responses and signals, not as behavioral *data* to be explained, but as objective indicators of the drive's presence and action. Today we know that a drive-establishing operation has among its consequences the creation of internal stimuli which can act as S^D's for operant responding. Stomach contractions are stimuli of this sort. They are one bodily result of fasting, and they are certainly discriminable by the organism, as Cannon and Washburn discovered when their signals 'I am feeling a hunger pang' were seen to be occasioned by the contractions. But, while the contractions are S^D's for the verbalization or the report of a 'sensation' or 'experience' of hunger, they are not the drive itself.

The 'feeling' of hunger is not hunger, or, to say it differently, hunger is not in the feeling of it.

The Measurement of Hunger

As with any drive, the measurement of hunger is made possible by any response change which co-varies with the degree of the drive-establishing operation—amount of deprivation. The *general activity* method gives the needed relation between deprivation and response change. In a crude way, it provides a measure of response rate, since with it one obtains the total of response emissions over a rather broad period of time. Both these things are true of the second technique, the *activity wheel*. The *obstruction* method is one in

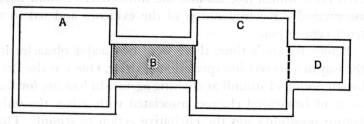

FIG. 67. Floor plan of the Columbia Obstruction Box. The labeled parts are: *A*—starting chamber; *B*—passage-way with grid floor; *C* and *D*—reinforcement chambers. (After Warden, 1931.)

which the response must be made in the face of a deterring or opposing 'resistance' like electric shock. That is, the animal must submit to a negative reinforcement before he can proceed to the positive. The animal is acclimatized in a box, with two chambers, and allowed first to run from one to the other across an uncharged grid to a reinforcement, such as food. Then the shock is turned on, and a test period of, say, twenty minutes is given to see how many times he will take the shock to reach the food. After each crossing, he is allowed a nibble and then quickly transported back to the starting chamber for another trial. This method has features which complicate the data got from it. Principally, one must remember that it depends upon a *conflictful* situation in which positive and negative reinforcement are combined and in which two drives, an aversive and an appetitive, are always operating together.

A more recent, and very satisfactory, method employs response rate under P-R. Co-variation between deprivation and response is shown in the *emission rate* of the response, which is a fundamental indicator of operant strength. Figures 62 and 63 (pages 267 and 268) have already illustrated this method as it was first used by its originator with the bar-pressing response. If you will look back at these graphs, you will see that the changing slope of a P-R curve is admirably suited to measuring degrees of hunger. The measure is uncomplicated by a simultaneous aversive drive; it is sensitive to small changes in drive level; it is applicable to a single reflex rather than a mass of reflexes; the emission pace is not restricted by arbitrary trial imposed on the organism by the experimenter; it is useful with a single animal, and does not require the averaging of data for many; and, finally, it yields a measure of reflex strength at any desired moment, instead of a gross one for a long test period which may run to a full day. Such a procedure is superior to the use of *eating* curves (which may have suggested itself to you) because, in the latter, the rate of responding depends so much upon the rate at which the animal can eat (see Figure 7, page 43). Above a certain point of deprivation, the animal eats as fast as he can anyhow, with the result that the slope of an eating curve is a relatively insensitive measure of drive strength. P-R curves depend less upon eating time, and their slopes are freer to vary.

Hunger Drive in Man

As is true of so many behavioral problems, direct experimentation upon human subjects is very difficult to arrange in the case of hunger. Social pressures militate against the use of infants, and adults are poor material because of their long and unknown personal histories of conditioning and motivation. Yet, there is no reason to believe that hunger is any less important for man than for lower organisms. History records huge migrations in search of food, and wars over bountiful lands; there are reports of human cannibalism under extreme starvation despite all previous training; and there is, of course, Napoleon's classic and highly credible statement that "an army travels on its stomach." The psychologist, Wada (1922), who studied the relation of hunger contractions to activity in infants, felt that hunger was initially the strongest of all drives, since the child when not hungry is usually asleep.

Several studies have shown that, among the human responses which a drive like hunger can affect, we must include the verbal. Discriminative stimuli normally insufficient to evoke food-word responses may become increasingly effective under stronger degrees of hunger. Thus, Sanford (1936) sought to find the relation of hunger to the number of food words (names of foods, meals, etc.) emitted by a group of college students. Tests of word association, word completion, and the like, were given (without the subjects' knowledge of their true purpose) at various between-meal periods and after a twenty-four-hour fast. Results indicated an increase in food words as a function of increased time since eating. In a similar type of experiment (Levine, Chein, and Murphy, 1942), volunteer adults underwent food deprivations of one, three, six, and nine hours, after which they were shown various ambiguous or 'nonsense' figures briefly behind a ground-glass screen and asked to name the 'objects pictured.' The percentage of the times that foods were 'seen' was greater for the hungrier subjects.

Such results remind one of the great amount of sexual conversation heard among the members of isolated and sex-deprived groups—soldiers, convicts, and others. Also in line with this, it is well-known that extreme degrees of drive may precipitate 'illusions' wherein very weak or usually non-generalizing stimuli may be responded to in a manner that seems pathological to the unmotivated onlooker. A point may be reached, in fact, where drive is so strong that no external S^D at all may be required for the response to appear: a starving man may 'see' his favorite dishes before him.

THE SUB-HUNGERS

The possibility of demonstrating sub-hungers depends on the fact that the withholding of food need not be an all-or-none matter, but can be limited to particular constituents. In place of total deprivation, an animal is offered all he can eat of a diet which is unbalanced or deficient in some respect. The question is whether such operations (selective deprivations or selective satiations) have effects on subsequent responses which warrant our speaking of various sub-hunger drives.

Testing for Sub-Hungers

There are several ways in which sub-hungers have been demonstrated. In the *satiation* method, as used by Bousfield (1938), the animal is first allowed to eat until sated with one food, after which that food is removed and one or more others are offered one at a time. When cats were used as subjects and four kinds of food were rotated in order of presentation on successive days, he found that satiation with one food might lead to no further eating when the others were presented, whereas satiation with another might be followed by successive satiations on all those that followed.

A second procedure is that called the *free choice* or *selective eating* method. This gives the animal an opportunity to select, in any amount he wishes, from among two or more foods made available at the same time. The method can be used on animals that have been held for some time to a diet deficient in some elements, or with animals that, although reared on an adequate diet, have created their own selective deprivation by virtue of one-sided choices from among foods offered. Numerous experiments with a number of animals (pigs, cows,

chickens, mice, etc.) agree quite well in leading to the conclusion that, given a choice, organisms will tend to select the one
food needed for an optimal diet or will draw in time from
many sources to maintain normal health and growth. Moreover, the choice among rations is governed by the changing
requirements of the organism during maturation, pregnancy,
illness, and so on.

Table XI

DATA FROM ONE CAT IN AN EXPERIMENT USING THE SATIATION METHOD
IN THE STUDY OF SUB-HUNGERS

(Data from Bousfield, 1938)

	Number of Grams of Other Food Eaten after Cat Was Satiated with the Food at the Left			
	Milk	Milk, cooked oatmeal, raw ground beef	Ground fish and milk	Ground beef-kidney and milk
Milk	—	52	12	130
Milk, cooked oat-meal, raw ground beef	0	—	30	0
Ground fish and milk	36	40	—	42
Ground beef-kidney and milk	0	0	0	—

An experiment, performed by Davis (1928) on three infants, supports the surmise that the phenomenon of sub-
hunger is not limited to lower animals. Just after weaning,
the children were started on a selective eating procedure
which lasted six months for two of them and an entire year
for the third. At each mealtime, a number of natural and
cooked foods, including liquids, were placed on a tray before
them. They ate with their fingers, or spoons, or more directly,

as they wished, choosing freely from among the offerings. Over the long course of the experiment, they showed themselves to be omnivorous, and their choices were nutritionally broad enough to promote health, energy, good sleeping, and some· what better than normal weight increases. Occasionally, one

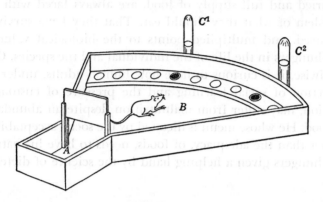

FIG. 68. Model of an apparatus used by Young for studying food preferences and sub-hungers. *A*—entrance chamber; *B*—choice chamber; *C¹* and *C²*—proffered foods. (From Harlow, in T. G. Andrews, *Methods of psychology* [John Wiley & Sons, Inc., 1948]. By permission.)

of the children would develop a strong preference for one food (e.g., cereal or meat) which would last for days, but would then ease off in favor of a wider selection. It was even recorded that one infant, who had rickets at the beginning of the study, took cod-liver oil until the condition disappeared, and then stopped taking any more!

Some Final Observations

These findings lend credence to non-experimental reports of the way men and animals adjust their eating to their dietary needs. Deer travel far to reach licks when they require salt; cattle in phosphorus-poor areas will gnaw on bones to supply the lack; dogs may eat grass when ill; malnourished children are said to eat earth or schoolroom chalk because of the min· erals they contain. Within the laboratory, if rats in a colony are not properly fed, cannibalism may appear as a means of dietary compensation; and the same reason may lead parturient female rats to devour their new-born litters.

Although these things seem dramatic at first reading, it should be recognized that animals in the wild state, granted a varied and full supply of food, are always faced with the problem of what they should eat. That they have survived, matured, and multiplied points to the biological value of sub-hungers in the life of the individual and the species. Contrariwise, it is curious to note how human adults, under the direction of social learning and the pressure of custom or fashion, may suffer from malnutrition despite an abundance of food. He whose menu is dictated by the social acceptability, rather than the adequacy, of foods, needs to have his natural sub-hungers given a helping hand by the science of dietetics.

SEX DRIVE

There is a large amount of scientific information and general misinformation concerning sex—more than we can outline (or counteract!) here. We must limit ourselves to some introductory facts.

The sex drive is classed with the appetites because it involves responses which change in strength as a function of deprivation and satiation. With the females of many species, the drive is marked by temporal cycles so long as satiation (or insemination) is not provided. Seeking, approaching, courting, and copulating are broad categories of responses affected by sex drive. Changes in the strength of such responses are fairly clear in lower organisms, but obscure in man owing to long and meticulous social training. As a basic motive in animals, sex has been investigated with methods similar to those employed with hunger and other drives.

In our short treatment of sex drive, we shall refer often to physiological correlates of the drive. Much work has been done by other sciences on sexual mechanisms. But sex *drive* is still a *behavioral* matter, and a stimulus or glandular theory of sex behavior would be as extraneous here as a stomach-contraction theory of hunger.

Some Classical Studies of Sex Behavior

A few pioneer studies may be cited, both for the information they supply and as illustrations of the experimental approach to the problem. These studies may logically, and for historical continuity, be organized around the apparatus and methods employed. Two lines of development will suffice for our purposes.

1. *Studies with the activity wheel.* In 1923, Wang, working in the same laboratory with Richter, reported his findings in an experiment on the activity of adult female white rats. In the wheel, each female showed a highly consistent cyclical rise and fall in her activity, with peaks every four to five days and declines on intervening days. Wang followed up this observation, and proved that the cycle was intimately correlated with events in the reproductive organs of the female, events called the oestrus rhythm. Activity is greatest at the height of oestrum, at which time there is a flow from the vagina and the female is said to be 'in heat.' At this time, too, ovulation occurs so that the female is maximally ready for insemination, is most receptive to sexual advances by the male (when not in oestrum, she is likely to resist copulation and fight off the male), and is most stimulating to the male by way of olfactory cues given off by the vaginal discharges. The rise to, and recession from, the peak of oestrum coincides with increasing vaginal discharge (and the cellular content of the flow is a continually changing index of oestrus stages), while between peaks there is no discharge at all. (An interesting comparison may be noted here parenthetically. The rat's oestrus period does not correspond functionally to the menses of human females. In contrast with the rat, the latter are fertile approximately midway between menstrual periods, and infertile at menses when the ovum is being discarded in the vaginal flow.

Also, for most human females, the susceptibility to fertilization is low just before menses when the uterus is preparing for menses, and again just afterward when ovulation may not yet have occurred. It is these features of human fertility that are the basis of the so-called 'rhythm method' of birth control. Some of the higher apes are thought to resemble the human female in this respect, but it is not yet clear just where in the evolutionary scale, and why, this curious reversal occurred.)

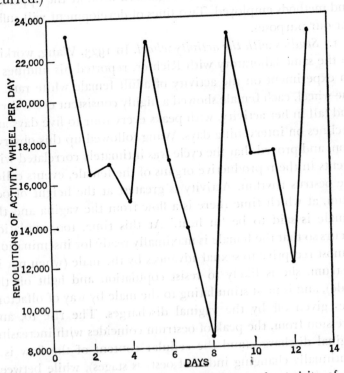

Fig. 69. The effect of the oestrus cycle upon the activity of the female white rat. Notice the regularity with which the peaks of activity occur coming at the height of oestrum. (After Wang, 1923.)

Wang and later workers went on to show a number of other correlations. The characteristic activity cycle of the adult female rat is missing before puberty, and commences at puberty when oestrum does; it is absent during pregnancy, and after parturition (while lactation is going on), two periods when the oestrus rhythm is in abeyance; it is restored after weaning of the litter, when oestrus rhythm reappears; it can be permanently erased, just as oestrum is, by surgical excision of the ovaries, an event that also lowers all activity and renders it more uniform from day to day.

The male rat does not exhibit the sex-activity cycle seen in the female. Male rats, like human males and others, differ in this regard from many species in which males as well as females have special mating seasons. Strength changes in all sex reflexes are the result of deprivation and satiation. The male's sex drive is lowest right after a period of free access to a female in heat, but recovers much of its strength within a few hours following.

2. *Studies with the obstruction method.* The first to devise an obstruction apparatus using electric shock for the study of drive was Moss (1924). His apparatus was a forerunner of later improved models such as the Columbia apparatus constructed by Warner and described earlier (page 288). With Moss's ideas of drive (namely, that drive is an "impelling force" the strength of which could be measured by the amount of "opposing resistance" or "repelling force" it would overcome) we are no longer concerned. But his device and his findings were the instigators of much worthwhile research and are still, therefore, of interest. Having undertaken to measure the sex drive of the rat by its "willingness" to undergo electric shock in order to reach a sex-object, he compared sex and seventy-two-hour hunger by permitting rats to choose between a compartment containing food and one containing a mate. His observations (on too small a number of animals to be significant) were that females in heat cross the grid more often to reach the male than the male does to reach the female; and also that hunger could be a stronger motive than sex, since about 80 per cent of the males chose food rather than a female. Tsai (1925), using a method of simple choice

without any shock, came to a similar conclusion. His male rats, only twenty-four-hours hungry, chose food rather than a female in about 75 per cent of the chances given. While sex has been condemned or extolled as the most powerful of drives, this is apparently not true even of infra-human animals.

The strength of sex drive as related to length of sex deprivation was investigated by Warner (1927) with the Columbia obstruction apparatus. Male rats under six degrees of sexual deprivation were tested for grid crossings to a female in oestrum within a standard observation period of twenty minutes. The six deprivation periods, timed from the last session of unrestricted copulations, were 0, 6, 12, 24 hours, 4 and 28 days. He concluded that maximal drive was reached after about twenty-four-hours' deprivation, with subsequent slight decline to the twenty-eighth day. A breakdown of Warner's data by Leuba (1931), however, raised some doubt about the decline after maximum. If the grid crossings are tabulated for the four 5-minute parts of the whole 20-minute session, the crossings after 24 hours and 28 days distribute themselves as follows:

AVERAGE NUMBER OF CROSSINGS FOR GROUPS OF ANIMALS

	First 5-minute period	Second 5-minute period	Third 5-minute period	Fourth 5-minute period	Total
24 hours of deprivation	3.6	3.2	3.0	3.5	13.3
28 days of deprivation	.8	2.0	2.7	5.1	11.6

The acceleration of crossings by the 28-day group within the 20-minute test period, despite its smaller total indicates two things: (1) after 28 days, adaptation to the shock builds up more slowly; and (2) that a 20-minute test period is too short to have a full indication of drive strength. There is reason to believe that sex drive in male rats does not decrease after a maximum, but instead that after the first rapid increase there are diminishing increments with prolonged deprivation. It may be mentioned incidentally that Warner, too, showed that sex can be outweighed by both hunger and thirst as motives.

The obstruction method has also been used to study 'maternal behavior.' In the female white rat, this is a complex of many activities. Objectively, it appears as nest-building, nursing, retrieving the young or returning to the litter when separated from them, and more. Nissen (1930) found that the number of grid crossings a parturient female would make in order to reach her litter was maximal just after birth, and decreased until the young were of weaning age. Many observers have recorded their belief that reinforcement is the basis of this reaction: regular suckling by the young relieves breast congestion in the mother, and allows normal functioning of the milk glands; the decline in lactation coincides with weaning time (about twenty-one days after birth), and return-to-litter behavior fades out. Although physiological correlates are not known as yet for the other components of maternal behavior, it is a fact that they all lose strength up to weaning time, after which the female's oestrus rhythm re-emerges. We may note in passing that the principles of stimulus generalization and discrimination show themselves in the operant reactions that compose the maternal pattern. Females will retrieve, and carry back to the nest, not only their own wandering offspring, but will take young from the litters of other mothers if the age-size difference from their own young is not too great. When the difference is large, say ten days or more, they show some discrimination and will reject the strange young. Moreover, females will cross a grid to litters not their own, will suckle other young, and, more strikingly, will retrieve even inanimate objects like a piece of wood or a sandbag if it approximates the size of their offspring.

Because of our social training, we tend to think of 'maternal behavior' as tender, loving, protective and care-providing. We call women who act otherwise 'unnatural mothers.' But the female rat, though she will take many shocks to return to her litter, will also on occasion, if severely upset emotionally or subjected to dietary deficiencies, kill or devour her young. And if we get outside the confines of our society, we find practices like infanticide acceptable under certain circumstances. It is always dangerous to mistake our individual ethical ideals for either the facts or the potentiality of human and animal behavior. A practical program of ethical training must take account of fact, but fact pays no heed to our ethical goals.

Human Sexuality

Although the sex drive was always accepted as important for infra-human organisms, the emphasis upon its significance in human living has come about in relatively recent times. At times its rôle among men has been greatly, even grotesquely, exaggerated. Controlled studies of sex among human beings are naturally difficult. Society's laws, personal reluctance, and the researcher's own sympathies stand in the way of experimentation; and field studies are handicapped by socially induced attitudes that block the information-seeker. The result is that real evidence on the characteristics and modes of human sex behavior and development is very scanty. Yet it is just here that interest is greatest, so that speculations and theories are put forth in bewildering and distorted profusion. Where facts are few and interest is high, the temptation to make a guess and to voice an opinion is hard to resist. Only in the last few years has there been in progress (Kinsey, Pomeroy, and Martin, 1948) the first large-scale attempt to get some elementary statistics on the sex activities of typical Americans of all ages, social levels, educational backgrounds, and of both sexes. This study, it is estimated, will take some ten to fifteen years, will cost some millions of dollars, and will end up with a sample of 100,000 persons in the total population of 140,000,000. While this return may seem small, it far surpasses any effort to date, and represents the lengths to which one must be prepared to go for statistics on human sexuality.

Beyond the statistical tabulations, however, remains the problem of how sex activities reflect behavioral principles. A premonition of the complexity and multiple causality of copulation by human males, for example, can be got from castration studies of the male rat (Stone, 1927). The effect of castration on the rat depends principally on two factors, the age and amount of previous experience with sex at the time of castration. Castration before puberty eliminates copulation after puberty; and castration of an adult male who had been raised in isolation, will keep him from copulating when he is later given access to a female. If, however, an adult male with ample previous experience is castrated, his sex behavior may continue for some time albeit at diminished frequency. Medical literature contains very few post-castration studies of men injured accidentally or operated on for medical necessity. Those available indicate that frequency of intercourse, and the pleasure reported, may be little, if any, reduced by the operation. The action of secondary reinforcements in these instances shows that there are other reasons than glandular for sexual intercourse, just as there are other reasons than stomach contractions for eating. These sexual S^r's probably include both exteroceptive and proprioceptive stimulation.

Sexual Discriminations and Differentiations

Among infra-human animals, it is frequently seen that the stimuli and responses which are correlated with sexual reinforcement may be operative with a minimum of conditioning. It is often so difficult to tell whether the stimuli are eliciting or discriminative, that instances have sometimes been called "unlearned behavior." Some European zoologists have simply spoken of "innate releasing mechanisms" in their attempt to explain the interaction of certain animals (e.g., the male and female stickleback fish) in their sexual behavior. Animals at the mammalian level may show a similar quick establishment of sexual chains. The fact is that one cannot yet tell with assurance when he is dealing with accounts of speedily conditioned operants or of respondents requiring no conditioning at all.

Male rats raised in isolation from females will mount and copulate, without overmuch delay, when eventually paired with a female in heat. The S^D's for the male rat are largely olfactory, but anosmic males (with the sense of smell destroyed) will still copulate, since there are other S^D's—for example, the short, jerky movements and leaps of the female in oestrum. Before puberty, male rats are not responsive to the smell cues of oestrum nor any other S^D's from the female. At the human level, males respond to secondary sexual characteristics of the female, such as shape, contour, voice and others, as S^D's, and in addition are affected by social S^D's like fashionableness of dress, skill with cosmetics, flirtatiousness, and so on. In contrast with the rat, too, the human male may need some time to learn the responses involved in copulation.

Under certain conditions, sexual discriminations and differentiations of higher animals, and especially man, are not only 'incorrect,' but may take a turn conventionally termed 'abnormal.' These deviant responses are learned in accordance with the same laws which govern the acquisition of 'normal' behavior, but are deemed queer because they are out of step with more common patterns or conflict with the codes of the society in which they occur. Thus, in one of Moss's studies, male rats were reared together for 50-150 days without females, with the result that they seemed to lose interest in females and mounted each other in preference. A similar finding has been reported for birds, with males reared together preferring males to females. Another example of early reinforcement interfering with 'normal' sexuality is that in which birds raised with members of another but related species may later prefer them as mates rather than their own species. Human homosexuality involves much more intricate sets of personal relationships, but there is little doubt that discriminative training plays an important rôle in it.

As with other motives, high sex drive may produce responses to stimuli which are not ordinarily sexual. Deprived persons may see a sexual symbolism in things like mountains and valleys, guns and targets, ladders and windows, and many other objects. Under high drive, stimuli of all sorts may generalize as S^D's and become metaphors, as it were, of true sexual S^D's for evoking sex talk or action that is bizarre to an observer. A phrase with *double entendre,* an unconscious pun, a mispronounced or misspelled word, oftimes embarrassingly reveals the motive underlying a speaker's or writer's avowed intention. Such 'slips' of the tongue or pen were cited by Freud as the "psychopathology of everyday life," and he ascribed them to the workings of a "subconscious mind." There is, however, nothing esoteric about motivational strengthening of reflexes, even when the person cannot tell us, or is 'unaware of,' his present motives.

THE AVERSIVE DRIVES

Aversions, like appetites, form a major class of drives. There are two criteria for determining whether a given stimulus is aversive: (1) a response made in its *presence* should be strengthened by its *removal;* and (2) a response made in the *absence* of the stimulus should be depressed if it is followed by the *administration* of the stimulus. You will note, of course, that these are also the criteria for a negative reinforcer. In this chapter, however, our interest will be in the motivating function of such stimuli, which may, therefore, be named aversive stimuli. The three aversions chosen for comment here—light aversion, sound aversion, and shock aversion—by no means exhaust the list. Others are known, still others are suspected, and the total number of them, as in the case of appetites, is a matter of empirical discovery for each species of organism.

Light Aversion

This drive can be demonstrated rather easily in the white rat. Richter, it will be recalled, found that the rat, a 'nocturnal' animal, is less active in light than in dark, suggesting the depressive action which we now expect of an aversive stimulus; and several experiments in recent years have shown that light-removal may constitute a positive reinforcement for conditioning a response (Keller, 1942). The second criterion of an aversion to light can be met by administering the stimulus whenever a given response is made. In a trial experiment, Schoenfeld (1946) used a hungry rat daily in one-hour sessions in a bar-pressing apparatus with no positive reinforcement given for pressings. When each response to the bar was immediately followed by five flashes of a bright light the rate of operant-level pressing dropped swiftly and remained low for some days after the punishing stimulus was discontinued.

A combination of the above-mentioned procedures can be very strong in its effect. Hefferline (see page 312) rigged his apparatus so that a rat's depression of the bar would turn off a light, but release of the bar would bring it back on again. He reasoned that the bar-pressing response has two components, an 'up' and a 'down' response. The 'down' received a positive reinforcement (light-removal) and the 'up' a negative (light-onset); the positive reinforcement could be obtained, and the negative reinforcement avoided, only by pressing and *holding* the bar down. The rats in this situation conditioned quickly to prolonged holding, so that they were immobilized on the bar for as much as 95 per cent of each experimental hour. This failure to 'unmake' a response is related to those preference situations in which animals move into, and stay in, dark rather than lighted areas, as well as to other instances of sticking to 'safe' environments. It also helps us to see why, in experiments using aversive stimuli, some animals cannot be conditioned at all. If a partial reinforcement can be obtained in some other way, as by hiding one's head or covering one's eyes in a light-aversion situation, the animal may be immobilized through the combination of this reinforcement with the punishment consequent upon moving from the position—with the result that a more effective rein- forcement is never achieved.

An amusing aspect of the effect of combining positive with negative reinforcement in the manner just described is that provided by a simple experiment routinely carried out by first-year students of psychology in Columbia College. Some object like a metal coin or piece of wood is placed in the rat's cage and a bright light is turned on overhead. As soon as the animal, in moving about, makes contact with the coin, the light is diminished; and, as soon as he leaves the coin, the light returns. Within a few minutes, the animal shows a proto- typical 'fetishism': he stays close to his coin, taking it in his teeth, chewing on it, and carrying it about with him wherever he goes. Although one would hesitate to say that the rat wor- shipped the object for its magical powers, one cannot but be reminded of the rabbit's feet and lucky coins at a higher evolutionary level.

Sound Aversion

An aversion to certain sounds is found in many animals, including the student who is annoyed by such things as the squeak of chalk on a blackboard. Among rats, 'audiogenic seizures' are known to result from stimulation with escaping air, jangling keys, electric bells, and the like. These seizures are marked by periods of wild, erratic behavior alternating irregularly with trembling, prostration, and bodily rigidity; an unnatural lack of sensitivity to other stimulus influences (as when the animal is poked with a stick); and a condition somewhat like the "waxy flexibility" of certain patients in mental hospitals whose limbs and body are passive and may be molded into various positions. Recovery may seemingly be complete on the day following the seizure, but a new episode is more easily induced on later occasions.

In an exploratory experiment, two rats were trained in a working-box that contained a loud buzzer. In daily one-hour sessions, the buzzer was sounded and bar-pressings were regularly reinforced by sound-removal for one-minute periods. The response was quickly strengthened and soon came to be very stereotyped in appearance, with the animal remaining close to the bar in the silent periods. The latencies of the response to sound, which were characteristically short, showed an interesting cyclical effect that may also be observed occasionally under light aversion. In a short series of stimulus presentations, they became gradually of shorter and shorter duration; then they would suddenly lengthen and begin another gradual decrease; with such lengthenings and shortenings continuing throughout most of an experimental hour. Apparently, the latency decreased to a point at which the escape response came so closely on the heels of the stimulus onset that the response was virtually punished, thus bringing about a temporary depression of the sound-removing behavior that showed itself in a lengthened latency.

As in other aversion experiments, those with sound require rapid conditioning if the animal is not to be 'beaten down' by the stimulus and fail to respond in the desired manner. It would probably be of advantage in such experiments to use as the to-be-conditioned response one which is easier still than bar-pressing and has a higher operant level. The faster the conditioning, the less should be the likelihood of producing audiogenic seizures.

Shock Aversion

Electric shock is perhaps the most generally aversive of all stimuli for most organisms. In the rat, it easily satisfies both criteria for an aversive stimulus: a response removing it is strengthened, and one that brings it on is depressed. We may take Mowrer's (1940) study as an example since his results resembled those obtained under light aversion. He used a box in which electric shock to the animal's feet built up gradually from zero intensity to one that was highly upsetting, with the 'pain threshold' reached at approximately the end of the first minute of application. As the shock increased above this point, the rat became very active, even frantic. If, during this activity, he bumped or pushed a panel at one end of the box, the shock returned to the zero level and gradually built up again in intensity. Conditioning was rapid; the successful response became very stereotyped; 'freezings' to the panel were often observed following shock-removal. All these phenomena are equally typical of light-aversive behavior. It is important when using shock for conditioning, even more than in the case of light or sound, to avoid over-stimulation, else the organism may be immediately thrown into a flurry of convulsive activity which precludes any form of adaptive behavior.

Human Aversions

That human beings possess aversive drives seems beyond question. Infants, by their squirmings and wailings, and adults, by their verbal reports, indicate that they find some stimuli noxious, painful, or unpleasant. They easily learn to get rid of strong shocks, glaring lights, grating noises, putrid odors, pricking pins, and the like. Yet, when brought into the laboratory, their aversion is not always obvious. When we attempt, for example, to condition a finger-withdrawal under shock-aversion, our subject may thwart us by taking the shock without complaint unless it is of exceptional severity. Our experiment has perhaps not taken into account the subject's reinforcement history, in which there may have been given much positive reinforcement for stoical behavior.

It is a commonplace of human experience that stimuli which were once unpleasant can lose this character and become acceptable, even sought after, as a result of training. Adults may like bitter and spicy foods that infants will reject; they come to enjoy music that is cacophony to children or other adults; they welcome such otherwise annoying stimuli as the vibrations applied by the barber to a balding head. We have already mentioned such matters in our chapter on secondary reinforcement. It is not simply that the aversion is outweighed by conflicting drive, but rather that the aversive stimulus becomes a secondary reinforcement. This is related, not only to our subject's failure to withdraw his finger from shock, but to the aging boxer's refusal to quit the ring, and the neurotic's masochism.

A simple experiment, easily carried out in an undergraduate laboratory, provides the prototype of masochism. Hungry rats are conditioned to bar-pressing for food pellets, some receiving regular and others periodic reinforcement. Each reinforcement is accompanied by a mild electric shock. After an hour of such training, extinction of bar-pressing is begun, with neither food nor shock given for the response. When extinction is well advanced, the shock alone is reintroduced as an accompaniment of bar-pressing. The result is commonly a rapid acceleration in response rate, which appears as a sizable bump in the cumulative response curve. To an uninformed bystander watching the animal's behavior, it appears that the rats enjoy the shocks and are deliberately punishing themselves

ANXIETY AND AVOIDANCE

Pavlov once wrote: "... it is evident that under natural conditions the animal must respond ... to stimuli which signal the approach of harm or good...." We now ask what happens when a discriminative stimulus precedes an aversive one. We approached this problem in the preceding chapter, in our discussion of secondary negative reinforcement. Two experiments can be designed. In one, the S^D is followed inevitably by the aversive stimulus; in the other, some response to the S^D suffices to keep the aversive stimulus from coming. These two arrangements provide operational definitions of "anxiety" and "avoidance" respectively.

Anxiety

In an investigation of anxiety, Estes and Skinner (1941) dealt with the problem in the following way. At intervals during periodic reconditioning of the bar-pressing response, a soft tone came on and sounded for a period of five minutes, at the end of which an electric shock was delivered. The tone, at the outset, had no appreciable effect upon bar-pressing rate, but very soon it took on a markedly depressant character at each presentation, from which there was immediate recovery as soon as the shock had been given. Bar-pressing during the tone ceased almost entirely, with the undoubted accompaniment of other reflex changes which might easily be labeled 'anxious.' Extinction of this effect was accomplished by presenting tone continuously, without shock, during a thirty-three-minute period of P-R in which the rats gradually returned to their normal rate of responding. Spontaneous recovery of the effect, on the following day, was, however, practically complete, suggesting that the tone had by no means lost its power to set up the anxiety.

We may speak of this anxiety as a state induced by a stimulus which, in the past, has preceded negative reinforcement. It arises from experience and, *if* it is to be classed as a drive, it should be regarded as secondary. It begins with an S^D that has become a secondary negative reinforcer and ends with the primary aversive stimulus. When the warning is over and the punishment borne, normal behavior is restored—reminiscent of the way men describe their relief when a period of anxious waiting is ended: "Well, *that's* over!"

Anxiety is, unfortunately, more common in men than in rats. Daily, and in many ways, we are subjected to punishment and threats of punishment. Law-abidance and education are both fields in which it is often difficult to achieve results without recourse to such motivation. Children are all too often made literate by the same aversive motivation that is used to keep men out of jail—this is the philosophy upon which a whole society may stand. Is it odd that such a society is plagued by a high incidence of anxiety-ridden members who may, at one time or another in their lives, need therapeutic assistance? If threats from one's personal environment and society in general become excessive, an individual's every day and every act may be dominated by anxiety. And if, as a child,

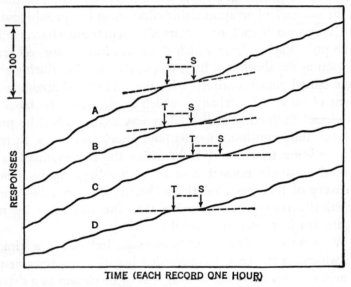

Fig. 70. The effect of an anxiety-inducing stimulus on rate of bar-pressing under P-R. *T* denotes the onset of a 5-minute tone; *S*, the occurrence of shock. The four curves (A, B, C, D) are for four successive days. The response rate declines during successive periods of anxiety until, by the fourth day, it is almost zero during the presentation of the tone. Each cumulative response curve is an average for the group of six rats. (After Estes and Skinner, 1941.)

he does not know what responses may be punished, but only that it will be strong, frequent, and inevitable, all the ordinary stimuli about him become 'dangerous' and anxiety-producing. The files of psychological clinics are filled with cases of morbid and obsessive anxieties which are clearly the outcome of disciplinary and social training overburdened with threats of punishment. As compared with others, including so-called inferior or primitive cultures, our society is sorely beset in this respect.

Avoidance

In ourselves, in others, and in many animals, we seem to see responses that are made to prevent the impact of noxious stimuli. It would appear that such avoidance responses depend on some S^D or other that signals the imminent arrival of a negative reinforcer—or, more concisely, that these responses are discriminative operants. But what is the reinforcement for them? Any answer that proposes the response's "actual success in avoiding the stimulus" is inadequate because it glosses over the difficulty itself, to wit, how the absence or non-occurrence of a stimulus can be reinforcing. Were it not for very strong evidence that avoidance can be manifested by an organism, one would be inclined to deny its very possibility.

A partial answer to this question has been suggested in Chapter 8, where we saw that the removal of a conditioned negative reinforcement could act as a positive reinforcer. There are many situations in which we commonly speak of avoidance when an animal escapes from such an S^D—for example, in the experiments of Mowrer (1939) and Miller (1941). In these cases, the best avoidance results are apparently obtained when the S^D is continuously present until brought to an end by some response. But there are other cases in which the S^D is of short duration and the primary negative reinforcement does not follow until some time has elapsed. Warner (1932) taught rats to escape shock by jumping over a barrier in an experimental chamber. When the response was well established, he introduced a one-second warning buzzer that preceded the shock by intervals of 1, 10, 20, and 30 seconds. Using different groups of rats with each delay interval, he gave fifty trials per day under these conditions for a period as long as twenty days. The rats in the 1-second group required, on the average, three days to meet a criterion of six successive avoiding responses—that is, they jumped the barrier within the 1-second interval and did not receive the shock. In the 10-second group, the median animal reached this criterion in the fourth day and one animal failed to solve the problem. The 20-second group required seven and a half days, with four animals unsuccessful; and all of the animals in the 30-second group failed. In addition to demonstrating avoidance in the absence of a continuous external S^D which could be terminated by the response, Warner's experiment shows us that whatever discriminative or noxious value the S^D acquired was dependent on the temporal remoteness of the negatively reinforcing stimulus with which it was correlated.

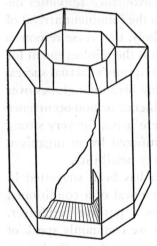

FIG. 71. Four-chambered octagonal box used in studying escape and avoidance behavior by rats. The animal, when shocked by the floor grid in any compartment or warned by some signal, can move into an adjoining chamber. (After Hunter, 1935.)

Hunter (1935), employing a similar experimental procedure with white rats, sounded a buzzer for one-fifth of a second; two seconds later a shock was presented unless the animal jumped into an adjacent compartment during the period between the two stimuli. Trials were spaced by 58 seconds and a maximum of 150 trials was allowed per animal for meeting a criterion of ten successive avoidances. Of 91 rats, only six failed to reach the criterion. The average number of trials was a little over sixty.

Hefferline (1950) showed that rats, with long training, could be taught to avoid another type of noxious stimulus, strong light, when it was preceded for fifteen seconds by a series of clicks at half-second intervals. This is hardly comparable to the studies just described, since the S^D was essentially continuous, but Hefferline was also able to show avoidance conclusively when no change at all occurred in the external situation. This was in his "holding" experiment, wherein rats were noted to keep a bar in a "down" position for stretches of forty minutes or more, when 'letting go' of the bar was always followed by the onset of a negatively reinforcing light. Hefferline ascribed this holding behavior to the fact that *proprioceptive* stimuli, aroused when the rat began to let up on the bar, had come to be noxious and "anxiety-inducing" in themselves. Maintenance of the "down-response" was thus treated essentially as an escape from the stimuli aroused whenever the "up-response" began.

Hefferline's explanation has much in common with the view, expressed by Mowrer and Lamoreaux (1947), that avoidance behavior is reinforced by anxiety-reduction; but it gives us a clue as to the possible stimulus factors involved. Further research will undoubtedly clarify this situation, but at present we seem to be justified in saying that the most common acts of avoidance are positively reinforced by the termination of an *external* S^D which is also a secondary negative reinforcer, as in the experiments by Miller, Mowrer, and others (pages 250-253). Other avoidances, like that described by Warner, in which there is a lapse of time between the S^D and the primary negative reinforcer, are conceivably reinforced by the removal of *proprioceptive* stimuli or other parts of the external stimulus compound (Schoenfeld, 1950). For convenience of expression, we may also speak of avoidance as anxiety-reducing, just as we sometimes speak of a food-reinforced response as hunger-reducing. This accords well with the teachings of some psychotherapists who insist that a wide diversity of behavioral symptoms are to be understood as 'escape mechanisms'—ways of alleviating anxiety or avoiding 'unpleasant thoughts or ideas.' You will correctly infer, from this line of reasoning, that the extinction of avoidance responding depends on the extinction of anxiety-inducing stimuli. So long as the S^D is capable of exciting anxiety, just so long will an avoidance response which cuts off these stimuli be positively reinforced.

The extinction of avoidance responding may be carried out in two ways. First, we may have the S^D always followed by the noxious stimulus, with the response no longer effective in removing the S^D. This is, of course, a return to the original anxiety situation, and will result in a weakening of the avoidance response as well as a resumption of the customary anxiety symptoms—depressed activity, cowering, and so on. Secondly, we could have the S^D presented on schedule, but never followed by the noxious stimulus. This case duplicates the situation that prevails when the organism is successfully avoiding; and you might be led to wonder how the animal would ever 'discover' that the noxious stimulus would not come. You would have to recall that the reinforcement for avoidance behavior does not lie in the non-appearance of anything; rather, it lies in stimulus removal.

Actually, extinction occurs in this second case, because the S^D maintains its negatively reinforcing status only when it is at least occasionally followed by the primary reinforcer. Without the shock or other noxious stimulus, its power dissipates (along with its anxiety-producing function). This is related to the experimental observation (Schlosberg, 1936, 1937; Sheffield, 1948) that the latency of the avoidance response to the S^D goes through a cyclical lengthening and shortening. In the course of a string of successful avoidances, the latency increases from trial to trial as the S^D's anxiety-producing power extinguishes. When, finally, the response comes too late, the noxious stimulus strikes the animal, and acts to restore the S^D's power. The next latency 'snaps back' to a low value, only to go through another lengthening phase with each successful avoidance. However, in extinction, it has been observed (Culler, Finch, Girden, and Brogden, 1935) that if an avoidance response passes by the time when shock is customarily given, it will continue to weaken. This weakening is sometimes strikingly rapid and it may be that it depends upon the violation of a temporal discrimination built up by the training schedule.

We have a great deal to learn about avoidance behavior and anxiety. Our present knowledge, gleaned mainly from animal study, indicates that the extinction of an avoidance response is often extremely difficult, even in well-controlled experimental situations. It suggests that, at the level of human behavior, where all manner of stimuli may, by design or caprice, accompany punishment, the problem of eliminating anxiety is one of the first magnitude. This is especially true of our own society, which so wantonly, deliberately, or systematically relies on punishment in the control of behavior. Ideas on the subject abound, among laymen as well as professional workers in psychotherapy, but the scientific validation of most of them still lies ahead. Is it wise to send the aviator aloft immediately after the crash? Should we force the person with a phobia to face the feared object? Can a child's dread of darkness be removed by keeping him in a dark room? These and related questions are of deep concern to the mental hygienist, who has evolved his own set of rules for the prevention or removal of behavioral 'maladjustments'—rules that have a pragmatic basis in the benefits sometimes derived from their use, but which as yet have only been partially subjected to analysis.

The Conflict of Drives

The laboratory, which permits the analysis of natural processes into components rarely or never seen in the massive events of daily life, also permits us to re-create the more complex events step-by-step for deliberate study. Although we have so far dealt mainly with motives operating singly, it must be evident to all that in the usual affairs of animals and men more than one drive may be present at any time. Before this already lengthy chapter is closed it may be worthwhile to look briefly at some of the known effects of co-existing motives upon behavior. In this connection, attention has often been focussed upon the *conflict of drives*.

A word of explanation is needed about "conflict of drives" lest we lose contact with our earlier discussions. A moment's consideration will disclose that it is not drives that conflict, but rather responses or response tendencies. As Shaffer (1936) has put it: "The term *conflict* means that the individual confronts a complex situation to different aspects of which he has learned to make antagonistic responses ... [which] cannot be made at the same time...." We speak of drive conflict when opposition between incompatible responses arises from drive operations like deprivation or stimulation. This is in contrast with conflicts originating in other ways—for example, from the direct stimulation of antagonistic muscles simultaneously, or the simultaneous use of S^D's for incompatible responses. Direct stimulation has been investigated mainly by physiologists; the "conflict of cues" (or S^D's) has been of interest in the study of special discrimination problems (e.g., Nissen and Jenkins, 1943) like sensory "illusions." Always, however, 'conflict' refers to the instigation of incompatible movements, movements which cannot occur together and may be thought of as competing. In the discussion which follows, therefore, our use of 'drive conflict' will mean "response conflict created by drive operations"; and when we speak here of 'response conflict' we shall intend this to mean competition that is drive-induced.

The co-existence of several drives can mean harmonious performance if the responses involved are simultaneously possible; or it can mean, if the responses are incompatible, the kind of behavioral upset that all of us have experienced at one time or another. The signs of conflict, which are also the response characteristics measured in experiments, include increased hesitation or latency of response, vacillation or alternation between responses, frequency of 'blocking' or failing to respond at all. These measures have been used by several researchers who, within recent years, have begun a promising line of experimental attack upon the problem.

Conflict situations differ in complexity depending upon the number and variety of competing responses. Two experimental arrangements, however, because of their simplicity, provide a good starting point. In each case let us assume that the response is fully conditioned, and that other variables are kept constant, so that only the experimenter's drive operation is manipulating the strengths of the responses involved. (In this way, we avoid the complications that responses with unequal training are differently affected by the same drive operation (Sears and Hovland, 1941), and so forth. While these are doubtless important variables, we may for simplicity's sake ignore them here.)

1. An animal is placed into an alley apparatus in which he is trained to move toward or away from either end by the positive or negative reinforcements placed in the ends. Locomotion is a kind of response, and this situation is often described in terms of "approach and avoidance." This arrangement is valuable because it affords a good picture of conflicting responses and allows relatively easy measurement. The student should remember, however, that the spatial results of the animal's responding are not the prime consideration, and that analysis could as well be made of responses that do not require travel by the organism (Miller, 1948). Brown (1948), using white rats and such an alley, attached a small harness to his animals and was able to measure the pull exerted by the animals as they tried to move toward a positive reinforcer (food) and away from a negative (electric shock). The graphs in Figure 72 show how the force of the pull varied with distance of the rat in the alley from the point of reinforcement. The two gradients of approach and avoidance, each obtained from animals who had had only one type of reinforcement, led to the following observations (Miller, 1944): (a) the tendency to approach a goal is stronger the nearer the subject is to it ("approach gradient"); (b) the tendency to go away from a place or object avoided is stronger the nearer the subject is to it ("avoidance gradient"); (c) the strength of avoidance increases more rapidly with nearness than does the strength of approach. With this known, we may go on to establish three conflictful situations by simul-

taneously placing reinforcement in the alley ends according to three combinations.

a. Both alternatives positively reinforced. Thus, we could use food and water with animals both hungry and thirsty; or even food at both ends, with only hunger drive present. This is an "approach-approach" conflict like that of the mythical ass between two bales of hay. The ass, it is told, starved to death, but you will readily agree that this is not a likely outcome! The story's humor arises from the fact that its ingredi-

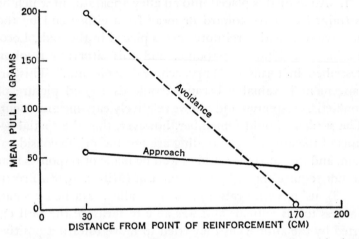

FIG. 72. The intersecting approach and avoidance gradients obtained by Brown (After Miller, in J. McV. Hunt, 1944.) In connection with these graphs, see also Figure 59, page 253.

ents are conceptually possible, but their attainment actually impossible: the ass is not a point in space equidistant from the bales; the bales are not equal S^D's, nor do they occupy mere points in space. In actuality, the slightest departure from ideal conditions means an increasing pull in one direction with a correspondingly decreasing pull in the other as the distance from it increases (see Figure 72). Conflicts like these are easily resolved for the organism. When men speak of being torn between equally attractive courses of action, there is usually the unspoken element that one course will be rewarding and the other not, so that there is an undercurrent of anxiety lest the wrong choice be made. But in a world where all choices are rewarded, the approach-approach situation should produce none but fleeting conflicts.

b. Both alternatives negatively reinforced. Thus, either end of the pathway might be charged to give a painful shock. The organism tends to retreat from either end, but cannot get out of the dilemma. Movement away from the center, in either direction, increases the repelling power of the approaching aversive spot, so that he is caught and suspended between them in an agitated and conflictful immobility. If he were not confined to the alley, the animal would flee from the situation altogether, probably in a compromise direction at right angles to the line connecting the two aversive spots. A phenomenon similar to this was demonstrated by Hovland and Sears (1938) with human subjects. The instructions were to draw on a square sheet of paper a diagonal line from the midpoint of the near side to one of the far corners. Each far corner had a light which could be flashed at the will of the experimenter, and the subject was to respond to the light which did flash by drawing the line as quickly as he could. After training to both corners, a conflict was set up by flashing both lights at once. The result in many cases was a blocking that caused lines to be drawn straight ahead *between* the two far corners rather than diagonally. In contrast with this, we can easily suppose that if an organism were ringed by an aversive circle with escape impossible, he would bog down at the center, just as in the alley where the walls prevent leaving the situation. The effect of hemming an organism in on all sides by negative reinforcements is of great interest to students of abnormal behavior. The "escape from reality" and "retreat into phantasy" which they observe in many patients seem to be consequences of life situations in which punishment awaits every move. Where there is no escape, something is bound to give way.

c. One alternative positively, one negatively, reinforced.

Thus, a choice of one direction is favored by both its own positive value and the negative value of the other. This is clearly a combination in which no conflict resides. One has only to answer such questions as how the two response tendencies summate, whether arithmetically or in some other fashion.

2. The alley apparatus can be used for a conflict arrangement that is even simpler than the above. This involves locating the reinforcements, whether positive or negative, at only one end so that we can consider locomotion toward that end as a single response that may be rewarded or punished. No problem arises when: (a) only positive reinforcements have been given at that end; or (b) when only negative reinforcements have been given. In either case, there is no conflict about approaching, or retreating from, the place of reinforcement. The instance that most concerns us is that in which the animals have on some occasions been rewarded for approaching, and on other occasions punished for the same response. The result is that he has tendencies both to approach and avoid, and we should be able to deduce in part from Figure 72 what his behavior will be like. Since the approach and avoidance gradients differ in steepness and the point of intersection, we might expect that there will be a place in the alley at some distance from the end, where the animal will tend to come to rest. Thus, if we put the animal down in the alley beyond that point, he would approach until the avoidance force exceeded that of approach. His approach momentum would probably carry him past that point, whereupon he would slow up and begin to retreat; the retreat momentum would again take him too far away, and he would then begin to approach once more; and so on. In short, there should appear not only a point of equilibrium but also a vacillation of movement direction around that point, with the animal unable to advance or retreat decisively. Just this type of thing has been obtained experimentally (Miller, Brown, and Lipofsky, 1943; Rasmussen, 1940). As Miller has written (1944), the

situation is reminiscent of human dilemmas like that of the hard-hit but bashful lover who vacillates helplessly at a distance from his loved one; or like that of a man eager for a higher salary but afraid to approach a 'tough' employer.

Of the situations outlined above, there are two that seem to be outstanding generators of conflict and probably contain the germ of the admittedly more complex conflicts of daily life. They are, if we may recapitulate, the double avoidance case where either of two alternate responses is punished, and the case where a single response has had both positive and negative reinforcement applied to it. Before taking up some examples of conflict that are on the next level of complexity, it may be noted that the amount of conflict engendered between two response tendencies is inversely related to the difference in strength of the two tendencies; or, the amount of conflict increases as the strengths of the opposing responses approach equality. This has been tested and confirmed in several studies (Sears and Hovland, 1941; Godbeer, 1940; see also a review by Bitterman, 1944). Barker (1942), for example, gave ten-year-old boys the task of indicating which of two proffered liquids they would choose to drink. In one part of the experiment, both alternatives were unpleasant (as determined in advance of the experiment), but differentially so. Barker found that the more the alternatives differed in attractiveness, the faster the choice was made and the fewer the vacillations in making the final decision. This example is one of the double avoidance type, but the available evidence shows that the hypothesis is probably valid for a single response with a combined history of reward and punishment (Miller, 1944).

Our final case of conflict involves two incompatible reactions, either of which is reinforced but at the same time results in the loss of the other reinforcement or is punished. In other words, one positive reinforcement must be foregone (or punishment endured) when the subject chooses the other. The situation comprises two interacting instances of a single

response that is both rewarded and punished. It has been rec·
ognized (e.g., Hovland and Sears, 1938) that the case resembles
more closely the conflictful contingencies of real life, and it
has been studied by several investigators. In a series of experiments with conflicting light-aversion and hunger drives in
the white rat, Tolcott (1949) employed an apparatus in which
two incompatible responses were available for separate rein·
forcement with darkness or food. Located at one end of a box
was a bar that, when pressed, delivered food pellets, while at
the other end was a platform or pedal which controlled a
flashing bright light placed directly over the box. The animals
were first trained, in separate preliminary sessions, to procure
food by bar-pressing and to keep the light off by stepping or
sitting on the platform, when getting off the platform meant
the immediate return of the light. The bar and platform were
separated by a distance greater than the length of the animal's
body, so that in the conflict sessions when they were hungry
they could not maintain platform contact while stretching
over to press the bar at the same time (as many tried to do).

In one experiment, Tolcott compared the behavior of his
subjects in the conflict situation with that under hunger alone
and under light aversion alone. Two of his interesting findings may be quoted.

1. When the two drives are aroused simultaneously (conflict) the
typical behavior pattern is an alternation between the responses—short
periods of pedal-holding alternate with brief flurries of bar-pressing.

2. During these conflict sessions, more than half the experimental
interval is spent on the pedal; nevertheless the same number of bar-
responses are made as occurred during the sessions of appetite alone.
This is accomplished by an increase in the net rate, or rate at which
the bar is pressed during the spurts of bar-pressing.

The latter is an interesting point and is in line with the finding that punishment is not necessarily sufficient to reduce the
strength of a response. Indeed, it looks as if it is this very
inefficacy of punishment that allows the conflict to continue
unabated.

In another experiment, Tolcott lessened the degree of con-flict systematically by lowering the hunger drive, and com-pared behavior under the various strengths of hunger as it competed with the light aversion that was held constant. The use of light aversion was somewhat different here, since it involved the periodic and signalled presentation of light rather than continuous light. He was able to demonstrate that with increased pre-feeding, the warning signal for onset of light came to have a greater effect. Lowered hunger meant less conflict, more frequent returns to the platform in the warning period, less vacillation between the two incompatible re-sponses, and so on. The data, therefore, once more support the hypothesis that the amount of conflict is inversely related to the difference in strength of competing incompatible responses.

A later study by Winnick (1950) produced data that are significant for our understanding of conflictful behavior, and that are relevant to our earlier discussion of experiments like Hefferline's on avoidance behavior. She replaced the platform of Tolcott's apparatus with a small vertical hinged panel against which the rat pushed to keep off the aversive light. The panel could be pushed some distance beyond the point at which a switch broke the light circuit, and a pen was at-tached to the panel that gave a continuous record of its movements on a kymograph tape. As before, a bar at the other end of the box, whereby food could be obtained, created a conflict situation when the animals were placed in the box hungry. As Tolcott had observed, animals vacillated between panel-pushing and bar-pressing in the conflict sessions. But the record of panel-pushing revealed that conflict was present even when no oscillation was apparent to the eye. The panel-pushing was not steady in force or extent, but was marked by large variations even though the animal might not for a long time release it sufficiently to allow the light to come on. Incipient movements toward the bar that stopped short of the light-switching-on point, alternated with retreats from the switching-on point and pushing with renewed vigor. Figure 73 is a sample bit of Winnick's records of this conflict.

This ingenious experiment deserves to be followed up because of what it reveals about conflict and the way it bridges the topics of proprioceptive S^D's, covert response, anxiety and avoidance, and conflict behavior. The beginnings of one response, as we have said elsewhere, can generate proprioceptive S^D's which serve as anxiety arousers because they are cor-

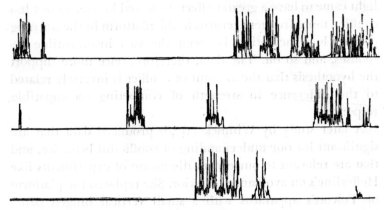

FIG. 73. Sample records of panel-pushing behavior by rats in a conflict situation. When the recording pen was at the base line, the aversive stimulus (light) was present. The animals were hungry and the jagged records show that, though they often kept the light off, there was considerable vacillation of pushing behavior because the food-getting bar was present at the opposite end of the response chamber. The records are to be read from right to left. Three 4-minute samples of behavior are shown. (From Winnick, 1950.)

related with ensuing punishment if the response goes to completion. In this way, anxiety S^D's of muscular origin give rise to 'inhibition' or 'repression' of behavior. A similar emphasis on the rôle of proprioception is to be found in the writings and actual therapeutic practices of some psychoanalysts (e.g., Wilhelm Reich, 1949). We shall not digress into this area, but there can be little doubt that the work of the clinician awaits the fruitful touch of the laboratory scientist. Studies like those of Luria (1932), Godbeer (1940), and others, show that laboratory studies with human subjects in conflict situations are feasible. Some of the findings with animals have already been corroborated with human beings. In the end, however, our knowledge of man, though it may start with humbler organisms, must be rounded out by studying man himself.

NOTES

Our chapter has been long, but it would have been longer if we had paid attention to non-experimental studies of motivation, especially to the work of Sigmund Freud (1856-1939) who, more than any other, is identified with the modern emphasis upon the sexual drive in human beings. For Freud, this drive was the foundation for his general theory of psychoanalysis, the basic tenets of which are now available in many books and articles written for laymen as well as students and professional psychotherapists. We cannot go into the intricacies of this theory here, but we may note that many of its concepts (e.g., regression, symbolism, and repression) have found their parallels in experimental research, even at the sub-human level. The future may show that this development has even more points of contact with behavioral science than are now apparent.

The best single text on motivation to which we can direct you is P. T. Young's *Motivation of behavior* (1936) which contains an excellent account of the research in this field prior to 1936. Young has himself made significant experimental contributions to our knowledge, especially in studying the sub-hungers.

The distinction between appetites and aversions is an old one, going back at least to the time of Thomas Hobbes (1651). Young, in the book mentioned above, treats these as two classes of drives, and so does E. C. Tolman, in a thought-provoking little book called *Drives toward war* (1942). Tolman's book, which leans heavily upon observations of animal behavior, also includes some interesting speculations concerning the relation of basic motives to several psychoanalytic concepts and to certain sociological and economic teachings.

10

EMOTION

THE TYPICAL varieties of emotion are each connected with certain characteristic . . . trends of activity. Anger involves a tendency to destroy and
forcibly to break down opposition. . . . Joy involves what we may call
expansive activity. . . . In grief there is a general depression and disturbance of the vital functions. . . . Fear . . . arises in a situation which
demands action for averting, evading, or escaping a loss or misfortune
which has not yet taken place.

G. F. Stout, *The Groundwork of Psychology*, 1903

A Preliminary Question

In this chapter, as in the preceding, we are concerned, not
with a principle, but a problem. The problem, in large part,
is that of deciding what to do about the term *emotion*. Is this
word to be kept in service as an aid to our understanding of
behavior, or should we retire it from active scientific duty?
The question may strike you as a foolish one. Emotion, one
hears, is something that colors human life from birth until
death. It is the essence of pleasure and the companion of pain;
it is the spirit of ecstasy and the soul of despair; it is the friend
of creative effort; it promotes well-being and ruins digestion.
Do without it? Would we not be left with a colorless and cold
existence?

This attitude misses the point of our problem. We did not
propose to shirk our obligation to deal with those aspects of
behavior which, in common speech throughout the ages, have
been called 'emotional.' We asked only if a clear and useful
meaning could be given to the word. What we sought to emphasize was the danger that lies in adopting, for scientific
purposes, a term that has such a variegated history of usage

as this one. Other terms of ancient lineage, such as *instinct*, have suffered from the same defect, and have been dropped from the vocabulary of many present-day psychologists. Still others seem destined for a similar fate. If we are to retain this one (as we really intend to do), we shall have to hedge it about carefully. We must restrict and qualify its use in a way that leaves no room for misunderstanding. At the same time, we must not strip it so bare of meaning that it no longer pertains to the countless observations from which it originally stemmed.

Some Observations

It has been profitable for us, in preceding chapters, to take, as a starting-point for discussion, the bar-pressing behavior of the white rat. Suppose we return to the laboratory again, this time with an eye to any details of his responding which we may have slighted in our earlier descriptions. What will we find that is relevant to the topic now at hand?

A number of items immediately present themselves. We note, for example, that an initial period of *'acclimatization'* to the experimental situation is generally provided before any attempt is made to condition the bar-pressing response. Without such a period, or periods, the time required to set up the habit is often quite prolonged. Familiarizing procedures are used in almost every type of animal experimentation. 'Gentling' subjects before training; giving them unreinforced 'pre-trials' in runways and mazes; acquainting them with food-boxes; accustoming them to clicks, buzzes, and other apparatus noises—all these devices are conducive to rapid learning. A similar effect has also resulted from the use of sound-proof experimental rooms, constant conditions of illumination, and so forth. In the absence of such precautions, rats are not only slowed down in their rate of learning, but may also be seen to react in unusual ways. When introduced to the experimental situation, they may wash or groom excessively, crouch in corners, and void urine or feces. Movements of exploration may be slow and cautious or absent entirely; and the slightest alteration of stimulus conditions may startle them or cause them to 'freeze' in position.

A second item of interest turns up in connection with the *extinction* of Type R responses after a period of regular reinforcement. Here, as we remarked earlier (page 71), three things are obvious: (1) an initial high rate of bar-pressing; (2) recurrent periods in which bar-pressing may be completely absent or much reduced in frequency; and (3) corresponding periods of rapid responding which seem to compensate, in decreasing measure, for the periods of no response (see Figure 16). If we watch the animal closely, again we note bar-gnawing, urination, defecation, grooming, and other responses, together with attempts to get out of the situation. These responses, and the cyclical deviations in bar-pressing rate, are *not* so typical of extinctions that follow periodic (or aperiodic) reconditioning (see page 90).

Easily observed changes of a similar sort appear when some *negatively reinforcing stimulus* is applied to our animals during periods of reinforced or non-reinforced bar-pressing. Besides the more or less complete suppression of the operant itself when the animal is slapped or shocked, he shows crouching, climbing, jumping, approaching and retreating, rapid breathing. These and other movements are characteristic of his behavior when the negatively reinforcing stimuli are frequent or intense.

Weak but clearly discernible effects upon bar-pressing rate may appear under other experimental conditions. The introduction of a dim light within the response chamber will regularly produce a lowered frequency of response during P-R sessions; and even a mild tone or buzz, to be used as an S^D or an S^Δ in a discrimination experiment, may halt responses completely during their first few presentations. Extreme intensities of these stimuli may render the animal incapable of any movement whatever. They are no longer useful as S^D's, nor can they serve as aversive stimuli, the termination of which is reinforcing—the animal cannot make the coördinated movements which would remove them.

These behavioral changes are not peculiar to any one experimental situation. Many studies have been made of the effects of lights, tones, shocks, withdrawal of reinforcement, and so forth, upon other animals than the rat, and in relation to other activities than bar-pressing. Our own observations merely confirm those which have been described by various investigators.

It requires no great imagination for one to draw up comparable examples of his own or others' behavior. Who has not been upset in strange surroundings or in the face of unexpected change? Who has not been frustrated by his inability to meet a familiar situation with an accustomed mode of action? And who has not experienced, at least for a moment, the behavioral disruption which can follow an injury, an explosion, a loss of equilibrium, or some other form of sudden, intense stimulation? We would hardly say that our rat's behavior is unique.

Such phenomena as those we have described above lead us to a few general statements. Certain experimental operations, such as the taking away of positive reinforcement or the giving of negative, result in certain operant and respondent changes. These effects sometimes fade out gradually with continued exposure to the situation or with removal of the noxious stimuli. When one observes all or some of them, he feels fairly safe in saying that emotion exists. This is not the entire story, but it gives us a point of departure for what follows.

Emotion and Drive

If we were to define emotion tentatively, and broadly, as a state inferred from the change in strength of a number of reflexes as a result of certain operations, we should not only epitomize the foregoing discussion, but we should also be making a statement that applies equally well to the concept of *drive* as we treated it in the preceding chapter. Moreover, we would not be the first to recognize this similarity. Many students, ancient and modern, have noted as much. Descartes, in the seventeenth century, argued that "the principal effect of the passions [emotions] in man is that they incite and dispose [motivate] the mind to will the things to which they prepare the body." William James (1890) asserted that "instinctive reactions [read motives] . . . shade imperceptibly into each other. Every object that excites an instinct excites an emotion as well. . . ." And William McDougall (1923) postulated for most of the basic 'instincts' (again, motives) a closely related emotional counterpart—flight, an 'instinctive' impulse, was associated with fear, an "affective state"; pugnacity was associated with the emotion of anger; and so on.

In our own discussion of aversions, it must have occurred to you that the effects of such stimuli as electric shocks were certainly 'emotional' in the everyday sense of the word; and to this we are forced to agree. In addition, we would have to admit that the scientific, no less than the popular, distinction between emotion and aversion is perhaps insupportable. The line of demarcation is at best very faintly drawn. The operation by which we define aversion is that of presenting stimuli —shocks, slaps, lights, tones, and so on; but this is also one of the operations we use to define emotion. One difference between aversion and emotion seems to lie in the *intensity* of stimuli that we present.

This difference leads us to look at the matter in another way. On page 232 we stated that stimuli have different functions. Beyond their *reinforcing* status, they may be *elicitative* (the respondent case), *discriminative* (setting the occasion for reinforcement of an operant), *drive-inducing* (aversive), and *emotionalizing*. We now suggest that the intensity continuum cannot be ignored. Mild or moderately intense stimuli readily become S^D's; stronger, negatively reinforcing stimuli, the removal of which is positively reinforcing, may be called *aversive;* and extreme intensities are those we commonly treat as *emotional*. Take a weak light as an S^D (a shock or tone would serve as well). A rat can be easily trained to press a bar whenever such a stimulus is presented. If, however, we increase the intensity of this stimulus, we have trouble in separating the purely discriminative or eliciting status from the aversive—that is, we find that the animal can be taught to turn off this light. Now, if the intensity is still further increased, the motivating function of the stimulus is obscured—the animal may respond for a while in an adaptive fashion, but gradually his behavior becomes more and more disorganized. He runs this way and that; he leaps and climbs and falls about in his cage; and he may even end by lying prostrate on the floor, unable to make any movement that would free him from his plight.

We begin to see, then, why it is that emotions and drives have so long and so persistently been confused with each other. Ultimately, we may decide that the fence between the two concepts does not justify the labor spent in its upkeep. For the present, however, we shall assume that the suggested difference in operations and behavior are great enough to warrant a distinction.

Emotion as an Inferred State

In our tentative definition, we spoke of emotion as an 'inferred state.' We should now add, as in our discussion of drive, that such inferring is convenient, but not strictly necessary, and sometimes dangerous. If we slip into the practice of assigning to this hypothetical state any properties not given in our observations, we jeopardize the clarity of our thinking. It is especially necessary to avoid treating the state as something 'mental' that causes our behavior. In so doing, we may be merely trying to lift ourselves by our own bootstraps—we infer something *from* behavior which we then use to *explain* the very behavior from which the inference came.

When we think of the state as *physiological* or *neurological*, rather than mental, we would seem to be on better ground.

There is indisputable evidence of widespread organic changes which accompany responses regularly called emotional. Yet, even here we must be wary. Our lack of detailed knowledge, both physiological and behavioral, does not permit us to go very far in relating the two areas. We are on much better footing at present if we consider an emotional state as a behavioral construct, keeping uppermost in mind the operations that provide for changes in response.

Three Theories

To illustrate the complexity of our problem, with reference to the points just made, let us consider briefly three ways in which the emotion of 'fear' has been treated by psychologists and physiologists. A very old, and still popular, view runs something like this. Fear is an episodic *mental* state—an unpleasant, all-pervasive, and 'stirred-up' consciousness, known at first hand only to its possessor. It is *aroused* by certain objects, events, or ideas; and it *is expressed* by various 'involuntary' or 'voluntary' changes in behavior. It arises *naturally*, as when one quakes at a loud sound heard in the night, or *through training,* as when one trembles at the prospect of making a speech before a large audience. In its extreme form, terror, its expression is very dramatic. The eyes and the mouth open wide; the skin pales and cools and sweats; breathlessness occurs, and the heart beats against the ribs; saliva stops flowing and the mouth becomes dry and sticky; the voice becomes husky and indistinct, or fails entirely; the pupils of the eyes enlarge and the hairs stand erect on the head and body surface. The normal digestive functions are halted and bowel or bladder control may be lost. The hands may be raised high, flight may ensue, or one may stand, trembling, rooted to the spot.

In this classical picture, the sequence of events is (1) stimulation, (2) subjectively 'felt' emotion, and (3) bodily 'expression'—behavior. The same sequence, with differences in content, would be characteristic of joy, sorrow, anger, and other time-honored categories. (We ignore, for the present, the problem of how an 'idea' may be a stimulus, how a 'mental' state may be known except through behavior, or why 'introspective' descriptions of the emotions seem always to point to S^D's arising from the bodily response itself.)

William James, in 1884 and later, proposed a drastic revision of the earlier theory. Supporting his view by an appeal to a similar position arrived at by the Danish physiologist, Lange, he argued that the felt emotion *follows,* rather than precedes, the bodily expression. For him, the stimulating object or event led first to the *expressive movements* which themselves *produced* the 'awareness' of the emotion. "Common sense says, we lose our fortune, are sorry and weep; we meet a bear, are frightened and run; we are insulted by a rival, are angry and strike. . . . The more rational statement is that we feel sorry because we cry, angry because we strike, afraid because we tremble." Stated more baldly than James would perhaps have liked, his position was this: a stimulus (e.g., a bear) sometimes elicits widespread changes in a person's behavior, and these changes in turn become discriminative stimuli which prompt us, or the individual himself, to assert that fear exists.

The James-Lange doctrine no longer upsets us. The objectively oriented person, trained to distinguish between what is observed and what is merely inferred, even finds it easier to understand than its predecessor. But a vigorous attempt has been made to turn our thoughts in a third direction—toward brain physiology. In 1927, Walter B. Cannon and two associates demonstrated that the surgical removal of the sympathetic division of the autonomic nervous system did not eliminate the overt responses 'expressive' of rage, fear, or joy in cats. The same investigator adduced evidence to show that there are no response changes (in heart-rate, digestive activity, sweating, hair-erection, and the like) which are distinctive for the various emotions. All of them are characteristic of strong excitement, and many of them are present in fever, strong exercise, and other presumably non-emotional states. From such considerations, Cannon was led to reject the James-Lange view that emotion, in general, is the 'awareness' of response, and that different response patterns give rise to the specific emotions of rage, fear, and so on. Instead, he offered a theory which relates the emotional 'consciousness' to the activity of a special brain center (the thalamus) which may be excited by stimuli independently of any expressive reactions of the muscles or glands.

We need not enter into the intricacies of these theories or the debates which have revolved about them. Rather, let us remind ourselves that all three suffer from the defect that we described in the preceding section. In ascribing either a 'mental' or a physiological character to emotion, they do not clarify our thought. The basic facts are these: something is done to an organism—a stimulus is presented or withdrawn, a reinforcement is given or taken away; and, as a result, widespread changes in reflex strength occur. Some of these changes, like those of digestive activity, are detectible only with the tools of the physiologist; others, like the depressions or accelerations of on-going operants, are visible to anyone's naked eye. In order to circumvent the round-aboutness of this account, we say that the organism is *emotional*. To assert that the emotion is *mental*, does not advance our scientific understanding, since there is no known procedure for investigating the mental as distinct from the behavioral. To say that it is *physiological*, has more justification, since we have some independent evidence of physiological changes which accompany the behavioral, but we still have a long road to travel before all the physiological 'correlates' of behavior are determined. Certainly, the *prediction* and *control* of behavior is not far advanced by the assumption that either a 'felt' emotion (mental) or its 'expression' (behavioral) is caused by brain processes (physiological).

Response Patterns and Emotion

For many generations, men have treated certain responses or groups of responses as indicative of emotion; and, down through the years, attempts have regularly been made to distinguish one emotion from another on such a basis. The classical theory was oriented in this direction, and so was the James-Lange view that followed it. Each major emotion was to be defined, at least in part, in terms of a pattern of bodily changes, alike in all individuals, with components that were presumably apparent to any naïve observer. It behooves us, therefore, to ask whether this practice is sound, whether emotions *can* be described as specific response patterns.

1. *Facial expression.* The answer to this question is not as simple as you might think. It seems obvious that the face of an enraged man is unlike that of a frightened one; and, seemingly, no one could mistake the face of joy for that of sorrow. Yet, when we look at the matter closely, we find ourselves in trouble. Is my expression of fear or joy like yours? Does the anger of the Asiatic resemble that of the European? Are these expressions 'natural' or are they 'acquired'? How can we tell whether they are 'real' or 'feigned'? Are the responses "universal and immutable," as argued by Duchenne (1862), or was William James right in saying that "everyone of us, almost, has some personal idiosyncrasy of expression?"

The history of facial-expression studies gives us a rather confused picture, but one or two conclusions may today be drawn with some assurance. First, it would appear that a certain limited number of facial response patterns are recognizable in human children shortly after birth. A clearly distinguishable *smile,* which precedes and is closely related to the *laughing* response, may be evoked after two to fifteen weeks of infancy (Jones, 1926). It has been pointed out by Young (1943) that both smiling and laughing tend to occur with (a) the satisfaction of hunger or thirst, (b) relief from discomfort, (c) presentation of certain colors, sounds, tastes, and contacts, and (d) the free movements of play or dancing. In a word, they come as a consequence of presenting positive reinforcers or removing negative reinforcers. *Frowning,* which is related to *crying* as the smile is related to the laugh, also occurs in infancy as a recognizable pattern. Young says that this response accompanies (a) hunger or thirst, (b) painful stimulation, (c) dazzling lights, loud sounds, or other intense stimuli, and (d) frustration or blockage of response. That is to say, negative reinforcement or the withdrawal of positive reinforcement.

Secondly, we note that such expressions can apparently be strengthened and modified operant-wise. The child, we say, comes to 'use' an expression 'for his own purposes.' He develops an 'ingratiating' or a 'disarming' smile; he 'gets his own way' by crying; and so on. His facial expression, like his vocal, is shaped in one way or another by the selective reinforcement which his family, his friends, and others provide. The 'natural' smile of babyhood may be displaced almost entirely by a smile that is 'artificial,' 'studied,' or 'forced.' So powerful are these strengthening influences that the naïve expression is often obscured. In some adults, a fairly complete immobility of features—for example, the 'dead pan' of the professional card-player—may be achieved when it is of advantage to do so. Or, at the other extreme, as in the expressions of the skilled actor, a variety of subtle variations of response may be developed through their effectiveness in molding the reactions of others. As with many common forms of behavior, facial responses come under the control of the organism's social environment. It should, therefore, occasion little surprise to find that the facial habits of adult Chinese are as different from our own as forks are different from chopsticks (Klineberg, 1940).

Thirdly, we may say that, as far as the adult human being is concerned, facial expressions are poor indices of the prevailing emotional state. A well-known study by Landis (1924) points this up rather dramatically. Mature human subjects were presented with a variety of presumably emotion-arousing stimuli (electric shocks, explosions, etc.). Resultant changes in pulse, respiration, and heart-beat were recorded and, in addition, photographs were made of the facial expression of each subject in each emotional situation. Analysis of these

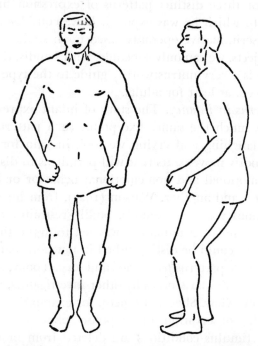

FIG. 74. Two representations of "startle," an unconditioned pattern of muscular responses to such stimuli as pistol shots. This is one of the few relatively stable 'emotional' patterns in human adults. This characteristic spasm is over in less than a second. (From Landis and Hunt, *The startle pattern* [Farrar & Rinehart, 1939].)

photographs showed that there was no facial expression typical of any stimulus situation or any verbally reported emotion. Nor was there any relation between reported emotion and the recorded internal changes. Landis was led to conclude that the behavioral distinction between emotions lay, not in the facial response pattern or the organic changes, but in the nature of the stimulus situation and the degree of general disturbance evoked. Verbal reports of such states as surprise, anger, exasperation, and disgust were paralleled mainly by a decrease in the *amount* of facial movement, in the order here named; and each individual characteristically used no more than two or three distinct patterns of expression in all the situations to which he was exposed. If we consider these reports as discriminative operants based upon similar states in all the subjects, we can only conclude, with Landis, that facial expression is a very untrustworthy guide to the type of emotion involved, at least for adults.

2. *Patterns in infancy.* The story of infant expressions of emotion is much the same. Except for such patterns of response as laughing and crying we look in vain for specific facial or bodily movements that will permit us to distinguish between emotional and non-emotional behavior or between one emotion and another. Watson (1924), from his study of infant responses to loud sounds, bodily restraint, fondling, and other forms of stimulation, was led to argue that three basic patterns could be distinguished in newborn babies, and he named these patterns *fear, rage,* and *love.* Today, however, in the light of similar studies by other investigators, we question Watson's view. Sherman (1928), for example, has shown us that the observation of response patterns *alone* (as when the stimulus conditions are deleted from moving-picture records of the experiments) provide for a great deal of disagreement among observers as to the emotions actually displayed. Unanimity of judgment by nurses, medical students, and others, depended largely upon their knowledge of the circumstances in which the behavior took place. In this field, as in that of adult facial expression or of 'physiological' reactions (blood-pressure, respiratory, and other changes), the attempt to find uniform emotional patterns of response has been singularly unsuccessful.

You may have anticipated such findings because of the way in which we approached our problem. We said that emotion is to be distinguished from motivation on the basis of the operations involved and the widespread changes in reflex strength observed, but we did not attempt to specify any particular responses or patterns of response that were uniquely emotional in their nature. Perhaps there *are* such, observable at the sub-human level and in the early years of human growth. A pattern of 'rage,' for example, has been observed in cats, dogs, and other animals, and we have already mentioned the smiling and frowning responses of babies. But there is little reason to believe that we shall ever be able to classify man's emotions exclusively in terms of his behavior.

Table XII

THE IDENTIFICATION BY ADULTS OF EMOTIONS "EXPRESSED" BY INFANTS
(Data from Sherman, 1928)

Names Given	Initiating Conditions							
	Not Shown				Shown			
	Hunger	Dropping	Restraint	Needle-pricking	Hunger	Dropping	Restraint	Needle-pricking
Anger	13	15	16	9	15	5	29	13
Fear	7	5	5	9	0	27	4	7
Hunger	7	6	2	2	7	0	0	0
Pain	3	3	4	3	2	2	1	13

Some of the names given by graduate students in psychology to infant "emotional" behavior (as seen in moving pictures) when (a) the initiating conditions were *shown* (or named, as for "hunger") and (b) when the initiating conditions were *not shown*. The table may be read as follows: 13 students called the infant's behavior "anger" when the behavior was aroused by "hunger" but the initiating conditions were not shown, etc.

Specific Emotions

What, then, can we say about the traditional categories of emotion that we commonly respect in our everyday speech and which have been the subject matter of so many psychological treatises? Are we justified in talking of fear, rage, joy, sorrow, and the like, when they have never been defined to the satisfaction of the objectively oriented scientist? It will not do, in answering these questions, to argue that, since we have used such words or their equivalents down through the ages and in many lands, they *must* represent fundamental realities; nor will it do to appeal to personal 'experience' or 'consciousness' of these different emotions. Error, no less than truth, may persist for long periods of time; and one's report of an 'experienced' emotion does not ordinarily tell us what S^D's determined it. We might rather take the same path that we followed in our treatment of motivation. Let us ask about the effect of specific operations upon the changes in strength of groups of reflexes. Perhaps, in the end, we shall be able to justify the popular distinctions, but we ought not to begin by accepting them too readily.

1. *Fear.* In our discussion of anxiety in Chapter 9, it may have struck you that we could as easily have used the word *fear* for this inferred state and called it *emotional*. This is, indeed, the case. It is difficult to draw a sharp line between the motivational and emotional aspects of anxiety, and the difference between *fear* and *anxiety* is hardly worth arguing about. The important thing is not the name that we use but the fact that some originally neutral stimulus comes to be a secondary negative reinforcer and *alters the probability that certain responses will occur*. A distinction between fear as emotion and as drive is possibly useful in some cases, as when the organism seems unable to make the responses which would remove the activating stimuli. Fear then qualifies as distinctly emotional and is sometimes called *terror*. However, we could study the matter in detail without ever mentioning any of these words;

the experimental operations and the behavioral changes are the truly significant things. If we choose to apply these classical terms, it is only because serious students of motivation and emotion have often used them in connection with situations and behavior that are indistinguishable from those with which we are concerned.

From the earliest days of theorizing about fear, emphasis has been placed upon responses mediated by the autonomic nervous system—respondents, like paling, sweating, shivering, and so on. But these responses, as Cannon has made clear, are not sufficient to define the emotion adequately. They may occur in other states, some of which, like fever, would not be called emotional. The changes in strength which help us most are those depressions of on-going operant behavior which are obvious to any observer. The organism shows a marked decrease in the frequency of many of his normal, everyday responses. The rat, for example, at the sound of the tone which was followed by shock in the Estes-Skinner experiment (page 309), no longer pressed the bar at his accustomed rate; and we have reason to believe that all of his other operant behavior in the experimental chamber was similarly affected. The human being, in a comparable situation, talks less, makes fewer movements, is hyper-sensitive to small stimulus changes, approaches new objects gingerly, or brings his routine activities to a complete standstill. These are some of the changes which serve as S^D's for us in ascribing fear to another.

The operation we have selected in defining fear is the *presentation of a secondary negative reinforcer*. It is unlikely that this is the only effective condition. Primary negative reinforcers (shocks, loud sounds, etc.) may have the same behavior outcome; and there may be still other inducing factors. It is best, however, to leave it for future research to broaden the group of operations and to make further distinctions.

In line with the present analysis, any stimulus situation may become fear-instigating if associated with aversive stimuli.

This has long been recognized by specialists in the study of morbid fears or 'phobias.' Scarcely an object or event can be named which has not been for some person at some time a source of overpowering fear. Sharp objects, open spaces, running water, horses, dirt, automobiles—these, and countless other components of our everyday outside world may come, through conditioning, to alter severely our response tendencies. Even internal, response-produced stimuli may be effective, as when we are said to fear a 'thought,' an 'idea,' or the performance of some act. When the circumstances of life have conspired to give a negatively reinforcing status to too many of the aspects of the environment, outer or inner, it may even make sense to speak of 'generalized fear.'

2. *Anger.* When positive reinforcement is suddenly withdrawn, a rat's bar-pressing, as well as his general activity in the experimental situation, will show a quick acceleration, and he may even be seen to 'attack' the bar vigorously with his teeth. Pigeons, when crowded into narrow quarters or confronted by trespassers upon their well-staked-out preserves, will fight each other viciously (Craig, 1921). Other animals respond similarly in similar situations. Hebb (1946) has recently given us an especially interesting account of chimpanzee behavior, from which it appears that the *breaking of an operant chain* is a fundamental factor in producing sudden and violent attack behavior, self-injury (pounding the head on the floor), screaming, and, on some occasions, a response depression or 'negativity' which may reach the point where the ape will turn away entirely from some formerly positive reinforcer. Hebb applies the words *rage, temper tantrums,* and *sulking* to such behavior, and speaks of the initiating circumstances as "the removal of a desired object," the "failure to get something," and the "frustration of an expectation." The breaking of a chain of on-going responses may, however, apparently be effected by the withdrawal of positive reinforcers and the presentation of negative. Thus, Hebb speaks also of *teasing,* as when one ape repeatedly interrupts

another's activity-in-progress by screaming, spitting at him, or making threatening gestures. (It seems obvious that 'teasing' might also be applied to those cases in which an 'expectation' is set up and then 'frustrated.')

In his treatment of infant emotions, Watson (1924) cited 'restraint of movement' as the principal cause of rage. We can see in physical restraint another way of interrupting a chain, and some credence may therefore be given to Watson's position. But it should be noted that the restraining action must be imposed upon movement-in-progress—it must be truly 'thwarting.' Dennis (1940) has pointed out that a new-born infant's random movements may be restricted greatly and for long periods of time, as by swaddling clothes or cradle-boards, without noticeable emotional upset unless the 'restraint' is forceful enough to constitute a negatively reinforcing stimulation.

The operation of chain-breaking may be detected or suggested in many everyday situations allegedly productive of anger. In a study by Gates (1926), women students were asked to report all instances of this emotion during a one-week period of self-observation, giving in each case an account of the precipitating circumstances. Among the situations mentioned by these subjects were scoldings, criticisms, refusals of requests, tardiness of friends in keeping appointments, getting a wrong number on the telephone, failure in operation of such objects as watches, fountain-pens, and typewriters, delays in bus or elevator operation, clumsiness in dressing or sewing, disobedience of dogs or children, interrupted sleep, and loss of money. These occasions were reported to engender "impulses" to (a) make verbal retorts, (b) do physical injury to the offender, (c) injure inanimate objects, (d) get out of the situation, and (e) cry, scream, or swear. The order of frequency with which these tendencies were reported is indicated by the order of mention. The verbal retort was specified five times as often as crying, screaming, or swearing. Also, *persons*, rather than *things*, were reported as the main source of anger.

Obviously no one pattern of responses for all subjects was peculiar to any one situation, since the responses involved were dependent upon the individual's history of conditioning, yet some similarity of outcome is indicated by the fact that the responses fall into these five groupings.

In spite of the fact that no two persons react in exactly the same way as a result of the anger-producing operation, there appear to be certain fairly common elements of such behavior as we ordinarily observe it. Increased muscular tension (sometimes seen in the clenched fist, the grimly set jaw, and the rigid posture of an angry man), movements of advance or attack, stamping of the feet, elevation of the voice, and so on, are often enough seen to suggest the state even when we are unaware of the initiating conditions.

3. *Sorrow and joy.* The changes in rat behavior resulting from stimuli that have been regularly associated with electric shock often lead observers to attribute *fear* to these animals. The sudden burst of bar-pressing and biting responses at the beginning of an extinction session is frequently said to show *anger.* We now see that the use of these two terms is justified in some degree. *Sorrow and joy,* on the other hand, are seldom imputed to the rat in any situation, even by persons who regularly employ such terms in connection with the behavior of dogs, chimpanzees, and human beings. Are there operations, different from those we use to define anger and fear, which are related to special changes in reflex strength?

We are loath to reply to this question, for several reasons. Psychological literature does not abound with treatment of these concepts. One of the most authoritative discussions in recent years (Young, 1943) gives them barely a mention; and most textbooks do little more than assume their existence. Unlike anger, and especially fear, they have seldom been the subject of scientific investigation. Moreover, those who attempt to give meaning to these terms are in no great agreement, possibly because they have so often been concerned with the fruitless task of identifying these emotions by facial expression. Yet, it is improbable that the present reader will have the least doubt about the existence of sorrow and joy.

It would perhaps be wise to say nothing more about the matter here. Yet we cannot resist mention of two possibilities that present themselves in connection with familiar descriptions of sorrow and joy. To us it seems clear that the *complete removal of secondary positive reinforcers* occasions a widespread behavioral depression which involves changes commonly referred to as those of grief, sadness, or sorrow. The irretrievable loss of money, home, possessions, family, or friends seems to bring an obvious altering of muscular tonus (one is 'bowed down' under the 'weight of sorrow'), a slowness or absence of reaction to customary social stimuli, and a decrease in the frequency and force of speaking, not to mention the appearance of sobbing and moaning.

The withdrawal of strong secondary reinforcers implies the breaking of response chains, and this is an anger-producing operation. How, then, can we call it a condition of sorrow? The answer here may be that anger is the first stage in the production of sorrow. If the loss of secondary reinforcement is impermanent or restricted to but a few chains of action, anger may be the result, but if the loss is prolonged and related to many chains sorrow will ensue. Accounts of sorrowful behavior seem to be in part accounts of anger. Thus, Foley (1935) has described the grief of chimpanzees as due to such factors as a refusal or delay in complying with their expressed wants or desires, operations which Hebb (page 342) treats as productive of anger. And have we not all observed that great losses are commonly met at the outset by cries of rage and resentment, to be followed soon by the deepest of depressions? Perhaps, even, the 'sulkiness' so often taken to be a form of anger is, in good part, the beginning of sorrow.

If the removal of secondary positively reinforcing stimuli is important for sorrow, certainly the *presentation* of such stimuli should facilitate those responses we call *joyful*. Again, we have little evidence to present, but the non-experimental

observation of human beings and certain animals points convincingly in this direction. Almost everyone has noted the
changes in the behavior of children at the approach of a dot-
ing relative or family friend, the announcement of an unexpected holiday, the promise of a trip to the beach or the
zoo, or the sound of the bell that signals a recess from school.
The reaction picture on such occasions is one of excitement,
just as marked in its own way as the depression of sorrow.
Lively, free, and extensive movements of arms and legs (the
child 'dances for joy'), smiling, laughing, excessive vocaliz-
ing—these and other activities are commonly observed when
a child is presented with verbal or other stimuli that have in
the past been followed by strong positive reinforcement.
Adults are usually less expressive, and react in a less diffuse,
more differentiated fashion than do youngsters, but some
changes in tendency to respond are usually apparent.

These suggestions are put down with hesitation, because
the problem of identifying specific emotions is a complex one.
We have not made an exhaustive attack upon this problem,
but an important aim will have been accomplished if we have
shown the way in which an objective, experimental approach
must proceed. One thing is certain: there are operations,
involving stimulus presentation and removal, which do more
than change the strength of a single response (as in conditioning and extinction); they change the strength of *many* responses. We have argued that these latter changes, taken in
conjunction with the operations involved, seem to be related
to traditional descriptions of fear, anger, sorrow, and joy. But,
even if this were not entirely true, we would still have the
problem of accounting for the changes resulting from the
operations.

Emotional Conditioning

It is unnecessary to say much about the conditioning of
emotions, in view of the instances of it which have already
accumulated in this text. It has long been recognized that

emotion involves a great deal of autonomically governed behavior; and, since Chapter 2, you have known that this kind of behavior is readily conditioned in Type S fashion. Our treatment of the effects of punishment, in Chapter 4, made explicit note of emotional conditioning; and statements of similar import have occurred in our discussion of several other topics. Emotional conditioning is a fact, and so is emotional extinction, although our knowledge of these processes is still at a fairly primitive level.

A classic instance of conditioned emotion may be cited here. Watson and Rayner (1920) presented a nine-months-old boy with a white rat at the same time that a loud sound was produced by hammering on a steel bar. The rat had not previously disturbed the child, whereas the noise had elicited a violent 'fear reaction.' Only a few combinations of the two stimuli were required to give the rat a strong conditioned-stimulus function. Moreover, the effect was shown to generalize to other furry animals and several inanimate objects of a 'furry' nature—even to cotton wool.

Criticism was later launched at Watson's *definition* of fear (see page 338), but several studies have confirmed the fundamental observations of a conditioned emotional change, and a few investigators have gone further. Jones (1924a, 1924b), working with a three-year-old boy who came to her with an already well-established emotional reaction to rabbits, rats, and other animals, undertook to eliminate this effect. The procedure first employed was that of introducing the rabbit to the the child gradually while the latter was playing with three other, unafraid, children. This technique was working well when an unfortunate experience with a large dog served to recondition the emotion. The method then adopted was that of presenting the rabbit at times when the child was eating a highly desired food. In order to avoid a violent upset on any test occasion, the animal was never brought so near to the child as to depress his eating behavior. This procedure of combining the extinction of some responses with the positive reinforcement of others was successful in eradicating the fear. In addition, Jones found that the extinction generalized to such a degree that the other, formerly frightening, animals and objects lost their power to evoke the emotion.

In view of such findings as these, you may be surprised to learn that very few follow-up studies of the conditioning and extinction of human emotions have been made. Obviously, much work remains to be done in this area. It is understandable, however, that experimentalists (and parents) hesitate to subject children to emotional conditioning unless there is a control of factors, in the home and elsewhere, such that the often lengthy process of extinction can be carried to completion. The usefulness of preliminary research with animals is clearly indicated. We do well, perhaps, in following the lead of medical scientists and others who test out their procedures at a phylogenetic level where it will not endanger human health and development.

Observing Our Own Emotions

It was stated earlier (page 340) that our 'consciousness' of our own fear, joy, and so forth was not a satisfactory reason for assuming the reality of these states of reflex strength. Before leaving the topic of emotion, something further should be said about this statement.

When we say that we *observe* anything, we mean no more than that we make a specific response to a discriminative stimulus or stimulus compound. Such stimulation may, in psychology, arise from the behavior of *other* organisms, in which case we ordinarily speak of 'objective' observation. It may also arise from *our* own responses, affecting us through our eyes, ears, or the sense-organs in our muscles (proprioceptors). When you say, of another person, "He is angry," you are behaving in much the same way as when you respond to your own behavior by saying "I am angry." The difference lies mainly in the discriminative stimuli. Moreover, your responses to either of these two stimulus situations are made

because they have in the past been *reinforced* in their presence—you have actually been *taught* to discriminate by someone in the course of your behavioral development.

If this is clear, let's go a bit further. When you were taught
to say "I am angry," your teacher could not himself observe
(respond to) all the stimuli present, because some of them
were produced by your covert responding. He could observe
the external stimulus situation and *some* of the changes in
your behavior that followed, but not all. Which stimuli became important for you as S^D's he could not tell. Your teacher
may have said only "You're angry, aren't you," when he saw
your overt behavior. When you come to say "I am angry,"
your S^D's may not be limited to those which led to his response. The astonishing fact is that, after such training, there
is so often good agreement between one's own report of anger
(or some other state) and the report of an onlooker—not seldom is the assertion "You look angry" answered by the assertion "I *am* angry."

We have already said, however, that the response "I am
angry," as well as such typical non-verbal accompaniments as
fist-clenching, may be made independently of any anger-producing operation whatever. The use of these words and
gestures may be effective in producing other kinds of reinforcement than that provided by our 'teacher.' They may be
used, for example, because they have been reinforced by flight,
or some form of compliance, in another. In such cases it is
sometimes hard for us to say whether a person is 'really angry,'
'just bluffing,' or 'hunting for sympathy' unless we know his
history very well and the situation in which he is behaving.

By now you should be able to see why psychologists have
hesitated to lean upon verbal reports of emotion. These reports are discriminative responses as much as any other, but
some of the S^D's are *private* and one cannot be sure that they
always go hand in hand with those that are *public*. In any
case, you should appreciate that one's reports of his own emotions are derived initially from the discriminative training

given by someone else. Hence, they can hardly be used as the test of any *objective* distinction between anger, joy, and any other states.

Emotion and Feeling

In Chapter 8 (pages 254-256), we noted that the problem of reported 'feelings' is similar to that of reported 'emotions.' When someone tells us that an object, a color, or a design is 'pleasant' or 'unpleasant,' he is reporting upon his own reactions to that object, color, or design. A positive, or a negative, reinforcer has been presented or withdrawn; a change in behavior has taken place, including, perhaps, incipient movements of approach or withdrawal; these movements (or others) provide the S^D's for his verbal responses—his 'affective judgments.' The situation is undoubtedly similar to that which obtains when we ask subjects to identify their emotions. We can easily understand why feelings and emotions are characteristically lumped together, and why people have often tried to classify emotions as 'pleasant' or 'unpleasant.' The operations of giving and taking away reinforcement are important in both emotion and feeling; whether we report one or the other depends upon the particular S^D complex (as well as the request for a report) that is operative at the moment.

Finally, we can see why feelings and emotions are generally treated as 'subjective.' We might suggest that you extend this line of thought a little farther. Where, in essence, would "beauty" and "ugliness" lie? And what is the basis for our ethical judgments of "good" and "bad"? These are interesting questions, in psychology as in other disciplines, but this is hardly the place for their discussion. We have perhaps equally interesting matters for consideration in the chapter to come. Let us, then, move on.

NOTES

An excellent review of past treatments of emotion by psychologists and physiologists may be found in Chapters XI and XII of Woodworth's *Experimental psychology* (1938); and you may find interesting the related chapters (X and XIII) dealing with *feeling* and the *galvanic skin response*. It will also pay you to read the discussions of emotional 'expression' (Landis) and the physiological theory of emotion (Bard) in the *Handbook of general experimental psychology*, edited by Carl Murchison. For an account of the James-Lange theory of emotion, you ought to go to that written by James himself in his *Principles of psychology*, Vol. II, Chapter 25 (1890). The most inclusive modern text on emotion is Young's *Emotion in man and animal* (1943). The intrinsic interest and readability of these accounts should not blind you to the fact that they do not attempt a systematic *behavioral* analysis of the problem—one that is free of mentalism and physiology.

11

SOCIAL BEHAVIOR

SOCIAL BEHAVIOR comprises the stimulations and reactions arising between an individual . . . and his fellows. . . . Social psychology must not be placed in contradistinction to the psychology of the individual; it is a part of the psychology of the individual, whose behavior it studies in relation to that sector of his environment comprised by his fellows. . . .

F. H. Allport, *Social Psychology*, 1924

Introduction

In one sense, this chapter is anti-climactic; in another, it is preparatory. Your introduction to the problems of general psychology was essentially completed with the discussion of motivation and emotion. The present chapter represents in a small way how our basic principles may be extended into areas of behavior which, though complex, are compelling in interest and importance. Psychologists have painstakingly amassed a large body of information about the social conduct of animals and human beings. It will be our task here to show how this area may be approached with the analytical tools now at your command. Only considerations of space prevent our doing the same thing for other special areas, such as abnormal psychology, developmental psychology, and so on.

We have said before (page 257) that social stimuli do not differ from other stimuli in their dimensions. Rather, the difference is one of *origin*. They arise from other organisms, their behavior, or the products of their behavior. Moreover, social stimuli do not differ in their *function* from those of inanimate origin; they act as eliciting, reinforcing, discriminative, and so on. Social life arises because *social* stimuli come to exercise these functions. These facts give us a solid step-ping-off point for the discussion to come. It will help, too, to recall that sub-human organisms, no less than man, exhibit social behavior. Indeed, from them we may learn a number of things that will enable us to see man's social activities in a more objective light.

In venturing to extend our principles into social behavior, we must be cautious because the experimental or field data under examination have often been gathered under complex conditions. Complex studies, in which many (and sometimes unknown) variables are at work, allow only general inter-pretations and force any detailed analysis to be too speculative for scientific comfort. The *details* of data may resist analysis even when we discern in them the operation of some underly-ing principle that we know well.

Social Behavior in Animals

Behavioral interaction may be observed at the biological level of single-celled creatures. The plant *Volvox*, for ex-ample, lives in a colony to which the offspring remain con-nected until they break away to form their own aggregations; and *Paramecia*, which are normally solitary animals, come together for the purposes of sexual reproduction. At this level, actions probably depend on physico-chemical changes that function exclusively in an eliciting fashion.

Higher in the animal scale, *insects* have long provided us with complicated examples of social interaction. Everyone has heard of the division of labor and specialization of func-tion which characterize ant and bee communities. Some species of ants even protect and rear other organisms (aphids) within their nests, and 'milk' them later for the nutritive liquid they secrete. Much of this and other insect behavior is probably elicited respondent-wise. Nevertheless, insects can also learn in Type R fashion. We know that they may be taught to run simple mazes for food and to escape from noxious stimuli; and it may be that social stimuli, such as those involved in return to the nest, may also act as operant reinforcers.

Birds provide further examples of socially mediated reinforcement. Many species habitually live in flocks, but even where this is not the case, they may form groups under certain conditions, as at times of migration. Seasonal changes in temperature and in diurnal illumination produce bodily effects (e.g., in the sex organs) that raise the activity level. The gathering of a migratory group at given locations, the formation of typical flight patterns in the air, the flight leadership by older and more experienced birds—all of these probably involve operant-respondent overlap, but social interaction is obvious. Most birds show a degree of care for the young, and they may prolong this care beyond the time when the offspring are capable of independent flight and self-support. Even the songs and call-notes of birds may be in part a product of social control. In the oft-cited experiment by Scott (1901), young orioles were separated from their parents and raised in isolation, so that they would not be exposed to the normal oriole song, with the result that a new kind of song appeared. Conradi (1905), later, placed sparrows with canaries and observed that the sparrows tended to reproduce the canary calls. In such creatures, there may be a natural tendency to echo sounds, but even if there were not, it is possible that, through socially-given differentiation training, such behavior might arise, with the parent bird providing food for the young when certain sounds were approximated. In this way, a young stranger in the nest might gradually be taught the 'language' of his foster parents, even as we do with our own children.

Social behavior is, of course, found in extraordinary richness among *mammals,* particularly the *primates.* Habitual living may be in herds, flocks, and packs; family units are often clearly defined; and sexual attachments may be monogamous or polygamous, seasonal or perennial, and sometimes even homosexual. One has but to think of domesticated animals like the dog and horse to realize that social stimuli may become powerfully discriminative, reinforcing, and drive-arousing for sub-human behavior. Monkeys, baboons, and the anthropoid apes have been studied in some detail by psychologists and zoologists, and much is known about their actual or potential social activity. Investigators all attest to the strength of friendships and enmities among these animals, and to various other well-delineated inter-personal relations.

The exigencies under which social stimulation controls animal behavior are numerous. Sexual needs give reinforcing value to the mate who mediates the reinforcement. Parental care, especially among animals in which the young go through a long period of dependency, also favors the development of social S^D's and S^r's. Huddling behavior, whereby physical warmth is provided, may lead to the same end. Even food-getting may give rise to behavioral control by such stimuli, as when predatory animals hunt in packs and work together in running down their prey.

In a famous experiment by the Kelloggs (1933), a seven-months-old chimpanzee, *Gua,* was brought into their family and raised with a ten-months-old child of their own, *Donald,* during a period of nine months. Every attempt was made, during this period, to treat the youngsters in identical fashion. They lived and played together like any ordinary pair of children, even as twins might; they wore the same clothes, followed the same daily schedules, ate the same foods, slept in similar beds, were spoken to in the same way, and so on. The 'children' accepted each other fully and affectionately; and Gua's development testified clearly to the potentiality of chimpanzee behavior. She was hardly to be outdone by Donald in a number of activities. She acquired, for example, a good 'passive' vocabulary, reacting consistently and correctly to many words used by the Kelloggs. In other respects, she definitely surpassed Donald, as in her climbing ability. The experiment could not, of course, be continued indefinitely, since the child had clearly less to gain from the association;

but it provides us with a clear indication of almost-human social capacity at the sub-human level.

Sample Analyses of Social Interaction

Of the several types of social relation among animals that have received the attention of psychologists, we may select as examples for our closer attention those of *dominance, co-operation,* and *imitation.*

1. *Dominance.* An animal may achieve dominant status over another by virtue of the actual or threatened negative reinforcement it applies. In competition for food, mates, sleeping quarters, or whatever, the dominant individual wins out by lowering response strength in a rival through punishment. He may thus become a strong secondary negative reinforcer and S^D, to the extent that a mere gesture will lead the submissive animal to beat a hasty retreat. Schjelderup-Ebbe (1935) has noted that dominance may often be established at the first meeting of two birds, with the dominant animal driving away or pecking the other at will. The avoidance and escape reactions of submissive birds may persist even when the dominant birds have become old and weak, if only the battle posturings of the latter maintain their S^D and S^r functions. The fact that submissive animals sometimes 'rebel' is consistent with our knowledge of the impermanence of the effect of punishment; and we may suspect that rebellions are more likely to occur when motivation is high and the dominant animal blocks the way to reinforcement like food or a mate.

Dominance through physical force has also been observed among baboons by Maslow (1936a, 1936b) and among rats by Seward (1946), and has been seen to involve stimulus generalization. A badly-thrashed animal will transfer his submissiveness to other animals than the one that first defeated him. A single thrashing, if severe enough, will bring about submission to all comers, even when the loser in a fight has previously been the champion.

Dominance-submission relations, it is often said, may be

based upon other factors than general physical strength. This is true, since the application of punishment by one individual is not related solely to over-all physique. The determining factors are the *histories* of the interacting organisms. Thus, an old bird, or a relatively feeble young one, may be dominant by virtue of the submissive one's experience with similar war-like stances assumed by a former victor; and a nimble or resourceful ape may dominate a stronger one because he is nevertheless more adept in applying punishment. Circumstances like these are not far different from those of human experience. However, there is no reason why, in human as well as in animal life, dominance-submission need not be based on a combination of positive and negative reinforcement, or on positive reinforcement alone. Any definition of dominance is arbitrary. In some animal species, for example, a normally submissive female may gain marked control, in mating season or at other times, because of sexual changes in the male which raise her reinforcement value for him. Or, if a person's own efforts often result in failure and there is someone who unfailingly supplies rewards, independent efforts may cease and excessive dependence on the willing benefactor may develop. Furthermore, the dominance of one individual and the submission of another may be specific to certain situations and actions, in accordance with the histories of both individuals. It is not always the same man in a college class who dominates in both the classroom and the gym.

2. *Coöperation.* Coöperation, like dominance, is not a single response entity, but denotes many kinds of responding in many types of situation. It may be defined as the case in which the *combined behavior of two or more organisms is needed to procure positive, or remove negative, reinforcement for either.* Two organisms may perform the same act, like hauling together on a rope to obtain food, or different acts, as when one steps on a treadle to open a door while the other pulls in food. This sort of coöperation is easily obtained in human adults, by verbally instructing them in their rôles

or by letting them discover the efficiency of joint action. With animals, as well as young children, we have to train them from the start and can, therefore, observe how coöperation develops. The effectiveness of verbal instruction in the human adult depends, of course, upon a long history of training, from childhood on; and, even with us, coöperative endeavor in some activities is often achieved only with difficulty—sometimes never. In any case, whether with human beings or animals, and whatever the task, coöperation involves two things: (1) each organism's action must be discriminative for the other's performance; and (2) each organism must be reinforced for the part it plays in the coöperative scheme.

The investigations of Daniel (1942, 1943) are good illustrations of the way in which coöperation is acquired by animals difficult to train in such behavior. In his studies, rats were first taught to obtain food from a dish on the floor of their experimental chamber, and then to turn off an electric shock from the grid floor by climbing on to a small platform. The platform was eight inches from the food dish, making it impossible for the animal to eat and avoid shock simultaneously. When the two responses had been independently well established in each rat, training in coöperation began. Two hungry animals were placed in the chamber at the same time, with the floor electrified and food in the dish. Thus, one rat was able to eat without being shocked only if his partner stayed on the platform. If both went to the food dish, both were shocked. Experimentation took place during a forty-day period. As training progressed, Daniel observed that the rats came to exchange positions with considerable regularity, and with such efficiency that both got plenty to eat and were able to avoid shock on 94-99 per cent of all the times that either animal left his position. Seldom did they waste feeding time by sitting on the platform together; and more and more their behavior came to be directed by the stimulation they received from each other. Keeping at least one foot on the platform, the shock-avoiding rat would nudge, paw, or even bite the tail of the feeding rat until the latter left the dish and gave him his 'turn' at eating.

A sketchy analysis of such coöperative behavior might run as follows. The platform rat, though hungry, stayed in place because shock was thereby avoided. As his anxiety abated, his

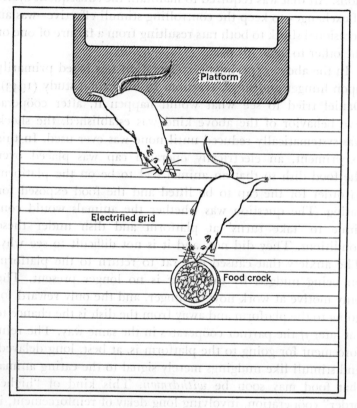

FIG. 75. Plan of the apparatus used by Daniel (1942) in studying coöperative behavior in rats. (After Dashiell, 1949.)

food-getting behavior became prepotent and he attempted to produce the S^D for approach to food—to bring the other rat beside him on the platform. His nudgings, pawings, and bitings served in turn as anxiety-arousing stimuli for his partner, since they had in the past been followed by electric shock if he delayed in returning to the platform rat's side. The only escape from this stimulation for the feeding rat was, of course, by leaving the food and going to the platform; whereupon the platform rat, having its S^D for 'safety,' was free to eat, and the entire process was repeated with the animals in reversed positions. All that was required to maintain the subsequent cycles of exchange—to keep the controlling stimuli effective—was an occasional shock to both rats resulting from a failure of one or the other to 'play his part.'

In the above experiment, coöperation was based primarily upon hunger and shock-aversion. In his second study (1943), Daniel tried to see what would happen if, after coöperative behavior of the above kind was established, the shock was systematically reduced until none was ever used. In this experiment, an electrically operated cap was placed over the food dish so that an animal had to be on the platform in order for the cap to be lifted and the food exposed for eating. The question was whether the animals would continue to 'take turns' at platform and dish under these conditions. They did not, and it is not difficult to see why. The anxiety that caused one rat to return to the platform on being nudged by the other is no longer present. The only motive at work now is hunger, and the only reward for going to the platform and away from the dish is the chance to eat later *if* the partner coöperates in the same way. The reinforcement for going to the platform is, at best, long delayed, and stimuli like nudgings merely signal to the eating animal that food may soon be *withdrawn*. This kind of "higher order" coöperation, involving long delay of reinforcement, is apparently very difficult, if not impossible, to obtain in a rat, whereas it is characteristic of many everyday human activities such as budgeting one's income in order to save for desired things like a car or the family's own home. Nevertheless, you can see that coöperative behavior at all levels of organismic life follows our basic principles, and that the functions of social stimuli are the same as those of non-social.

3. *Imitation.* Our third illustration of social relations among animals is that of imitation, and it, too, can give us an opening into human social behavior. We need not go into the centuries-long discussion of imitation. It is enough to say that, for a long time, many outstanding men like Charles Darwin and William James believed that imitation was simply a natural or "instinctive" thing. Early social psychologists like Gabriel Tarde (1890) regarded imitation as a fundamental trait of behavior, and used it as an explanatory principle in itself when discussing the regulation of human custom and the development of human society. Experimental attempts to measure "unlearned" imitation in man or animals never gave an unequivocal answer, and there has been an increasing reluctance on the part of psychologists to appeal to imitation as the explanation of any case of one animal's duplicating the behavior of another. They feel that behavioral duplication can arise from many causes, so that not all cases ought to be classed together. Moreover, not all behavioral duplication is "imitation," since there are many duplications no one would be inclined to class as imitation; for example, people walking to the morning bus, or a defensive fullback chasing the ball carrier.

Whether or not there is any such thing as unlearned or innate imitation, one thing is sure. Imitation can be *taught.* Through the use of conditioning procedures—by making reinforcement contingent upon repeating another's act—an organism can be made to imitate. An act of one organism is made the S^D for an act of another, so that the action of the leader must be repeated if the follower is to get his reinforcement.

As an example of this leader-follower relation, we may cite an experiment by Miller and Dollard (1941) who worked with both human and animal subjects. Once more, we choose an animal illustration because of its relative simplicity and dramatic clarity. The animal (a rat) who was to act as leader, was first and separately taught to run down the stem of an elevated T-maze, and at the choice point to turn down the

arm marked by a black card. In the usual discrimination
training procedure, the position of the white and black cards

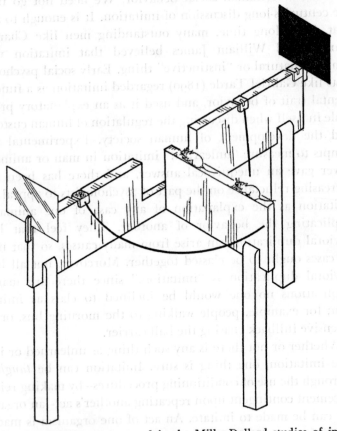

FIG. 76. The apparatus used in the Miller-Dollard studies of imitation. The stem of the T is 18 inches long and the running surface is 1⅛
inches wide. The gap to be jumped at the choice point is 4¾ inches
in either direction. The food-cup for the leader is 16½ inches from the
gap; for the follower, 8½ inches and is covered by a hinged cap which
is removed after the leader has passed over it. (After Miller and Dollard,
1941.)

was exchanged in random order from trial to trial on the arms
of the T, but a turn toward the black card (S^D) always brought
the animal to food, whereas a turn to the white card (S^Δ) went

unreinforced. After the leader had mastered this discrimination well, a potential follower (a rat without any previous training, but hungry) was placed directly behind him on the stem of the T. The follower received reward only if he turned into the same arm of the T as did the leader; if he turned into the opposite arm, he got no food. The experimental results left no doubt that imitative responding was learned: the response of the leader became an S^D for the follower who came practically always to make the same turn he did. This finding was not dependent on accidental cues from the black and white stimuli reaching the follower, as proved by the production of imitative responding without cards being present at all. For this check, some leaders were trained always to turn right in the T, others always to turn left. The tested animals were well-trained followers, but had learned their following with leaders who had themselves obeyed card cues. With the new leaders who required no cards, and who sometimes were right-turning animals and sometimes left-turning animals, the followers continued to use the leader's response as S^D. You will not have missed the added implication of this finding that leaders will generalize for followers, so that a well-trained follower will trail after many leaders indiscriminately! In the light of recent and tragic historical examples we would hardly care to train into our children such discriminative dependence upon others or the generalized tendency to follow any would-be leader who happens along.

Human Behavior and the Cultural Environment

The community in which men and women live makes up an important part of their total environment. It is difficult, if not impossible, to think of a single operant activity of the individual which does not show in some degree the pervasive influence of his community's teaching. The full recognition of this we owe to the efforts of anthropologists and social psychologists who have devoted themselves to the study of the form and content of human societies around the world, and to the interaction between the individual and his cultural environment. From earliest times, men knew, and were interested in, the fact that neighboring or distant communities existed that were different from their own, and that people behaved differently in those communities. During the nineteenth and twentieth centuries, anthropology developed as a social science, an important sector of which came to be known as *comparative ethnology,* or the comparative study of human behavior and customs in different societies. From such study, we have been led to discard some old conceptions and attitudes towards human communities.

The new conception may be called *cultural relativity.* Where once we were inclined to think of other peoples as strange, backward, and inferior to ourselves, the conclusions of anthropologists lead us to think otherwise. They point out that even the so-called *primitives* think the same things about us. In some societies, even the word *human* is limited to one's own group, while other peoples are described as "non-men" or "sub-human." Furthermore, the primitive is not, as was once thought, childlike in his simplicity and illogical in his reasoning; in fact, he thinks the same things of us and easily picks out weaknesses in our culture and inconsistencies in our social behavior. Nor does he concede any ethical superiority to us. There are instances, for example, where he has reproached us for our wholesale slaughters in war and has offered to send missionaries to teach us how conflicts among men may be settled without bloodshed. He is amused by some of our customs, and revolted by others. Sometimes he is impressed by our gadgets and material achievements; or he may be singularly unmoved by tall buildings and ships, or airplanes, pointing out that such things, while perhaps useful, are no guarantee of a peaceful and abundant span of years. All in all, the comparative study of cultures leads us to conclude that such differences as exist among human groups do not form a basis for making *value* judgments concerning them. Differences in customs, folk-ways, manners, religious practices, ideals, beliefs, and so on, are simply differences in the way men may grow up in diverse physical environments, out of diverse historical streams, and out of a total potential repertory of behavior that is far greater than any one culture can explore to the full. Each human society is to be approached in a spirit of objectivity and accorded the tolerance (which we would wish for ourselves) that comes from an understanding of its origins, values, and methods of molding the lives of its members.

Understandably enough, this contribution of anthropology has, in its dissemination, sometimes been misconstrued. The underlying conception of man's *alikeness* must not be lost in the recognition of *differences*. What men learn in different societies ought not to obscure the basic facts that all men learn in the same way and are subject to the same drives. The principles of reinforcement, extinction, discrimination, and the like, operate universally, though the *form* of the response to be learned, or the special type of S^D to be obeyed, may be selected by the community. Similarly with the motives of men: all men eat, though they differ in how and what; all men drink, perform sexual acts, and breathe. Further, all men have similar eyes and ears and noses for the reception of exteroceptive stimuli, though they may be taught to respond differently to those stimuli, through conditioning procedures that are the same for everyone. We need to hold onto the idea of human *absolutes* as much as to that of cultural relativity.

The cultural environment (or, more exactly, the members of the community) starts out with a human infant formed and endowed along species lines, but capable of behavioral training in many directions. From this raw material, the culture proceeds to make, in so far as it can, a product acceptable to itself. It does this by training: by reinforcing the behavior it desires and extinguishing others; by making some natural and social stimuli into S^D's, and ignoring others; by differentiating out this or that specific response or chain of responses, such as manners and attitudes; by conditioning emotional and

anxiety reactions to some stimuli and not others. It teaches
the individual what he may and may not do, giving him norms
and ranges of social behavior that are permissive or prescrip-
tive or prohibitive. It teaches him the language he is to speak;
it gives him his standards of beauty and art, of good and bad
conduct; it sets before him a picture of the ideal personality
that he is to imitate and strive to be. In all this, the fundamental laws of behavior are to be found.

Personality and History

While all human beings obey the same laws of behavior,
each individual ends up with a unique behavioral equipment
that defines his 'personality.' The emergence of uniqueness
from uniformity is possible because of the variations in circumstance under which the basic processes are worked out.
The uniqueness stems from the reinforcement and motivational history of the individual which is different from that
of others. We may think of the individual as a special (and
very large) set of parametric values of basic functions. Thus,
persistence in the face of failure may vary greatly from one
person to another, depending upon the amount and variety
of periodic reinforcement one has had in the past. Again, one
may be more or less dominant or submissive in the presence
of friends and strangers, depending upon his experience with
other people.

The fact that the individual's present personality is related
to his biography leads to an interest in behavioral development from birth through infancy, childhood, adolescence,
adulthood, and old age. Students of psychopathic behavior
know the importance of the early years in forming habits that
may last for life. In tracing behavioral disorders of adults they
are often led back to childhood experiences as the sources of
instability and disturbance. The importance of biography has
long been known by politicians, fanatics, and all manner of
special-interest groups, each of whom, in seeking to manage
society, sought either to control the family in which the child

grows up, or to gain outright possession of the child. The tenacity of early training has been made the topic of bitter wit, as when William James said, "People often think they are thinking, when they are merely re-arranging prejudices"; or, as a student once wrote in a term essay, "A college education does not eradicate prejudices, it merely makes them more subtle." He who would control society must ultimately reach the youth, and there is psychological soundness in the old slogan, "Give me the child until seven, and you can do with him as you wish thereafter." We need not agree with the complete pessimism of this opinion, nor vouch for the age seven, but the idea is not without basis.

Consider the "Oedipus complex" of psychoanalysis. The general idea, as the reader probably knows, is that the son tends to rebel against his father, and wishes to overcome or destroy him, because the father is a powerful and pre-empting rival for the affection of the mother whom the son covets. This competition with, and fear of, the father colors the whole psychological development of the child, and may be reflected in many ways in the adult character. The Oedipus relation was thought to be an innate, motivating reaction of the son to the father. This view of the father-son relation seems, however, to arise within families in which the father is the disciplinarian who applies negative reinforcement. Study of other kinds of family organization, and in some non-European cultures, shows that the father-son relation can be quite different (Malinowski 1929, Kardiner 1939, Linton 1945). In some societies, the father has little or no disciplinary jurisdiction over the child, and acts mostly as a beneficent supplier of comforts and affection. It may be the mother's brother who acts as head of the family and administers discipline. In this case, we would have an "uncle-Oedipus complex." There is little reason to resist the conclusion that the personality development of the individual is a function of his own conditioning history.

After the time when the rôle of the family is at its peak,

formative influences continue to work upon the maturing child through his friends and his school. The currents and counter-currents of conditioning and extinction that stem from social origins do not stop. Joined with the reinforcement history of an individual are such factors as his general health, physique, personal appearance, social and economic position. Other things equal, a strong and healthy child is more likely than a weak and sickly one to develop physical self-reliance through the success of his running and jumping and climbing and pushing. In our society, where 'good looks' are highly prized, a handsome child can quickly acquire social suavity and self-assurance (or a 'spoiled brat' character) because of the partiality and indulgence shown by his elders. Persons of high socio-economic status are often the victims of obeisance and flattery—and what is flattery but the indiscriminate use of positive reinforcement? Obstinacy and arrogance may be the result. The 'cute' child who is encouraged again and again to recite, to tell jokes, or dance, may continue to do so as long as he wins approval, until he ends up making his living at it. With such examples, we do not, of course, intend to oversimplify the factors that contribute to any personality. The phrase "other things equal" seldom holds outside the laboratory where things are kept equal by experimental devices. It must be admitted at once that the detailed analysis of any personality is an extremely complex matter because of the multiplicity of co-acting variables, past and present. In broad outline, nevertheless, we can see how such variables exert their force by determining *when* reinforcement and extinction will be applied, *how often,* and by *what schedule,* and similar questions.

Of great importance to the formation of personality, is the fact that human beings can discriminate their own actions, appearance, feelings, and successfulness. In the course of growing up, the child comes to 'know' about himself; he becomes at least partially 'aware' of his capacities and weaknesses, his likelihood of winning or losing in given situations, his physical and social attractiveness, his characteristic reactions. This is sometimes spoken of as the development or emergence of the "Self," a word that is meant to designate the ability to speak of (be "aware" of) one's own behavior, or the ability to use one's own behavior as the S^D for further behavior, verbal or otherwise. The sociologist Mead spoke of the "Self" as a social product, that is, it arises out of social interaction; but more specifically, we can say today that the individual is *taught* by his fellows to respond discriminatively to himself and his behavior. He can observe himself and judge himself with words like "good" and "bad." He can estimate his own efficacy as a social agent in pleasing people and in striving for social success; and if he discriminates what in his behavior is causing failure, he may switch to new responses, that is, "improve" or "snap out of it." The "Self," in short, is the person, his body and behavior and characteristic interactions with the environment, taken as the discriminative objects of his own verbal behavior. They are made discriminative for him by his social community, as it teaches him his language, because (*a*) his behavior is itself important to the community, and (*b*) it is also important to the community that he 'know' about his behavior. By *important*, here, we mean that the smooth living of both the individual and the community depends on his conduct toward others as well as his discriminative self-control.

We can deduce two things from the fact that the "Self" arises out of discrimination training and out of verbal behavior. First, the child starts out in life without a "Self," and must build one up through stages of dim realization by a continuous learning process. "Self"-learning probably never ends, nor is it ever perfect. There are times in life when new requirements are imposed upon the individual and new behavioral possibilities open up to him for exploration. At such times, the "Self" may come in for searching examination, and may grow rapidly as the individual recognizes new talents and capacities; or it may suffer as the individual fails to measure up to what is expected of him by the community. Thus, in adolescence, as we usually consider it, we see a transition (often attended by social rituals and ceremonies) from childhood to adulthood, with the consequent expectation that the person will thereafter exhibit the bearing and behavior of an adult, and take on the adult's responsibility for his own behavior. Yet the adolescent does not know what an adult has to be and do, and the learning of it is not easy in a society that does not planfully allow its children to assume adulthood by graduated steps. In our society, we speak of "adolescence" as though there could be only one, and that combining both physical and social maturation. In truth, however, we prolong social adolescence long after sexual adolescence is complete, and this creates problems not necessarily encountered in societies that recognize the difference. Other societies may have many "adolescences," or transitions between recognized stages of social responsibility, rather than a single leap from childhood to adulthood. But, regardless of the number of transitions, at each one there are newly learned increments to the "Self," as well as some sloughing off of old parts; and while the emergence of the "Self" is expected to come in large steps at these official transitions, there is in fact a continual and progressive flux in self-discrimination going on at all times. When the process is arrested or seriously distorted, society may judge the individual's lack of self-control or self-knowledge as pathological. Psychotherapy is then brought to bear upon him in the hope that, with special tutoring, the growth of the socialized "Self" may be resumed.

A second deduction: a person possessing no verbal behavior of any sort would not have a "Self," or any 'consciousness.' His reactions to the world would be like those of any animal, though he might be more "intelligent," that is, he could learn more things and faster than could lower animals. He would go after positive reinforcements, and would avoid negative reinforcements, but would do so directly, without "reflection." To ask whether he "feels" this way or that, whether he "knows" that he is being pained, whether he "realizes" that what he has done is good or bad, and so on, is as idle as to ask the same question of a rat. Without verbal behavior which is discriminatively conditioned to come out (i.e., to "describe," or "report" or "introspect") at the occurrence of stimuli, or at the occurrence of some of his own behavior or behavior tendencies, there is no "conscious awareness" and no "Self." It is not that he possesses these things but cannot speak of them; it is simply that the question of whether he possesses them is meaningless. They are the *products* of verbal behavior, not the causes. In the last analysis, the "Self" and "consciousness" are the creations of human society operating on the individual by means of verbal training.

In passing, it is perhaps worth noting that because the "Self" is a constellation of discriminative operants, it is under some motivational control. We pointed out in Chapter 5 that high motivation may distort discrimination to a point where a discriminative response may be emitted in the presence of remotely similar stimuli or even in the absence of any stimulus. Some writers speak of this as "autism" or "wishful thinking." We see 'wishful thinking' when a person speaks of (i.e., responds to) his "Self" as though he had traits he does not really possess. Thus, he may say of himself "beautiful, witty, and wise," when he possesses, not these features, but only the desire!

Consistency and Integration of the Personality

Because personality is the outcome of reinforcement history, and because an individual is capable of behaving in many ways, there arise the two problems of *consistency* and *integration*. Behavior is always consistent with the laws of behavior, but not always with logic. A man may act in two logically inconsistent ways with respect to the same subject matter, but if he does so it is because he has been separately reinforced for both ways of acting. Thus, in one company, a man may decry greed or gossip or intolerance; yet at another time, in another setting, he may practise any one of them. He has been reinforced for speaking one way, and for acting another. It is as if different response systems, each capable of separate reinforcement and extinction, exist within a single person's behavioral repertory, with the several systems operating in ways that may be consistent or inconsistent as judged by some outside logical criterion. Oftimes, when an individual has had an inconsistency in his behavior or attitudes pointed out to him, he will summon reasons which we suspect are not the real ones but are only "rationalizations" for his inconsistency. Rationalizations are usually unsuspected by the one who uses them, but serve as effective smoke screens for the real causes of his conduct.

Overlapping the question of consistency is the broader concept of *integration* of personality, or that harmonious functioning of all the response systems within the individual which is necessary for good adjustment to his social and natural environment. Persons who are psychologically "normal" have a certain oneness about their behavior, a continuity or wholeness, that indicates coördination and coöperation (not necessarily perfect) among their several response systems. They seem to be "in touch with" most of their behavior tendencies or attitudes, in the sense that they can speak of them on demand, or be taught to recognize them. Integration is not a clearly defined behavioral concept, but it figures importantly in the way clinical psychologists and other students of personality think about the organization and functioning of an individual's reaction repertory. In one form or another, clinical evaluations of personality are likely to include observations upon the harmony of interaction of whatever "segments" or response systems have been identified in the personality. An integrated personality does not exhibit responses that are severely out of joint with the circumstances in which the individual finds himself, or out of joint with one another; nor is the individual entirely unaware of the consistencies and inconsistencies among his response tendencies.

There is a thread of continuity and self-control running through integrated behavior that makes one feel that he is dealing with a single, articulated, unitary person. On the other hand, personalities said to be poorly integrated give the opposite impression. In them, it seems as though the response systems have no contact with one another; as though there were no over-all direction to the individual's behavior that gets his actions to cohere, or to correspond with what is called for in a given situation. Thus, a patient with hysterical symptoms, such as functional paralysis, is said to suffer from impaired integration; that is, his bodily and behavioral segments seem to be going along independently, without relation to the personality's unity. Again, pathological cases of multiple personality, amnesia, somnambulism, and the like, represent failures of integration. It is difficult to convey the intention of the concept of "integration" because it is not a rigorously definable term. Yet clinicians and psychiatrists find it useful, and you would do well to become acquainted with it if you expect to read further in the field of abnormal psychology. It should be made clear, however, that "inadequate integration is a developmental defect" (Shaffer, 1936, page 384). We might add, also, that it may show up only when some precipitating circumstance befalls the individual (such as emotional shocks, severe negative reinforcement, or threat of punishment) that he cannot cope with. At such times, personality may disintegrate, producing the neurotic and psychotic maladjustments that are the specialized subject matter of abnormal psychology.

Social Motives—Are There Any?

The heading of this section is put as a question, because that is probably the best way to approach the matter of social motives. The answer must depend on the elementary considerations about drive that occupied us at the opening of Chapter 9. There we saw that the concept of drive has three sources: (a) an establishing operation; (b) the effects of that operation upon the momentary strength of reflexes apart from further operations of reinforcement; and (c) the possibility of reinforcement that the establishing operation creates. It is against these criteria that the student must weigh the status of any proposed "social" motive. To put the question a bit differently, we ask what is intended by the adjectival use of the word *social* as applied to motives.

On taking thought, the student ought to come to these conclusions: (1) A motive may be called social if its establishing operation and appropriate reinforcement involve the withdrawal or supplying of social objects or stimuli. Thus, a female rat separated from her litter for a time may have a response conditioned if return-to-litter is used as the reinforcement. Some have argued that the social aspect of this motive is incidental to the underlying factor of pain in the filled mammary glands which is alleviated by the draining of milk by the unweaned litter, and therefore that the sociality of the motive is specious or entirely derived from a non-social drive. Counter-arguments have likewise been made against other proposed social motives such as gregariousness and sex. With further thought, however, you will not fail to see that (2) the distinction between drives as social and non-social is not a critical one. Classifying drives as of one type or the other is not nearly so important as recognizing that many commonly supposed social drives are not drives *at all*.

When we speak casually of a person "striving for," or "desiring," this or that, it is plain that we mean there is some motive present. The layman's error, however, comes in his assumption that the things striven for *identify* the motives. Take, as examples, the desires for prestige and social approval, which the layman might propose to include among his social motives. The reflective student will sooner or later ask himself what are the establishing operations and drive-reducing reinforcements for the "prestige motive" or "approval motive"; and, failing to see an answer, will wisely decide that they are doubtful candidates. The many forms that prestige and approval take—awards, smiles, words, deference, invitations, money, and so forth—are enough to make us wonder in the first place how such diverse items ever came to be grouped together. It is likely that they are all secondary reinforcements because of their correlation with positive primary reinforcers, or because they stave off anxiety about possible punishments. Stripped of these correlations, the tokens of prestige and approval become empty, and ineffective as controllers of behavior. The tokens, furthermore, probably serve as the S^D's for the next things to do in our enormously complex chains of social activity, since they indicate what behavior, successful in the past, is worth doing again. Here, too, when the behavior occasioned by past success is no longer reinforced secondarily or primarily, the tokens extinguish as do any S^D's that are no longer correlated with reinforcement.

Other candidates for the position of social motive, such as the popular one of "mastery," are subject to the same reservations mentioned above. In each case, the difficulty of finding the establishing and reinforcing operations, as well as the infinite variety of forms the "motive" takes, makes us reluctant to accept them. Concerning dominance, coöperation and imitation, enough has already been said to indicate that none of these can be subsumed under the drive concept.

Perhaps a word ought to be said about romantic love as a possible social motive since it figures so large in our literature, art, and folklore. It is certain that two persons in love have more between them than the sex drive alone, since for the latter any partner would serve; and an aged couple may be in love when sex is no longer a factor in their lives. Yet what it *is*, and even how it is recognized by lovers, cannot easily be put down either introspectively or by direct examination of specimens. Nevertheless, many people unhesitatingly call love a motive, partly because of our literary tradition that tells of its force. We may doubt that love is a motive, although the behavior involved still interests us. The dramatic case is that of "love at first sight," and we can make some guesses about it. Here, each lover at once presents to the other an array of discriminative, reinforcing, and drive-arousing stimuli that are effective for him. These stimuli have a history, and there is undoubtedly a large element of stimulus generalization or transference involved. The more of these each lover embodies for the other, the deeper the attraction, until the ideal of the story-teller is reached in the all-inclusive love. Thus, the bond that unites lovers may be tied at their first meeting, but its strands were aweaving long before. The matching of life-histories in this way is bound to be a rare event in human experience, but it need not happen often for the ideal to suggest itself. Less dramatically, love may be the outcome of a felicitous life spent together. In the course of time, each of a pair comes to possess positive stimulus values that may not have been present at the start and that give rise to mutual devotion and dependence.

In either event, however, the stimulus rôles played for each other by lovers are basically the same. Always, of course, the continuance of these stimulus functions in love depends on the ultimate primary reinforcements provided or shared by lovers, including food and drink, play activities, rest and sleep, reduction of anxiety, and the relief of the sex drive. But whatever true motives become involved in it, love is not itself a motive.

VERBAL BEHAVIOR
Introduction

No account of human behavior can be complete that overlooks man's verbal activity. It is his highest and most valuable form of behavior; more than any other, it distinguishes him from lower animals; in it are treasured up man's cultural heritage of philosophy and science and art and technology, and by it the transmission of this accumulated knowledge is effected from generation to generation. Indeed, verbal behavior has made such knowledge *possible*. The layman may take his verbal behavior for granted, but to the scientific mind the forms, functions, and influences of language constitute phenomena of the grandest magnitude.

The analysis of language's forms and functions has been approached from many angles in years past. One after another, the grammatical, linguistic, semantic, and still other approaches have sought to clarify the origins and development of language, in the belief that thereby they could clear away obstacles to thinking, avoid needless disputes of understanding, make for better communication among men, and provide a better basis for dealing with human behavior. All of these varied attempts have in common a fundamental assumption, or set of assumptions, about man and his language which the science of behavior finds quite unacceptable. This assumption holds that a man has "ideas" which he "expresses" in language "in order to communicate" them to another person; his language is simply a *medium* wherewith he *clothes* his ideas so as to project them through space to someone else who, hearing the words, "interprets" or undresses them back into the underlying "ideas." The assumption is that a man is an *agent* who manipulates words—finds the "right words"—for purposes of communication, and that the words are *indicators* of ideas outside themselves. Such views are essentially mystical, as well as logically circular. In explaining verbal behavior, such views assert the existence of things which cannot be either proved or disproved, and for which the only evidence is the very language behavior which the things are invented to explain in the first place. The dual classification of man into "mental" and "behavioral" components has been a stumbling block for theories of both language and behavior. Scientific psychology has profitably discarded this dualism.

You will probably find the problem of verbal behavior the most difficult one in this text. The mind-body dualism is deeply ingrained in our habits of thinking, and a new viewpoint which does not comport with the old is hard to achieve and tempting to resist. Nevertheless, it is in this direction that we must go, and the last major topic of this text will be to show

how verbal behavior can be subsumed within objective psychological science. Our phrase "verbal behavior" covers all aspects of language—spoken, written, and gestural—but we shall limit ourselves to the spoken, since the extension of our analysis to the other types would introduce further complexity in detail but no new principle.

The Nature of a Behavioral Theory of Language

Verbal behavior (spoken) is composed of responses of muscles in the mouth, throat, and chest which we may call the vocal apparatus. These responses produce various combinations of sounds which serve as exteroceptive stimuli for the person hearing them and the one emitting them. In addition, the responses produce proprioceptive stimuli in the speaker that play a part in directing chains of verbal responses. Spoken sounds, or the muscular responses causing them, do not 'naturally' indicate objects or events in the outside or inner world. The fact that adult speech bears relation to the environment in a more or less lawful manner is something to be scientifically explained, rather than taken for granted. *How* such a correspondence arises is a central problem for analysis, just as it is with an animal whose operant responses become conditioned and extinguished so that they finally provide a commerce with the world that is based on its actual features and requirements.

A behavioral treatment of language will, then, take as its data the sounds emitted by the human organism, just as it takes any observable behavior, like the rat's bar-pressing. When a person says something, our concern is with the *saying* and with the conditions that *control* the saying. Enunciation is an act, and to relate this act to its controlling factors is to understand the 'meaning' of speech. Our treatment will start with the young child and show the processes whereby its sounds become transformed into language. Our interest will not be in the historical origins of verbal behavior in the human species, but in the genesis and development of language in the individual as an outcome of present and past variables working upon him.

That verbal responses were to be regarded as raw data was one of the remarkable things proposed over thirty years ago by John B. Watson (1919). Watson asserted that when a human subject in an experiment spoke of his 'awareness,' or 'consciousness,' or 'perceptions,' it is a mistake to hypothesize the *reality* of these things. The subject's 'introspective' words do not objectively 'report' anything, but should be recorded as additional data in themselves, though Watson was not clear on how they could be analyzed in any useful way. He argued that inner mental events have no independent observable existence, that we have only the subject's words to deal with as our data, and that there is no necessary reason to erect a human psychology on the supposed presence of an inner controlling *psyche*. Watson's views were received with hostility by most of his contemporaries because they were radical for that time, and because they were not developed to a stage where their fruitfulness could silence criticism. Moreover, as we shall see, they were wrong in one important way. Verbal responses *do* become correlated in the course of training with interoceptive and proprioceptive stimuli, so that verbal reports of inner events acquire some degree of credibility. A behavioral account of how these correlations are set up does not, however, depend on psychic forces that supposedly employ words as a medium of communication. Watson was thus correct in his general approach, though he erred in detail. After all these years, we can more justly appreciate the soundness of his thinking, and the acuteness of thought which led to his beliefs.

There are many aspects of verbal behavior about which we have no experimental data at present. Even so, the principles with which we are already familiar enable us to dissect verbal processes in a way that conforms neatly with what is known about behavior generally. Perhaps the most valuable thing you will get from our discussion is a perspective and an attitude toward verbal behavior that will help you avoid some of the mystery in this field and help you think about language in a scientific way.

The Emergence of Verbal Behavior in Childhood

Vocalization alone does not constitute language, and the sounds an infant makes are only the raw material from which his verbal behavior is formed. At first, his repertory of sounds is limited, but as he matures the range of vocal responses increases. No one language makes use of all the basic sound units (*phonemes*) that the human vocal apparatus can produce, but each selects out a number which go into its words and ignores others. Thus, the English language makes no use of a phoneme like the *ch* in the German *nicht,* or of the nasalized *on* of French. The infant's repertory of sounds grows rapidly from birth and includes more than his own native tongue will need, so that, in his language training, part of his repertory is retained and strengthened, and other parts extinguished. You may recall your own amusement, and your teacher's horror, when you tried to pronounce a foreign word in high school or college language courses.

It is, of course, of interest to know how phonemes become available in the child's repertory, since this availability is related to the rate at which we can expect children to acquire proper pronunciations. Data of this kind for English-speaking children were recorded by Irwin and Chen (1946), in usual home environments, and represent the normal phonemic growth that occurs without special training in differentiation. Irwin and Chen determined the number of native-tongue phonemes spontaneously uttered by infants, and plotted the growth curve (Figure 77) for the number of types of speech sounds appearing at various ages. A total of 95 infants from middle-class homes was studied during the first 30 months after birth. At a given visit, a child's sample vocalization, as uttered on 30 respirations or breaths, were transcribed in the International Phonetic Alphabet. The data are plotted for time units of two months, so that the developmental curves for the 30 months are based upon 15 points, each point representing the mean number of types of speech sounds for the corresponding two-month period. The curve for all children shows that from the first to the last two-month period the child passes from 7.5 to 27 of the 35 sounds present in adult English speech.

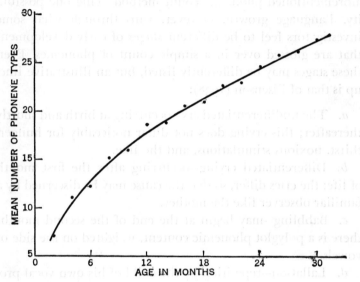

FIG. 77. The increase in number of English-language phonemes emitted by infants at different ages. (After Irwin and Chen, 1946.)

In addition to variety of sounds, an infant's vocalizations may be analyzed with respect to the *frequency of appearance* of each type. It has been found (Irwin, 1947) that, whereas the mastery curves for phoneme types show a decreasing rate with age, the frequency of production is a positively accelerated function. Thus, as the child grows older, he not only makes regular progress in mastering his native tongue's phonemes, but his *use* of these sounds increases at a faster rate. While the available data for any given age do not permit analysis of speech sounds into discriminative and non-discriminative operants, it is plain that opportunities for elaborate verbal conditioning are present in the early months of life.

The first few years' growth of the child's language is swift, with so many facets developing from week to week that a close, deliberate analysis of the individual case is rendered extremely difficult. Different workers in this field have often used different schemes for classifying early language, the aforementioned phonemic count method being one possibility. Language growth, however, runs through what some investigators feel to be different *stages* of early development that are glossed over in a simple count of phonemes. Even these stages may be differently listed, but an illustrative line-up is that of Eisenson (1938):

a. The undifferentiated cry—occurring at birth and shortly thereafter; this crying does not differ noticeably for hunger, thirst, noxious stimulations, and the like.

b. Differentiated crying—occurring after the first month of life; the cries differ, so that the cause may be discerned by a familiar observer like the mother.

c. Babbling—may begin at the end of the second month; there is a polyglot phonemic content, weighted on the side of vowels.

d. Lallation—repetition by the child of his own vocal production, leading to perseverative vocalization; begins about the sixth month or soon after.

e. Echolalia—repetition or imitation by the infant of sounds made by other persons; begins at about the ninth or tenth month and lasts indefinitely, perhaps throughout life.

f. Verbal utterance—the use of recognizable words in response to stimuli or to control the actions of people; usually begins in the first half of the second year.

The flow of speech development is, of couse, divisible into as many stages as we wish, and only practical or theoretical considerations can inform us when we are to stop. At the present time, any segregation of stages is of limited fruitfulness, although all attempts of this kind emphasize the large changes going on in the early years. That all children go through roughly similar changes is itself a provocative observation, since it indicates that there are probably uniform underlying processes at work. For example, there is the long-known fact that congenitally deaf children do not learn to speak. They reach the babbling stage, and probably get to a limited lallation, but never progress further. Apparently the hearing of speech is a condition for language development. Special coaching methods have been worked out, however, for teaching deaf children to speak, and there are a few institutions for this purpose in the United States. These methods represent the educational art at a high level, but a scientific survey of the principles involved could well lead to a better understanding of language behavior as well as possible further refinement in the methods themselves. This is almost unexplored territory awaiting the attention of trained psychologists.

Two Functions of Language: The Mand and the Tact

Phonemic availability and the listing of developmental stages do not, of course, give us information about some things. More important for our understanding of verbal behavior are the *processes* by which it is *learned,* and the *conditions* under which it is *used*. The forms and *functioning* of language are our central problems. We take the operant speech repertory as the raw material on which our principles operate, and ask how the specific characteristics of verbal behavior arise. We note, first, that the individual's speech results from the training given him by those who make up his "verbal community." Without a verbal community to teach him, an individual would never develop verbal behavior. In asking how the individual acquires speech, therefore, we shall find ourselves dealing with other people who are his "hearers," and who are the instruments for training his vocalizations.

Given, then, the phonemic raw material, the principles of conditioning and an appropriate teacher, our analysis of language can get under way. We may identify two basic categories of verbal behavior which appear early and remain fundamental throughout an individual's lifetime. These are the *mand* and the *tact*.

1. The mand (from the Latin *mando,* to order or command) is an utterance which procures a specific type of reinforcement from the hearer. A child can reach for his milk or he can make a sound *milk* and the two responses are not different in any *functional* way. Both are reinforced in the same manner except that in the latter case the reinforcement is mediated by another organism. The mand as a response is strengthened by its consequences just as any operant such as bar-pressing, chain-pulling, or running through a maze. In the grammarian's terms, the mand is in the imperative mood, and it includes demands, entreaty, commands, requests, and so forth. Mands are probably the first functional elements to appear in the language behavior of the child. They are developed under the instigation of primary drives and are the first verbal responses to be reinforced by hearers like the mother or nurse. When an infant is hungry, for example, his general activity, including the vocal, is heightened, and different sounds, interpreted by the mother as approximating intelligible words, are fastened upon by her for differential reinforcement. She proceeds to condition these sounds by supplying milk when the infant says something vaguely resembling *milk,* supplying a toy for a sound like *tuh,* and so on. Jespersen (1922, pages 154-155) has put it in these words:

. . . The baby lies and babbles . . . without associating the slightest meaning with his mouth-games, and his grown friends, in their joy over the precocious child, assign to these syllables a rational sense. . . . It is very natural that the mother who is greeted by her . . . child with the sound 'mama' should take it as though the child were *calling* her 'mama,' and since she frequently comes to the cradle when she hears the sound, the child himself does learn to use these syllables when he wants to call her.

The conditioning of mands, therefore, is one in which the *form of the response is specific to the particular reinforcement obtained.* The 'meaning' of a mand is given by what consequences follow its emission in a particular verbal community. Mand emission is controlled by the organism's needs since these mands have a history of appropriate reinforcement under those needs. Mands are not originally discriminative operants, but they usually become discriminative because the likelihood of reinforcement is greater in some circumstances than in others. Thus, manding food or drink usually occurs in the presence of certain people and in certain places. Nevertheless, as with other discriminative operants, if the drive becomes strong enough, they may be emitted, even by adults, in the absence of the customary S^D's. Sometimes, by extension or generalization, manding will occur in situations where the local S^D's have never themselves been reinforced. The "magical mand" is of this variety, an example being that of the bowler who calls after his swerving ball "get in there!"

We have said that mands are conditioned by the verbal community which gives specific reinforcement to specific sounds or to words of a specific form. The sounds or words selected from the child's repertory for mand training depend on the conventions of the verbal community, that is, the native language. There is nothing inherent in the sounds that necessarily places them in the mand category. Any words can serve as mands if they are so conditioned and if they function that way upon hearers. Mands are made so by their past history of specific reinforcement, and they disclose their character in the behavior of the hearer whose reactions are thereby controlled in specific ways. In the case of high drive or stimulus generalization, manding responses may appear that are not actually effective in procuring reinforcement, but the behavior is traceable to prior history of the sort we have indicated.

2. The richness and versatility of language in human life would be greatly restricted were its content limited only to

mands. Of greater importance is the *tact* function of verbal responses (*tact* from the past participle, "tactus," of the Latin, "tango," to touch). Whereas the mand is only incidentally under the control of S^D's, and is a response whose form determines a specific reinforcement, the tact is of a different complexion. The tact relation is one in which the form of the verbal response which the community reinforces is related to *particular discriminative stimuli,* and the response is given, not specific reinforcement, but *generalized* reinforcement. We may think of tacting as a 'naming' function: if the speaker emits the required sound when a given S^D is present, he is reinforced. The tact is not motivated by a special need of the speaker, and it does not call for a special reinforcement. The correlation between the response and its proper S^D must, however, be reinforced somehow, and what we observe is that the reinforcement provided by hearers is a *general* one. This reinforcement may be in the nature of smiles, approval, or money, all of which have in the past been associated with many types of primary reinforcement and are now, on that account, secondary positive reinforcers operating effectively in a wide range of situations. It has been said that the notion of generalized reinforcement is probably the most important single characteristic of verbal behavior, since it gives the verbal community almost unlimited power to train the individual. The vital result of this training is that the verbal responses of the individual are made to stand in a dependable relation to the environment. In the grammarian's terms, the tact relation is that of the declarative sentence; it is an announcement of "fact" representing relatively disinterested behavior on the part of the speaker, behavior for which he gets nothing in particular but only something in general.

Of all the verbal behavior acquired by the individual, the tact relation is of the deepest value both to himself and to the community. By teaching him to correlate words with facts and states of affairs, both inside and outside himself, the community opens up for him the opportunity to participate in, and contribute to, human discourse and human wisdom. If human language were limited to mands alone, it would differ little (except for size and clarity of the vocabulary) from the grunts and barks of lower animals. With mands alone, we would never rise above the level of making our personal needs and states discriminable to other persons who might then (were they reinforced for doing so) act to alleviate our hunger or thirst. It is the tact relation, however, that makes man able to speak of, to 'know,' and be able to 'think' about, the world and himself.

The Speaker-Hearer Relation

In any verbal community, the rôle of speaker changes hands continually, as does that of hearer, so that a given person is now one and now the other. An analysis of verbal behavior must cover this double-ended process if we are to glimpse the full scope of verbal functions. A key question we can take off from is, what reinforcement does the hearer afford the speaker for speaking, and what is afforded the hearer for listening and reinforcing the speaker? Who profits, and how? Clearly, both speaker and hearer must profit if they are to act as either, but we must see how this is effected.

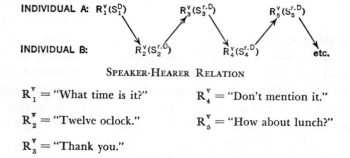

INDIVIDUAL A: $R_1^v(S_1^D)$ $\qquad$ $R_3^v(S_3^{r.D})$ $\qquad$ $R_5^v(S_5^{r.D})$

INDIVIDUAL B: $\qquad$ $R_2^v(S_2^{r.D})$ $\qquad$ $R_4^v(S_4^{r.D})$ $\qquad$ etc.

SPEAKER-HEARER RELATION

R_1^v = "What time is it?" $\qquad$ R_4^v = "Don't mention it."

R_2^v = "Twelve oclock." $\qquad$ R_5^v = "How about lunch?"

R_3^v = "Thank you."

The speaker's speaking is reinforced by the hearer in two ways. His mands are specifically reinforced according to his needs, while his tacting secures generalized reinforcement from the hearer who thus "encourages" him to go on. The hearer has his own reasons for listening and reinforcing the speaker. If he reinforces the speaker's mands, he gets reinforced himself in one or both of two ways: generalized reinforcement from third parties for doing the "proper thing," and somewhat more specific, though delayed, reinforcement from avoiding trouble caused by *not* meeting the speaker's needs. A mother, for example, responds to her child's mands as she is "expected to" by the community which requires her to be a dutiful mother; but she may also do so because she thereby prevents such later troubles as coping with an undernourished or injured child.

An interesting problem, however, is why a hearer reinforces a speaker's *tacting*. Hearers reinforce tacting because they *make use* of the information they obtain from the tacting. Thus, a speaker may say "there is food in the refrigerator," or "fire!" with resulting reinforcement to the hearer if he bases his own behavior on these tacts. The hearer gets an ultimate reinforcement for giving a speaker immediate reinforcement, since good tacting provides guides or S^D's for the hearer's own successful responding. Each hearer obtains from many speakers in his community much more knowledge than he could obtain by himself; each person in a community benefits all others by acting as additional eyes and ears for all, and this is as true for opinions and meditations as for straight reporting of environmental facts. Because of this mutual profit, the community plenteously reinforces tacting in the verbal behavior of its members. Note that we are considering the "informative or communicational value" of speech, without resort to the dualistic notion that speech is merely a medium for expressing 'ideas' in the 'mind.' Tacting responses are acquired according to conditioning principles, and the behavior of hearers may be explained in the same way.

We have pointed out earlier that verbal behavior would never develop without a verbal community which mediates the reinforcement for it. The fact that reinforcement is at the disposal of the hearer means that the hearer is the one who acts as the teacher of speech. Any speech response is a complex pattern of muscular action in the vocal apparatus, and as we all know it takes a long time to acquire acceptable pronunciations and inflections, in addition to grammatical forms and sentence structures. Involved here is the matter of response differentiation, for which the responsibility lies in the hands of the hearer-teacher. As the child matures, hearers use the devices of selective reinforcement for, and successive approximations to, the desired sounds. By this social insistence, the child's speech is gradually molded into accepted forms. "It is not *yeah,* son, but *yes*—can't you say it properly?", we tell our youngsters. Or we may grow angry and threaten to withhold some desired thing unless the child abandons his baby talk and speaks as "a big boy should." Furthermore, children are soon conditioned to imitate the sounds of adults so that the active rôle of the hearer as a differentiator may be reduced to the point where he is unaware that he has done anything. You have undoubtedly observed, as did Mark Twain, that French children learn French and Chinese children Chinese, without any trouble!

An interesting and extremely important variety of tacting is that which has *internal* stimuli as the discriminative source. From childhood on, the individual is taught by the community to report to hearers on his interoceptive and proprioceptive stimuli. The adult can, for example, tact the location of pain, whereas the child may be in obvious distress and yet unable to say even what part of his body hurts. Many expressions beginning with "I feel . . ." are tacts of internal stimuli and states like pain, sleepiness, fatigue, tension, hunger. Such tacts are an essential source of information about goings-on inside the individual which are otherwise inaccessible to an observer. To the community, this information is necessary for meeting the individual's needs, assuring his survival, and predicting what he is going to do. The individual learns such tacting because it is heavily reinforced: if he says his tooth aches, it can be relieved; if he says he is melancholy, he can be cheered; if he speaks his fear, he can be calmed. "Introspective" reports of feelings, thoughts, and the like, are what have led to the dualistic conception of an internal mind as separate from the language expressing it. No one doubts that hidden internal S^D's for such tacting exist, and that as a result of training the tacts *do* serve to give information about them. But a scientific theory of verbal behavior takes the tact relation as a datum, and refers its origin to known principles, rather than to some mind-agency within the individual that somehow knows which word should go with which stimulus, and thereupon sorts them into meaningful speech. The dualistic view takes the existence of referents for words, the correspondence of speech with fact, and the conveying of information to hearers, as matters that need only to be logically or grammatically formalized. The science of behavior asks *how* these things come about.

You may ask at this point what makes us decide that some introspective tacts are valid and others not. Why, for example, do we question "mind" if a person says, "My mind is working"? To this and many similar questions, we can reply that there is no doubt the speaker is *saying* something, but he is not necessarily tacting what he *supposes* he is. Thus, a person who says "I am thinking" does not have ghostly thoughts as his S^D, but rather muscular responses of the vocal apparatus (and perhaps other parts of the body) which he tacts as "thinking." A child wrestling with a problem is told by his parent "My, but you're thinking hard, aren't you?" and he gropingly replies "am I *thinking*?"; thereafter, similar activity will also be called thinking although he learns in later life to make vague statements about the "nature of thought." We all think, but we do so with our muscles which provide the only S^D's for the tact "thinking." If we are asked, however, to *describe* thinking we do so incorrectly because we have learned to talk about thinking in a certain way. We may say that we "feel our brains working," but this is not a valid tact since neural activity in the brain is not itself perceptible and no discriminative response can be anchored to it. We could examine in this manner all the misconceptions about themselves that men evince in their verbal responding. For the moment, it will suffice if the basic viewpoint is grasped to some extent, for this is perhaps the most difficult reorientation of all for beginning students in psychology.

Distortions of the Tact Relation

Ideally, the tact relation would contain a response made discriminatively to a single S^D. In actuality, this relation is subject to many deflections, and some of the more important kinds may be noted. In the following cases, you might provide your own running commentary on the social acceptability of the distortions, and of the way they are learned, extinguished, or punished.

1. *Generalizations of the S^D*. Since the tact is a discriminative operant, generalization of the S^D is naturally to be expected. Such generalizations may have practical use. They get information to a hearer more briefly than otherwise, or perhaps more comprehensively than by direct statement, because the hearer's own background of experience is called into play.

a. Metaphorical extension: this is used not only by poets but in ordinary conversation. "Thin as a reed," or "strong as a horse," or "fast as a deer," are commonplace similes. Contractions may occur if the speaker is sure his hearer will understand, as with "she is a flower."

b. Generic extension: here the generalization is sanctioned by the usage of the community. We speak of "players" in different sports and games, yet some are professionals who are clearly not 'at play.'

c. Redintegration: a form of generalization in which a part of a stimulus complex is used to stand for the whole (see page 152 in Chapter 5). "Counting noses," "reciting Shakespeare," are such expressions in which noses stand for people, and one recites only what Shakespeare wrote.

2. *False and non-existent S^D's*. These are instances where

a speaker pretends to tact although there is no S^D for it, or where the speaker tacts incorrectly.

a. Lying, or contrary-to-fact: this may be done to avert the punishment that a truthful tact would incur. "No, I did not break that, Mother." A false tact may also be used to obtain specific positive reinforcement. "I got an A in arithmetic today," says John, if that is the only method he has to get his candy. Of all people, we depend on our *scientists* to be truthful tacters without specific rewards or inducements. Imagine the catastrophe if they had to fabricate data in order to eat. A scientist must be free of pressures that turn tacts into concealed mands, and society sets before him standards of honesty that are more heavily reinforced than standards of success.

b. Exaggeration or invention: this is a way of obtaining generalized reinforcement from an audience that would otherwise withhold it. We have all listened to tall stories, embellished autobiographies, and dubious tales of personal conquest.

c. Distortions that produce special effects on the hearer: telling jokes and 'tear-jerkers,' 'crying wolf' to make a person do something we want, and telling stories with a moral are instances where the hearer's behavior is to be manipulated in special ways.

A listing like the above does not avoid some overlapping between types of tacting. Its purpose is to point up different ways that tacting appears in the stream of speech activities, so that you may get a feeling for the processes involved.

Other Controlling Factors in Speech

Whereas mands are of value most directly to the speaker whose needs they serve, the tact relation is of greater value to the verbal community. Tacting is the quintessence of social behavior, and of all verbal behavior it is the part we are most concerned to understand. We may, therefore, take a bit more time on some factors that control responses of the tact class.

Some of these factors may be obvious, but even they are worth making explicit.

1. *Textual factors.* Verbal responses are made to certain stimuli by way of *reading*, that is, we tact the marks on paper that make up writing. Here, the form of the response has a particular conventionalized relation to the written symbols. Schools devote much of their curriculum to the teaching of reading. Moreover, some written matter gives directions for continued verbal responding by the reader—for example, mathematical symbols like $\div$, $\dfrac{dy}{dx}$, $\sqrt{}$ — and we then get into the problem of how such follow-up responses are taught to the individual.

2. *Echoic responses.* We mentioned earlier that there seems to be a stage when the child begins to imitate or echo the sounds made by others. But even before he learns to speak words, his babbling acquires the inflectional pattern of his native tongue, so that he babbles English, as it were, even before he can speak it. These observations indicate the importance of the *heard* sound. Later on in life, it is easy to evoke echoic behavior by simply instructing a person, "repeat after me." Moreover, it is likely that all of us tend to repeat speech we are listening to even without being told to do so. We murmur to ourselves as the speaker talks; we use his words to introduce our own sentences; we go along with him and complete his sentences for him. In an exploratory study of this problem, Ritter (1949), using adults as subjects, had them memorize nonsense syllables. The instructor then called out one of these syllables, with the subjects instructed to respond as quickly as possible with the first syllable they thought of. They could respond with any of the memorized syllables including the one called out. The data showed a notable tendency for them to repeat the heard one despite the fact that they had a number of other well-learned choices available. Echoic control over verbal responding seems real enough, but

we need to know much more about it before we understand it fully or can estimate its magnitude.

3. *Audience.* The speaker's audience provides an immediate control over his verbal responding. A given part of the verbal repertory may be activated by one audience and left untouched by another. We would not address a minister as we do our fraternity brothers—the tone and content alike of our speaking would differ. Recall that a hurt child will cry more when there are people about than when alone, and still more when, of all people, its mother is there. Where audience control of speaking fails conspicuously, we have a symptom of psychopathological behavior in which verbal output is, we say, not 'in contact' with the immediate social situation.

4. *Motivation.* Variations in drive strength affect the strength of verbal responses just as they do any other kind of behavior. This is quite clear with respect to mands, but tacts are also susceptible. Slips of the tongue, unwitting puns, and so forth, in a speaker's output often indicate some motive at work *in him* that has taken priority over the usual S^D's. Freud has made extensive use of this observation, but it would be unwise to conclude that every slip or pun has a motivational basis. There is multiple causality in speech, and sometimes errors and distortions occur because the tongue is sidetracked by similar phonetic words or by the intrusion of related themes from the speaker's history. An invention (Skinner, 1936) called the "verbal summator" brings out many of the factors mentioned here. Combinations of vowels are played from recordings at a low loudness, each combination being repeated a number of times. The subject is told that "this is a test in the clarity of speech" and is asked to listen carefully and to put down, as soon as he thinks he has detected it, "what the man is saying." Of course, the man is not actually saying anything but a vowel series like "uh-ee'-uh-uh-uh," but this acts to select out of the subject's repertory words or sentences that are, for him, the stimulus. He reports "hearing" the man say such and such, but what he really hears is *himself* saying

such and such in response to the meaningless sounds of the recording. It is as if the repetition of incoming stimuli builds up the strength of the subject's latent speech, and soon those items that are closer to the emission threshold "come to the surface" and are spoken out. The verbal summator is related to testing methods which have been called "projective techniques" in the study of personality. Different subjects respond in different ways to the same meaningless stimuli, and their responses are often revealing of their motives and their history. Tabulations of response frequencies to the summator often show that the most common responses refer to the opposite sex, to worries, the wish to go home, and so on. When normal persons are compared with mental hospital patients (Shakow and Rosenzweig, 1940) gross differences appear in their responses to the summator. This is not wholly unexpected, since we already know something of how these contrasted groups perform on many other tests. The investigation indicated, however, that the summator technique deserves to be explored more thoroughly in the analysis of normal speech and psychopathic deteriorations.

Further Characteristics of Verbal Behavior

Broadly considered, verbal behavior is subject to greater delays in reinforcement than are some other ways of responding. Mands, for example, require action by hearers who mediate the reinforcements, and often the speaker could get his reinforcement more quickly by reaching or moving himself. Children must learn to ask for bread rather than grab for it. Moreover, in both manding and tacting, we may frequently be disappointed by our hearers who fail to supply any reinforcement whatever. Even our polite requests may often be rebuffed. The result is that we often speak with less assurance than we *act*.

Vocal language has special advantages for the range and utility of our verbal behavior. There is no necessary reason why language could not originally have been gestural or tactile. As we may conceive it, however, the speech type was selected out owing to its greater versatility and value in procuring reinforcement (perhaps by leaving the hands free). Constructed as we are, olfactory, heat, or radiational language would not be an effective basis for a verbal community. Sight or hearing would be more likely bases for interstimulation at a distance. Of these two, however, a language of seen movements is limited by the necessity of looking and by its ineffectiveness in the dark. Moreover, a vocabulary of movements-to-be-seen would be restricted to the number of discriminably different movements made by the 'talker,' and this number is not large. Finally, such a vocabulary is not easy to execute but requires considerable expenditure of energy that is negatively reinforcing to some degree. On the other hand, speech gets around most, if not all, these difficulties and is, in addition, capable of an indefinitely large vocabulary. Responses of the vocal apparatus can be differentiated very finely to produce an enormous number of sound combinations that are discriminably different to the hearer. Speech movements are small and cost little energy, they can be rapidly made, their intensity can be varied as well as their pitch, they are easily combined into chains, and so on. We may think of language functions as having located themselves in the vocal apparatus by virtue of a kind of natural selection that we can describe in terms of reinforcement principles.

The first years of language development in children are commonly characterized by the fact that their verbal behavior is *audible,* that is, children do all their talking aloud. It needs schooling and social pressure to quiet down their speech so they do not say aloud everything that 'comes into their heads.' Even as seemingly simple a thing as silent reading takes up a good deal of teaching time in the early grades. And, even as adults, we may talk aloud to ourselves when we are alone; and, by the same token, mental patients showing 'withdrawal from society' (i.e., a loss of control over behavior by social S^D's) talk to themselves aloud without regard for the presence of others. Silent speech is an important part of thinking. When engaged on difficult tasks like mathematical problems, we are likely to abandon silent speech and revert to 'thinking aloud.' Perhaps the suppression of talk is not altogether good for our intellectual efficiency. It does, of course, conceal from our neighbors things we do not want them to know. Yet, from the standpoint of mental hygiene, it may be better to talk out our feelings than to let them rankle.

In general, speech uses only the smaller muscles of the body, and in silent speech or thinking still smaller movements of these small muscles are involved. But man's speech is a mighty lever, and one may truly say that never did such small muscles move such large worlds.

Consciousness and Understanding

Verbal behavior can itself act as the S^D for further verbal behavior. That is, we can talk about our talking, or think about our thinking. We may use the term *secondary language* to designate verbal behavior that has verbal behavior as its S^D. As we have said, "consciousness" is probably reducible in the end to the ability of a person to verbalize adequately his own actions, including his prior verbal responses. We say he is 'oriented' or 'self-aware' when he can tact his own behavior in about the same way that we would.

We are satisfied, also, that a person comprehends or understands us, not if he echoes what we have just said, but more by his ability to say it in a different way. Merely to repeat our words verbatim tells us only that our own verbal chains were memorized. If he can start with our words and go on to further statements that we ourselves might make, we conclude with more confidence that he has understood us. Understanding is a verbal activity, for the person who understands us *talks as we do.* Like all behavior, understanding needs reinforcement if it is to be made firm. This being so, one may examine various forms of instruction used in schools, for example, to see which provides the best reinforcement for comprehension, that is, proper speaking or thinking. From such an examination, the lecture method of teaching, so common at the college level, emerges with a poor recommendation. The lecture method provides no reinforcement for the hearer's speech except the long-delayed one of examination and final grade. It is not to be wondered that, with the small comprehension achieved by lectures, students often aim on examinations only to reproduce verbatim the lecturer's words. The notes that he takes are a means of stimulating talk in himself after he is alone (a kind of lecturer-student conversation without the lecturer present), but can only partially succeed in filling the gap left by the absence of immediate reinforcement for the hearer's talking. On the other hand, the laboratory method of instruction, and the discussion-group method, hold out the possibility of superior learning if they are well used. One danger in discussion groups that are not skillfully conducted is the tendency to reinforce every discussant for saying almost anything as his "contribution," so that no one carries away any more comprehension than he brought with him. But the lecture method inherently promises little for any but selected audiences already so well trained in a special subject matter that the heard words fit into, and generalize with, a verbal repertory prepared in advance and primed at high strength while listening.

Problems of individual understanding are joined with those of common understanding in the community, that is, with verbal usages that are expected to have a common meaning for all persons. The "meaning" for a speaker of a word or sentence is, of course, defined by the sum total of conditions under which it is emitted; while the "meaning" for a hearer is defined by the behavioral consequences it induces in him. As background and training differ or agree for different speakers, the conditions evoking a given word from them will overlap but perhaps not coincide exactly. Similarly with the partial coincidence of reaction on the part of hearers. The study of *semantics* centers on questions of meaning like this, and it seems probable that the behavioral and semantic approaches to language will draw closer together in the future.

It is interesting, finally, to conjecture what the impact may be upon philosophy when the behavioral analysis of language reaches a more formidable stage than at present. Language is, in a way, both the medium and substance of philosophy. It would be strange indeed if an inquiry into the nature and origins of verbal behavior had no bearing upon the import or validity of that same verbal behavior. For, even if it is true that an idea may be valid without our knowing its source, it is also true that in many cases we cannot judge its validity except from its source. In like manner, it would be strange if our knowledge of the medium in which philosophers speak, take issue, or agree with one another, did not help us also know when their talking is sound and fury, and when it signifies something. No one can say how far in the future lies the first strong impact of behavioral science upon philosophy, but that it will come seems certain. In a science that takes the whole of behavior as its province, what part of man's activities shall be said to lie out of bounds and be exempt from scrutiny? Who can justly deny her the right of passage through any meadow, and on what basis declare that she trespasses?

NOTES

Social psychology is such a large and inclusive province that there is often little similarity in the content of textbooks within the field. An interesting approach is that provided by Klineberg's *Social psychology* (1940), the material of which may be used to supplement some of the topics we have treated in this chapter. *A handbook of social psychology,* edited by Murchison (1935), is also to be recommended, especially for its description, by various authorities, of sub-human social behavior.

An enlightening experiment on coöperative behavior in chimpanzees has been carried out by Crawford (1937). This investigator's exposition lends itself readily to the type of analysis you have been using, and supplies a splendid approach to the complexity of human coöperation. Maslow's (1936a, 1936b) observations on the dominance-submission relation among baboons serves a similar purpose. With respect to imitation, we have already mentioned (page 361) the studies reported by Miller and Dollard (1941).

In our treatment of verbal behavior, we have leaned primarily upon the analysis recently presented by Skinner (1948b) in a series of formal lectures at Harvard University. Skinner's approach amounts to the first important extension of reinforcement theory into the realm of human language function, and is an impressive attempt to free the problem of language from mind-body dualism.

A LAST WORD

The power of science is nowhere in history more stirringly revealed than in its first victories over the most difficult and defiant subject matter ever presented to it—the behavior of organisms. This book has attempted to plot, in general fashion, some of the paths that have been opened up in man's study of his own behavior and that of his fellow-creatures. Starting with the humble analysis of simple bits of behavior, modern psychology has extracted a few shining conclusions that dispel somewhat the mists which once shrouded human and animal behavior and made an understanding of its laws a seemingly impossible goal.

All behavior, as we can now discern it, is composed of variations on a few basic themes. For the first time in mankind's saga, these themes are open to all who wish to see them in the steady light of science, rather than by the rare illuminations of intuitive minds. We are on the frontier of an enormous power: the power to manipulate our own behavior scientifically, deliberately, rationally. How this power will be used—whether for good or ill—no one of us can tell. Certain it is that whatever use is made of it will be determined by the character of the persons using it. But character itself is open to a science of behavior. We need to hasten and train a generation of men of good will. How this is to be done may be mankind's last desperate question of all. Without a science of psychology, no answer is possible; but psychology, while offering the methods, cannot ensure their use. It is to the latter that we finally commend our readers.

REFERENCES AND AUTHOR INDEX

The numbers in italics at the end of each reference indicate the pages in this text on which the reference is cited.

1. ALLPORT, F. H. (1924) *Social psychology.* Boston, Houghton Mifflin, xiv, 453 pp.—*35*
2. ANDERSON, O. D., and LIDDELL, H. S. (1935) Observations on experimental neurosis in sheep. *Arch. Neurol. Psychiat.,* Chicago, 34, 330-354.—*29*
3. ANREP, G. V. (1920) Pitch discrimination in the dog. *J. Physiol.,* 53, 367-385.—*18*
4. ANTONITIS, J. J. (1950) Variability of response in the white rat during conditioning and succeeding extinction and reconditioning. Ph.D. dissertation, Columbia Univ.—*181, 182, 183, 185*
   ANTONITIS, J. J., *see also* Nos. 226, 227.
5. ARNOLD, W. J. (1947) Simple reaction chains and their integration. *J. comp. physiol. Psychol.,* 40, 349-363.—*203, 205*
6. BARD, P. (1934) Emotion: I. The neuro-humoral basis of emotional reactions. In Murchison, C. A. (ed.), *A handbook of general experimental psychology.* Worcester, Mass., Clark Univ. Press. —*351*
   AYLESWORTH, M., *see* No. 282.
7. BARKER, R. G. (1942) An experimental study of the resolution of conflicts in children. In Q. McNemar and M. A. Merrill (eds.), *Studies in personality.* New York, McGraw-Hill.—*321*
8. BASH, K. W. (1939) An investigation into a possible organic basis for the hunger drive. *J. comp. Psychol.,* 28, 109-135.—*287*
9. BASS, M. J., and HULL, C. L. (1934) The irradiation of a tactile conditioned reflex in man. *J. comp. Psychol.,* 17, 47-65.—*127*
10. BEEBE-CENTER, J. G. (1932) *The psychology of pleasantness and unpleasantness.* New York, Van Nostrand, viii, 427 pp.—*255*
11. BECHTEREV, V. M. (1932) *General principles of human reflexology.* New York, International, 467 pp.—*34*
    BERNSTONE, A. H., *see* No. 185.
12. BERSH, P. J. (1950) The influence of two variables upon the establishment of a secondary reinforcer for operant responses. *J. exp. Psychol.* in press.—*243, 244*
    BERSH, P. J., *see also* Nos. 226, 227.
13. BITTERMAN, M. E. (1944) Behavior disorder as a function of the relative strength of antagonistic response-tendencies. *Psychol. Rev.,* 51, 375-378.—*321*

14. Boring, E. G. (1929) *A history of experimental psychology.* New York, Appleton-Century-Crofts, xvi, 699 pp.—*163*

15. Bousfield, W. A. (1938), *see* B. F. Skinner (1938).—*291, 292*

16. Bray, C. W. (1928) Transfer of learning. *J. exp. Psychol.,* 11, 443-467.—*170*

17. Brogden, W. J. (1939a) The effect of frequency of reinforcement upon the level of conditioning. *J. exp. Psychol.,* 24, 419-431.—*99, 113*

18. Brogden, W. J. (1939b) Unconditioned stimulus-substitution in the conditioning process. *Amer. J. Psychol.,* 52, 46-55.—*49*

Brogden, W. J., *see also* No. 40.

19. Brown, J. S. (1948) Gradients of approach and avoidance responses and their relation to level of motivation. *J. comp. physiol. Psychol.,* 41, 450-465.—*317*

Brown, J. S., *see also* No. 170.

20. Brown, R. H. (1936) Color vision in the rabbit. *J. gen. Psychol.,* 14, 83-97.—*133*

21. Bruce, R. H. (1932) The effect of removal of reward on the maze performance of rats. III. *Univ. Calif. Publ. Psychol.,* 6, 75-82.—*235*

22. Bryan, W. L., and Harter, N. (1899) Studies on the telegraphic language. The acquisition of a hierarchy of habits. *Psychol. Rev.,* 6, 345-375.—*153*

23. Bugelski, R. (1938) Extinction with and without sub-goal reinforcement. *J. comp. Psychol.,* 26, 121-134.—*235*

24. Bugelski, R., and Miller, N. E. (1938) A spatial gradient in the strength of avoidance responses. *J. exp. Psychol.,* 23, 494-505.—*253*

25. Bullock, D. H., and Fischer, L. (1949) The effect of repeated conditioning and extinction of an operant response. (To be published).—*83*

26. Bunch, M. E. (1928) The effect of electric shock as punishment for errors in human maze learning. *J. comp. Psychol.,* 8, 343-359.—*111*

27. Bunch, M. E. (1935) Certain effects of electric shock in learning a stylus maze. *J. comp. Psychol.,* 20, 211-242.—*111*

28. Burnham, W. H. (1917) Mental hygiene and the conditioned reflex. *J. genet. Psychol.,* 24, 449-488.—*35*

Campbell, R. K., *see* No. 94.

29. Cannon, W. B. (1927) The James-Lange theory of emotions: a critical examination and an alternative theory. *Amer. J. Psychol.,* 39, 106-124.—*333*

30. Cannon, W. B. (1929) *Bodily changes in pain, hunger, fear and rage.* New York, Appleton-Century, xvi, 404 pp.—*286*

31. Cannon, W. B., and Washburn, A. L. (1912) An explanation of hunger. *Amer. J. Physiol.,* 29, 441-454.—*285*

32. Cason, H. (1922) The conditioned pupillary reaction. *J. exp. Psychol.,* 5, 108-146.—*25, 35*

CHEIN, I., *see* No. 147.
CHEN, H. P., *see* No. 114.
CHRISTO, I. J., *see* No. 131.
CLAYTON, F. L., *see* No. 120.
33. COFER, C. N., and FOLEY, J. P. (1942) Mediated generalization and the interpretation of verbal behavior: I. Prolegomena. *Psychol. Rev.*, 49, 513-540.—*160, 163*
COMMINS, W. D., *see* No. 257.
34. CONRADI, E. (1905) Song and call notes of English sparrows when reared by canaries. *Amer. J. Psychol.*, 16, 190-198.—*354*
35. COWLES, J. T. (1937) Food-tokens as incentives for learning by chimpanzees. *Comp. Psychol. Monogr.*, 14, No. 71, 96 pp.—*248*
36. CRAFTS, L. W., SCHNEIRLA, T. C., ROBINSON, E. E., and GILBERT, R. W. (1938) *Recent experiments in psychology.* New York, McGraw-Hill, xiv, 417 pp.—*14, 136, 137*
37. CRAIG, W. (1921) Why do animals fight? *Int. Jour. Ethics*, 31, 264-278.—*342*
38. CRAWFORD, M. P. (1937) The coöperative solving of problems by young chimpanzees. *Comp. Psychol. Monogr.*, 14, No. 68, 88 pp. —*399*
39. CRUTCHFIELD, R. S. (1939) The determiners of energy expenditure in string-pulling by the rat. *J. Psychol.*, 7, 163-178.—*196*
40. CULLER, E., FINCH, G., GIRDEN, E., and BROGDEN, W. J. (1935) Measurements of acuity by the conditioned response technique. *J. gen. Psychol.*, 12, 223-227.—*314*
41. DANIEL, W. J. (1942) Coöperative problem solving in rats. *J. comp. Psychol.*, 34, 361-369.—*358, 359*
42. DANIEL, W. J. (1943) Higher order coöperative problem solving in rats. *J. comp. Psychol.*, 35, 297-305.—*358, 360*
43. DASHIELL, J. F. (1949) *Fundamentals of general psychology.* 3rd ed., Boston, Houghton Mifflin, x, 690 pp.—*17, 359*
44. DAVIS, E. A. (1937) The development of linguistic skill in twins, singletons with siblings, and only children from age five to ten years. (*Inst. Child Welfare Monogr. Ser.* No. 14), Minneapolis, Univ. of Minn. Press, ix, 165 pp.—*205*
45. DAVIS, C. M. (1928) Self selection diet by newly weaned infants. *Amer. J. Dis. Child.*, 36, 651-679.—*292*
46. DAVIS, R. C. (1948) Responses to 'meaningful' and 'meaningless' sounds. *J. exp. Psychol.*, 38, 744-756.—*230*
47. DENNIS, W. (1940) Infant reaction to restraint: an evaluation of Watson's theory. *Trans. N. Y. acad. Sci.*, 2, No. 8, 202-218.—*343*
48. DINSMOOR, J. A. (1950) A quantitative comparison of the discriminative and reinforcing functions of a stimulus. *J. exp. Psychol.*, in press.—*237*
49. DODSON, J. D. (1932) The relative values of satisfying and annoying situations as motives in the learning process. *J. comp. Psychol.*, 14, 147-164.—*111*

DOLLARD, J., *see* No. 171.

50. DUCHENNE, G. B. A. (1862), *see* Dumas, G. (1923) .—*335*

51. DUMAS, G. (1923) *Traité de psychologie.* Vol. I. Paris, Alcan, xiv, 964 pp.—*335*

52. EBBINGHAUS, H. (1885) *Memory* (Trans. H. A. Ruger and C. E. Bussenius), New York, Teachers College, 1913, viii, 123 pp. —*78, 229*

53. EISENSON, J. (1938) *The psychology of speech.* New York, Appleton-Century-Crofts, xiii, 280 pp.—*382*

54. ELDER, J. H. (1934) Auditory acuity of the chimpanzee. *J. comp. Psychol.,* 17, 157-183.—*135*

55. ELLIOTT, M. H. (1934) The effect of hunger on variability of performance. *Amer. J. Psychol.,* 46, 107-112.—*179*

56. ELLSON, D. G. (1938) Quantitative studies of the interaction of simple habits: I. Recovery from the specific and generalized effects of extinction. *J. exp. Psychol.,* 23, 339-358.—*77*

57. ELLSON, D. G. (1939) The concept of reflex reserve. *Psychol. Rev.,* 46, 566-575.—*77*

58. ESTES, W. K. (1943) Discriminative conditioning: I. A discriminative property of conditioned anticipation. *J. exp. Psychol.,* 32, 150-155.—*243*

59. ESTES, W. K. (1944) An experimental study of punishment. *Psychol. Monogr.,* 57, No. 263, iii, 40 pp.—*107*

60. ESTES, W. K. (1948) Discriminative conditioning: II. Effects of a Pavlovian conditioned stimulus upon a subsequently established operant response. *J. exp. Psychol.,* 38, 173-177.—*243*

61. ESTES, W. K. (1949a) Generalization of secondary reinforcement from the primary drive. *J. comp. physiol. Psychol.,* 42, 286-295. —*241*

62. ESTES, W. K. (1949b) A study of motivating conditions necessary for secondary reinforcement. *J. exp. Psychol.,* 39, 306-310.—*241*

63. ESTES, W. K., and SKINNER, B. F. (1941) Some quantitative properties of anxiety. *J. exp. Psychol.,* 29, 390-400.—*309, 310*

64. EWERT, P. H. (1933) Eye-movements during reading and recall. *J. gen. Psychol.,* 8, 65-84.—*216*

65. FIELDS, P. E. (1932) Studies in concept formation: I. The development of the concept of triangularity by the white rat. *Comp. Psychol. Monogr.,* 9, No. 2.—*158*

66. FINAN, J. L. (1940) Quantitative studies in motivation: I. Strength of conditioning in rats under varying degrees of hunger. *J. comp Psychol.,* 29, 119-134.—*112*

FINCH, G., *see* No. 40.

FISCHER, L., *see* No. 25.

FLETCHER, F. M., *see* No. 186.

67. FOLEY, J. P. (1935) Judgment of facial expression of emotion in the chimpanzee. *J. soc. Psychol.,* 6, 31-67.—*345*

FOLEY, J. P., *see also* No. 33.

68. FRICK, F. C. (1948) An analysis of an operant discrimination. *J. Psychol.*, 26, 93-123.—*127, 128*

GAGNÉ, R. M., *see* No. 81.

69. GALTON, F. (1883) *Inquiries into human faculty and its development.* London, Macmillan, xii, 387 pp.—*221*

70. GARRETT, H. E. (1941) *Great experiments in psychology.* Rev. ed., New York, Appleton-Century-Crofts, xxi, 452 pp.—*14*

71. GATES, G. S. (1926) An observational study of anger. *J. exp. Psychol.*, 9, 325-336.—*343*

72. GELLERMANN, L. W. (1931) The double alternation problem: III. The behavior of monkeys in a double alternation box-apparatus. *J. genet. Psychol.*, 39, 359-392.—*203*

73. GENGERELLI, J. A. (1930) The principle of maxima and minima in animal learning. *J. comp. Psychol.*, 11, 193-236.—*196*

74. GENGERELLI, J. A. (1933) The principle of minimum path in the ringtail monkey. *Publ. U.C.L.A. Educ. Philos., Psychol.*, 1, No. 13, 165-187.—*176*

75. GHISELLI, E. E. (1936) Changes in neuromuscular tension accompanying the performance of a learning problem involving constant choice time. *J. exp. Psychol.*, 19, 91-98.—*196*

76. GIBSON, E. J. (1939) Sensory generalization with voluntary reactions. *J. exp. Psychol.*, 24, 237-253.—*129*

77. GILBERT, R. W. (1936) The effect of non-informative shock upon maze learning and retention with human subjects. *J. exp. Psychol.*, 19, 456-466.—*111*

78. GILBERT, R. W. (1937) A further study of the effect of non-informative shock upon learning. *J. exp. Psychol.*, 20, 396-407.—*111*

GILBERT, R. W., *see also* No. 36.

79. GILHOUSEN, H. C. (1931) An investigation of "insight" in rats. *Science*, 73, 711-712.—*178*

80. GODBEER, E. (1940) Factors introducing conflict in the choice behavior of children. Ph.D. dissertation, Yale University.—*321, 324*

GIRDEN, E., *see* No. 40.

81. GRAHAM, C. H., and GAGNÉ, R. M. (1940) The acquisition, extinction, and spontaneous recovery of a conditioned operant response. *J. exp. Psychol.*, 26, 251-280.—*53, 55*

82. GRICE, G. R. (1948) The relation of secondary reinforcement to delayed reward in visual discrimination learning. *J. exp. Psychol.*, 38, 1-16.—*209, 210*

83. GRINDLEY, G. C. (1929) Experiments on the influence of the amount of reward on learning in young chickens. *Brit. J. Psychol.*, 20, 173-180.—*73, 234*

84. GUTHRIE, E. R. (1935) *Psychology of learning.* New York, Harper, viii, 258 pp.—*113, 196*

GUTHRIE, E. R., *see also* No. 247.

85. GUTHRIE, E. R., and HORTON, G. P. (1946) *Cats in a puzzle box.* New York, Rinehart, 67 pp.—*164, 165, 166*

86. HARLOW, H. F. (1948) Studying animal behavior. In T. G. Andrews (ed.), *Methods of Psychology.* New York, John Wiley, xiv, 716 pp.—*293*

HARTER, N., *see* No. 22.

87. HAYS, R., and WOODBURY, C. B. Unpublished study reported by C. L. Hull (see No. 104).—*171, 172*

88. HEATHERS, G. L. (1940) The avoidance of repetition of a maze reaction in the rat as a function of the time interval between trials. *J. Psychol.,* 10, 359-380.—*177*

89. HEBB, D. O. (1945) The forms and conditions of chimpanzee anger. *Bull. Canad. psychol. Ass.,* 5, 32-35.—*342*

90. HEFFERLINE, R. F. (1950) An experimental study of avoidance. *Genet. Psychol. Monogr.,* in press.—*113, 250, 312*

91. HEIDER, F. K., and HEIDER, G. M. (1940) A comparison of sentence structure of deaf and hearing children. *Psychol. Monogr.,* 52, No. 1, 42-103.—*205*

HEIDER, G. M., *see* No. 91.

92. HENMON, V. A. C. (1906) The time of perception as a measure of differences in sensations. *Arch. of Phil., Psychol. and Sci. Meth.,* New York, The Science Press, 75 pp.—*143*

HERON, W. T., *see* No. 215.

93. HILGARD, E. R. (1937) The relationship between the conditioned response and conventional learning experiments. *Psychol. Bull.,* 34, 61-102.—*66*

94. HILGARD, E. R., CAMPBELL, R. K., and SEARS, W. N. (1938) Conditioned discrimination: the effect of knowledge of stimulus-relationships. *Amer. J. Psychol.,* 51, 498-506.—*121, 122*

95. HILGARD, E. R., and MARQUIS, D. G. (1940) *Conditioning and learning.* New York, Appleton-Century-Crofts, xi, 429 pp.—*13, 34, 35, 66, 169*

96. HOBBES, T. (1651) *Leviathan.* London, Oxford Univ. Press, Part I, Ch. VI.—*325*

HORTON, G. P., *see* No. 85.

97. HOVLAND, C. I. (1937a) The generalization of conditioned responses: I. The sensory generalization of conditioned responses with varying frequencies of tone. *J. gen. Psychol.,* 17, 125-148.—*127*

98. HOVLAND, C. I. (1937b) The generalization of conditioned responses: II. The sensory generalization of conditioned responses with varying intensities of tone. *J. genet. Psychol.,* 51, 279-291.—*127*

99. HOVLAND, C. I. (1937c) The generalization of conditioned responses: III. Extinction, spontaneous recovery, and disinhibition of conditioned and of generalized responses. *J. exp. Psychol.,* 21, 47-62.—*127*

100. HOVLAND, C. I. (1937d) The generalization of conditioned responses: IV. The effects of varying amounts of reinforcement upon the degree of generalization of conditioned responses. *J. exp. Psychol.*, 21, 261-276.—*26*

HOVLAND, C. I., *see also* No. 229.

101. HOVLAND, C. I., and SEARS, R. R. (1938) Experiments on motor conflict: I. Types of conflict and their modes of resolution. *J. exp. Psychol.*, 23, 477-493.—*319, 322*

102. HUDGINS, C. V. (1933) Conditioning and the voluntary control of the pupillary light reflex. *J. gen. Psychol.*, 8, 3-51.—*25*

103. HULL, C. L. (1920) Quantitative aspects of the evolution of concepts; an experimental study. *Psychol. Monogr.*, 28, No. 123. —*154*

104. HULL, C. L. (1943) *Principles of behavior.* New York, Appleton-Century-Crofts, x, 422 pp.—*14, 26, 69, 74, 171, 172, 178, 196, 209, 261*

HULL, C. L., *see also* No. 9.

105. HULL, C. L., et al. (1940) *Mathematico-deductive theory of rote learning.* New Haven, Yale Univ. Press.—*229*

106. HUMPHREYS, L. G. (1939) The effect of random alternation of reinforcement on the acquisition and extinction of conditioned eyelid reactions. *J. exp. Psychol.*, 25, 141-158.—*99, 113*

107. HUMPHREYS, L. G. (1940) Extinction of conditioned psychogalvanic responses following two conditions of reinforcement. *J. exp. Psychol.*, 27, 71-75.—*100*

108. HUMPHREYS, L. G. (1943) The strength of a Thorndikian response as a function of the number of practice trials. *J. comp. Psychol.*, 35, 101-110.—*100*

109. HUNT, J. McV., and SCHLOSBERG, H. (1939) The influence of illumination upon general activity in normal, blinded, and castrated male white rats. *J. comp. Psychol.*, 28, 285-298.—*282*

HUNT, W. A., *see* No. 142.

110. HUNTER, W. S. (1920) The temporal maze and kinaesthetic sensory processes in the white rat. *Psychobiol.*, 2, 1-17.—*177*

111. HUNTER, W. S. (1928) The behavior of raccoons in a double-alternation temporal maze. *J. genet. Psychol.*, 35, 374-388.—*177, 207*

112. HUNTER, W. S. (1935) Conditioning and extinction in the rat. *Brit. J. Psychol.*, 26, 135-148.—*312*

IREY, E., *see* No. 187.

113. IRWIN, O. C. (1947) Development of speech during infancy: curve of phonemic frequencies. *J. exp. Psychol.*, 37, 187-193.—*381*

114. IRWIN, O. C., and CHEN, H. P. (1946) Development of speech during infancy: curve of phonemic types. *J. exp. Psychol.*, 36, 431-436.—*380, 381*

115. JACKSON, T. A. (1939) Studies in the transposition of learning by children: III. Transpositional response as a function of transposed dimensions. *J. exp. Psychol.*, 25, 116-124.—*158*

116. JACOBSON, E. (1932) The electrophysiology of mental activities. *Amer. J. Psychol.*, 44, 677-694.—*213*

117. JAMES, W. (1884) What is an emotion? *Mind*, 9, 188-205.—*333*

118. JAMES, W. (1890) *Principles of psychology*. New York, Holt, II, vi, 704 pp.—*330, 351*

JENKINS, T. N., *see* No. 283.

119. JENKINS, W. O. (1950) A temporal gradient of derived reinforcement. *Amer. J. Psychol.*, 63, 237-243.—*245*

JENKINS, W. O., *see also* No. 194.

120. JENKINS, W. O., and CLAYTON, F. L. (1949) Rate of responding and amount of reinforcement. *J. comp. physiol. Psychol.*, 42, 174-181.—*100, 112*

121. JESPERSEN, J. O. (1922) *Language: its nature development and origin*. New York, Holt, 448 pp.—*384*

JONES, H., *see* Nos. 177, 178.

122. JONES, M. C. (1924a) The elimination of children's fears. *J. exp. Psychol.*, 7, 382-390.—*347*

123. JONES, M. C. (1924b) A laboratory study of fear. The case of Peter. *J. genet. Psychol.*, 31, 308-315.—*347*

124. JONES, M. C. (1926) The development of early behavior patterns in young children. *Ped. sem. & J. genet. Psychol.*, 33, 537-585. —*335*

125. JUNG, C. G. (1919) *Studies in word association*. New York, Moffat, Yard, ix, 575 pp.—*225*

126. KANTOR, J. R. (1924) *Principles of psychology*. New York, Knopf, xix, 473 pp.—*230*

KAPLON, M. D., *see* No. 297.

127. KARDINER, A. (1939) *The individual and his society: the psycho-dynamics of primitive social organization*. New York, Columbia Univ. Press, xxvi, 503 pp.—*367*

KATZ, A., *see* No. 222.

128. KELLER, F. S. (1937) *The definition of psychology*. New York, Appleton-Century-Crofts, vi, 111 pp.—*220*

129. KELLER, F. S. (1940) The effect of sequence of continuous and periodic reinforcement upon the 'reflex reserve.' *J. exp. Psychol.*, 27, 559-565.—*77*

130. KELLER, F. S. (1941) Light-aversion in the white rat. *Psychol. Rec.*, 4, 235-250.—*62, 304*

131. KELLER, F. S., CHRISTO, I. J., and SCHOENFELD, W. N. (1946). Studies in International Morse Code: V. The effect of the "phonetic equivalent." *J. appl. Psychol.*, 30, 265-270.—*149*

132. KELLER, F. S., and SCHOENFELD, W. N. (1944) Studies in International Morse Code: III. The efficiency of the code as related to errors made during learning. *J. appl. Psychol.*, 28, 254-266.—*148*

133. KELLOGG, W. N. (1939) "Positive" and "negative" conditioning, without contraction of the essential muscles during the period of training. *Psychol. Bull.*, 36, 575.—*169*

KELLOGG, L. A., see No. 134.

134. KELLOGG, W. N., and KELLOGG, L. A. (1933) *The ape and the child.* New York, Whittlesey, xiv, 314 pp.—*355*

135. KENT, G. H., and ROSANOFF, A. J. (1910) A study of association in insanity. *Amer. J. Insan.,* 67, 37-96; 317-390.—*222*

136. KINSEY, A. C., POMEROY, W. B., and MARTIN, C. E. (1948) *Sexual behavior in the human male.* Philadelphia, W. B. Saunders, xv, 804 pp.—*300*

137. KLINEBERG, O. (1940) *Social psychology.* New York, Holt, xii, 570 pp.—*336, 399*

KOERNER, L., see No. 187.

138. KÖHLER, W. (1925) *The mentality of apes.* New York, Harcourt Brace, viii, 342 pp.—*59, 65*

139. KONORSKI, J., and MILLER, S. (1937) On two types of conditioned reflex. *J. gen. Psychol.,* 16, 264-272.—*63*

LAMOREAUX, R. R., see Nos. 179, 180.

140. LANDIS, C. (1924) Studies of emotional reactions: II. General behavior and facial expression. *J. comp. Psychol.,* 4, 447-501.—*336*

141. LANDIS, C. (1934) Emotion: II. The expressions of emotion. In Murchison, C. (ed.), *A handbook of general experimental psychology.* Worcester, Mass., Clark Univ. Press.—*351*

142. LANDIS, C., and HUNT, W. A. (1939) *The startle pattern.* New York, Farrar and Rinehart, xvi, 168 pp.—*337*

143. LASHLEY, K. S. (1916) The human salivary reflex and its use in psychology. *Psychol. Rev.,* 23, 446-464.—*35*

144. LASHLEY, K. S. (1929) *Brain mechanisms and intelligence.* Chicago, Univ. of Chicago Press, xiv, 186 pp.—*137*

145. LASHLEY, K. S. (1930) The mechanism of vision: I. A method for rapid analysis of pattern vision in the rat. *J. genet. Psychol.,* 37, 453-460.—*136*

146. LEUBA, C. J. (1931) Some comments on the first reports of the Columbia study of animal drives. *J. comp. Psychol.,* 11, 275-280.—*298*

147. LEVINE, R., CHEIN, I., and MURPHY, G. (1942) The relation of intensity of a need to the amount of perceptual distortion: a preliminary report. *J. Psychol.,* 13, 283-293.—*290*

148. LIDDELL, H. S. (1938) The experimental neurosis and the problem of mental disorder. *Amer. J. Psychiat.,* 94, 1035-1043.—*29, 139*

LIDDELL, H. S., see also No. 2.

149. LINTON, R. (1945) *The cultural background of personality.* New York, Appleton-Century-Crofts, xix, 157 pp.—*367*

LIPOFSKY, H., see No. 170.

150. LORGE, I. (1936) Irrelevant rewards in animal learning. *J. comp. Psychol.,* 21, 105-128.—*175, 196*

151. LURIA, A. R. (1932) *The nature of human conflicts, or emotion, conflict, and will; an objective study of disorganization and*

control of human behavior. (Trans. by W. H. Gantt) New York, Liveright, xviii, 431 pp.—*324*

152. Lyon, D. O. (1917) *Memory and the learning process.* Baltimore, Warwick and York, 179 pp.—*228*

153. MacDuff, M. M. (1946) The effect on retention of varying degrees of motivation during learning in rats. *J. comp. Psychol.,* 39, 207-240.—*112*

154. MacFarlane, D. A. (1930) The rôle of kinesthesis in maze learning. *Univ. Calif. Publ. Psychol.,* 4, 277-305.—*169*

155. Malinowski, B. (1929) *The sexual life of savages in northwestern Melanesia: an ethnographic account of courtship, marriage and family life among the natives of the Trobriand Islands in British New Guinea.* New York, Liveright, 506 pp.—*367*

Marquis, D. G., *see* Nos. 95, 299.

Martin, C. E., *see* No. 136.

156. Maslow, A. H. (1936a) The rôle of dominance in the social and sexual behavior of infra-human primates: I. Observations at Vilas Park Zoo. *J. genet. Psychol.,* 48, 261-277.—*356, 399*

157. Maslow, A. H. (1936b) The rôle of dominance in the social and sexual behavior of infra-human primates: IV. The determination of hierarchy in pairs and in a group. *J. genet. Psychol.,* 49, 161-198.—*356, 399*

158. Masserman, J. H. (1946) *Principles of dynamic psychiatry.* Philadelphia, W. B. Saunders, xix, 322 pp.—*82, 203*

159. Mateer, F. (1918) *Child behavior, a critical and experimental study of young children by the method of conditioned reflexes.* Boston, Badger, v, 239 pp.—*35*

160. Max, L. W. (1935) An experimental study of the motor theory of consciousness: III. Action-current responses in deaf mutes during sleep, sensory stimulation and dreams. *J. comp. Psychol.,* 19, 469-486.—*214*

161. Max, L. W. (1937) Experimental study of the motor theory of consciousness: IV. Action-current responses in the deaf during awakening, kinaesthetic imagery, and abstract thinking. *J. comp. Psychol.,* 24, 301-344.—*214*

162. McCarthy, D. A. (1930) *The language development of the preschool child.* Minneapolis, Univ. Minn. Press, xiii, 174 pp.—*204, 205*

163. McDougall (1923) *Outline of psychology.* New York, Scribner, xvi, 456 pp.—*330*

164. Menzies, R. (1937) Conditioned vasomotor responses in human subjects. *J. Psychol.,* 4, 75-120.—*26*

165. Merkel, J. (1885) Die zeitlichen verhältnisse der willensthätigkeit. *Philos. Studien,* 2, 73-127.—*143*

166. Miles, W. R. (1931) Studies in physical exertion: II. Individual and group reaction time in football charging. *Res. Quar.,* 2, 6-13.—*146*

167. MILLER, N. E. (1941) An experimental investigation of acquired drives. *Psychol. Bull.*, 38, 534-535.—*311*. See Miller, (1948)

168. MILLER, N. E. (1944) Experimental studies of conflict. In J. McV. Hunt (ed.), *Personality and the behavior disorders*. Vol. I. New York, Ronald Press.—*317, 318, 320, 321*

169. MILLER, N. E. (1948) Studies of fear as an acquirable drive: I. Fear as motivation and fear reduction as reinforcement in the learning of new responses. *J. exp. Psychol.*, 38, 89-101.—*250, 251, 252, 317*
MILLER, N. E., *see also* No. 24.

170. MILLER, N. E., BROWN, J. S., and LIPOFSKY, H. (1943) A theoretical and experimental analysis of conflict behavior: III. Approach-avoidance conflict as a function of strength of drive and strength of shock. Reported in Miller (1944).—*320*

171. MILLER, N. E., and DOLLARD, J. (1941) *Social learning and imitation*. New Haven, Yale Univ. Press, xiv, 341 pp.—*196, 361, 362, 399*
MILLER, S., *see* No. 139.

172. MITRANO, A. J. (1939) Principles of conditioning in human goal behavior. *Psychol. Monogr.*, 51, 230 pp.—*82*
MORGULIS, S., *see* No. 300.

173. MOSS, F. A. (1924) Study of animal drives. *J. exp. Psychol.*, 7, 165-185.—*297*

174. MOWRER, O. H. (1939) A stimulus-response analysis of anxiety and its rôle as a reinforcing agent. *Psychol. Rev.*, 46, 553-565.—*311*

175. MOWRER, O. H. (1940) An experimental analogue of "regression" with incidental observations on "reaction-formation." *J. abn. (soc.) Psychol.*, 35, 56-87.—*61, 81, 306*

176. MOWRER, O. H. (1947) On the dual nature of learning—a reinterpretation of "conditioning" and "problem solving." *Harvard Educ. Rev.*, 17, 102-148.—*66*

177. MOWRER, O. H., and JONES, H. (1943) Extinction and behavior variability as functions of effortfulness of task. *J. exp. Psychol.*, 33, 369-386.—*196*

178. MOWRER, O. H., and JONES, H. (1945) Habit strength as a function of the pattern of reinforcement. *J. exp. Psychol.*, 35, 293-311. —*100, 207*

179. MOWRER, O. H., and LAMOREAUX, R. R. (1942) Avoidance conditioning and signal duration—a study of secondary motivation and reward. *Psychol. Monogr.*, 54, No. 247, iii, 34 pp.—*251*

180. MOWRER, O. H., and LAMOREAUX, R. R. (1946) Fear as an intervening variable in avoidance conditioning. *J. comp. Psychol.*, 39, 29-50.—*251*

181. MUENZINGER, K. F. (1928) Plasticity and mechanization of the problem box habit in guinea pigs. *J. comp. Psychol.*, 8, 45-70. —*167*

182. MUENZINGER, K. F. (1934a) Motivation in learning: I. Electric shock for correct response in the visual discrimination habit. *J. comp. Psychol.*, 17, 267-277.—*113*

183. MUENZINGER, K. F. (1934b) Motivation in learning: II. The function of electric shock for right and wrong responses in human subjects. *J. exp. Psychol.*, 17, 439-448.—*113*

184. MUENZINGER, K. F. (1942) *Psychology: The science of behavior.* New York, Harper, xi, 441 pp.—*14*

185. MUENZINGER, K. F., BERNSTONE, A. H., and RICHARDS, L. (1938) Motivation in learning: VIII. Equivalent amounts of electric shock for right and wrong responses in visual discrimination habit. *J. comp. Psychol.*, 26, 177-185.—*113*

186. MUENZINGER, K. F., and FLETCHER, F. M. (1936) Motivation in learning: VI. Escape from electric shock compared with hunger-food tension in the visual discrimination habit. *J. comp. Psychol.*, 22, 79-91.—*113*

187. MUENZINGER, K. F., KOERNER, L., and IREY, E. (1929) Variability of an habitual movement in guinea pigs. *J. comp. Psychol.*, 9, 425-436.—*195*

188. MUENZINGER, K. F., and NEWCOMB, H. (1935) Motivation in learning: III. A bell signal compared with electric shock for right and wrong responses in the visual discrimination habit. *J. comp. Psychol.*, 21, 95-104.—*113*

189. MUENZINGER, K. F., and WOOD, A. (1935) Motivation in learning: IV. The function of punishment as determined by its temporal relation to the act of choice in the visual discrimination habit. *J. comp. Psychol.*, 20, 95-106.—*113*

190. MUNN, N. L. (1946) *Psychology: the fundamentals of human adjustment.* Boston, Houghton Mifflin, xviii, 497 pp.—*14*

191. MURCHISON, C. A. (ed.) (1935) *A handbook of social psychology.* Worcester, Clark Univ. Press, xii, 1195 pp.—*400*

MURPHY, G., *see* No. 147.

192. MURPHY, M. J. (1943) The differentiation of a response—An exploratory study with human subjects. *Abridgement of Ph.D. dissertation, New York University*, 23 pp.—*188*

NEWCOMB, H., *see* No. 188.

193. NISSEN, H. W. (1930) A study of maternal behavior in the white rat by means of the obstruction method. *J. genet. Psychol.*, 37, 377-393.—*299*

194. NISSEN, H. W., and JENKINS, W. O. (1943) Reduction and rivalry of cues in the discrimination behavior of chimpanzees. *J. comp. Psychol.*, 35, 85-95.—*316*

195. NOTTERMAN, J. M. (1950) The interrelationships among aperiodic reinforcement, discrimination, learning, and secondary reinforcement. Ph.D. dissertation, Columbia Univ.—*235, 245, 246*

196. PAVLOV, I. P. (1923) In Holt, E. B. (1931) *Animal drive and the learning process.* New York, Holt, vii, 307 pp.—*19*

197. PAVLOV, I. P. (1927) *Conditioned reflexes.* (Trans. by G. V. Anrep) London, Oxford Univ. Press, xv, 430 pp.—*24, 34, 68, 83, 117, 126, 134, 138, 162*

198. PAVLOV, I. P. (1928) *Lectures on conditioned reflexes.* (Trans. by W. H. Gantt) New York, International, 414 pp.—*34*

199. PERIN, C. T. (1942) Behavior potentiality as a joint function of the amount of training and the degree of hunger at the time of extinction. *J. exp. Psychol.,* 30, 93-113.—*75, 266*

200. PIAGET, J. (1929) *The child's conception of the world.* New York, Harcourt, ix, 397 pp.—*154*

201. PLOTKIN, L. (1943) Stimulus generalization in Morse Code learning. *Arch. Psychol.,* 40, No. 287.—*124*

POMEROY, W. B., *see* No. 136.

202. RABEN, M. W. (1949) The white rat's discrimination of differences in intensity of illumination measured by a running response. *J. comp. physiol. Psychol.,* 42, 254-272.—*54, 129*

203. RASMUSSEN, E. W. (1940) The shock method as a measure of hunger and of the intensity of a conflict. *Acta. psychol., Hague,* 5, 63-78.—*321*

RAYNER, R., *see* No. 290.

204. RAZRAN, G. H. S. (1939a) The law of effect or the law of qualitative conditioning. *Psychol. Rev.,* 46, 445-463.—*66*

205. RAZRAN, G. H. S. (1939b) A quantitative study of meaning by a conditioned salivary technique (semantic conditioning). *Science,* 90, 89-90.—*160*

206. RAZRAN, G. H. S. (1939c) Studies in configural conditioning: I. Historical and preliminary experimentation. *J. gen. Psychol.,* 21, 307-330.—*35*

207. REICH, W. (1949) *Character analysis.* New York, Orgone Institute, xxvi, 516 pp.—*324*

208. REINWALD, F. L. (1938) Personal communication.—*29*

209. REINWALD, F. L. (1941) Personal communication.—*64*

210. REYNOLDS, B. (1949) The relationship between the strength of a habit and the degree of drive present during acquisition. *J. exp. Psychol.,* 39, 296-305.—*112*

RICHARDS, L., *see* No. 185.

211. RICHTER, C. P. (1922) A behavioristic study of the activity of the rat. *Comp. Psychol. Monogr.,* 1, No. 2, 55 pp.—*279, 280*

212. RIESS, B. F. (1940) Semantic conditioning involving the galvanic skin reflex. *J. exp. Psychol.,* 26, 238-240.—*160*

213. RIESS, B. F. (1946) Genetic changes in semantic conditioning. *J. exp. Psychol.,* 36, 143-152.—*160, 161*

214. RITTER, A. M. (1949) Some conditions influencing the incidence of response duplication of verbal stimuli. *J. Psychol.,* 28, 93-118. —*393*

ROBINSON, E. E., *see* No. 36.

416 REFERENCES AND AUTHOR INDEX

215. ROBINSON, E. S., and HERON, W. T. (1924) The warming up effect. *J. exp. Psychol.*, 7, 81-97.—*188*

ROSANOFF, A. J., *see* No. 135.

ROSENZWEIG, S., *see* No. 232.

216. RUCH, F. L. (1948) *Psychology and Life.* New York, Scott, Foresman, xvi, 782 pp.—*14*

217. SALTZMAN, I. J. (1949) Maze learning in the absence of primary reinforcement: a study of secondary reinforcement. *J. comp. physiol. Psychol.*, 42, 161-173.—*235*

218. SANFORD, R. N. (1936) The effects of abstinence from food upon imaginal processes: a preliminary experiment. *J. Psychol.*, 2, 129-136.—*290*

219. SCHJELDERUP, EBBE T. (1935) Social behavior of birds. In Murchison, C. (ed.), *A handbook of social psychology.* Worcester, Mass., Clark Univ. Press. Pp. 947-972.—*356*

220. SCHLOSBERG, H. (1936) Conditioned responses in the white rat: II. Conditioned responses based upon shock to the foreleg. *J. genet. Psychol.*, 49, 107-138.—*314*

221. SCHLOSBERG, H., (1937) The relationship between success and the laws of conditioning. *Psychol. Rev.*, 44, 379-394.—*66*

SCHLOSBERG, H., *see also* No. 109.

222. SCHLOSBERG, H., and KATZ, A. (1943) Double alternation lever-pressing in the white rat. *Amer. J. Psychol.*, 56, 274-282.—*203*

SCHNEIRLA, T. C., *see* No. 36.

223. SCHOENFELD, W. N. (1946) Unpublished study.—*304*

224. SCHOENFELD, W. N. (1947) Unpublished study.—*62*

225. SCHOENFELD, W. N. (1950) An experimental approach to anxiety, escape, and avoidance behavior. In *Anxiety: Proc. Amer. psychopathol. Ass.*, New York, Grune and Stratton. In press.—*313*

SCHOENFELD, W. N., *see also* Nos. 131, 132.

226. SCHOENFELD, W. N., ANTONITIS, J. J., and BERSH, P. J. (1950a) A preliminary study of training conditions necessary for secondary reinforcement. *J. exp. Psychol.*, 40, 40-45.—*236*

227. SCHOENFELD, W. N., ANTONITIS, J. J., and BERSH, P. J. (1950b) Unconditioned response rate of the white rat in a bar-pressing apparatus. *J. comp. physiol. Psychol.*, 43, 41-48.—*113*

228. SCOTT, W. E. D. (1901) Data on song in birds. *Science*, 14, 522-526.—*354*

SEARS, R. R., *see* No. 101.

229. SEARS, R. R., and HOVLAND, C. I. (1941) Experiments on motor conflicts: II. Determination of mode of resolution by comparative strengths of conflicting responses. *J. exp. Psychol.*, 28, 280-286.—*317, 321*

SEARS, W. N., *see* No. 94.

230. SEWARD, J. P. (1946) Aggressive behavior in the rat: IV. Submission as determined by conditioning, extinction, and disuse. *J. comp. Psychol.*, 39, 51-76.—*356*

231. SHAFFER, L. E. (1936) *The psychology of adjustment.* Boston, Houghton Mifflin, xix, 600 pp.—*316*

232. SHAKOW, D., and ROSENZWEIG, S. (1940) The use of the tautophone ("verbal summator") as an auditory apperceptive test for the study of personality. *Character & Pers.,* 8, 216-226.—*395*

233. SHAW, W. A. (1940) The relation of muscular action potentials to imaginal weight lifting. *Arch. Psychol.,* No. 247, 50 pp.—*215, 216*

234. SHEFFIELD, F. D. (1948) Avoidance training and the contiguity principle. *J. comp. physiol. Psychol.,* 41, 165-177.—*314*

235. SHERMAN, M. (1928) The differentiation of emotional responses in infants: I. Judgments of emotional responses from motion picture views and from actual observation. *J. comp. Psychol.,* 7, 265-284.—*338, 339*

236. SKINNER, B. F. (1930) On the conditions of elicitation of certain eating reflexes. *Proc. nat. Acad. Sci.,* Wash., 16, 433-438.—*42*

237. SKINNER, B. F. (1932) On the rate of formation of a conditioned reflex. *J. gen. Psychol.,* 7, 274-285.—*43*

238. SKINNER, B. F. (1933) The rate of establishment of a discrimination. *J. gen. Psychol.,* 9, 302-350.—*99*

239. SKINNER, B. F. (1935) Two types of conditioned reflex and a pseudo type. *J. gen. Psychol.,* 12, 66-77.—*47, 66*

240. SKINNER, B. F. (1936) The verbal summator and a method for the study of latent speech. *J. Psychol.,* 2, 71-107.—*394*

241. SKINNER, B. F. (1937) Two types of conditioned reflex: a reply to Konorski and Miller. *J. gen. Psychol.,* 16, 272-279.—*47*

242. SKINNER, B. F. (1938) *The behavior of organisms: an experimental analysis.* New York, Appleton-Century-Crofts, ix, 457 pp.—*14, 20, 30, 44, 45, 46, 50, 71, 77, 80, 85, 87, 88, 90, 91, 92, 95, 98, 106, 107, 108, 119, 120, 121, 162, 171, 186, 202, 207, 234, 267, 268, 282*

243. SKINNER, B. F. (1948a) "Superstition" in the pigeon. *J. exp. Psychol.,* 38, 168-172.—*103*

244. SKINNER, B. F. (1948b) William James Lectures on verbal behavior. Harvard University.—*400*

245. SKINNER, B. F. (1950) Unpublished study.—*100*
SKINNER, B. F., *see also* No. 63.

246. SMALL, W. S. (1901) An experimental study of the mental processes of the rat. *Amer. J. Psychol.,* 12, 206-239.—*56, 57*

247. SMITH, S., and GUTHRIE, E. R. (1921) *General psychology in terms of behavior.* New York, Appleton, xii, 270 pp.—*35*

248. SMOKE, K. L. (1932) An objective study of concept formation *Psychol. Monogr.,* 42, No. 4, 46 pp.—*157*

249. SOLOMON, R. L. (1946) Time and effort factors in the avoidance of repetition of responses. *Amer. Psychologist,* 1, 291-292.—*177*

250. SOLOMON, R. L. (1948) The influence of work on behavior. *Psychol. Bull.,* 45, 1-40.—*177, 196*

251. SPENCE, K. W. (1936) The nature of discrimination learning in animals. *Psychol. Rev.,* 43, 427-449.—*158*

252. SPENCE, K. W. (1947) The rôle of secondary reinforcement in delayed reward learning. *Psychol. Rev.,* 54, 1-8.—*209*

253. SPRAGG, S. D. S. (1943) The relative difficulty of Morse code alphabet characters learned by the whole method. *J. exp. Psychol.,* 33, 108-114.—*148*

254. STARCH, D. (1910) A demonstration of the trial and error method of learning. *Psychol. Bull.,* 7, 20-23.—*169*

255. STONE, C. P. (1927) The retention of copulatory ability in male rats following castration. *J. comp. Psychol.,* 7, 369-387.—*301*

256. STONE, C. P. (1937) A sand-tube obstruction apparatus. *J. genet. Psychol.,* 50, 203-206.—*96*

257. STONE, C. P., and COMMINS, W. D. (1936) The effect of castration at various ages upon the learning ability of male albino rats: II. Relearning after an interval of one year. *J. genet. Psychol.,* 48, 20-28.—*301*

258. STRASSBURGER, R. C. (1950) Resistance to extinction of a conditioned operant as related to drive level at reinforcement. *J. exp. Psychol.* (in press).

259. STROUD, J. B. (1931) The rôle of muscular tensions in stylus maze learning. *J. exp. Psychol.,* 14, 184-185; 606-631.—*196*

260. SWINDLE, P. F. (1917) The term reaction time redefined. *Amer. J. Psychol.,* 28, 508-518.—*229*

261. SWINDLE, P. F. (1919) Some forms of natural training to which certain birds are subjected. *Amer. J. Psychol.,* 30, 165-172. —*229*

262. TARDE, G. (1903) *The laws of imitation* (Trans. by E. C. Parsons). New York, Holt, xxix, 405 pp.—*361*

263. THORNDIKE, E. L. (1898) Animal intelligence. An experimental study of the associative processes in animals. *Psychol. Monogr.,* 2, No. 8, 109 pp.—*36, 38, 40*

264. THORNDIKE, E. L. (1911) *Animal intelligence: experimental studies.* New York, Macmillan, viii, 297 pp.—*14, 39, 61*

265. THORNDIKE, E. L. (1913) *The original nature of man* (Educational psychology, I.) New York, Teachers College, vii, 327 pp.—*40*

266. THORNDIKE, E. L. (1931) *Human learning.* New York, Appleton-Century-Crofts, 206 pp.—*104, 172, 173, 176*

267. THORNDIKE, E. L. (1932) *The fundamentals of learning.* New York, Teachers College, xvii, 638 pp.—*14, 40, 61, 105*

268. THORSEN, A. M. (1925) The relation of tongue movements to internal speech. *J. exp. Psychol.,* 8, 1-32.—*230*

269. TITCHENER, E. B. (1908) *Lectures on the elementary psychology of feeling and attention.* New York, Macmillan, ix, 404 pp.—*255*

270. TITCHENER, E. B. (1915) *A beginner's psychology.* New York, Macmillan, xvi, 362 pp.—*219*

271. TOLCOTT, M. A. (1948) Conflict: a study of some interactions between appetite and aversion in the white rat. *Genet. Psychol. Monogr.*, 38, 83-142.—*322*

272. TOLMAN, E. C. (1937) The acquisition of string-pulling by rats—conditioned response or sign-gestalt. *Psychol. Rev.*, 44, 195-211. —*96*

273. TOLMAN, E. C. (1942) *Drives toward war.* New York, Appleton-Century-Crofts, xv, 118 pp.—*325*

274. TSAI, C. (1925) The relative strength of sex and hunger motives in the albino rat. *J. comp. Psychol.*, 5, 407-415.—*297*

275. TSAI, L. S. (1932) The laws of minimal effort and maximal satisfaction in animal behavior. *Monogr. Nat. Res. Instit. Psychol.*, Acad. Sinica, No. I, 47 pp.—*196*

276. VERPLANCK, W. S. (1942) The development of discrimination in a simple locomotor habit. *J. exp. Psychol.*, 31, 441-464.—*129*

277. WADA, T. (1922) An experimental study of hunger in its relation to activity. *Arch. Psychol.*, 8, No. 57, 65 pp.—*290*

278. WALKER, K. C. (1942) The effect of a discriminative stimulus transferred to a previously unassociated response. *J. exp. Psychol.*, 31, 312-321.—*242*

279. WANG, G. H. (1923) The relation between 'spontaneous' activity and oestrus cycle in the white rat. *Comp. Psychol. Monogr.*, 2, No. 6, 27 pp.—*295, 296*

280. WARDEN, C. J. (1924) The relative economy of various modes of attack in mastery of a stylus maze. *J. exp. Psychol.*, 7, 243-275. —*60*

281. WARDEN, C. J. (1931) *Animal motivation.* New York, Columbia Univ. Press, xii, 502 pp.—*288*

282. WARDEN, C. J., and AYLESWORTH, M. (1927) The relative value of reward and punishment in the formation of a visual discrimination habit in the white rat. *J. comp. Psychol.*, 7, 117-128. —*111*

283. WARDEN, C. J., JENKINS, T. N., and WARNER, L. H. (1935-1940) *Comparative psychology*, 3 vols. New York, Ronald Press. —*58, 163*

284. WARNER, L. H. (1927) A study of sex behavior in the white rat by means of the obstruction method. *Comp. Psychol. Monogr.*, 4, No. 22, 68 pp.—*298*

285. WARNER, L. H. (1932) The association span of the white rat. *J. genet. Psychol.*, 41, 57-90.—*311*

WARNER, L. H., *see also* No. 283.

WASHBURN, A. L., *see* No. 31.

286. WATERS, R. H. (1937) The principle of least effort in learning. *J. gen. Psychol.*, 16, 3-20.—*196*

287. WATSON, J. B. (1916) The place of the conditioned reflex in psychology. *Psychol. Rev.*, 23, 89-116.—*35*

288. WATSON, J. B. (1919) *Psychology from the standpoint of a behaviorist.* Philadelphia, Lippincott, ix, 429 pp.—*7, 379*

289. WATSON, J. B. (1924) *Behaviorism.* New York, People's Institute, 248 pp.—*338, 343*
WATSON, J. B., *see also* No. 301.

290. WATSON, J. B., and RAYNER, R. (1920) Conditioned emotional reactions. *J. exp. Psychol.,* 3, 1-14.—*347*

291. WELLS, F. L. (1908) Normal performance in the tapping test. *Amer. J. Psychol.,* 19, 437-483.—*188*

292. WHEELER, R. H. (1929) *The science of psychology.* New York, Crowell, xvii, 556 pp.—*196*

293. WILLIAMS, K. A. (1929) The reward value of a conditioned stimulus. *Univ. Calif. Publ. Psychol.,* 4, 31-55.—*234*

294. WILLIAMS, S. B. (1938) Resistance to extinction as a function of the number of reinforcements. *J. exp. Psychol.,* 23, 506-522. —*72, 73*

295. WINNICK, W. A. (1949) Response vacillation in conflict situations. Ph.D. dissertation, Columbia Univ. (to be published).— *323, 324*

296. WOLFE, J. B. (1936) Effectiveness of token-rewards for chimpanzees. *Comp. Psychol. Monogr.,* 12, No. 60, 72 pp.—*247*

297. WOLFE, J. B., and KAPLON, M. D. (1941) Effect of amount of reward and consummative activity on learning in chickens. *J. comp. Psychol.,* 31, 353-361.—*74*
WOOD, A., *see* No. 189.
WOODBURY, C. B., *see* No. 87.

298. WOODWORTH, R. S. (1938) *Experimental psychology.* New York, Holt, xi, 889 pp.—*163, 226, 230, 351*

299. WOODWORTH, R. S., and MARQUIS, D. G. (1947) *Psychology.* New York, Holt, x, 677 pp.—*14*

300. YERKES, R. M., and MORGULIS, S. (1909) The method of Pawlow in animal psychology. *Psychol. Bull.,* 6, 257-273.—*35*

301. YERKES, R. M., and WATSON, J. B. (1911) Methods of studying vision in animals. *Behav. Monogr.,* I, No. 2, iv, 90 pp.—*137*

302. YOUNG, P. T. (1936) *Motivation of behavior.* New York, Wiley, xviii, 562 pp.—*325*

303. YOUNG, P. T. (1943) *Emotion in man and animal.* New York, Wiley, xiii, 422 pp.—*344, 351*

304. YOUTZ, R. E. P. (1938) Reinforcement, extinction, and spontaneous recovery in a non-Pavlovian reaction. *J. exp. Psychol.,* 22, 305-318.—*76*

305. ZEAMAN, D. (1949) Response latency as a function of the amount of reinforcement. *J. exp. Psychol.,* 39, 466-483.—*73*

306. ZIPF, G. K. (1949) *Human behavior and the principle of least effort.* Cambridge, Addison-Wesley, xi, 573 pp.—*196*

SUBJECT INDEX